*Other Guides in the
Discovering Historic America Series*

CALIFORNIA & THE WEST

MID-ATLANTIC STATES

NEW ENGLAND

Text:

Vicki Brooks
Martin Greif
Lawrence Grow
Laura McPhee

Design:

Frank Mahood
Donald Rolfe

Cover illustration: *The Governor's Palace, Williamsburg,
Virginia, courtesy of the Virginia State Travel Service.*

DISCOVERING HISTORIC AMERICA

THE SOUTHEAST

- **Virginia**
- **West Virginia**
- **North Carolina**
- **South Carolina**
- **Georgia**
- **Florida**
- **Alabama**
- **Mississippi**
- **Tennessee**
- **Kentucky**

General Editor: S. Allen Chambers

E.P. DUTTON, INC. · *NEW YORK*
1983

Published in the United States by E. P. Dutton, Inc.,
2 Park Avenue, New York, NY 10016

Library of Congress Catalog Card Number 82-71548
ISBN 0-525-93260-7 Volume 4

Published simultaneously in Canada by Clarke, Irwin &
Company Limited, Toronto and Vancouver

10 9 8 7 6 5 4 3 2 1

First Edition

Contents

Introduction

EACH of the titles in the *Discovering Historic America* series brings together the rich and varied resources available to the traveler in an historic region of the United States. In whatever season of the year, the traveler may journey into a past that is alive today and not an ocean or oceans away from home. History may have begun on the other side of the Atlantic or Pacific, but it is abundantly and colorfully displayed in the highways and byways of rural and urban America, in historic homes, museum villages, state and national parks, inns and churches, courthouses and city halls, hotels and libraries, museums and environmental centers, battlefields and archaeological sites, mills and manors.

This comprehensive guide to the historic Southeast, organized state by state, offers the traveler hundreds of opportunities to step away from the frenzied pace of everyday life — to enjoy the quiet of a country inn, to trace the path of Revolutionary or Civil War soldiers, to experience the delights of a ride in a horse and buggy or on an old-fashioned carousel, to discover our heritage in the folk arts and crafts. For families with small children, *Discovering Historic America* provides useful information on activities which are not only entertaining but educational, whether on a day trip, weekend, or extended vacation. For every traveler there is a rich selection of historical treasures to be explored and enjoyed in almost every corner of the ten tradition-rich states that make up the region.

Many of the places described in this book are listed in the National Register of Historic Places; some are also official National Historic Landmarks. These listings have been supplemented with historical museums, reconstructions such as museum villages, excursion railroad lines, traditional craft workshops, state and national parks, and monuments of historic interest. And there are, of course, hundreds of historic properties included here which have yet to reach the official listings in Washington or elsewhere. Because the southeastern region is so full of history, the selections have been necessarily limited, the prime consideration given to those which are open to the public.

For the traveler heading out from one of the major metropolitan areas of the Midwest or East, a one-volume guide which includes information on all of these features in addition to a selection of historic accommodations is of considerable value. Whether a trip is undertaken as a family activity or as a get-away-from-it-all escape for a weekend or a week, there is much pleasure to be gained in discovering the treasures of this culturally-rich region. Discerning travelers, dismayed by today's slick commercial tourism, will delight in the authentic and will find exploration of America's past a satisfying experience.

Dozens of people associated with the region's historical societies, preservation organizations, and tourist authorities have provided generous suggestions and expert background material for this volume. In addition, the records of the National Register, Washington, D.C., have been made available for checking facts. Although it is impossible to name everyone who has offered assistance, several people merit very special thanks. I wish particularly to thank the members of the National Register staff who made the task of gathering data pleasant and rewarding; thanks also, to Carolyn Dobel, Tourist/Communications Division, Georgia Dept. of Industry & Trade; Jenny Stacy, Travel Industry and Media Development, Savannah Area Convention & Visitors Bureau; Jane Brown, Director of

Public Relations, Shakertown at Pleasant Hill, Ky.; Libby Hitt, Tourism Development, Dept. of Economic Development, State of Mississippi; Donald R. Taylor,
administrator, Tryon Palace Restoration Complex, New Bern, N.C.; John J.
Little, administrator, Archaeology and Historic Preservation Section, N.C. Dept.
of Cultural Resources; Mrs. Armistead Bond, executive secretary, Association for
the Preservation of Tennessee Antiquities; and Martha W. Steger, Virginia State
Travel Service.

How to Use This Book

Discovering Historic America: The Southeast is a useful book to consult and a
very easy book to use. It is organized by state, starting with Virginia and West Virginia, and then moving clockwise through the region until reaching Kentucky.
These states are further broken down into geographic regions, beginning with
those settled first. North Carolina, for example, is divided into coastal, Piedmont,
and western sections. These smaller areas make the planning and execution of
trips easier and enable the traveler to choose from a wide variety of historic sites
and attractions concentrated within a self-contained geographic region. A state
map, indicating the key regions, appears at the beginning of each chapter of the
book. The listings for each of these regions are broken down by town or city in
alphabetical order.

Information on the historical, architectural, or other cultural significance of a
place is given along with essential facts on hours of operation, address, telephone
number, and admission fee if any. Some of the historic places listed and described
remain in private hands but are still accessible for viewing from the public way or
are open on special occasions. These are so designated.

Special letter code and symbols are used with many of the listings. **NR** means
that the property has been nominated and accepted as an historic property by the
National Register of Historic Places, National Park Service, Department of the Interior, Washington, D.C. **NHL** is the designation for a National Historic Landmark, an honor reserved by the National Park Service for properties and
geographic districts of exceptional significance to the nation. All these landmarks
are automatically included in the National Register. Places of special interest to
families with children are marked with the symbol ✔. Historical sites of military
interest are indicated with the symbol ★. Abbreviations are used in some in-
stances to indicate properties maintained by two preservation organizations:
APVA, Association for the Preservation of Virginia Antiquities; **APTA**, Association for the Preservation of Tennessee Antiquities.

Selective listings of historic accommodations are included at the end of each
state's entries. Only properties which can be considered of historic interest have
been included. In every case, modern improvements have been made, but these
have been designed with consideration for the architectural integrity of the
original building or buildings. Those hotels and inns which serve meals are indicated with an asterisk.

Although every effort has been made to insure the accuracy of addresses,
telephone numbers, hours of operation, and admission fees appearing in this
book, these are all subject to change over time. In planning a trip, it is always wise
to call or write ahead for the latest information.

THE SOUTHEAST

1. VIRGINIA

During the 16th century various attempts were made by Sir Walter Raleigh and other adventurous Englishmen to establish new colonies along the coast of what is now North Carolina, immediately south of the Old Dominion. Raleigh named the new country Virginia in honor of his sovereign, Elizabeth I, who was known as "the virgin queen." It was not until 1607, however, that three small ships put in at Jamestown and the first permanent English settlement in America was founded. Plantations were established along the James River, and trade in agricultural goods, especially tobacco, was begun with the mother country.

Virginians are justly proud of their position in American history and diligent in preserving their heritage. Wherever one travels in the state, whether to visit famous popular attractions such as Colonial Williamsburg, Mount Vernon and Monticello or to explore the sleepy villages along peaceful country roads, there is history almost everywhere. Nearly every small town has some historic building worth exploring, be it a lovely early courthouse such as King William's — a Colonial brick structure dating from about 1725 — or a well-preserved 18th-century church such as the Aquia Church near Garrisonville (1751), which retains its original triple-tier pulpit, reredos, gallery, and pews.

Many of Virginia's oldest and most beautiful historic homes and churches are open to visitors year round; still more welcome travelers during the state's famous Historic Garden Week, held each year at the end of April. The Association for the Preservation of Virginia Antiquities (APVA) administers many of the dominion's finest landmarks; others are carefully tended by local historical societies, and museums; but everywhere is the sense that heritage really matters in Virginia — a statewide enthusiasm for preserving ancestral building and decorative arts that is too often lacking in other areas of the country.

Virginia's soldiers played important roles in both the Revolutionary and Civil Wars: at Appomattox, Yorktown, New Market and other locations across the state, battlefields have been carefully preserved and clearly interpreted.

To facilitate travel throughout Virginia's nearly 41,000 square miles, the listings which follow are divided into four geographic areas: Northern Virginia, including the communities nearest Washington, D.C.; The Tidewater, stretching from the sparsely populated Eastern Shore on the north down to the North Carolina border, and inland along the James and Appomattox Rivers to Petersburg and Richmond; Central Virginia — the Piedmont — home of Thomas Jefferson and James Monroe; and Western Virginia, where small cities and towns are still widely separated and fir-covered mountains are preserved in national and state parks.

Woodlawn Plantation, Middletown vicinity

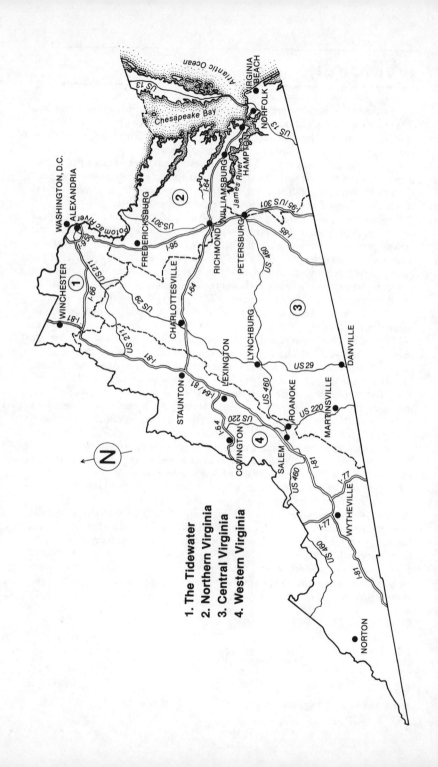

1. The Tidewater
2. Northern Virginia
3. Central Virginia
4. Western Virginia

The Tidewater

Along Virginia's scenic coast and beautiful river the first documented English settlements in America were established, predating the more famous pilgrims' landing in Massachusetts by more than a decade. Three tiny ships landed at Jamestown in 1607, having first stopped farther south at what is now Virginia Beach. The Tidewater saw some of the most decisive battles of the Revolutionary and Civil Wars; it was here in 1781 that Cornwallis was finally defeated, and Richmond's evacuation in 1865 presaged the Confederacy's surrender by only a few days.

Bacon's Castle

BACON'S CASTLE, off VA 10, c. 1655. Built by immigrant Arthur Allen, this wonderful gabled, multi-chimneyed Jacobean manor house is one of the oldest brick houses in English North America. It took its name from an episode in which supporters of the rebel Nathaniel Bacon seized the estate from Arthur Allen's son in 1676, fortified it, and held it for four months in their battle against the tyrannical rule of Royal Governor William Berkeley. Operated by the APVA, Bacon's Castle is undergoing complete restoration, but is open by appointment. NR, NHL. (804) 357-5976.

Beaverdam

SCOTCHTOWN, VA 685, c. 1719. Charles Chiswell, a Scottish immigrant who had arrived in Virginia in the late 17th century, was deeded nearly 10,000 acres of prime farmland in 1717 and built his frame plantation house shortly thereafter. Roughly sixty years later, Patrick Henry purchased Scotchtown and some of the surrounding acreage at auction, and it was his home during his most active political years. Operated by the APVA, Scotchtown has been painstakingly restored and is furnished with 18th-century antiques. Henry's nearby law office, a separate kitchen, and a guesthouse have been reconstructed. NR, NHL. Open Apr-Oct, M-Sa 10-5, Su 2-5. $2 adults, 75¢ children under 19, group rates. (804) 227-3500.

Charles City vicinity

North of Williamsburg along VA 5 are the well-marked entrances to a number of historic James River plantations, which could easily occupy a full day or more on the traveler's itinerary. They are listed in order from southeast (Williamsburg) to northwest (Richmond).

SHERWOOD FOREST PLANTATION, VA 5, 1780. John Tyler, President of the

Scotchtown

United States, lived in this 2½-story frame gabled house for the last two decades of his life. After purchasing the estate in 1842, he added a covered colonnade to connect the main house with the kitchen and laundry, and a corresponding wing to serve as a ballroom and private office. Original china, books, and furniture from Tyler's time are still in place. NR, NHL. Open all year, daily 9-5. $3.50 adults, $3 senior citizens, $1.75 children 6-12, group rates. (804) 829-5377.

BELLE AIR, north of VA 5, c. 1700. The oldest house on the old Williamsburg to Richmond road, Belle Air is a frame residence surrounded by beautifully manicured grounds and furnished with 18th-century antiques. NR. Open during Historic Garden Week at the end of April and to groups by appointment. (804) 866-8486.

Not far from Belle Air, off VA 5, is **Westover Church** (1731), a brick Georgian structure whose parish is one of the oldest in the country, documented as having been established as early as 1625. NR.

WESTOVER, VA 5, 1730-34. A noted example of early Georgian domestic architecture, Westover is a 2½-story brick mansion built by William Byrd II, tobacco planter and founder of nearby Richmond. Although the house itself is open only during Historic Garden Week in April, the beautiful grounds overlooking the James River, with their sweeping lawns, old shrubs, and lovely plantings, are accessible all year. NR, NHL. Open daily 9-6. $1 adults, 50¢ children 7-15. (804) 866-8486.

BERKELEY PLANTATION, VA 5, 1726. Berkeley, built by Benjamin Harrison, fourth in a family line so named, was the birthplace nearly fifty years later of President William Henry Harrison and, two generations later, of his grandson, who became President Benjamin Harrison. As the ancestral home of two presidents, Berkeley has a distinction shared only with the Adams House in Massachusetts. **Harrison's Landing**, below the large Georgian brick manor house, was for most of the 18th century one of the chief shipping points on the James River, and the house was the scene of lavish entertaining: every president from Washington to Buchanan enjoyed the Harrison hospitality at one time or another. NR, NHL. Open all year, daily 8-5. $4.50 adults, $3.50 senior citizens, $1.75 children 6-12, group rates. (804) 795-2453.

SHIRLEY PLANTATION, VA 5, 1770. Shirley Plantation was part of a large tract of land patented by Edward Hill in 1660; Anne Hill Carter, mother of Robert E. Lee, was born in the two-story brick manor house in 1773. The 800-acre James River estate on which the Georgian main house stands is still owned and operated by descendants of the original owners; furnishings and family possessions of the Hills and Carters remain in the mansion, many in the same places they have occupied for more than two centuries. NR. Open all year, daily 9-5. $2.50 adults, $1.50 students, $1 children, group rates. (804) 829-5121.

The Eastern Shore

Virginia's Eastern Shore is a long, narrow peninsula connected not to the rest of the state, but to the southern border of Maryland. Accessible either from Maryland or via the Chesapeake Bay Bridge-Tunnel from Norfolk, the sparsely-populated area is bisected by US 13, which connects small hamlets and villages along the way.

Chances are you won't come to this

beautiful area for its history, but for the quiet and the chance to dabble in the Atlantic or the more tranquil waters of Chesapeake Bay. But the first English settlers arrived here in 1614, and there are reminders of this and of other early periods throughout the peninsula. **Assateague Island,** which parallels the shore, is administered by the states of Virginia and Maryland and by the federal government, which has designated it a national seashore and wildlife refuge. Legend says that the wild ponies which roam the island are descendants of horses carried in a Spanish galleon which was wrecked 400 years ago; each July they are rounded up and sold at auction in nearby **Chincoteague.** The seashore visitor center is open all year, daily 8:30-5. Nominal admission to wildlife tours on Assateague. (804) 336-6122.

Also in Chincoteague is the **Oyster Museum of Chinco,** Beach Rd., whose displays depict the seafood industry so vital to residents of the area. The children will enjoy the live marine life exhibits. Open Apr, Oct-Nov Sa-Su 10-5; May-Sept daily 10-5. $1 adults, 25¢ children. (804) 336-6117.

Fredericksburg

Fredericksburg was first settled in 1671 just below the falls of the Rappahannock River. By the mid-18th century it had evolved into a commercial center of note, and its 40-block historic district (see following) includes both the old downtown commercial center and several residential areas as well. As an important colonial port city, Fredericksburg was a center of Revolutionary War preparations and figured prominently in the Civil War as well: four of the war's major battles were fought here, and the city changed hands no fewer than seven times during the conflict.

FREDERICKSBURG HISTORIC DISTRICT, 18th-20th centuries. Any tour of the central downtown area, where hundreds of 18th- and 19th-century buildings are still in use as homes, shops, and museums, should begin at the **Bicentennial Visitor Center,** 706 Caroline St., where brochures and maps are available and a

short film which introduces many of the city's historic sites is shown. The center itself is an early residence, the **George Norwood House** (c. 1817). (703) 373-1776.

Historic Fredericksburg Foundation Museum, 623 Caroline St., 1771. **The Chimneys,** a two-story Georgian frame house so named because of the massive

twin chimneys at its ends, is now home to the Foundation's fine collection of costumes, Civil War artifacts, antique furnishings, and personal objects once owned by many of Fredericksburg's outstanding citizens. NR. Open Mar-Dec, daily 9-5. $1.50 adults, 50¢ children over 6. (703) 371-4504.

Kenmore, 1201 Washington Ave., c. 1750. This handsome Georgian home was built by Fielding Lewis, brother-in-law of George Washington, for his bride, Betty. Lewis served in the Virginia House of Burgesses, was a member of a local committee of correspondence, and superintended the manufacture of small arms in Fredericksburg during the Revolution. The mansion reflects the status and taste of the Lewis family, with decorative plasterwork seldom seen in Virginia houses of the time. NR, NHL. Open Apr-Oct, daily 9-5; Nov-Mar, daily 9-4. $2.50 adults, $1 children 6-15. (703) 373-3381.

Masonic Lodge No. 4, 803 Princess Anne St., 18th century. George Washington was initiated a Mason at this two-story brick lodge in 1752. The bible used during his initiation, along with the minute book recording the event, are displayed. Open all year, M-Sa 9-4, Su 1-4. $1.50 adults, 50¢ children 6-12. (703) 373-5885.

Hugh Mercer Apothecary Shop, 1020 Caroline St., c. 1761. Silver-plated pills, a rose-water "still," and hand-blown glass apothecary jars painted on the inside are just a few of the interesting items on display in this early doctor's office and apothecary. Operated by the APVA. Open winter, daily 9-4; summer, daily 9-5. $1.50 adults, 50¢ children 5-17, group rates. (703) 373-3362.

James Monroe Law Office-Museum, 908 Charles St., 1758. In the early 1780s James Monroe studied law with Thomas Jefferson; he opened his own practice in this small brick building in 1786, but was here only three years before returning to politics and eventually the presidency. A modern museum building attached to the old office contains many exhibits relating to Monroe and his long political career. Operated by Mary Washington College. NR, NHL. Open all year, daily 9-5. $1.50 adults, 50¢ children. (703) 373-8426.

Rising Sun Tavern, 1306 Caroline St., 1760. Built by the youngest brother of George Washington, Rising Sun Tavern fulfilled an important function in 18th-century life as a political and social meeting place for leading figures of the day. Here in 1776, a group led by Thomas Jefferson outlined the bill that he later phrased as the Virginia Statute for Religious Liberty. Operated by the APVA. NR, NHL. Open Mar-Nov. daily 9-5; Nov-Apr. daily 9-4:30. $1.50 adults, 50¢ children, group rates. (703) 371-1494.

Mary Washington House, 1200 Charles St., c. 1761. Mary Ball Washington spent the last seventeen years of her life in this comfortable frame home bought for her by her son, George. It was here that the new president came to receive his mother's blessing before his inauguration in 1789; many of Mrs. Washington's favorite possessions are on display. Operated by the APVA. NR. Open Mar-Nov, daily 9-5; Dec-Feb daily 9-4:30. $1.50 adults, 50¢ children, group rates. (703) 373-1569.

FREDERICKSBURG/SPOTSYLVANIA NATIONAL MILITARY PARK, 1862-64. This national park contains nearly 7,000 acres of land on which four major Civil War battles were fought. For a park service map of the area and the many historic sites within it, your first stop should be the **Fredericksburg Battlefield Visitor Center,** Lafayette Blvd. at Sunken Rd., whose exhibits include a diorama outlining the battles, many Civil War relics, and photographs. Open all year, daily 9-5. Free. (703) 373-4461. Across Sunken Rd. from the Visitor Center is **Fredericksburg National Cemetery,** where more than 15,000 troops killed during the Civil War are interred. ★

On the east side of the Rappahannock is **Chatham** (1771), 120 Chatham Ln., a Georgian mansion which served as Union headquarters during the war. Clara Barton and Walt Whitman are known to have nursed the wounded here. Open all year, daily 9-5. Free. (703) 373-4461.

Fredericksburg vicinity

BELMONT, 224 Washington St., Falmouth, 1761. Situated on a hill overlooking the Rappahannock to the north of Fredericksburg, Belmont was the home of Gari Melchers, landscape and portrait painter, who is best known for the murals he executed for the Library of Congress. Many of Melchers' works are on display here, along with fine European and American antiques collected by his family. NR, NHL. Open all year, M, W, F-Su 1-4 and by appointment. $1.50 adults, 50¢ children 6-18, guided tours additional. (703) 373-3634.

Glen Allen

MEADOW FARM MUSEUM, Mountain and Courtney Rds., c. 1810. Meadow farm is one of the last remaining 19th-century farms in Henrico County and was owned by the same family for four generations. The house sits on 150 bucolic acres, planted with old fruit and shade trees and laced with nature trails. Inside are many Sheppard/Crump family furnishings and early farm tools. NR. Open all year, Tu-Su 10-4. $1 adults, 50¢ children. (804) 788-0391.

Gloucester

GLOUCESTER COUNTY COURT HOUSE, Court House Sq., c. 1766. This brick T-shaped colonial courthouse is the focal point of an historic square which contains a number of 18th- and 19th-century buildings, including the jail and small law offices necessary to an early county seat. Visit the court house for information about the area and to see portraits of Gloucester's famous native sons — among them Major Walter Reed, conqueror of yellow fever, and Nathaniel Bacon, leader of the 1676 rebellion against the Crown. NR. Open all year, M-F 8:30-4:30. Free. (804) 693-2502.

Gloucester vicinity

Walter Reed's Birthplace, a 19th-century frame residence, is about 5 miles southwest of Gloucester at the junction of VA 614 and VA 616. It may be toured upon request. NR. 50¢ adults, 10¢ children 6-12. (804) 693-3693. Nearby is Rosewell (c. 1725), the seat of the Page family and most notably the home of John Page, a member of Congress and governor of Virginia. Although the brick house was burned in 1916, enough remains to indicate that this was once one of the state's largest and finest colonial mansions, noted for its architecture and its extraordinary brickwork. The ruins can be toured. (804) 693-5380.

The Page family tombs, which were originally at Rosewell, have been moved a few miles away to Abingdon Church (c. 1755), a brick Georgian church which is only the second to serve a parish established in the mid-17th century. Located near White Marsh on US 17, Abingdon Church is open on a regular basis. (804) 693-3035.

If you haven't tired of ecclesiastical architecture, just north of Gloucester on VA 14 is one of the earliest churches in Virginia, Ware Parish Church (1715), a well-preserved Georgian building where American infantry camped during the Revolutionary War, and Union troops during the Civil War. NR. (804) 693-3821.

Hampton

Hampton, one of the oldest English settlements in North America, traces its beginnings from the early village of Kecoughtan in 1610. The town was burned in 1861 to prevent its falling into the hands of Union forces and rebuilt after the war by energetic citizens and veterans. The town's Information Center, 413 W. Mercury Blvd., offers maps of the area, and drivers will find clearly posted markers identifying the route of the Hampton Tour, along which major sites are located. (804) 877-0522.

FORT MONROE (Fortress Monroe), Old Point Comfort, 1819-34. As the nearest continuously-held Union stronghold to the Confederate capital, Fort Monroe played an important role in the Civil War. From its ramparts spectators watched the epic battle between the U.S.S. Monitor and the C.S.S. Virginia (Merrimac). Jefferson Davis was imprisoned here after the fall of the Confederacy. The oldest building on the fort grounds is Quarters Number One, built shortly after 1819. President Lincoln stayed here in May, 1862, planning operations which led to the fall of Norfolk. The Casemate Museum, located within the old fort's walls, displays the cell in which Davis was imprisoned; other exhibits document the history of the fort. Chapel of the Centurion, dedicated in 1858, is still the Protestant chapel of the current Continental Army Command. It was named for the Roman centurion, Cornelius, who was converted to Christianity by the Apostle Peter. NR, NHL. Open all year, daily 10:30-5. Free. (804) 727-3391. ★

HAMPTON INSTITUTE, NW of US 60 and Hampton Roads Bridge Tunnel, 19th century. The town of Hampton became a gathering place for freed slaves at the close of the Civil War; Hampton Institute was opened in 1868 with the primary goal of teaching those freedmen. Outstanding among the campus's early buildings are the **Mansion House** (now the president's house), originally a plantation residence; **Virginia Hall** (c. 1871), designed by Richard Morris Hunt in the French Renaissance style; and the Romanesque **Memorial Church,** designed by J. C. Cady. A museum in the old **Academy Building** includes Indian and African artifacts and displays featuring such prominent alumni as Booker T. Washington. NR. (804) 727-5254.

ST. JOHN'S CHURCH, W. Queen and Court Sts., c. 1728. St. John's, the fourth building to serve Hampton's Episcopal parish, is a colonial brick structure whose interior decor dates from Victorian times. NR. Open all year, daily 9-4. Free. (804) 722-2567.

SYMS-EATON MUSEUM, 418 W. Mercury Blvd. Named for Benjamin Sims and Thomas Eaton, who are credited with developing free public school education in America, the museum features historical exhibits on education and on Hampton history. Open winter, M-F 8-4:30; summer, M-F 8:30-5, Sa-Su 10-5. Free. (804) 727-6248.

Hanover

HANOVER COUNTY COURTHOUSE HISTORIC DISTRICT, 18th-20th centuries. The focal point of tiny Hanover is its courthouse, built c. 1735, a one-story Georgian brick building famous as the site where Patrick Henry pleaded his first well-known case, the Parson's Cause, in 1763, by attacking the "misrule of the King and the greed of the clergy." Many of the battles north of Richmond during the Civil War were fought in the vicinity of the courthouse; it was there in 1862 that

J.E.B. Stuart received his commission as a Major General in the Confederate Army. The building has been in continuous use for nearly 250 years. NR, NHL. (804) 798-6081.

Nearby is the old **jail,** built around 1835, and opposite the courthouse the venerable 18th-century **Hanover Tavern,** a rambling, picturesque frame building now a dinner-theater called the **Barksdale Theater.** NR. Open all year, W-Sa 6-10:30 pm. (804) 798-6547.

Hopewell

WESTON MANOR, off VA 10, c. 1780. One of the few plantation houses remaining on the lower Appomattox River, this early Georgian frame dwelling is on land granted to the Eppes family by the British Crown in 1635. Interior features include carved paneling, a 25-foot entrance hall, and heart pine flooring. NR. Open all year by appointment. (804) 458-5536.

Hopewell vicinity

FLOWERDEW HUNDRED, VA 639. Located on the south bank of the James River, this site was originally inhabited by American Indians. Excavations have uncovered ancient artifacts dating from 9000 B.C. to the Civil War period. The area's odd name stems from Governor George Yardly, granted the land in 1618, who called his estate Flowerdew after his wife's English family. Archaeological work continues here today; and a fully-operational reconstruction of an 18th-century windmill has recently been completed on the property. NR. Open Apr-Nov, Tu-Su 10-5. $2.50 adults, $1.50 children 6-12. (804) 541-8897.

MERCHANT'S HOPE CHURCH, VA 641 and VA 10. This 17th-century church is notable both for its age and for its colonial brickwork, rather elaborate for the period. Although most of the interior dates from an extensive renovation in 1870, the original Portland stone flooring tiles are intact, and one roof timber of the structure has the date 1657 (or 87, it's difficult to tell) carved on it. NR. Donations accepted. (804) 458-8657.

Jamestown

COLONIAL NATIONAL HISTORICAL
PARK, Colonial Pkwy., 17th century.
This is where it all began: the site of the
first permanent English settlement in
America. "James Cittie," which has long
since disappeared, was the capital of the
colony of Virginia during its first century
of development, 1607-98. In 1619 the first
meeting of the House of Burgesses, the first
representative legislative assembly in the
New World, was held here. Among the
well-known persons associated with the
colony's early years are Captain John
Smith, John Rolfe, and his wife, the Indian
maiden Pocahontas—names that every
school child learns today. With the exception of the **Old Church Tower,** which dates
from the 1640s, there are no remains of the
settlement above ground. But archaeological excavations have uncovered foundations of houses and public buildings, remains of streets, and many small artifacts
of the 17th-century settlement. Jamestown
and Yorktown (which see) make up Colonial National Historical Park. Administered by the National Park Service, it has
been filled with interpretive markers point-
ing out key sites of Jamestown, which is a
small island in the James River separated
from the mainland by narrow Back Creek.
The **visitor center and museum** should be
your first stop—you can arrange for a
guided tour, pick up maps to make your
visit more meaningful, and look at the
17th-century artifacts on display. NR.
Open all year, daily 8:30-4:30. $2 per
vehicle. (804) 898-3400.

JAMESTOWN FESTIVAL PARK, VA 31.
Not far from archaeological excavations
of Jamestown Island is an ambitious full-
scale replica of James Fort, which the first
English settlers erected on their arrival in
1607. Moored on the James are accurate
reproductions of the colonists' three ships.
A reconstruction of Chief Powhatan's
17th-century lodge has displays of artifacts
discovered nearby. The park is not truly
historic, but it's fun for the kids. Operated
by the state. Open all year, daily 9-5.
$2.50 adults, $1.25 children, group rates.
(804) 229-1607. ✔

Kilmarnock vicinity

CHRIST CHURCH, 3 miles S. via VA 3,
1732. The history of this early brick
church is linked with the Carter family,
particularly Robert "King" Carter, whose
tomb, together with those of his two
wives, is a feature of the quiet churchyard.
Carter was agent for Lord Fairfax, proprietor of the Northern Neck—all the land
lying between the Potomac and Rappahannock Rivers. He was at one time treasurer
of the colony, and served successively as
speaker of the House of Burgesses,
member of the council, and acting governor of Virginia. Christ Church was erected
on the site of an earlier wooden church
built about 1669; Carter offered to build
the new church at his own expense as long
as the identical site was retained and the
family grave of his parents remained in the
chancel, as it does today. The beautiful
Georgian church has been completely
restored, and is operated as a museum by
the Foundation for Historic Christ
Church. NR, NHL. Open all year, daily
9-5. Donations accepted. (703) 438-6855.

New Kent vicinity

ST. PETER'S CHURCH, county road
642, 18th century. This early Colonial

brick church is one of the oldest in Virginia, thought to have been constructed in the early 1700s. Much of both the interior and exterior have been restored to a condition approximating the original; there is some speculation that George and Martha Washington were married here, as she once lived not far away and St. Peter's was her parish church before she moved to Mt. Vernon. NR. Open all year. Call (804) 932-4846 for information.

Newport News

THE MARINERS MUSEUM, Museum Dr. Old salts of all ages will enjoy a visit to this museum, whose collection of maritime artifacts is one of the most extensive in the world. Its small craft collection brings together over 100 boats from many ports; there is a superb display of miniature ships, decorative arts, paintings, and relics from the sea floor. Open all year, M-Sa 9-5, Su 12-5. $1.50 adults, 75¢ children, group rates. (804) 595-0368. ✔

THE WAR MEMORIAL MUSEUM OF VIRGINIA, 9285 Warwick Blvd. Thousands of artifacts representing every American conflict from Revolutionary times to Vietnam—weapons, posters, uniforms, aircraft, tanks, artillery and more —will make this a required stop for the military buff. Open all year, M-Sa 9-5, Su 1-5. 50¢ adults, 25¢ children and senior citizens, group rates. (804) 247-8523. ★ ✔

Norfolk

The port of Norfolk was founded by decree of King Charles II in 1682, and by 1736 it was the largest town in Virginia. During the Revolutionary War, however, Norfolk was almost totally destroyed by the British, and thus most of its historic buildings date from the last years of the 18th century or later. 20th-century bulldozers have destroyed a great deal of the city's early architecture in the name of progress: for a glimpse of the town that used to be, you might want to wander through the West Freemason St. Area Historic District, located mainly on W. Freemason and Bute Sts., near the Elizabeth River. Norfolk's other historic attractions are centered in the downtown area, but there are a number to the north as well. The city has posted markers clearly delineating the route of the Norfolk Tour along which most of these attractions are located.

THE CHRYSLER MUSEUM, Olney Rd. and Mowbray Arch. This superb general art museum is considered to be one of the finest in the country. The museum also administers three of Norfolk's finest historic landmark homes—the Adam Thoroughgood, Willoughby-Baylor, and Moses Myers houses, which are treated separately in these listings. Open all year, Tu-Sa 10-4, Su 1-5. Free. (804) 622-1211.

GENERAL DOUGLAS MacARTHUR MEMORIAL, 421 E. City Hall Ave., 1847-50. Norfolk's old city hall and courthouse, a granite faced Greek Revival building, was renovated as a memorial to MacArthur in 1960 when he agreed to house his papers and memorabilia in the city. After MacArthur's death four years later, the great marble rotunda was adapted to serve as his tomb. NR. Open all year, M-Sa 10-5. Su 11-5. Free. (804) 441-2382. ★

MOSES MYERS HOUSE, E. Freemason and N. Bank Sts., c. 1792. The Norfolk home of merchant Moses Myers was one of the first brick houses built after the British destroyed the city in 1776. The Federal-style residence retains many of its original furnishings. NR. Open Apr-Nov, Tu-Sa 10-5, Su 12-5; Dec-Mar, Tu-Su 12-5. $2 adults, $1 children. (804) 622-1211.

Diagonally across the street from the Myers House is the Gothic Revival Freemason Street Baptist Church (1850), designed in stuccoed brick by Thomas U. Walter. NR.

NORFOLK NAVAL STATION AND NAVAL AIR STATION, Hampton Blvd. and I-564. Norfolk is home for over 100 ships of the Atlantic and Mediterranean fleets and for 38 aircraft squadrons. Within the confines of the huge military base are a group of buildings dubbed the **Jamestown Exposition Site**. Constructed in 1907, these 23 frame and brick buildings, most in the Georgian Revival style, were originally exhibition pavilions for an exposition organized to celebrate the tercentennial of the founding of Jamestown. The **Pennsylvania Building**, more or less a replica of Independence Hall, houses the **Hampton Roads Naval Museum**, whose collections include ship models, photographs, naval prints and other artwork, and nautical artifacts. NR. Open all year, M-F 9-5, Sa 9-4, Su 10-4. Free. (804) 444-3827. Tours of the base are available mid Apr-Oct, daily 10:30-2:30. $2 adults, $1 children 6-12. (804) 444-7955. ★ ✔

ST. PAUL'S CHURCH, 201 St. Paul's Blvd., 1739. St. Paul's is the oldest building in the city; badly damaged during the British bombardment in 1776 (a cannonball is imbedded in one wall), the Georgian brick building was restored after the Revolution. Today the venerable structure is operated as a museum, but Sunday services are still held. NR. Open all year, Tu-Sa 10-4:30, Su 2-4:30. Free. (804) 627-4353.

ADAM THOROUGHGOOD HOUSE, 1636 Parish Rd., c. 1636. This small brick house is one of the oldest in the country; built by Thoroughgood, who came to Virginia in 1621 as an indentured servant and eventually became a member of the House of Burgesses and a large landowner, the house, beautifully restored, and with a lovely 17th-century garden adjacent, is a mainstay of the Norfolk Tour, though it is in fact just across the town line in Virginia Beach (which see). NR, NHL. Open Apr-Nov, Tu-Sa 10-5, Su 11-5; Dec-Mar, daily 12-5. $1 adults, 50¢ children. (804) 622-1211.

WILLOUGHBY-BAYLOR HOUSE, 601 E. Freemason St., c. 1794. This detached two-story brick town house was built by Captain William Willoughby on the site of America's first Freemason lodge, which had burned during the Revolution. The house reflects both Georgian and Federal architecture and is furnished with 18th-century pieces. NR. Open Apr-Nov, M-Sa 10-5, Su 11-5; Dec-Mar, Tu-Su 12-5. $1 adults, 50¢ children. (804) 622-1211.

Petersburg

Petersburg was founded in 1645 as a frontier fort (Fort Henry), but not incorporated as a city until 1850, by which time the thriving industrial and commercial center was approaching its heyday. Nearby plantations depended on its tobacco warehouses, cotton and flour mills, and iron foundries; many of their products were shipped from the city's docks down the Appomattox and James rivers to Europe.

CENTRE HILL MANSION, Centre Hill Ct., c. 1820. After the siege of Petersburg, Major General G. L. Harsuff, district commander of the Union forces, made this elegant brick Greek Revival mansion his headquarters. President Lincoln is known to have visited here in 1865; many of the furnishings which decorated the house at his visit are on display. Operated by the state chapter of the Victorian Society in America. NR. Open all year, M-Sa 9-5, Su 1-5. Free. (804) 732-8081.

OLD BLANDFORD CHURCH, 321 S. Crater Rd., 1736. This small unprepossessing brick church contains surprising treasure: fifteen stained-glass windows designed by Louis Comfort Tiffany in 1901. Each state of the former Confederacy paid for a window as part of the church's restoration and rebirth as a Confederate memorial. An information center on the grounds provides details about the church's varied history (it was used as a field hospital during the Civil War) and the many old gravestones in its cemetery. NR. Open all year, M-Sa 9-5, Su 12-5. Free. (804) 732-2230.

PETERSBURG OLD TOWN HISTORIC DISTRICT, 18th-20th centuries. "Old Towne," as the natives call it, is Petersburg's most historic area, a mix of public, religious, commercial, and residential buildings representing a variety of architectural styles, from the early Georgian and Federal to Greek Revival, Italianate, and Queen Anne. **City Market** (1878), at

Rock and W. Old Sts., is a one-story brick structure whose location has been an important site for buying and selling since the late 1700s. NR.

Farmers Bank, 19 Bollingbrook St., is a Federal brick building completed in 1817. The bank failed at the end of the Civil War, but its old double vault, gold-measuring scales, and the press and plates used to print money have been preserved, along with many other remnants of the financial boom years. Operated by the APVA. NR. Open all year, Tu-Su 10-5. Free. (804) 861-1590.

The old **Exchange Building** (1841), 19 W. Bank St., a brick and stucco Greek Revival landmark built by members of the Petersburg Exchange to house tobacco and cotton displays, auctions and sales, has been transformed into the **Siege Museum**, which documents town life during the last months of the Civil War. NR, NHL. Open all year, M-Sa 9-5, Su 1-5. Free. (804) 861-2904. ★

As you wander through the streets of the Old Town District, make a point of stopping at **Trapezium House** on North Market St., a town house built c. 1816 by an eccentric Irish bachelor whose West Indian servant encouraged his superstitions. Charles O'Hara became convinced that right angles harbored ghosts and evil spirits, so he ordered his home built in the form of a trapezium—with no parallel sides and no right angles. This architectural oddity is currently being restored by the city. NR. (804) 861-8080.

Petersburg vicinity

PETERSBURG NATIONAL BATTLEFIELD, S and W off VA 36, 1864-5. In a grim ten-month struggle, Ulysses S. Grant's Union army gradually but relentlessly encircled Petersburg and cut Robert E. Lee's railroad supply lines from the south. The decisive Confederate defeat at

Richmond

Five Forks and Petersburg in early April, 1865, led to the city's evacuation, and only a week later to Lee's surrender at Appomattox. The National Park Service operates a **visitor center** east of Petersburg off VA 36; this is a good first stop for maps of the battlefield, a look at war relics, and an introductory presentation explaining the campaign. NR. Open Sept-mid June, daily 8-5; summer, daily 8-7. Free. (804) 732-3531. ★

Portsmouth

HILL HOUSE, 221 North St., early 19th century. Owned by one prosperous Portsmouth family for more than 150 years, this handsomely furnished residence is a fine example of the "basement house" prevalent in the port city because of its low-lying topography. Basements could not be dug because of the high water table; serving and dining areas, ususally sited underground, therefore had to be located on the first floor. Operated by the Portsmouth Historical Society. NR Open all year, Tu-Su 2-5. Nominal admission. (804) 393-0241.

PORTSMOUTH NAVAL SHIPYARD MUSEUM, High St. This maritime collection traces the history of the shipyard, the Portsmouth area, and the armed forces of the locality, including the history of the ship that changed the course of naval history, the world-famous C.S.S. *Virginia (Merrimac)*. Open all year, Tu-Sa 10-5, Su 2-5. Free. (804) 393-8741. ★ ✔

Just to the west, at London Blvd.'s meeting with the Elizabeth River, is berthed the **Portsmouth Lightship Museum**, a former U.S. Coast Guard vessel permanently moored here in the 1960s after nearly fifty years of active service. The ship exhibits artifacts relating to lightship service, including photographs, uniforms, and Coast Guard equipment. Open all year, Tu-Sa 10-4:45, Su 2-4:45. Free. (804) 393-8741. ✔

Virginia's capital and largest city celebrated its official bicentennial in 1982, *though settlements were known on this part of the James River as early as 1609*

and it became the seat of Virginia government in 1780. Colonel William Byrd, who owned much of the land along the James in the early 18th century, named the town Richmond because of its similarities to Richmond on the Thames, which he had become familiar with during his school years in England. By the outbreak of the Civil War, Richmond was an important port city, and was named capital of the new Confederate States of the Union under President Jefferson Davis. Although the city was high on the Union Army's list for capture, it withstood siege after siege until late in the war, and was not evacuated until April, 1865. Today the capital sprawls out from both banks of the James, but its major attractions are all located on the northern side of the river. The listings which follow are arranged within five geographic sections to make touring easier.

Capitol Square

VIRGINIA STATE CAPITOL, 1785-92. The focal point of Capital Square, and of Richmond, was the first public building in America to be designed in the Classical Revival style and was a collaboration between Thomas Jefferson and French architect Charles-Louis Clerisseau. The original white-painted brick building is today the center of the capitol — the wings were added in the early 20th century to accommodate new House and Senate chambers. The imposing central **rotunda** is the setting for one of the most famous and historic

marble statues in the United States, Jean Antoine Houdon's life-sized **statue of George Washington,** completed in 1788. Houdon executed the statue from life — it is the only sculpture of Washington so created, and as such is thought to be the most perfect likeness of the first president. The old **Hall of the House of Delegates,** located off the Rotunda opposite the portico entrance, was the meeting place of the Virginia House from 1788 until 1906. It was here in 1807 that Aaron Burr was acquitted of treason; the Hall is now a museum of state treasures, including statues of many of Virginia's most prominent citizens. NR, NHL. Open Apr-Nov, daily 9-5; Dec-Mar, M-Sa 9-5, Su 1-5. Free. (804) 786-4344.

On the capitol grounds is the **Executive Mansion,** a two-story Federal brick building designed by Alexander Parris that has been home to every Virginia governor since it was completed in 1813. NR. Open in Apr during Historic Garden Week. (804) 644-7776.

ST. PAUL'S CHURCH, 815 E. Grace St., 1845. This stuccoed brick Episcopal church was constructed in the style of a Roman temple with a Greek Corinthian portico, the whole designed by Thomas B. Stewart. During services here on Sunday, April 2, 1865, President Jefferson Davis received word that General Robert E. Lee could no longer hold the nearby city of Petersburg, and that he should therefore

evacuate Richmond. NR. Open all year, M-Sa 10-4, Su 1-4. Donations accepted. (804) 643-3589.

North and East Richmond

JOHN MARSHALL HOUSE, 9th and Marshall Sts., 1790. As chief justice, John Marshall presided over the United States Supreme Court during its formative years, 1801-35, and is credited with helping to weld what had been a weak compact of sovereign states into a truly national government. Marshall owned this square brick house for nearly half a century, and it remained in the possession of his descendants until the early 1900s, when it was acquired by the city. Both the house and its small garden have been restored; many of the furnishings are original, and a comprehensive collection of Marshall memorabilia is on display. Operated by APVA. NR, NHL. Open all year, Tu-Sa 11-4. Free. (804) 648-7998.

MUSEUM OF THE CONFEDERACY, 12th and Clay Sts., 1818. This Federal brick mansion, designed by Robert Mills, architect of the Washington Monument, was built for Dr. John Brockenbrough, a Richmond physician and banker. In 1861, when Richmond became the capital of the Confederacy, the city rented the house to the Southern government for the use of Jefferson Davis and his family. Known as the White House of the Confederacy, the mansion has been meticulously restored; within it and a new adjacent museum building is housed an outstanding collection of material relating to the Civil War. NR,

NHL. Open all year, M-Sa 10-5, Su 2-5. $1 adults, 50¢ children, group rates. (804) 649-1861. ★

Nearby is another landmark designed by Robert Mills: Monumental Church (1812), 1224 E. Broad St., is an octagonal stuccoed building erected as a memorial to the 72 people, including Governor George William Smith, who died in a fire during a theater performance in December, 1811. NR. Behind the church is the Egyptian Building (1845), an exotic Egyptian Revival structure erected as the first campus building for the Medical College of Virginia, the South's oldest such school. Note the iron fence, with its posts shaped like mummies. NR. Both of these historic buildings are now owned by the college. (804) 786-9734.

VALENTINE MUSEUM, 1005 E. Clay St., 1812, 1840, 1870. The repository for a superb collection of historic and cultural artifacts relating to the city of Richmond and the state of Virginia, the Valentine Museum is housed in three separate 19th-century landmarks. The principal building—and the earliest—is the Wickham-Valentine House, one of Richmond's finest Federal residences, designed by Alexander Parris and built for lawyer John Wickham, who served as one of the defense attorneys in Aaron Burr's trial. Mann Valentine II, a collector of historic artifacts, purchased the house in 1882, and at his death ten years later left both the house and his fine collection to the city. The two-story mansion has been restored and its rooms furnished to reflect the changes in decor over the course of the 19th century. NR, NHL. Three connected Italianate town houses, built around 1870, and the Greek-Revival Bransford-Cecil House (1840), moved to the site in 1954, contain the balance of the museum's extensive holdings. NR. Open all year, Tu-Sa 10-5, Su 1:30-5. $2 adults, $1 students, group rates. (804) 649-0711.

Northwest Richmond

BATTLE ABBEY, 428 North Blvd. Headquarters of the Virginia Historical Society, this museum contains a fine collection of

Confederate arms, a large group of portraits, a gallery of flags, and an extensive collection of manuscripts and maps. Open all year, M-F 9-5, Sa-Su 2-5. Admission $1. (804) 358-4901. ★

MONUMENT AVENUE HISTORIC DISTRICT, bounded by Grace and Birch Sts., Park Ave. and Roseneath Rd., 19th-20th centuries. This is undoubtedly Richmond's most impressive thoroughfare, a wide, tree-shaded avenue lined with elegant Georgian Revival and Second Renaissance Revival town houses and terrace rows, named for the statues and memorials to Confederate leaders placed at intervals along its grassy central strip. Equestrian statues of **J.E.B. Stuart** (1907) and **Robert E. Lee** (1890); memorials to **Jefferson Davis** (1907) and **Matthew Fontaine Maury** (1929); and the **Jefferson Davis Memorial** (1907) have all been placed along this beautiful avenue. NR.

SCIENCE MUSEUM OF VIRGINIA, Broad and Robinson Sts., 1919. The old Broad St. Railroad Station, designed by John Russell Pope in the Neoclassical style popular in the early 20th century, has been adapted for use as a science museum, featuring hands-on displays and space and aeronautical exhibits. NR. Open all year, Tu-F 10-5, Sa-Su 1-5. $1.50 adults, $1 children 6-17. (804) 257-1013. ✔

THE VIRGINIA MUSEUM, Boulevard and Grove Ave. This was America's first state-supported arts institution (1936), and it is the largest museum of its kind in the southeast, with extensive collections of painting, sculpture, and the decorative arts spanning many centuries and cultures. Open all year, Tu-Sa 11-5, Su 1-5. 50¢ adults, seniors and children under 16 free. (804) 257-0844.

The West End

AGECROFT HALL, 4305 Sulgrave Rd., 1926-28. Set above the James River in the fashionable Windsor Farms residential district, Agecroft is a striking Tudor-Revival dwelling built in part with fragments from a post-medieval English manor house. Prominent Richmond businessman

Thomas C. Williams arranged to have the original Agecroft Hall, a late 16th-century English house, dismantled and had parts of it shipped to Virginia, where they were incorporated in his new residence. Carved oak paneling, sculpted plaster ceilings, and old stained-glass panels are among the elements which decorate the interior. NR. Open all year, Tu-F 10-4, Sa-Su 2-5. $1 adults, 50¢ children. (804) 353-4241.

HOLLYWOOD CEMETERY, 412 S. Cherry St., mid-19th century. Among the notables buried in this picturesque cemetery are J.E.B. Stuart, Jefferson Davis, and President John Tyler. A stone pyramid at the north end of the grounds marks the burial place of 18,000 Confederate soldiers; President James Monroe was reinterred here in an elaborate tomb in 1858. NR, NHL. Open all year, daily 8-5. Free. (804) 648-1234.

MAYMONT, 1700 Hampton St., 1890. Maymont is an elaborate, massive three-story mansion built for Major James H. Dooley, a wealthy industrialist and member of the Virginia House of Delegates, as part of an estate whose outbuildings include a stone stable, carriage house, and a manager's cottage. Today the mansion is the historic centerpiece of **Maymont Park**, whose 105 acres were bequeathed to the city in 1925. The mansion features collections of 19th-century stained glass, porcelain, and tapestry; the carriage house displays early horse-drawn vehicles, and the surrounding park offers a nature center, children's farm, gardens, and an arboretum among its attractions. NR. The park is open daily 10-5; the mansion Tu-Su 12-5. Free. (804) 358-7166. ✔

WILTON, S. Wilton Rd., c. 1750-54. This stately Georgian brick house was the residence of Peyton Randolph, speaker of the House of Burgesses, chairman of the First Virginia Convention in 1775, and president of the First Continental Congress. All walls are panelled from floor to ceiling in every room, hall, and closet—an unusual feature for the time. Wilton was moved from its original location across the James in the 1930s and reconstructed as the Virginia headquarters of the National

Society of the Colonial Dames of America. NR. Open all year, Tu-Sa 10-4, Su 2:30-4:30. $1.50 adults, 75¢ students, group rates. (804) 282-5936.

South and East of Capitol Square

CHURCH HILL, bounded roughly by 22nd, Marshall, 32nd, Main, and Franklin Sts. and Williamsburg Ave., 18th-19th centuries. The Historic Richmond Foundation has been fighting to preserve and renew this historic district, the oldest residential area in the city. The focal point of the district, which contains numerous examples of Federal, Greek Revival, and Neoclassical architecture, is the Georgian St. John's Episcopal Church at E. Broad and 24th Sts. Built on land donated by Colonel William Byrd in 1740, St. John's was the meeting place for Virginia's General Assembly in 1775, where Patrick Henry delivered his famous words, "Give me liberty or give me death." NR, NHL. Open Mar-Nov, M-Sa 10-4, Su for 11 am service. Donations accepted. (804) 643-7407.

Edgar Allan Poe Museum, 1914 E. Main St. The Poe Museum occupies five buildings that open on enclosed gardens; the central building, the Old Stone House (c. 1736), is thought to be Richmond's oldest building and is a rare example of colonial stone construction. Within the museum are manuscripts, illustrations, furniture, personal artifacts, and portraits owned by the poet or by members of his family. A scale model of the Richmond Poe knew in the early 19th century is on display. NR. Open all year, Tu-Sa 10-4:30; Su-M 1:30-4. $2 adults, $1 students. (804) 648-5523.

JAMES RIVER AND KANAWHA CANAL HISTORIC DISTRICT, 12th and Byrd Sts., 18th-19th centuries. George Washington dreamed of a waterway system from the Atlantic to the Rockies and saw the James River as an important part of that system, but the falls at Richmond made the waterway impassable. Two locks from the first canal system in America, started in the late 18th century, have been preserved at this site, along with an irregular stone bridge which was built to span the canal in 1860. Today the locks are part of a park maintained by Reynolds Metals Company, which offers a narrated audiovisual presentation explaining the waterway's history. NR. Open all year, daily 9-5. Free

SHOCKOE SLIP HISTORIC DISTRICT, E. Cary between S. 14th and S. 12th Sts., 18th-19th centuries. The old warehouse district of Richmond, full of stone and brick industrial buildings centered around a triangular plaza which gives the area its name, is enjoying a new incarnation as Richmond's most popular dining and shopping area. Originally established as a trading center, the slip developed into a bustling center for banks, hotels, warehouses, stores and exchanges. Though much of its architecture was destroyed during the evacuation of Richmond in 1865, the district was quickly rebuilt, and many of its most notable cast-iron-front buildings, such as the Branch Building (1866), 1015 E. Main, and the Stearns Building (1865-69), nearby at #1007, date from the period immediately following the end of the Civil War. Most merchants in the district have brochures available which suggest walking tours and explain the history and significance of the colorful riverside area. NR.

Richmond vicinity

RICHMOND NATIONAL BATTLE-FIELD PARK, E. of Richmond and in Henrico County, 1862-65. Portions of several battlefields and other sites associated with Union attempts to capture the Confederate capital are now included in this wide-ranging national park. Richmond's fall on April 3, 1865, was followed only six days later by Lee's surrender to Grant at Appomattox Court House (which see). The National Park Service maintains two visitor centers, in Richmond at 3215 E. Broad St., and south, off the Osborne Tpke., at Fort Harrison. Both centers offer maps of the park, displays of military artifacts, and explanations of the battles fought over the Confederate capital during the course of the Civil War. NR. Open all year, daily 9-5. Free. (804) 226-1981. ★

TUCKAHOE PLANTATION, 7 miles W. on River Rd., early 18th century. Tuckahoe is a two-story Georgian frame house still in a plantation setting with a nearby complex of eight outbuildings. Much of the main house's interior and exterior detailing is original; the oldest portion may have been constructed as early as 1712. The property was first owned by William Randolph, who passed it on to his son Thomas. A grandson of Thomas fell heir to the land while still an infant, so his guardian Peter Jefferson, father of the future president, lived here and took care of the property for him. Thomas Jefferson studied here for a time as a child. NR, NHL. Open by appointment. Admission $3. (804) 784-5736.

Smithfield vicinity

ST. LUKE'S CHURCH, 4 miles S. on VA 10, 1632. St. Luke's, known familiarly as "Old Brick," is the oldest existing Anglican church in America. Among the treasures to be found within are an ancient rood screen, a 17th-century American silver baptismal basin, and other early pieces of silver. NR, NHL. Open Feb-Dec, Tu-Su 9:30-5. Nominal admission. (804) 795-2453.

After you visit St. Luke's, drive north to the town of Smithfield to see one of the best preserved, picturesque, and prosperous colonial port towns in Virginia. Most of the old town is included in the Smithfield Historic District, where you'll find a variety of buildings ranging from the mid-17th century Isle of Wight Courthouse and Syke's Inn (you might like to stop here for lunch) to the Romanesque Revival Smithfield Baptist Church, completed in 1904. NR.

Stratford

STRATFORD HALL, VA 214, 1725-30. Stratford Hall, a notable example of early Georgian architecture, is best known as the birthplace of Robert E. Lee. General Lee's father and grandfather lived here before him; among his uncles were three signers of the Declaration of Independence, several governors of Virginia, and members of the Continental Congress. Exquisitely furnished with 18th-century antiques and decorative arts, including a superb collection of American silver, Stratford Hall is maintained as a working plantation; a number of the outbuildings (including stable and gristmill) have been restored on the lovely grounds. NR, NHL. Open all year, daily 9-4:30. $2.50 adults, 75¢ children, group rates. (804) 493-8038.

Surry

CHIPPOKES PLANTATION, VA 634, 17th-19th centuries. Located on the south bank of the James River, opposite Jamestown, Chippokes is a 1,400-acre working plantation. Buildings on the plantation reflect its growth over three centuries: the brick kitchen dates to the 18th century, and was probably built as the summer kitchen for the main house, which was replaced in 1854 by the present two-story Greek Revival mansion. Chippokes was named for an early Indian chief who was friendly to the English; his lands included the present plantation, first owned by Captain William Powell, a shareholder in the Virginia Company of 1609. Today operated by the state, Chippokes is maintained as a state park. NR. Open Memorial Day-Labor Day, daily 9-6. Nominal admission. (804) 294-3625.

SMITH'S FORT PLANTATION, VA 31, early 17th century. John Smith is believed to have constructed this fort, of which only the earthworks remain, during the first two years of the Virginia colony's existence. Close to the fort is Warren House, built in the mid-17th century by Thomas Warren, who purchased the land from Thomas Rolfe, son of John Rolfe and Pocahontas. Warren's 1½-story brick home has been restored and furnished with 17th-century pieces. Operated by the APVA. NR. Open Apr-Sept, W-Su 10-5. $2 adults, $1 students. (804) 357-5976.

Urbanna

OLD TOBACCO WAREHOUSE, county

road T-1002, 1763-67. Built for Scottish merchants both for the storage of their tobacco crops and to house imported goods they bought on credit, this early brick building is a rare surviving example of its type. Operated by the APVA. NR. Open all year, Tu, Th 2-5; F-Sa 10-1. Free. (804) 357-5976.

Virginia Beach

OLD CAPE HENRY LIGHTHOUSE
1791
LAND GIVEN BY THE STATE OF VIRGINIA 1789
FIRST LIGHTHOUSE BUILT BY
THE UNITED STATES GOVERNMENT
DEEDED BY CONGRESS IN 1930 TO
THE ASSOCIATION FOR THE PRESERVATION OF
VIRGINIA ANTIQUITIES

CAPE HENRY LIGHTHOUSE, Fort Story, off VA 60, 1760. The first group of English settlers to reach America's shores landed at Cape Henry in April, 1607, and spent a few days in the area before moving on to Jamestown, where their colony was established. A memorial, part of **Colonial National Historical Park,** which includes Jamestown and Yorktown, marks the approximate site of the first landing. Near the memorial is the old Cape Henry Light, the first built by the federal government. The octagonal stone tower was designed by John McComb, Jr., and was in use until 1881, when a new lighthouse was erected nearby. Operated by the APVA. NR, NHL. Open Memorial Day-Labor Day, daily 9-5. Free. (804) 460-1688.

LYNNHAVEN HOUSE, Wishart Rd. and Independence Blvd., 17th century. A remarkably intact survivor from the early days of colonial Virginia, this small 1½-story brick house stands much as it did about 1650 when built as a plantation dwelling on the frontier. The household skills and crafts practised 300 years ago are demonstrated here today. Operated by the APVA. NR. Open late Apr-Labor Day, W-Sa 10-5, Su 1-5. $1 adults, 50¢ students. (804) 460-1688.

Washington's Birthplace

GEORGE WASHINGTON BIRTHPLACE NATIONAL MONUMENT, VA 204, 18th century. The site of George Washington's birthplace was on a 150-acre tract of land fronting on Pope's Creek, a plantation purchased by his father in 1718. Born on February 22, 1732, the young Washington spent only his first three years here, then returned at the age of eleven to study surveying. The house burned during the Revolutionary War; it is represented by a reconstructed mansion completed in 1932 and built of handmade bricks with construction methods as close as possible to techniques used in the 18th century. The National Park Service administers the plantation as a working farm, with kitchen garden, livestock, poultry, and crops tended according to methods common during colonial times. In the nearby burying ground are several original gravestones; thirty-two members of Washington's family are known to have been interred here. NR. Open all year, daily 9-5. Free. (804) 224-0196.

Williamsburg

Located on a peninsula between the James and York rivers, Williamsburg began as a tiny settlement called Middle Plantation, which grew up within the protective confines of a stockade erected in the 1620s to ward off Indian attack. Here in 1693 was founded the New World's second-oldest college, the College of William and Mary, named in honor of the reigning English sovereigns. The **Wren Building** (c. 1695) is still in use today.

In 1699 Williamsburg became the second capital of the Virginia colony following a disastrous fire which gutted the statehouse at Jamestown. The new capital

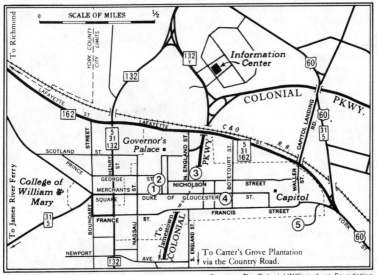

Courtesy The Colonial Williamsburg Foundation

Colonial Williamsburg

1. Bruton Parish Church
2. Wythe House
3. Peyton Randolph House
4. James Anderson House
5. Bassett Hall

was to remain the seat of Virginia's government until 1780, when Richmond was chosen to replace it. But it was in Williamsburg, in 1776, that the Virginia Convention passed a resolution directing its representatives at the forthcoming Constitutional Convention in Philadelphia to declare that the United Colonies announce their independence from English rule. Much of the language incorporated in that resolution found its way into the Declaration of Independence, drafted largely by Virginian Thomas Jefferson.

In 1926 John D. Rockefeller, encouraged by the Reverend William A. Goodwin, Rector of Bruton Parish Church (which see), established the Colonial Williamsburg Foundation to preserve and interpret what has become one of the most extensive restorations ever undertaken. All of the major public buildings of the original city plan laid out in c. 1700 by Lieutenant Governor Francis Nicholson have been refurbished or rebuilt, as have craft shops, homes, churches, taverns, and

more than 100 gardens and greens spread throughout the 173-acre historic area.

Demonstrations of many colonial crafts, such as wigmaking, blacksmithing, cabinetry, and leatherworking are given by costumed personnel; you may stop for lunch or dinner at one of three historic early taverns; and you might elect to stay at one of the old cottages operated by the Williamsburg Inn (see Historic Accommodations).

All of Colonial Williamsburg has been listed on the National Register of Historic Places and declared a National Historic Landmark. The listings which follow are intended merely to whet your historic appetite; they have been selected from Williamsburg's many outstanding attractions because of their historical significance and/or their architectural authenticity.

The first stop for all visitors to Colonial Williamsburg, regardless of the duration of one's stay, should be the **Information Center** just off Colonial Parkway. Here admission tickets are sold, excellent guide-books are available (including the highly-recommended and quite detailed *Official Guidebook* published by the Colonial Williamsburg Foundation), and introductory orientation films are shown. Colonial Williamsburg is open all year, daily 9-5. Fees vary according to the nature of the admission ticket requested; the Patriot's Pass is good for one year's unlimited admission to all of the buildings, including the Governor's Palace, $25 adults, $12.50 children 6-12. Other tickets include entrance to either 10 or 18 exhibition buildings and craft shops, $10 or $13 adults, $5 or $6.50 children 6-12. (804) 229-1000. ✔

JAMES ANDERSON HOUSE, Francis St., c. 1770. The 2½-story frame residence, once owned by Anderson, a blacksmith who served as public armorer of Virginia, replaced a tavern where Washington was known to have stayed when he visited the capital. Colonial Williamsburg's archaeology exhibits, including artifacts unearthed during restoration efforts, are housed here today.

BASSETT HALL, Francis St., 18th century. This stately frame house was the Williamsburg residence of Mr. and Mrs. John D. Rockefeller for a number of years. Its beautiful furnishings and grounds reflect the Rockefellers' personal tastes and enthusiasm for colonial art and design. Separate admission charges apply; $5 or $3 adults, $2.50 or $1.50 children (the lesser fee for general admission ticket holders).

BRUTON PARISH CHURCH, Duke of Gloucester St., 1712-15. Designed by Royal Governor Alexander Spotswood, this one-story brick church was for many years the principal house of worship in colonial Virginia and has been in continuous use since its construction. The adjacent old graveyard contains the headstones of many prominent Williamsburg residents.

THE CAPITOL, east end of Duke of Gloucester St. The capitol and the Governor's Palace (which see) are Colonial Williamsburg's most famous buildings; both are careful reconstructions based on historic plans, archaeological investigations, and accounts of the period. From its original completion in 1704 until the colonial government was moved to Richmond in 1780, this H-shaped Renaissance-style brick building was where Virginia's General Assembly convened.

THE GOVERNOR'S PALACE, Palace Green. Symbol of the power and prestige of the Crown, and considered the most elegant building in English America, this was the official residence of seven royal governors and was designed by one of them, Alexander Spotswood, in 1706. Dubbed "the palace" by embittered colonists who resented the extra levies imposed on them to pay for it, the elaborate mansion was burned during the Revolution; the superb reconstruction was begun in 1930 and included the reestablishment of the formal gardens surrounding the palace. Admission to the beautifully furnished palace is by reservation only and is not part of the general admission charges, although admission ticket holders pay the smaller noted fee. $6 or $3 adults; $3 or $1.50 children.

PEYTON RANDOLPH HOUSE, Nicholson St., c. 1715-25. Designed in the early Georgian style, the rambling two-story frame house was erected in three stages between 1715 and 1725. The east end was built separately in c. 1724 by Sir John Randolph, who later acquired the older house and united the two structures with a center section. Sir John's son Peyton, who inherited the residence, was speaker of the Virginia House of Burgesses and president of the First Continental Congress in Philadelphia. His former home is noted for its fine paneling, marble mantels, and heavy walnut doors.

WYTHE HOUSE, Palace Green, c. 1755. One of Virginia's finest Georgian brick houses, this was the home of George Wythe, a member of the House of Burgesses, signer of the Declaration of Independence, and mayor of Williamsburg. Wythe was also the first professor of law in an American college (William and Mary).

Williamsburg vicinity

CARTER'S GROVE, SE of junction of VA 667 and US 60, mid-18th century. Robert "King" Carter, probably the Virginia colony's wealthiest planter (owner of 300,000 acres and 1,000 slaves), was the founder of this James River plantation. His grandson, Carter Burwell, member of the House of Burgesses, built the existing brick Georgian country mansion around 1750. Thought to be one of the most beautiful homes in America, Carter's Grove is noted for its magnificent interior woodwork. NR. Operated by the Colonial Williamsburg Foundation. Open Mar-Nov, daily 9-5. $3 adults, $1.50 children 6-12. (804) 229-1000.

Yorktown

The tiny village of Yorktown, located at the mouth of the York River hard by Chesapeake Bay, is not much larger than it was during its heyday in the 18th century, when ships laden with tobacco from Tide-water plantations set off to distant ports. But it looms large in American history, for it was here, in 1781, that French forces under Lafayette and the Continental Army under Washington impelled Cornwallis's surrender and brought a virtual end to the Revolutionary War.

The best place to gain some perspective on the area is at the **Yorktown Victory Center,** VA 238. Opened in 1976, this was Virginia's major bicentennial project; unusual and comprehensive exhibits trace the events of the War from the Boston Tea Party in 1773 to the climactic battle fought nearby. Open all year, daily 9-5. $2 adults, $1 seniors, 75¢ children 7-12. (804) 887-2241. ★

COLONIAL NATIONAL HISTORICAL PARK, 18th century. The Yorktown section of this extensive park (see also Jamestown) features a **visitor center** with a fine museum displaying paintings, and relics relating to the Revolution in general and the battle of Yorktown in particular. Park Service personnel offer maps highlighting important sites throughout the area; guided tours may be arranged, or you may drive by the old fortifications yourself. At the edge of the battlefield is **Moore House,** a two-story frame residence constructed in the early 18th century, which was once part of a large plantation. Here in October, 1781, representatives of Cornwallis's British forces met with Colonel John Laurens of the Continental Army and the Viscount de Noailles, representing the French, to draft the articles of British surrender. Within the authentically-furnished house, guides offer narratives explaining how the surrender was accomplished. Colonial National Historical Park is open mid June-Labor Day, daily 8:30-6; otherwise daily 8:30-5. Free. (804) 898-3400. ★ ✔

Northern Virginia

The history of Virginia's northern section is inextricably linked to that of the neighboring District of Columbia: both Alexandria and Arlington County were originally part of the 10-mile square selected by George Washington in 1792 as the site of the nation's capital. Northern Virginia is a popular residential area for

Washington workers, as well as a tranquil weekend and vacation spot in its further reaches — a place to escape the politics and pressure of capital life. Even though some areas nearest Washington have been ruined by the encroachment of suburban tracts, there are many small towns and villages where the past has been lovingly preserved.

Alexandria

Founded in the 1730s by a group of Scottish merchants led by John Alexander, Alexandria was for a time one of the most important ports in the country, especially as a tobacco distribution center. The town was included in George Washington's 10-mile square for the new national capital, but was returned to the Commonwealth of Virginia in 1846. As a young man, Washington had helped to survey Alexandria, and the grid pattern he laid out is still much in evidence, especially in what is called "Old Town," the city's historic district (see following). Much of Alexandria's oldest history has been preserved, since the city was little damaged during the Civil War.

ALEXANDRIA HISTORIC DISTRICT, roughly bounded by the Capital Beltway, Alfred, Patrick, and Oronoco Sts. and the Potomac River, 18th-19th centuries. From shortly after its founding until the development of the railroads, Alexandria served as the principal commercial center of northern Virginia, as well as an important port. The historic district, also designated a National Historic Landmark, embraces nearly 100 blocks in the heart of the original town, many of whose cobblestone streets are lined with significant examples of colonial and Federal architecture. The attractions following are among the most important:

The Athenaeum, 201 Prince St., 1850. A stunning example of Greek Revival architecture, the Athenaeum was constructed as a banking house, later served as a place of worship, and today houses the art collection of the Northern Virginia Fine Arts Association. Open all year, Tu-Sa 10-4, Su 1-4. Free. (703) 548-0035.

Carlyle House, 121 N. Fairfax St., 1752. A mid-Georgian town house built for John Carlyle, one of the original incorporators of the city, this 2½-story stone mansion was the meeting place in 1755 of a council of colonial governors summoned by British General Edward Braddock to discuss strategy and funding for the French and Indian War. Recently restored and furnished with 18th-century antiques, Carlyle House is operated by the Northern Virginia Regional Park Authority. NR. Open all year, Tu-Sa 10-5, Su 12-5. $1.50 adults, $1 senior citizens, 75¢ children. (703) 549-2997.

Christ Church, Cameron and Columbus Sts., 1767-73. This Georgian brick church (with a wood and brick belfry added in the early 19th century) has been continuously in use as a house of worship since its completion. George Washington was a member of the building committee and worshipped here. NR, NHL. Open all year, M-Sa 9-5, Su 2-5. Free. (703) 549-1450.

Friendship Fire Company, 107 S. Alfred St., 1774. George Washington was a member of this volunteer fire company, which is housed in a two-story brick building with a tall cupola. Today the old pumpers are no longer in use, but are on display, along with a variety of other early fire-fighting equipment. Open all year, Tu-Sa 10-4. Nominal admission. (703) 549-0205. ✔

Gadsby's Tavern, 128 N. Royal St., 1752. One of the best-known inns in Virginia, Gadsby's Tavern comprises two adjoining buildings; the smaller coffee house, which was built first, and the adjoining three-story brick building added in 1792. Under both John Wise and John Gadsby, to whom Wise leased the tavern in 1794, the hostelry was renowned for its hospitality. Here George Washington recruited his first military command in 1754 in the campaign against the French and Indians. Restored in 1976 as a working tavern, Gadsby's is a popular restaurant again today. NR, NHL. Open all year, Tu-Sa 10-5, Su 1-5. Tours $1.50 adults, 75¢ senior citizens and children 6-17. (703) 838-4242.

Robert E. Lee Boyhood Home, 607 Oronoco St., 1795. "Lighthorse Harry" Lee, cavalry hero of the Revolutionary War and father of Robert E., brought his wife Ann and their five children here before the War of 1812. The 2½-story Federal brick house is furnished with 19th-century antiques and memorabilia of the Lee family and their descendants. Open Feb-mid Dec, M-Sa 10-4, Su 12-4. $1.50 adults, 75¢ children. (703) 548-8454.

Lee-Fendall House, 429 N. Washington St., 1785. This large frame house was built by Philip Richard Fendall on a half-acre lot purchased from "Light Horse Harry" Lee, a distant relative. The house was occupied by members of the Lee family until the early 1900s and is full of family heirlooms. Operated by the Virginia Trust for Historic Preservation. Open all year, Tu-Sa 10-4:30, Su 12-4:30. $1.50 adults, 75¢ children. (703) 548-1789.

Lloyd House, 220 N. Washington St., 1796. One of Alexandria's finest examples of late-Georgian architecture, this 2½-story brick home was built by John

Wise, who also built Gadsby's Tavern. In the early 1800s James Marshall, brother of Supreme Court Chief Justice John Marshall, lived here, followed by Jacob Hoffman, mayor of Alexandria. Benjamin Hallowell, tutor of Robert E. Lee, moved his school into the home's eight large rooms in 1826. A fine example of adaptive reuse, Lloyd House is now the repository for the Alexandria Library's extensive collection of rare books, documents, and records on city and Virginia history. NR. Open Sept-May, M-Sa 9-5; June-Aug, M-F 9-5, Sa 9-1. Free. (703) 838-4577.

Presbyterian Meeting House, 321 S. Fairfax St., 1774. Built by the Scottish founders of Alexandria, this brick church served as a meeting place for patriots in the turbulent months prior to the Revolutionary War. George Washington's funeral services were held here on December 29, 1799, when bad weather made roads to his own Christ Church impassable. In the cemetery stands the Tomb of the Unknown Soldier of the American Revolution. Open all year, M-F, Su 9-4. Free. (703) 549-0205.

Ramsay House, 221 King St., c. 1724. In the mid-18th century, William Ramsay, a Scottish merchant and friend of George Washington, is reported to have transported this small clapboard house, the oldest in Alexandria, from an early Northern Virginia settlement to its present site. Today Ramsay House is Alexandria's official visitor center, operated by the Alexandria Tourist Council, which offers maps of Old Town, brochures on the many historic attractions, an introductory film of historic sites, and other aids for the traveler. Open all year, daily 10-4:30. Free. (703) 549-0205.

Stabler-Leadbeater Apothecary, 107 S. Fairfax St., 1792. A fascinating collection of early medical ware and hand-blown glass containers is contained within this old brick apothecary shop, which was in business for nearly 150 years. Open all year, M-Sa 10-4:30. Free. (703) 836-3713.

George Washington Bicentennial Center, 201 S. Washington St., c. 1837. Benjamin

Hallowell, tutor to Robert E. Lee and other members of 19th-century Alexandria society, founded the Lyceum, a center for scholarly activities, whose members had this brick Greek Revival building constructed as a center for their meetings. Today the building houses artifacts, paintings, and antiques arranged to dramatize the story of the American Revolution. NR. Open all year, daily 9-5. Free. (703) 838-4994.

FORT WARD MUSEUM AND PARK, 4301 W. Braddock Rd. Fort Ward was one in an extensive chain of defenses built around Washington during the early days of the Civil War. Today a careful reconstruction of typical war headquarters buildings has been erected in this 40-acre park, the site of the original fort. Extensive exhibits—arms, uniforms and other military artifacts—are housed here. Open all year, Tu-Sa 9-5, Su 12-5. Free. (703) 750-6425. ★

GEORGE WASHINGTON MASONIC NATIONAL MEMORIAL, King St. Erected by American freemasons in honor of one of their earliest members, this huge memorial stands on Shooters Hill about a mile west of Old Town. A museum within the structure contains an eight-ton, seventeen-foot-high statue of Washington, and the trowel he used to lay the cornerstone of the nation's capitol. Open all year, daily 9-5. Free. (703) 683-2007.

Arlington

ARLINGTON NATIONAL CEMETERY, 19th-20th centuries. If you drive across the Arlington Memorial Bridge from the District of Columbia to Virginia, the beautiful grounds of the cemetery will appear to rise before you. By far the most outstanding landmark on the grounds is **Arlington House** (1802-17), a beautiful Greek Revival mansion which stands at the crest of a hill overlooking the cemetery grounds, the Potomac River, and the capital beyond. The two-story brick residence with its graceful Doric entrance portico was designed by George Hadfield for George Washington Parke Custis, adopted son of the first president. From 1831 until the outbreak of the Civil War it was the home of Robert E. Lee, who married Custis's daughter, Mary. Painstakingly restored and refurbished in the 1920s, the Lee Mansion is today a superb museum of 18th- and 19th-century furnishings, decorative arts, and Lee family memorabilia. NR. Open Apr-Sept, daily 9:30-6; Oct-Mar, daily 9:30-4:30. Free. (703) 557-0613.

In 1864 the grounds of the Lee Mansion became a military cemetery by order of the secretary of war, and so they have remained ever since. The first soldier buried here was a Confederate who had died in the mansion, which served for a time as a hospital. Today there are graves for nearly 200,000 men and women who have served in the Armed Forces of the United States, as well as two presidents William Howard Taft and John F. Kennedy. Aside from those for presidents, one of the most famous memorials is the **Tomb of the Unknowns,** a large solid marble block with an inscription which pays tribute to the unidentified American dead of 20th-century wars. Sentries stand watch over the memorial around the clock; the changing of the guard is a moving, dignified ceremony. Arlington National Cemetery is open Apr-Sept, daily 8-7; Oct-Mar, daily 8-5. Automobiles admitted by permit only. Guided tours leave from the visitors center. $2 adults, $1 children 3-11. (703) 545-6700. ★

Chantilly

SULLY PLANTATION, VA 28, 1794. Richard Bland Lee, builder of Sully, was a younger brother of "Light Horse Harry"

Lee and a member of the Continental Congress. The gable-roofed frame house he constructed is unusual because of the amount of original woodwork—floors, doors, and paneling—which survives today, and because it exemplifies the ongoing battle fought by preservationists against the encroachment of "progress": the house was saved from almost certain destruction when nearby Dulles Airport was built. NR. Open Mar-Dec, M, W-Sa 10-5, Su 12-5. $1.50 adults, 75¢ seniors and children 3-15. (703) 437-1794.

Leesburg

LEESBURG HISTORIC DISTRICT, centered at junction of US 15 and VA 9, 18th-19th centuries. Leesburg was established by the Virginia General Assembly in 1758 and designated as the Loudoun County seat. The town grew quickly during the late 18th century, but expansion slowed considerably after the Civil War. As a result Leesburg possesses an important collection of buildings dating from the late 1700s and the early 1800s, most of which are well-maintained. Especially notable is the **Laurel Brigade Inn,** (c. 1760) an early stone tavern still in operation (see Historic Accommodations). The **Loudoun Museum,** 16 W. Loudoun St., housed in two mid-19th-century buildings, is devoted to the history of Loudoun County. The museum staff offers a special audiovisual presentation about historic sites in the county, along with brochures describing those sites. Open all year, M-Sa 10-5, Su 1-5. Free. (703) 777-7427.

Leesburg vicinity

MORVEN PARK, 1 mile NW off US 15, c. 1780. This fieldstone and brick mansion is one of Virginia's most elaborate country estates. Built by the Swan family, the house was enlarged in the early 19th century and was owned in the 1920s by Westmoreland Davis, a Virginia governor. The mansion's 1,200 acres of grounds include a carriage museum with more than 100 vehicles, delightful boxwood gardens, and nature trails. NR. Open Memorial Day-Labor

Day, Tu-Sa 10-5, Su 1-5. $2.25 adults, $2 senior citizens, $1.25 children. (703) 777-2414.

OATLANDS, S. of Leesburg off US 15 and VA 651, c. 1800. One of the most notable Federal style mansions in Virginia, Oatlands was built from designs credited to George Carter, its builder-owner. The brick and stucco house boasts a large front portico and beautiful formal gardens. The interior is filled with French and American art and antiques. In spring and fall, point-to-point races and hunter trials are held here for equestrian enthusiasts. NR. Open Apr-Nov, M-Sa 10-5, Su 1-5. $3 adults, $2.50 seniors and students, group rates. (703) 777-3174.

Lorton

GUNSTON HALL, VA 242, 1755-58. Gunston Hall was the home of George Mason, a leading Revolutionary figure famed for his constitutional writings, including the Virginia Declaration of Rights (1776). The old kitchen and formal gardens have been restored and much of the original woodwork carved under the supervision of William Buckland, who was indentured to Mason, remains. NR, NHL. Open all year, daily 9:30-5. $2 adults, 50¢ students. (703) 550-9220.

POHICK CHURCH, 9201 Richmond Hwy., 1772. The two-story brick Pohick Church is attributed to James Wren; Washington was a member of the building committee and, together with George Mason, a member of the vestry. While little remains of the original interior woodwork, the building has been carefully restored to reflect its 18th-century appearance. NR. Open all year, daily 8-4. Free. (703) 399-6572.

Manassas

MANASSAS NATIONAL BATTLE-FIELD PARK, off VA 215, 1861. Manassas was the scene of the first and second battles of Manassas, usually called Bull Run, on July 21, l861, and August 28-30, 1862. The first encounter was one of the opening battles of the Civil War, pitting General Irvin McDowell's unseasoned Union troops against equally ill-trained, but victorious, Confederates under General P. G. T. Beauregard. The second battle, also a Confederate victory, cleared the way for General Robert E. Lee's first invasion of the North. Manassas is administered by the National Park Service; the **visitors center and museum** should be your first stop for maps of the area, audio-visual displays, and a look at Civil War relics. Several early structures survived the two bloody battles — **Stone House** (1828),

which was originally a tavern and served as a Union hospital during the conflict; **Stone Bridge,** where the first shots of the battle were fired; and **Dogan House,** the last surviving building of the little village of Groveton, which was caught between the battlelines in August, 1862. NR. Open all year, daily 9-6. Free. (703) 754-7107. ★

Middletown vicinity

BELLE GROVE, 1 mile S. on US 11,

1794. Isaac Hite, husband of Nelly Conway Madison, James Madison's sister, built this one-story limestone house during George Washington's administration; the porticos and west wing were added in the early 19th century. Union soldiers scrawled their names on the attic walls when General Philip Sheridan made his headquarters here during the Civil War. The surrounding farmland was the site of the **Battle of Cedar Creek,** which claimed the lives of more than 6,000 soldiers and gave the Union final control over the Shenandoah Valley. Now operated as a working farm and house museum, Belle Grove offers traditional weaving and open-hearth cooking workshops, rail-splitting contests, quilting bees, black-smithing, and other crafts of early America. NR, NHL. Open Apr-Oct, M-Sa 10-4, Su 1-5. $2 adults, $1.60 senior citizens, $1 children 6-18. (703) 869-2028. ✓ ★

Millwood

BURWELL-MORGAN MILL, VA 723 and 255, c. 1785. This two-story frame and stone mill was built by Colonel Nathaniel Burwell and General Daniel Morgan on property belonging to Burwell. Morgan and Burwell soon diversified their holdings, adding a tannery, another mill, and a distillery. The only structures which survive today, however, are the mill itself, which is restored and operating, and the nearby **Miller's House.** Before you leave you can pick up some stone-ground cornmeal or flour. NR. Open May-Oct, W-M 9:30-4:30. $1 adults, 50¢ children 6-12. (703) 837-1799.

Mount Vernon

MOUNT VERNON, George Washington Memorial Pkwy., 1743. Washington more than doubled the size of the modest house he inherited from his half-brother, Lawrence, in 1752. Besides enlarging the main house, he built a complex of outbuildings and landscaped the grounds during three separate periods of alteration over several decades. One of the most famous historic houses in the country,

Mount Vernon is noted for its beautiful position overlooking the Potomac, for its full-length two-story portico facing the river, and its well integrated service buildings, approximately a dozen of which are open to the public. The beautiful gardens remain substantially as they were in Washington's time. Within the mansion, fourteen rooms exhibit numerous original furnishings that have been returned to Mount Vernon since the Mount Vernon Ladies' Association, in a pioneering example of historic preservation, purchased the estate in 1858. NR, NHL. Open Mar-Oct, daily 9-5; Nov-Feb, daily 9-4. $3 adults, $2.50 senior citizens, $1 children 6-11 and students. Free Sept-Feb. (703) 780-2000.

WOODLAWN PLANTATION, US 1, 1800-1805. George Washington presented 2,000 acres of Mount Vernon lands, including Dogue Run Farm, a gristmill, and a distillery, to his foster daughter Eleanor Parke Custis upon her marriage to Lawrence Lewis, his nephew. The first architect of the U.S. Capitol, Dr. William Thornton, was engaged to design the Lewis home, a stately brick Georgian mansion that was later variously owned by Quaker and Baptist settlers from the North, a playwright, and a United States senator. Today Woodlawn is maintained by the National Trust for Historic Preservation and furnished with a variety of antiques reflecting its long and distinguished history. The grounds are traversed by nature trails designed by the National Audubon Society; the lovely gardens were designed by the Garden Club of Virginia.

Reconstructions of Washington's 18th-century gristmill and the miller's house are nearby. NR. Open all year, daily 9:30-4:30. $2.50 adults, $2 senior citizens, $1.25 students, group rates. (703) 557-7881.

On the grounds of Woodlawn is a vastly different landmark, moved to the site from Falls Church and also operated by the National Trust. The **Pope-Leighey House** (1940) was designed by architect Frank Lloyd Wright, who was concerned with the difficulty of providing middle-income Americans with well-designed housing at minimal cost. This small one-story house, constructed of wood, brick, and glass, with many of its furnishings built in, is an example of the "Usonian" style he developed to solve the problem. NR. Open Mar-Oct, Sa-Su 9:30-4:30. $2.50 adults, $2 senior citizens, $1.25 students. Combination ticket available with Woodlawn. (703) 780-3118.

Strasburg

STRASBURG MUSEUM, King St. Records indicate that the first potter came to Strasburg in 1765, and by the 1860s there were five pottery shops in the area. The Strasburg Museum, housed in a steam pottery (1890) which saw additional service as a railway depot, exhibits 18th-and 19th-century crafts, with the emphasis on the art of the potter, but also featuring blacksmith and cooper shops, Civil War and railroad artifacts, Indian artifacts, and fossils. NR. Open May-Oct, daily 10-4. $1 adults, 25¢ children. (703) 465-3428.

Warrenton

Warrenton, founded in the 1760s to serve as the county seat of Fauquier County, has developed over the years as a delightful small town, with just the right proportions between its governmental core and the adjoining business and residential areas. As would be expected, the focal point is the **courthouse**, with its classic portico and tall cupola, that faces Winchester St. where it intersects with Main St. The present building, which combines classical and Italianate details, was built in 1893 to replace an earlier building on the same site. Nearby is the former **Fauquier County Jail**, one of the most complete early county penal complexes in the state. The group consists of an 1808 brick jail, its 1822 stone replacement (built when the earlier jail was converted into a jailer's residence), and the stone-walled jail yard. The complex now serves as the museum and headquarters of the **Fauquier Historical Society**, which was formed to preserve the jail when it was threatened with demolition in the 1960s. NR. For information call (703) 347-5525.

Winchester

The first settlement of European colonists in the area which became Winchester took place about 1730, when a group of German and Scotch-Irish settlers migrated south from Pennsylvania to the Shenandoah Valley. The town was laid out in 1744 by Colonel James Wood, who named it for his English birthplace. Four years later George Washington began working here as a young surveyor for Thomas, Lord Fairfax. While the town was badly damaged during the Civil War much of Winchester remains as it was in the 18th

and early 19th centuries, and the downtown area has been designated an historic district.

ABRAM'S DELIGHT, 1340 Pleasant Valley Rd., 1754. Abraham Hollingsworth, a Quaker, settled in Winchester early in the 18th century, trading a cow, a calf, and a piece of red cloth to the Shawnee tribe for nearly 600 acres of land. The current colonial stone house replaced Hollingsworth's first log cabin (there is a restored log cabin on the site as well, although not the original one); the house has been restored and furnished with 18th-century pieces. NR. Open May-Nov, M-Sa 9-5, Su 2-5. $1.50 adults, 50¢ children under 12. (703) 662-6519.

STONEWALL JACKSON'S HEADQUARTERS, 415 N. Braddock St., 1854. This brick Gothic Revival house served as Confederate General Thomas J. "Stonewall" Jackson's Headquarters just prior to his famous Shenandoah Valley campaign of 1862. Essentially unaltered, it is today a museum of Jackson memorabilia; his office has been refurbished to look as it did more than a century ago. NR, NHL. Open all year, daily 10-4. $1 adults, 25¢ children under 12. (703) 667-3242. ★

GEORGE WASHINGTON'S OFFICE, Braddock and Cork Sts., 1750-64. This small log building is said to have served as Washington's military office and headquarters when he was a commissioned officer of the Virginia militia (1755-56). His responsibility was to protect Virginia's 300-mile frontier against French and Indian attack. A museum within the building contains relics from the French and Indian, Revolutionary, and Civil Wars. NR. Open May-Oct, M-Sa 10-5, Su 1-5. $1 adults, 25¢ children under 12. (703) 662-4412. ✓

Central Virginia

Linking the Tidewater on the east with the Blue Ridge Mountains to the west, Virginia's Piedmont is an interesting mix of thriving cities and sparsely populated

farmland, gently rolling hills and rugged mountains. Danville, in the south, is internationally-known as an important tobacco market, and throughout central

Virginia one comes across reminders of how the controversial but lucrative crop had its beginnings in colonial times. You may visit elegant plantations or more humble farms, or stop at Appomattox, where North and South finally ended the conflict which began over the right to use slave labor in running those farms. One of the state's most famous and important landmarks, Thomas Jefferson's Monticello, is located in the scenic hills of Albemarle County.

Amelia vicinity

HAW BRANCH PLANTATION, north via VA 667, late 18th century. Colonel Thomas Tabb, an early settler, purchased the nucleus of this plantation in 1743. A small house, believed to have been incorporated into the western part of the present 2½-story frame dwelling, was erected sometime prior to 1748. Outbuildings on the property, such as the early slave quarters, smokehouse, and outdoor kitchen, have been restored; the main house contains furniture and personal possessions of nine generations of the Tabb family. NR. Open Apr-Oct, daily 10-5; Nov-Mar by appointment to groups only. $2 adults, $1 children 6-12, group rates. (804) 561-2472.

Amherst

AMHERST COUNTY HISTORICAL MUSEUM, Old County Jail. The county historical society's collection of books, maps, and local artifacts is housed in the former jail, constructed in 1891. NR. Open all year, M-Sa 9:30-4:30. Free. (804) 946-2460.

The museum offers information about **Sweet Briar College,** just south of Amherst off US 29. The campus was designed by R. A. Cram in the beginning of the 20th century. **Sweet Briar House,** which serves as the president's home, was constructed in the early 1800s and owned for many years by the family of newspaper publisher Elijah Fletcher. Fletcher's daughter, Mrs. James Henry Williams, founded the college in memory of her only child.

Appomattox

APPOMATTOX COURT HOUSE NATIONAL HISTORICAL PARK, VA 24, 19th century. Originally the village of Appomattox Court House was known as Clover Hill — a small settlement with just a few houses centered around a tavern, which was the stopping-off point on the main Richmond to Lynchburg stage road. When the new county of Appomattox was formed in 1845, Clover Hill was chosen as the county seat and renamed. It was here on April 9, 1865, in the home of Wilmer McLean, that General Robert E. Lee surrendered his Army of Northern Virginia to General Ulysses S. Grant, thus ending the Civil War. The **McLean House,** destroyed in the 1890s, has been reconstructed, and surviving buildings of the small town, including a wheelwright's home, country store, and the Clover Hill Tavern, have been restored. NR. The reconstructed courthouse now serves as a **visitors center.** Open Apr-Oct, daily 8:30-5. $1 per car. (804) 352-8987. ★

Brookneal vicinity

PATRICK HENRY SHRINE (Red Hill), 5 miles SE via VA 600 and VA 619, 19th-20th centuries. Patrick Henry lived in several homes, including the Governor's Palace at Williamsburg. His favorite among them all, however, was this simple frame farmhouse and its surrounding dependencies, including a small law office, to which he retired in 1793. While the original buildings were destroyed by fire in the early 20th century, they have been reconstructed, using accurate drawings made before the fire, and some of the box hedges Henry planted, together with an osage orange tree some 300 years old, remain. The patriot's grave is located on the plantation; many of his personal possessions are on display in the main house. NR. Open Apr-Oct, daily 9-5; Nov-Mar, daily 9-4. $1.50 adults, 75¢ children, group rates. (804) 376-2044.

Charlottesville and vicinity

Charlottesville is distinguished historically

not only by the imprint left upon the city and surrounding Albemarle County by its most famous native son, Thomas Jefferson, but also as the home of President James Monroe and other illustrious Americans. Situated in the beautiful rolling hills of the Piedmont, ringed by the Blue Ridge Mountains, the Charlottesville area is noted for its fine estates, some of which are open to the public during Virginia's Historic Garden Week in late April. NR.

ALBEMARLE COUNTY COURT-HOUSE, Courthouse Sq., 19th century. The courthouse was the focal point from which the entire town developed. A portion of the T-shaped structure, built in the early 1800s, has been attributed to Thomas Jefferson. Its Federal northern wing was used as a place of worship until the first church was built in Charlottesville in 1824. Presidents Jefferson, Madison, and Monroe all attended services here. NR.

ASH LAWN, VA 6, 1799. James Monroe built this unprepossessing frame house on 550 acres near Jefferson's Monticello, and lived here until he became president in 1817. Ash Lawn has been restored by the College of William and Mary, Monroe's alma mater. Many of the fifth president's personal belongings are displayed; there are periodic spinning and weaving demonstrations given; and visitors are invited to stroll through the lovely boxwood gardens which Monroe laid out. NR. Open Mar-Oct, daily 9-6; Nov-Feb, daily 10-5. $2.50 adults, 75¢ children, guided tours $2 per person. (804) 293-9539.

GEORGE ROGERS CLARK MUSEUM, VA 20, 1740. A log cabin built in the first half of the 18th century and moved to the site commemorates the birthplace of George Rogers Clark, Revolutionary War hero, frontiersman, and explorer of the Northwest Territory. The rustic homestead has been furnished with furniture, china, pottery, and silver representative of the 18th century. Open Apr-Oct, daily 10-5. $1 admission. (804) 239-6789.

MICHIE TAVERN MUSEUM, VA 20, 18th century. In 1746 John Michie pur-

chased more than 1100 acres in northern Albemarle County from Major John Henry, father of Patrick. A dwelling which Major Henry had built was included in the sale; Michie made significant additions to the structure in 1763 and opened it as a tavern. The building was disassembled in the early 1900s and reconstructed near Monticello; a converted slave house, **The Ordinary**, is now a restaurant serving colonial-style luncheons. The tavern, known as "Inn of the Presidents" because Monroe, Jefferson, and Madison often rendezvoused there, is furnished with 18th-century furniture, silver, and pottery. Open all year, daily 9-5. $2 adults, $1.50 students, 75¢ children 6-12. (804) 977-1234.

MONTICELLO, VA 53, 1770-89. Thomas Jefferson spent many years designing and perfecting his estate, which he dubbed Monticello ("little mountain" in Italian) because of its hilltop location. His inventive genius can be seen throughout the brick and frame mansion: a dumbwaiter incorporated into the dining room mantle facilitated serving meals to the family's constant stream of guests; beds disappeared into walls; folding doors, not unlike those used a century later on streetcars, conserved space; and an early duplicating-writing machine eased Jefferson's correspondence. Among the outbuildings still standing on the estate is the first **guest house** Jefferson built in 1770. It is evident that Monticello was designed using elements of Roman, Palladian, and 18th-century French styles; the result, now called Jeffersonian Classicism, has been copied widely in the intervening two centuries. Operated by the Thomas Jefferson Memorial Foundation. NR, NHL. Open Mar-Oct, daily 8-5; Nov-Feb, daily 9-4:30. $3 adults, $1 children 6-11. (804) 293-2158. ✔

UNIVERSITY OF VIRGINIA HISTORIC DISTRICT, bounded by University and Jefferson Park Aves. and Hospital and McCormick Rds., 19th-20th centuries. Founded by Thomas Jefferson, the University of Virginia was granted a charter in 1819. The visual expression of his ideals is still present in **The Lawn and The Ranges,** the academic village which he planned and which still forms the physical heart of the campus. Dominating the area is the **Rotunda,** adapted from the Pantheon of ancient Rome. Designed by Jefferson in 1821 and begun the next year, the circular, white-columned brick structure was intended to be the university's library and served this purpose for more than a century. NR, NHL. Open all year, daily 10-4. Free. (804) 924-7116.

Cismont vicinity

CASTLE HILL, NE near junction of VA 231 and 640, 1764, 1825. Beautiful gardens, including some of the world's tallest boxwood, surround the 18th-century clapboard house of Thomas Walker, a physician and explorer noted for his discovery of Cumberland Gap (see Kentucky). His home, which remained in the family for five generations, was enlarged in the 19th century. Outbuildings include a carpentry shop, storehouse, smokehouse, dairy, and carriage house. NR. Open Mar-Nov, daily 10-5. $2 adults, 75¢ children 6-12. (804) 293-7297.

Clarksville vicinity

PRESTWOULD PLANTATION, US 15, c. 1795. Sir Peyton Skipwith, an American-born baronet, built Prestwould of native stone on a knoll overlooking the Roanoke River. Much of the Georgian

mansion's interior decoration remains intact, including important early wallpapers which enliven the high-ceilinged rooms. NR. Open May-Sept, W-Su 1:30-4; Oct-Apr, W-F 1:30-4. $1.50 adults, 50¢ children. (804) 374-8672.

Danville

DANVILLE MUSEUM OF FINE ARTS AND HISTORY, 975 Main St., 1857-58. Although the interior has been considerably altered, the **Sutherlin House,** which served for a time as Danville's public library, is one of Virginia's outstanding examples of the Italian Villa style. Major William Sutherlin, a member of the 1861 Virginia Convention, built the house which was occupied by Jefferson Davis for a week during his flight from Richmond in April, 1865. The ornate ante-bellum mansion is now the repository for a fine collection of paintings, furnishings, and local memorabilia. NR. Open all year, Tu-F 10-5, Su 2-5. Free. (804) 793-5644.

NATIONAL TOBACCO-TEXTILE MUSEUM, 614 Lynn St. Danville is a relatively young city by Virginia standards, having grown up around the vast tobacco warehouses and textile mills of the 1800s. Today the city boasts the largest textile plant in the country—that of Dan River—and is a booming mill center, but its humbler beginnings are explained in this museum, housed in a 1917 tobacco factory. Open all year, M-F 10-4, Sa-Su 2-4. $1.50 adults, 75¢ children. (804) 797-9437.

Ferrum

BLUE RIDGE FARM MUSEUM, VA 40. A working 1800 German farmstead, with a log house and kitchen, barn, outbuildings, gardens, and pasture, forms a living museum that interprets the daily life of colonists who came south from the German settlements of Pennsylvania and the Shenandoah Valley. This entertaining and informative farm is open June-Aug, Sa 10-5, Su 1-5 and by appointment. $1 adults, 50¢ children. (703) 365-2121. ✔

Lynchburg

Lynchburg, as any native will tell you, derives its name from John Lynch, who founded the city in 1786—not from any association with a rather severe form of corporal punishment. From its inception, Lynchburg flourished as a tobacco and trading center. While many of the city's landmarks date from these prosperous ante-bellum years, Lynchburg's primary architectural character dates from a later period—the turn of the last century, when new industry and development resulted in an enormous amount of building.

HILL NEIGHBORHOODS. Lynchburg claims to be a city of Seven Hills, though there has seldom been agreement on exactly which of the many hills comprise the original seven. One that must be considered is the eminence that rises just south of the central business district, known either as **Lynchburg** or **Courthouse Hill.** This hill is so steep that in several places stairs, rather than streets, connect the commercial center on the lower level with the houses and offices on the upper. Because it was relatively isolated from the business center of town, this hill developed early as a residential center. Now many of the houses along Court and Clay Sts. have been turned into professional offices. Located in this area are a remarkable collection of impressive churches, including the **First Baptist** (1884-86), Court and Eleventh Sts., one of the state's best examples of the High Victorian Gothic style, and **St. Paul's Episcopal** (1889-95), Seventh and Clay Sts., a sturdy Romanesque masterpiece by architect Frank Miles Day of Philadelphia. Next door to St. Paul's, and now serving as its parish house, is the **Carter Glass House** (1826), Lynchburg's only National Historic Landmark, so designated because it was Glass's home while he was secretary of the Treasury.

Just to the west of Lynchburg Hill is **Garland Hill.** Madison St. between First and Fifth Sts. is its major thoroughfare, and was known in the 1890s as "Quality Row" because of the scale of the mansions built on it. Particularly notable are the **A.H. Burroughs House** (1899) at 220 Madison and the adjacent **Craddock House** (1897), both huge Queen Anne mansions.

Washington and Pearl Sts. are the major thoroughfares of **Diamond Hill,** to the west of downtown. One of the most eclectic of the several hill neighborhoods, Diamond Hill contains excellent examples of Greek and Gothic Revival, Queen Anne, and Georgian Revival architecture. The area has a strong preservation society, and of all of Lynchburg's fine old neighborhoods shows the most encouraging signs of restoration and revitalization.

LYNCHBURG COURTHOUSE, Court St. at Monument Terrace, 1853-55. This handsome Greek Revival structure, along with the monumental stairway built in the 1920s as a World War I memorial which leads to it from Church St. a block away, was designed by a local architect, William S. Ellison. The pediment above the Doric portico contains the town clock, still operated by the original wooden gears and wheels. Inside, the building has been handsomely restored (as the city's major Bicentennial project) and serves as the headquarters of the **Lynchburg Museum System.** An informative display in the former witness and jury rooms and offices utilizes many objects of historic interest to tell the city's story. NR. Open Mar-Dec, Tu-Sa 1-4. $1 adults, 50¢ students. (804) 847-1459.

POINT OF HONOR, Cabell and "A" Sts., 1815. Dr. George Cabell built this impressive Federal house during the decade that Thomas Jefferson declared Lynchburg to be "growing more rapidly than any town I have ever known in any country." Its unique name derives from the fact that the extensive lawns were on occasion utilized as duelling grounds—where gentlemen of the day settled their "points of honor" with pistol or sword. The interior of the mansion displays some of the most accomplished woodwork in the city and is furnished with appropriate pieces and decorative objects. Operated as a unit in the Lynchburg Museum System. NR. Open Mar-Dec, Tu-Sa 1-4. $1 adults, 50¢ students. (804) 847-1399.

Point of Honor

OLD CITY CEMETERY, Fourth and Taylor Sts., 1806. Lynchburg's role during the Civil War was as a troop training and hospital center. Many of the wounded soldiers did not survive and were laid to rest in a special section of the city cemetery. Over 2,000 identical headstones mark their graves. Although in the middle of the city, the old cemetery remains a serene and peaceful spot, with a lovely view of the distant mountains. NR. Open all year, daily dawn-dusk.

ANNE SPENCER HOUSE, 1313 Pierce St., 1903. Anne Spencer, a noted poet and member of the literary movement termed the "Harlem Renaissance" lived in this simple frame house for more than seventy years. In it, she and her husband entertained many of the most noted black educators and leaders of the 20th century. The house and the small study in the yard are both furnished as they were at the time of her death. NR. Open by appointment. (804) 846-0517.

Rocky Mount vicinity

BOOKER T. WASHINGTON NATIONAL MONUMENT, 16 miles E. on VA 122, mid-19th century. The eminent black educator Booker T. Washington was born as a slave on the 200-acre Burroughs plantation in April, 1856. He spent his childhood in a one-room cabin, a replica of which has been constructed on the site. After the Civil War, Washington attended Hampton Institute, later teaching there from 1879-81. Then he was selected to establish a black normal school in Alabama, the now-famous Tuskegee Institute. The plantation is being reconstructed as a 19th-century farm with buildings, tools, crops, and livestock. NR. Open all year, daily 8:30-5. Free. (703) 721-2094. ✔

Washington

WASHINGTON HISTORIC DISTRICT, N. of US 211/522, 19th century. The seventy or so frame and brick buildings which comprise the Rappahannock County seat were constructed on a grid plan that had been laid out by George Washington in 1749 for a group of private proprietors; the town was named for him upon its organization by the General Assembly in 1796. Little has changed here for more than a hundred years: the early 19th-century **Inn at Little Washington** is a favorite dining spot among residents of the nation's capital, only an hour and a half away, and the Gothic-Revival **Trinity Episcopal Church** (1852) still holds Sunday services. The church and the Jeffersonian Classical **county courthouse** (1833), both on Gay St., were designed by James Leake Powers, reputed to have been one of Thomas Jefferson's workmen at the Uni- versity of Virginia. The courthouse and the adjacent **clerk's office** and **treasurer's office** are still used today for their original purposes. NR.

Western Virginia

The Old Dominion's westernmost reaches are also its least populous, settled far later than neighboring areas because of the for- midable Blue Ridge Mountains which pro- vide a natural barrier from north to south. To the west of the wooded range is the rich Shenandoah Valley, famous for its produc- tive apple orchards; farther south is the rugged Highland Region, where coal, rather than fruit, is the harvest. The **Skyline Drive** through **Shenandoah Na- tional Park** connects with the **Blue Ridge Parkway**, which winds for more than 400 miles southward into North Carolina along the crest of the mountains. Those who bypass the speedy interstates in favor of slower, less direct travel along the ridge will be rewarded by magnificent vistas throughout the parkways' course.

Abingdon

BARTER THEATRE OF VIRGINIA, Main St., 1932. Founded by Robert Porterfield, the Barter Theatre originally offered a haven for stranded Broadway ac- tors during the Depression. Tickets were bartered for produce, thus giving the fledgling organization its name. This was the first state theater in America; it oc- cupies three century-old brick buildings in the midst of Abingdon's **historic district,** a small area dotted with domestic and com- mercial buildings typical of a 19th-century rural Virginia town. NR. The theater is open Apr-Oct, Tu-Su for performances. Call (703) 628-3991 for ticket informa- tion.

Big Stone Gap

SOUTHWEST VIRGINIA MUSEUM, 10 W. 1st St. The **Ayers Mansion** (1888), an elegant Queen Anne residence built by state attorney general Rufus Ayers, is now home to this fine museum of rural Virginia history. Early farming tools, ingenious household gadgets, ancient firearms, and century-old handmade quilts are on dis- play. Open all year, Tu-Sa 9:30-5, Su 2-5. Free. (703) 523-1322.

Blacksburg

SMITHFIELD PLANTATION, off US 460 bypass, 1773-74. This was one of the earliest and largest estates west of the Blue Ridge Mountains, encompassing 120,000 acres granted to James Patton by the Crown in 1745. Patton's nephew, Col- onel William Preston, built the present co- lonial frame house and made it head- quarters for his family's extensive land operations in Virginia and parts of what are now West Virginia and Kentucky. Preston was a Revolutionary War hero and member of the House of Burgesses; his son and two later descendants were to become Virginia governors. Operated by the APVA. NR. Open mid Apr-mid Nov, W, Sa-Su 1-5. $1.50 adults, 50¢ children. (703) 552-2976.

Cumberland Gap

CUMBERLAND GAP NATIONAL HISTORICAL PARK (see Kentucky).

Fincastle

FINCASTLE HISTORIC DISTRICT, 18th-19th centuries. Fincastle, located in a beautiful setting of rolling hills and moun- tains, began as a colonial frontier outpost; the decrease in population during the late 1800s is largely responsible for its charm- ing 19th-century appearance today. The skyline is still dominated by the spires of its churches and the cupola of its Jeffersonian courthouse (1845). Its attraction lies not in superb museum houses or extensive historic collections open to the public, for there are none, but in its rural atmosphere: Federal and Greek Revival houses on generous lawns line the wide, shady streets. Wander about and discover your own favorites. NR.

Fort Defiance

AUGUSTA STONE CHURCH, US 11, 1749. This is the oldest Presbyterian church in continuous use in the state. The original 1½-story stone building has been enlarged several times. Even if you don't find the church open, stop and stretch your legs. NR. (703) 248-2634.

Lexington

This historic 19th-century college town was home to the two most famous Confederate generals, Robert E. Lee and "Stonewall" Jackson, and there is much to see here related to both men. Your best introduction to the community is the **Historic Lexington Visitor Center** (Sloan House,

c. 1844), 107 E. Washington St., where brochures suggesting various walking tours are available. Guided tours are offered during the summer months at no charge. (703) 463-3777.

LEXINGTON HISTORIC DISTRICT, 18th-20th centuries. Comprised of the campuses of Washington and Lee University and Virginia Military Institute (see following) as well as commercial and residential sections, Lexington's historic

district is a mix of simple board-and-batten cottages, elegant Queen Anne mansions, and utilitarian brick offices. One of the district's most notable attractions is **"Stonewall" Jackson House,** 8 E. Washington St., a simple two-story town house which dates from the early 1800s. Beautifully restored through the efforts of the Historic Lexington Foundation, it is furnished with many of the Jacksons' original pieces. NR, NHL. Open all year, M-Sa 9-4:30, Su 1-4:30. $1.50 adults, 75¢ children 6-11. (703) 463-2552.

VIRGINIA MILITARY INSTITUTE, US 11, 19th-20th centuries. Known as the "West Point of the South," VMI was formally organized in 1839 and quickly gained significance as a contributor of leaders to the Confederate Army, the most notable being Stonewall Jackson, who taught here for a decade prior to the outbreak of the Civil War. The Gothic Revival campus buildings were primarily the work of Alexander Jackson Davis. The **Barracks** (1851) and the mid-19th-century **Superintendent's and Commandant's quarters** were part of the original Davis design. NR, NHL.

The **VMI Museum,** located just north of the spacious parade ground, exhibits uniforms, arms, and various displays which interpret cadet life, among them a full-scale replica of a typical cadet room in Barracks. Open all year, M-F 9-4:30, Sa 9-12, 2-5, Su 2-5. Free. (703) 463-6232. ★

The **George C. Marshall Museum and Library,** to the south of the parade ground, is dedicated to one of VMI's most famous graduates, a U.S. Army chief of staff, secretary of state (1947-49), and secretary of defense (1950-51). Marshall was awarded the Nobel Peace Prize in 1953, the only professional soldier to be so honored. Museum exhibits trace the general's life and contributions; the library houses his personal and public papers. Open all year, M-Sa 9-5, Su 2-5. Free. (703) 463-7103. ★

WASHINGTON AND LEE UNIVERSITY, off US 11, 19th-20th centuries. Founded in 1749 as Augusta Academy, this is one of the nation's oldest colleges.

George Washington endowed it in 1796, and Robert E. Lee became president of the school after the Civil War. This is one of the most beautiful college campuses in America: its "Colonnade," a picturesque group of Neo-classical buildings, is a photographer's delight. The oldest of these columned structures is **Washington Hall** (1824), readily identified by the wooden statue of George Washington which crowns its three stories. NR, NHL.

about 25 years later Thomas Jefferson bought it and the surrounding acreage from King George III for a mere 20 shillings. But don't waste *your* shillings on the commercial trash that has sprung up around this Virginia landmark. Open all year, daily 7-dark. Nominal admission. (703) 291-2936. ✔

Lee Chapel, facing Washington Hall, is a Victorian Gothic brick building completed c. 1866 under Robert E. Lee's supervision. The chapel houses Lee's burial vault; a museum on the lower level includes Lee's office, preserved just as it was when he was president of the college. NR, NHL. Open mid Apr-mid Oct, M-Sa 9-5, Su 2-5; otherwise M-Sa 9-4, Su 2-5. Free. (703) 463-9111.

Natural Bridge

NATURAL BRIDGE OF VIRGINIA, US 11. A massive stone arch created by the action of water over millions of years, Natural Bridge stands 215 feet above Cedar Creek, is 90 feet long and from 50 to 150 feet in width. George Washington carved his initials into it in the mid-18th century;

New Market vicinity

NEW MARKET BATTLEFIELD PARK, US 11 and US 211, 1864. The northern campaign for Richmond in the spring of 1864 called for the advance of Union troops up the Shenandoah Valley to take possession of southwest Virginia. 6,000 Federal troops under Major General Franz Sigel met 5,000 Confederates under General John Breckinridge (aided by several hundred VMI cadets from nearby Lexington) in May, 1864. The lesser force managed to win, enabling southerners to harvest their crops and to keep the railroad running. **Bushong House** (1830), a two-story frame farmhouse in the middle of the fray, was used by both sides as a field hospital. A modern museum, the **Hall of Valor** contains extensive displays relating to the New Market Battle and to the course of the war. NR. Open all year, daily 9-5.

$2 adults, 75¢ children; tours $1.60 adults, 50¢ children. (703) 740-3101. ★ ✔

Pocahontas

POCAHONTAS HISTORIC DISTRICT, 19th-20th centuries. The history of this early boom town parallels that of other mining company towns of the period. Before the Southwest Virginia Improvement Company mines closed in 1955, more than 40 million tons of coal had been processed. Most of the frame and brick miner's homes and commercial structures remain, and visitors can drive through the **Pocahontas Exhibition Coal Mine** on VA 20 — the only mine in the world accessible by car. The mine is open May-Oct, M-F 10-5, Sa-Su 10-6. Nominal admission. (703) 963-3385. ✔

Roanoke

ROANOKE TRANSPORTATION MUSEUM, 802 Wiley Dr. This extensive collection of railroad memorabilia includes eight old steam locomotives and working scale models of old trains that traverse the museum grounds and provide a view of its many transportation exhibits. Open all year, daily 9-5. $2 adults, 75¢ children. (703) 342-5670. ✔

Staunton

WOODROW WILSON BIRTHPLACE, 20 N. Coalter St., 1846. Thomas Woodrow Wilson, 28th president of the United States, was born in this Greek Revival mansion in 1856. The spacious house was painstakingly restored in 1979, and the interior woodwork, mantels, and floors are all original, as are many of the furnishings throughout. Wilson family possessions, including china, silver, books, and musical instruments, are on display, as are many reminders of Wilson's prominence as president of Princeton University, governor of New Jersey, and head of state. NR, NHL. Open Mar-Nov, daily 9-5; Dec-Feb, M-Sa 9-5. $2 adults, $1 children 6-16, group rates. (703) 885-0897.

Mary Baldwin College, Frederick and New Sts., is close by Wilson's birthplace. Founded in 1842, the school has an extremely pleasant campus. Its chapel was formerly Staunton's Presbyterian Church, and Wilson's father was its pastor. NR. (703) 885-0811. Also worth visiting is the **Wharf Area Historic District,** a late-19th century area of warehouses and residences centered along Middlebrook Ave. which is enjoying a renaissance as a lively center for shops and restaurants. NR.

Steeles Tavern

CYRUS H. McCORMICK MEMORIAL MUSEUM, US 11 and County 606, early 1800s. Of all the inventions that revolutionized agriculture during the first half of the 19th century, Cyrus McCormick's mechanical reaper (1834) was probably the most important. Both McCormick's **workshop,** a small log building on a high stone foundation, and his large brick **farmhouse** are well preserved; replicas of his first reaper and subsequent inventions are displayed. NR, NHL. Open May-mid Oct, daily 8-5. Free. (804) 377-2255.

Tazewell vicinity

HISTORIC CRAB ORCHARD MUSEUM, VA 19 and 460. Archaeologists have discovered here the remains of no less than seven prehistoric Indian villages — including a burial cave and rock shelters — and two colonial settlements. Eight 19th-century log structures have been reconstructed, one of which houses a collection of Indian artifacts and colonial tools discovered nearby, Revolutionary and Civil War materials, and farming implements. NR. Open Mar-Oct, Tu-F 10:30-4, Sa 12-4:30, Su 2-4; Nov-Feb, Tu-F 10:30-4. Free. (704) 988-6755.

Warm Springs

Some of the most interesting chapters in Virginia's social history have been written in the Warm Springs Valley, which, since colonial times has been a fashionable spa resort. **The Homestead,** on U.S. 220 (see Historic Accommodations), is an internationally celebrated spa which operates **The Warm Springs Bathhouses,** off VA 220. The octagonal men's bathhouse (1761) and the 20-sided women's facility (1836) traditionally served as the starting point for annual tours of the Virginia hot springs, a social custom observed by southern aristocrats escaping the intense summer heat of the lowlands. Large pools within the frame structures are fed by the

steaming springs through loose cobbles at the bottom. NR. (703) 839-5500.

Wytheville

ROCK HOUSE MUSEUM, Tazewell and Monroe Sts. The **Haller-Gibboney Rock House** (1822-23), a two-story limestone residence, built during western Virginia's rugged frontier days, houses the antique furniture and decorative arts of the West County Historical Society. NR. Open all year, F-Su 2-4:30. $1 adults, 50¢ children. (703) 228-3841.

Wytheville vicinity

SHOT TOWER HISTORICAL STATE PARK, I-77, c. 1807. Built by Thomas Jackson, owner of nearby lead mines, the 75-foot tower conceals a shaft sunk an additional 75 feet. Molten metal was poured through a sieve down the tower. As it fell, it was rounded into the proper form for ammunition. NR. Open Memorial Day-Oct, W-Su 9-5. Free. (804) 786-2132.

Historic Accommodations

An asterisk (*) indicates that meals are served.

Abingdon

MARTHA WASHINGTON INN, 150 W. Main St., 24210. (703) 628-3161. Open all year. General Francis Preston and his wife, niece of Patrick Henry, built this rambling colonnaded mansion in 1832. The rooms still contain some original furnishings; a few have working fireplaces.*

Churchville vicinity

BUCKHORN INN, 6 miles W. via US 250, 24421. (703) 885-2900. Open all year. Built c. 1811 (and substantially enlarged in the 1920s), the Buckhorn Inn was a popular stopover for travelers en route to the hot springs of Virginia's beautiful mountain country.*

Hot Springs

THE HOMESTEAD, US 220, 24445. (703) 839-5500. Open Apr-Oct. The first part of this enormous resort hotel was built in 1891; it has been welcoming vacationers ever since. The food, the accommodations, and the beauty of The Homestead's 16,000 acres are legendary.*

Leesburg

LAUREL BRIDGADE INN, 20 W. Market St., 22075. (703) 777-1010. Open all year. It is said that President James Monroe was entertained at this 1760s stone inn and that Lafayette stayed here in 1825. Renowned for its fine cuisine, the Laurel Brigade also offers a few beautifully-decorated guest rooms. NR.*

Lexington

THE ALEXANDER WITHROW HOUSE, 3 W. Washington St., 24450. (703) 463-2044. Open all year. Located in the center of Lexington, this charming inn has had a colorful career—as school, bank, store and home—since its completion in 1789. NR.

Middleburg

THE RED FOX TAVERN, US 50, 22117. (703) 687-6301. Open all year. This venerable brick tavern has accommodated guests since the early 18th century. Superbly restored, it is handsomely furnished with period antiques.*

WELBOURNE, VA 743, 22117. (703) 687-3201. Open all year. Set in the middle of Virginia's famed hunt country, Welbourne is a gracious ante-bellum mansion which has been owned by the same family since the early 1800s.

Middletown

WAYSIDE INN, 7783 Main St., 22645. (703) 869-1797. Open all year. Once a relay station and stagecoach stop, the sprawling brick Wayside Inn (1797) was restored in the 1960s and furnished with hundreds of antiques appropriate to its long history.*

Roanoke

HOTEL ROANOKE, 19 N. Jefferson St., 24026. (703) 343-6992. Open all year. The Roanoke is one of the grand old hotels—a large Tudor-style landmark dating from the turn of the century, whose hallmarks are elegance and gracious service.*

Smithfield

THE SMITHFIELD INN, 112 Main St., 23430. (804) 357-4358. Open all year. Built in 1752 and expanded in the late 1800s, The Smithfield Inn is known for its fine dining and comfortable, antique-filled rooms.*

Staunton

THE STONEWALL JACKSON HOTEL, 28 S. Market St., 24401. (703) 885-1581. Open all year. This large cosmopolitan hotel was built in the 1920s; its spacious public rooms have been refurbished, and its location, within Staunton's historic district, is a convenience for leisurely touring. NR.*

Strasburg

HOTEL STRASBURG, 201 Holiday St., 22657. (703) 465-9191. Open all year. Built in the 1890s, the Hotel Strasburg was a private hospital for many years; it has been renovated and redecorated in the lush late-Victorian manner typical of its period.*

Trevilians

INN AT PROSPECT HILL, VA 613, Box 55, 23170. (703) 967-0844. Open all year. Formerly a working Virginia plantation, the Inn at Prospect Hill was built in 1732, and enlarged several times over the next 150 years. Guest rooms are located both in the main house and in the surrounding outbuildings; the fine restaurant is open to the public for dinner.*

Warm Springs

THE INN AT GRISTMILL SQUARE, Box 359, 24484. (703) 839-2231. Open mid Mar-Feb. The first mill on this site was built in the 1770s; the present one dates from the late 19th century. In clement weather alfresco dining is offered beside a picturesque stream.*

Williamsburg

WILLIAMSBURG INN AND COLONIAL HOUSES, S. Frances St., 23185. (804) 229-1000. The spacious, beautifully-decorated Williamsburg Inn was opened in 1934; rooms are available here or in one of many historic houses located throughout Colonial Williamsburg. NR.*

2. WEST VIRGINIA

SINCE colonial times West Virginia has appealed to adventurous people attracted to the rugged mountains and white water for which the state is now famous. The trans-Allegheny region of Virginia was not a place for refined ladies and aristocratic gentlemen, but for courageous and independent pioneers with a passion for the unpeopled wilderness. In 1670, Capt. Thomas Batts crossed the Blue Ridge and Allegheny ranges "for the finding out the ebbing and flowing of the water on the other side of the mountains." Other explorers followed Batts, but it was not until 1727 that Morgan Morgan built the first cabin in the northeast corner of what is now Berkeley County. Within a decade the fertile valley around the South Branch of the Potomac River had begun to fill with settlers from eastern Virginia, Pennsylvania, and Maryland. Many of the pioneers were immigrants from Europe who did not fit into Tidewater society. They sought undeveloped areas in which to build communities and develop a new way of life. Swiss, Irish, Scottish, and Germans, among others, have left their marks on this wonderfully diverse and surprising state.

From the time of the First Continental Congress, the people of trans-Allegheny Virginia yearned to be free of the state government in Richmond. Western Virginians complained that though they paid taxes, they received none of the benefits due them. The money was spent in the Eastern counties. In 1861, after representatives of twenty-four western counties voted to stay with the Union rather than secede, President Lincoln gave his attention to the motion for statehood. The state of West Virginia was officially recognized in 1863.

The Appalachian coal field, which extends from Pennsylvania to Alabama, reaches its greatest width in West Virginia. Of the state's fifty-five counties, forty-nine are underlaid with coal. The conditions associated with the mines and miners and the poor farming in mountain districts have led to West Virginia's reputation as a land of struggle. It is certainly a land of juxtapositions. Mineral springs have given rise to some of the country's oldest and most famous resorts, such as the elegant Greenbrier Hotel in Greenbrier County and Berkeley Springs in the northern part of the state. Coal, timber, and railroad magnates have built such lavish residences as Oglebay Mansion near Wheeling, Sunrise Mansion in Charleston, and Graceland in Elkins. The state abounds with examples of pioneer houses, mills, forts, and churches. Historic districts in Harpers Ferry, Lewisburg, Shepherdstown, and Wheeling illustrate the development of architecture in the state's towns. West Virginia is often thought of as Virginia's less endowed stepsister, a place of miners and hillbillies, but parts are both regal and beautiful: a state to discover.

For the convenience of the traveler, West Virginia's historic attractions have been divided into three areas: (1) the Eastern panhandle region, including the Allegheny Highlands and the area around the South Branch of the Potomac River; (2) the state's southern area, including the capital, Charleston; (3) the Ohio Valley region, including the northern panhandle.

State Capitol, Charleston

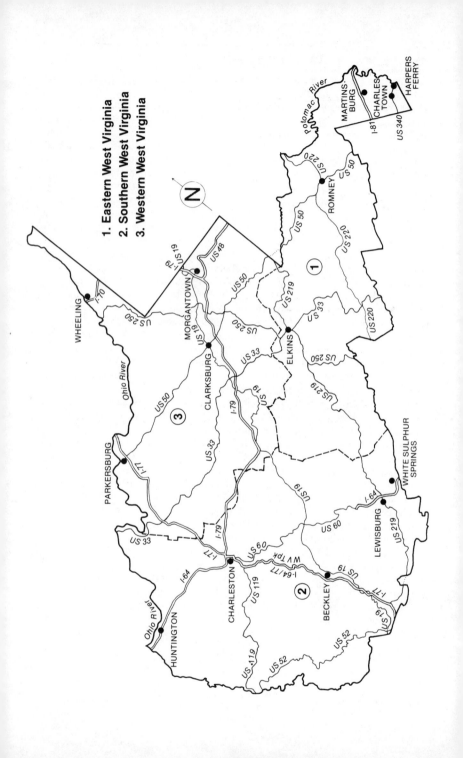

N

1. Eastern West Virginia
2. Southern West Virginia
3. Western West Virginia

Eastern West Virginia

In architecture and tradition the communities in this region of West Virginia derive more from their sister state than the more southerly and westerly reaches, which grew up independent of the aristocratic influences of tidewater Virginia. In colonial times, fashionable people from the eastern seaboard traveled here to visit the state's mineral springs, and many of those who were attracted to the spectacular landscape of the Blue Ridge and Allegheny mountains built mansions in places like Moorefield and Charles Town. Today, visitors to this area will discover a sophisticated, elegant, and extremely beautiful West Virginia.

Berkeley Springs

BERKELEY SPRINGS STATE PARK, S. Washington and Fairfax Sts., 18th-20th centuries. Officially named Bath for its famous English counterpart, the resort was fashionable throughout the mid-18th and 19th centuries. The oldest spa in the nation, this was the watering place of many notable Virginia and Maryland families. George Washington visited the springs for the first time in 1748 as a member of a surveying party and later had a house built here and returned numerous times with his family. Today the fresh warm spring water still flows at a rate of 2,000 gallons per minute. Baths, showers, and heat treatments are available to the public. Prices vary from $2 to $7 according to the treatment. NR. Open all year, M-Th 8:30-5, F 8:30-9, Sa 8:30-6, Su 12:30-6. (304) 258-2711.

Overlooking the springs is **Berkeley Castle,** ½ mile NW of town on WV 9, a turreted stone structure modeled on a fortified Norman manor house. The castle was built by 53-year-old Samuel Taylor Suit in 1887 to tempt beautiful young Rosa Pelham, daughter of an Alabama congressman, to marry him. The castle is now a museum. NR. Open daily 8-8. $3 adults, $2 senior citizens, $1.50 children. (304) 258-3274.

Cass

CASS SCENIC RAILROAD, off WV 28, 1902. The only part of 3,000 miles of West Virginia logging line still in use today, this eleven-mile strip of standard gauge railroad was constructed for the Chesapeake and Ohio Railway. Six of the "incomparable" Shay-type engines, invented for use in rugged mountainous areas, were renovated in the 1960s, and logging cars were converted to hold passengers. Today these steam locomotives still make the journey from Cass to Bald Knob, the state's second highest peak. Two trips are available, both offering spectacular views of the Allegheny mountains and Monongahela National Forest. Cass to Whittaker Station and return is a two-hour trip. $5 adults, $4 senior citizens, $1 children. Cass to Bald Knob and return takes 4½ hours. $7 adults, $6 senior citizens, $3 children. NR. Open the Sa before Memorial Day-Labor Day, Tu-Su; Labor Day-Oct, Sa-Su. The long trip leaves at noon, short trips at 11, 1, 3. (304) 456-4300. ✔

Charles Town

Founded in 1786, Charles Town bears the

Cass Scenic Railroad

name of George Washington's youngest brother, who platted the town and named many streets for members of his family. Many of the town's 18th-century residences are opened to the public each spring on the last full weekend in April. The self-guided **House and Garden Tour** of Jefferson and Berkeley Counties is sponsored by the Shenandoah-Potomac Garden Club. For details call (304) 876-2242.

CLAYMONT COURT, off US 340, early 19th century. The largest of the eight extant Washington family estates in Jefferson County, Claymont Court is reputed to be the grandest and most expensive house in the state's eastern panhandle. The original structure was built by George Washington's grand-nephew, Bushrod. When the mansion burned in 1838, it was immediately rebuilt. NR. Now run by the

Claymont Society for Continuous Education, it is open to visitors upon request. (304) 725-4437.

Just across the road is **Blakeley**, an estate built in 1820 by another of Washington's grand-nephews, John, who used it only as a summer house after he inherited Mount Vernon in 1829. The house burned in 1864 but was rebuilt. NR. Private, but visible from the road.

HAREWOOD, 3 miles W. of town on WV 51, c. 1770. This fine Georgian fieldstone house is the oldest of the Washington properties in the area. Dolley Payne Todd and James Madison were married here in 1794. Built for George Washington's brother Samuel, the house is occupied today by a direct descendant of his family. NR. Private, but easily visible from the highway.

Claymont Court

JEFFERSON COUNTY COURTHOUSE, corner of N. George and E. Washington Sts., c. 1837. The red-brick Greek Revival building is most famous as the site of John Brown's trial in 1859. Though the courthouse, badly damaged by shelling, was rebuilt after the Civil War, the original courtroom where Brown was tried for treason is still intact. NR. Open all year, M-F 9-5, Sa 9-12. (304) 725-9762.

ZION EPISCOPAL CHURCH, E. Congress, 1852. Over seventy-five members of the Washington family are buried in the cemetery adjacent to this vernacular Gothic Revival church. Open daily 8:30-4:30. (304) 725-3512.

Elkins

GRACELAND, Davis and Elkins College Campus, 1892. This massive and eclectic structure, built almost entirely of West Virginia granite, was the home of Henry Gassaway Davis, the man who was responsible for the construction of a large railroad network in the northern, central, and eastern regions of the state. In 1904 Davis and his son-in-law Stephen Benton Elkins, both of whom served as U.S. senators, founded Davis and Elkins College. NR. Tours available. (304) 636-1900.

RANDOLPH COUNTY COURTHOUSE AND JAIL, Randolph Ave. and High St., c. 1902. Designed by J. Charles Fulton, the courthouse and adjoining jail represent two of the state's most important examples of Richardsonian Romanesque architecture. In 1903 the *Randolph Enterprise* described the courthouse as "one of the most handsome, substantial, and conveniently arranged and furnished Temples of Justice in the state of West Virginia." NR. Open during regular business hours.

Fort Ashby

FORT ASHBY, South St., 1755. Fort Ashby is one of a score of forts constructed under the orders of Virginia's Governor Robert Dinwiddie following General Braddock's defeat in the battle of Monongahela in 1755. Named for its commander, Captain John Ashby, the fort was surrounded by a stockade within which the present building served as a barracks. Following the French and Indian War, the barracks was converted to a private home, but it was restored in the late 1930s. NR. The fort is open upon request. (304) 298-3319 or 3325. ★

Harpers Ferry

HARPERS FERRY NATIONAL HISTORICAL PARK, including most of the original town center and parts of the surrounding area, 18th-20th centuries. Situated on a point of land at the confluence of the Shenandoah and Potomac Rivers, the town is surrounded by the wild Blue Ridge Mountains. The first settlers stopped here in 1733, arrested by the extraordinary beauty of the landscape. In 1794, at the request of President Washington, Congress voted to build an armory in the growing town. The arrival of the Chesapeake & Ohio Canal and the Baltimore & Ohio Railroad in the 1830s seemed to guarantee economic success for Harpers Ferry.

On October 16, 1859, John Brown and his little army of eighteen abolitionists launched their attack on the thriving industrial town. Brown sought to liberate slaves by violence and set up a stronghold of free blacks in the Appalachian Mountains. Within hours, however, the alarm was spread, and at dawn on the 18th, Robert E. Lee, J.E.B. Stuart, and a detachment of marines stormed the armory. John Brown and six of his men were brought to trial in Charles Town. Brown was found guilty of murder, treason, and inciting slaves to rebellion and was hanged on December 2, 1859.

The park's **visitor center** is located in the **Stagecoach Inn** (c. 1830), Shenandoah St. Conducted and self-guided walking tours of the restored areas are available. (304) 535-6371. Among the buildings in the park are the **Master Armorer's House** (1859), Shenandoah St., now a museum with an exhibit on the production of firearms; **John Brown's Fort**, Arsenal Sq., a modern reconstruction of the building where Brown and his men took refuge from the villagers and the marines; **Harper**

Harpers Ferry

House (c. 1775), near High St., the oldest surviving structure in Harpers Ferry, built by the founder of the town and now restored and furnished with period pieces; and the **Lockwood House** (1848), Filmore St., originally the office and home of the armory paymaster. This building was later used as classrooms by Storer College, one of the nation's first institutions to offer higher education to blacks.

Several commercial establishments have been restored and are open to the public: the **Blacksmith Shop** (c. 1845), Shenandoah St.; the **Confectionery** (c. 1850), High St.; the **Dry Goods Store** (1812), Shenandoah St.; the **Pharmacy** (c. 1808), High St.; the **Post Office** (c. 1856), Potomac St.; **Whitehall Tavern** (c. 1856), Potomac St. NR. For information regarding tours, call (304) 535-6371. ✔ ★

Hillsboro vicinity

PEARL BUCK HOUSE (Stulting House), ½ mile N of Hillsboro on US 219, 1858. Built by Pearl Buck's great-grandparents,

this house was the birthplace of the Nobel and Pulitzer Prize winning novelist in June, 1892. The white frame house is now a museum which contains family and period furniture. NR. Open all year, M-Sa 9-5, Su 1-5. $1.50 adults, 75¢ students, children free. (304) 653-4430.

Marlinton and vicinity

FRANK AND ANNA HUNTER HOUSE, US 219 S., 1903. Now the Pocahontas County Historical Museum, this dwelling houses a good collection of county memorabilia from Indian times to the present, as well as an extensive photo collection. A log cabin, built around 1840, is also on the property. NR. Open June 15-Labor Day, M-Sa 11-5, Su 1-5; Sept-Oct, Sa 11-5, Su 1-5. 50¢ adults, 25¢ students 12-18, children free. (304) 799-5601 or 4973.

THE DROOP MOUNTAIN BATTLE-FIELD, 14 miles S of town on US 219, 1863. In November, 1863, Federal troops attacked the area in an attempt to drive the Confederates from the Greenbrier Valley. The Confederate defeat in the biggest battle ever fought in West Virginia marked the end of successful Southern campaigns in the state. Today the 288-acre battlefield has hiking trails and a small museum which contains Civil War artifacts. NR. Park open by appointment. Free. (304) 653-4254. ★

Martinsburg

ADAM STEPHEN HOUSE, 309 E. John St., 1772-89. Once the residence of the city's founder, Adam Stephen, who was an officer in both the French and Indian War and the Revolution, this native limestone house is now a museum furnished with fine antiques. NR. May 15-Oct 15, Sa-Su 2-5. Tours by appointment all year. (304) 267-4434.

TUSCARORA PRESBYTERIAN CHURCH, 3 miles W. on Tuscarora Rd., 1804. Scottish and Irish Presbyterians built this lovely native limestone church. The wooden pegs in the vestibule provided a convenient place for the settlers to hang their rifles during services. Open by appointment. (304) 263-4579.

Mathias vicinity

LOST RIVER STATE PARK, 5 miles from Mathias off WV 259. The two-story log **Lighthorse Lee cabin** situated in this forested park was built as a summer home

around 1800 by Revolutionary General "Lighthorse Harry" Lee. The house is now a museum. NR. Open Memorial Day-Labor Day, daily 10-6, other times by appointment. For the truly adventurous and those who like extraordinary natural settings, the 3,712-acre park also offers accommodations and a wide range of recreational activities. Open end of Mar-Dec 15. For information regarding the cabin and the park, call (304) 897-5372.

Moorefield and vicinity

Moorefield and the area which surrounds it prospered during the century before the Civil War. The rich land in the valley of the South Branch of the Potomac River provided ideal conditions for planters. A few of the plantation houses built during that time are still standing, and the town itself has retained its peaceful 19th-century ambience. The best time to visit Moorefield is during the **Hardy County Heritage Weekend** which takes place the last weekend in September. For two days the historic homes and buildings in Hardy and Grant counties are open to the public. A map, available at the Moorefield Library, and highway markers enable visitors to conduct self-guided tours. Sa 10-6, Su 1-6. (304) 538-6560.

MASLIN-GAMBLE HOUSE, 131 Main St., c. 1850. This house was built by a 19th-century land speculator and is a fine combination of traditional Federal and Greek Revival styles. NR. Private, but visible from the street.

MILL ISLAND, 1½ miles S. of Moorefield on an unmarked road, 1798, 1840. One of the most splendid structures in this area, this twenty-one room house is the product of the union of an early brick cottage with a Greek Revival mansion. The enormous addition was built by Felix Seymour as proof that he was worthy of his bride, Sidney McNeil of Willow Wall (see below). The interior of the mansion is light and airy with fifteen-foot ceilings on the first floor. Most of the enormous windows still hold their original glass, elaborate cornices crown each door and window, and a graceful oval staircase rises to the third floor. The 18th-century portion of the house now contains the dining room: the ceilings are not as high, nor is the woodwork as elegant. NR. Private, but open during the Hardy County Heritage Weekend.

WILLOW WALL, 5 miles N. of town off US 220 in Old Fields, c. 1812. When a sea captain named Daniel McNeil arrived in the South Branch Valley sometime around 1765, he built, on the site of the present mansion, a large log house. As his family grew, McNeil added two wings: one for the girls and one for the boys. It was with this U-shaped design in mind that Willow Wall was later built. Standing on a ridge and with a view of the river, Willow Wall is a Georgian Tidewater-style house built 200 miles from the sea. During the Civil War, McNeil's Rangers, a celebrated Confederate cavalry troop, used this property as a base for their activities, and the battle of Moorefield was fought on the plantation. NR. Private, but visible from the road and open during the Hardy County Heritage Weekend.

Shepherdstown

SHEPHERDSTOWN HISTORIC DISTRICT, bounded roughly by Mill, Rocky, Duke, and Washington Sts., 18th-19th centuries. Settled in 1719, Shepherdstown is one of West Virginia's oldest com-munities. Originally called Mecklenburg, the town later changed its name to honor Thomas Shepherd who built **Shepherd's Mill,** High St., in 1735. The mill was initially a two-story stone structure; the frame third story was added around 1880. The over-shot waterwheel is forty feet in diameter and is said to be one of the world's largest. Also on the property is a brick house erected by Abraham Shepherd in 1759. The rest of the district offers superb examples of Federal, Greek Revival, and Victorian houses. The residences, like the mill, are private, but a walking tour of the area is well worth the effort. During the last full weekend in April, many of the town's historic homes are open to the public. The **House and Garden Tour** of Jefferson and Berkeley counties is sponsored by the Shenandoah-Potomac Garden Club. Call for details. (304) 876-2242.

Southern West Virginia

Finding the area in the northeast of the state already settled, pioneers pushed southward, stopping at places like Lewisburg and White Sulphur Springs in mountainous Greenbrier County. Later, settlers followed the Kanawha River to the west, finally arriving at the Ohio River. For a century, this large southern section of the state remained relatively undeveloped. But when petroleum was discovered in the Little Kanawha Valley in 1860, industrialization began. With the ever-increasing demand for coal and improved mining techniques, the Cumberland plateau began to take on the characteristics it has today. Heavily industrialized, it is now the home of towns with names like Coal Fork, Coalwood, and Coal City.

Ansted

HAWKS NEST STATE PARK, US 60. From this lofty park one has a commanding view of New River Canyon, and an aerial tram offers visitors a spectacular ride from the park's lodge to a marina in the gorge below. On the mountain above the park is a rustic **museum** built of hewn logs during the Depression by the Civilian Conservation Corps. Displays concern Indian and pioneer life and coal and lumber production. Open Apr-Oct, daily 9-5. Admission to the park is free; the tram ride costs $1.50 adults, 75¢ children. (304) 658-9910. ✔

Also on US 60 in Ansted is **Contentment** (c. 1830). Built by Col. George Imboden, a local political figure, the one-story clapboard house with Greek Revival elements is typical of modest West Virginia dwellings of the period. Now a museum, the ante-bellum residence and nearby schoolhouse are furnished in period pieces. NR. Open May-Sept, M-Sa 10-5, Su 2-5. $1 adults, children under 12 free. (304) 465-5617.

Charleston

The capital of West Virginia since 1885, Charleston is the largest city in the state.

Situated on the banks of the Kanawha River, it is the most important trade center in the valley. Among its products are coal, oil, natural gas, and brine. One of Charleston's most renowned citizens, Daniel Boone, was elected to the state assembly in 1789 and was a resident until 1795.

MUSEUMS AT SUNRISE, 746 Myrtle Rd., across South Side Bridge. The highlight of this cultural complex is **Sunrise Mansion** (1905), built for William A. McCorkle, ninth governor of West Virginia. The 2½-story stone Classical Revival house is now used to exhibit paintings, decorative arts, sculpture, and graphics. Of interest to rock hounds is the wonderful mantel constructed of rocks from McCorkle's collection. Carved in each rock is the name of the place where it was found. There is also a **Children's Museum** and a **Garden Center**. NR. Open June-Aug, Tu-Sa 10-4; Sept-May 10-5; Su 2-5 all year. Free (304) 344-8035. ⌐

STATE CAPITOL, E. Kanawha Blvd., 1924-32. One of the country's most beautiful state capitols, the building was designed by architect Cass Gilbert in the Classical Revival style. A 3,300 piece handcut Czechoslovakian chandelier weighing more than two tons hangs from the central dome. NR. Open M-Sa 8:30-4:30, Su 1-4:30. Free. (304) 348-2286 or (800) 624-9110.

The museum in the **Cultural Center**, next to the Capitol on Washington St. E., houses collections of all kinds of artifacts of West Virginia life from Indian times to the present. A theater, two libraries, and a craft shop may also be of interest to the visitor. Open all year, M-F 9-5, Sa-Su 1-5. Free. (304) 348-0220 or 0162.

Huntington

West Virginia's second largest city, Huntington was founded in 1871 by Collis P. Huntington, the enormously wealthy Californian who was president of the Chesapeake and Ohio Railroad. He named the city for himself, of course.

BALTIMORE AND OHIO RAILROAD DEPOT, 11th St. and Veterans Memorial Blvd., 1887. For years the hub of Huntington and a whistle stop on several presidential campaigns, the Victorian station has been restored recently and is now a restaurant with a private backgammon room available to guests. NR. Open all year, M-Sa 10-5. (304) 696-5954.

THOMAS CARROLL HOUSE, 234 Guyan St., c. 1800. This two-story frame house with Italianate details is said to have been floated down river from Gallipolis, Ohio, piece by piece and reconstructed on its present site in 1810. Once an inn patronized by rivermen and travelers along the Kanawha and James River Turnpike, the house has been in the Carroll family since 1855. NR. Private, but visible from the street.

HARVEY HOUSE, 1305 Third Ave., c. 1873. This house is so wonderfully whimsical, with its flared eaves, fluted columns, and exaggerated voussoirs, that it must be seen, even if only from the outside. The curved stairs and original iron balcony were, unfortunately, removed. The house was designed by William Hope Harvey, a free-silver economist who ran as the Liberty Party's presidential candidate in 1932. NR. Private, but visible from the street.

OLD MAIN, 16th St., Marshall University Campus, 1870-1907. The focal point of the university, Old Main was built over a period of more than thirty years in five distinct parts, all Victorian in style. The university was named for John Marshall, Chief Justice of the U.S. Supreme Court from 1801-35. NR. (304) 696-3170.

Kesslers Cross Lanes vicinity

CARNIFEX FERRY STATE PARK, S. of town off WV 129, 1861. Union victory over Confederate troops at Carnifex Ferry in September, 1861, removed the threat of Confederate occupation of the Kanawha Valley and allowed area residents to participate in the West Virginia statehood movement. **The Patterson House**, a restored farmhouse in the 156-acre park, is now a museum which displays Civil War artifacts. NR. Open Memorial Day-Labor Day daily 10-6. (304) 872-3773. ★

Lewisburg

Andrew Lewis came into the Greenbrier Valley in 1751. He noted that the area around Lewis Spring, at the junction of two major Indian trails, the Seneca (now US 219) and the Kanawha (now US 60), would make fine farmland and a good place for a village. The first permanent settlements were made in the Lewisburg region around 1769, but local population did not begin to increase significantly until the State Road was built, opening the way to Ohio in 1786 and, by 1804, to Kentucky. In 1795, the town was described by a French traveler as a "village of considerable pretensions, a place noted for its intelligent and refined society."

LEWISBURG HISTORIC DISTRICT, off US 219, 18th-20th centuries. Before the 19th century, most of the town's dwellings were temporary pole or log structures, very few of which have survived. By 1810, good agricultural development had brought wealth to many Lewisburg citizens, and brick homes, public, and commercial buildings were erected prior to the Civil War. Of these buildings, many were designed and constructed by two architect/builders, John Weir and John Dunn, who arrived in the area about a decade apart, learned the trade of brickmaking and brickmasonry from slaves, and became contractors. Many of Dunn's houses are graced with elaborate interior woodwork carved by a local artisan named Conrad Burgess. A walking tour map of this historic town is available at the City Hall, 19 W. Washington St. Open M-F 9-4:30. (304) 645-2080.

GREENBRIER COUNTY COURTHOUSE, 200 N. Court St., 1837. One of the few surviving ante-bellum courthouses in West Virginia, this was designed by John Dunn and paid for by a county levy of $10,000. Dunn followed a pattern used for many early Virginia courthouses: an imposing square building with large brick columns topped, at the third story level, with a pediment and fanlight. NR. Open during regular business hours. (304) 645-2373.

JOHN NORTH HOUSE (Star Tavern), 301 W. Washington St., c. 1820. The North House floor plan is a good example of the Georgian layout most commonly used in the houses of architect/builder John Dunn. It includes a hallway running from the front to the back of the house with two large rooms to the left and right of the hall. The two front rooms are parlors or public rooms, where lovely examples of Conrad Burgess's handcarved woodwork grace the walls. North sold the house to James Frazier in the 1830s, and the new owner made additions and used it as a tavern for forty years. It is now the **Greenbrier Historical Society Museum** and contains a collection of colonial and 19th-century objects. NR. Open Apr-Sept, Tu-Su 1-5. $1 adults, 50¢ students 12-18, children under 12 free. (304) 647-9848.

OLD STONE PRESBYTERIAN CHURCH, 200 Church St., 1796. One of the few native limestone buildings in town, this lovely edifice with Georgian elements stands two-stories high and has an interior balcony on three sides. It has been continuously used since it opened almost two centuries ago. NR. Open daily 9-4. (304) 645-2676.

SUPREME COURT LIBRARY, W. Washington St. and Courtney Dr., 1834. The Virginia Supreme Court of Appeals was established in Lewisburg in 1831. Three years later, James Frazier had completed work on a two-story brick building to rent for use as a study and library. A good businessman, he had it built across the street from his Star Tavern. Today the building serves as a museum and library. Call for information regarding admission, (304) 645-2350.

Point Pleasant

POINT PLEASANT BATTLEGROUND, Main St., 1774. Also known as Tu-Endi-Wei, Indian for "point between two waters," the battleground is situated on a point of land at the confluence of the Ohio and Kanawha Rivers. Here 1,100 colonials and a lesser number of Indians fought over the traditional Indian hunting grounds to the west. Chief Cornstalk, in honor of whom a monument was later erected at Point Pleasant, was narrowly defeated. Today the battleground is a park within which the visitor will find the handsome **Mansion House.** Built around 1796, this is the oldest extant log building in the Kanawha Valley. The house now contains a collection of antiques and relics. NR. Park open Apr 1-Nov 15, M-Sa 9-5, Su 1-5. Tours by appointment. Donations accepted. (304) 675-3330. ★

Union vicinity

OLD SWEET SPRINGS, 9 miles E. of Union on WV 3, 19th century. One of the country's oldest mineral water resorts, Old Sweet Springs was well developed by 1790. In 1833, a large two-story brick Jeffersonian Neo-classical building was constructed, followed by an arcaded bathhouse with twin towers. Less than twenty years later a corporation was formed to improve the resort, but its plans were never realized. The beautiful main structure is now part of a state home for the elderly. NR.

REHOBOTH CHURCH, 2 miles E. of Union on WV 3, 1786. Probably the oldest Protestant church building west of the Alleghenies, this is a simple pioneer building constructed of hand-hewn logs. Inside are the original backless split-log benches and a handmade pulpit. NR. Closed, but visitors may walk around the grounds.

White Sulphur Springs

THE GREENBRIER, off US 60, 18th-20th centuries. A huge complex on 6,500 beautiful acres in the Allegheny mountains, The Greenbrier is a monument to gracious Southern living and hospitality.

One of the most famous spas in the country, it developed around three mineral springs and was used by settlers as early as 1772. Both before and after the Civil War, this sumptuous watering place attracted presidents, royalty, and other celebrated people. In 1816 the Greenbrier built a cottage for the presidents who visited here: Van Buren, Tyler, Fillmore, and Buchanan used it as a summer retreat. Today the cottage is a museum with collections of photographs, letters, furniture, paintings, etc. Open Apr-Oct, M-Sa 10-12 and 1-4; other times by appointment.

When the Chesapeake and Ohio Railroad Co. bought the resort in 1910, it hired New York architect Frederick J. Sterner to design the enormous Classical Revival central building which was finished in 1913. There is much to see and do at this luxurious resort, and even those who are not guests should drive up and have a look. NR, NHL. Open all year. (800) 624-6070.

Williamson

COAL HOUSE, Second Ave. and Court St., 1933. The object of Williamson's civic pride and a monument to coal mining and miners in the southern region of the state, the Tug Valley Chamber of Commerce building is made entirely of coal. In 1931, O.W. Evans, manager of Norfolk and Western Railroad's Fuel Department in Williamson, conceived the idea of a building of coal as a symbol of the area's major economic activity as well as the city's claim to being "The Heart of the Billion Dollar Coal Field." Every door and window in the building is arched, and the enormous front entrance is framed by two pseudo-pilasters. NR. Open during regular business hours. (304) 235-5240. ✔

The French laid claim to the fertile area around the Ohio River long before Europeans actually settled in the region. In the mid-18th century, when the first pioneers began to establish communities on the far side of the Allegheny mountains, the land became the property of those who lived here. In the 19th century, the western area began to develop rapidly as settlers ventured into the region from Virginia and Pennsylvania. Many were on their way west, but some came to stay. The historic sites in the cities and towns of this section of the state date largely from the last century, and travelers will find that reminders of the past range from the most rustic log structures to sophisticated mansions.

Bethany

ALEXANDER CAMPBELL MANSION, about 1 mile E. on WV 67, 1793. Built by Alexander Campbell's father-in-law, John Brown, the 2½-story frame house has a beautiful front porch supported by delicate columns and ornamented with elaborately carved balustrades and bracketing. Campbell, founder of Bethany College and intellectual leader of a religious denomination known as the Disciples of Christ, was married in this house and lived here until his death in 1866. The twenty-seven room dwelling is now a museum appointed with antique furnishings. NR. May-Oct, Tu-Su 10-12 and 2-5. Tours by appointment Nov-Apr. Free. (304) 829-7341.

OLD MAIN, Bethany College Campus, 1858-72. The largest of seven Gothic Revival buildings on the 300-acre campus, this U-shaped structure was designed by James Keys Wilson and William Walter. NR. Tours available year 'round. (304) 829-7341

Clarksburg and vicinity

STEALEY-GOFF-VANCE HOUSE, 123 W. Main St., c. 1807. Jacob Stealey, a successful tanner, built the first brick home in Clarksburg; it was well-made and sturdy, though essentially plain in style. Later owners, the Goffs, transformed the house by adding a high-pitched center gable, a porch, and fancy Victorian lacework around 1892. The house was later owned by Cyrus Vance, former U.S. Secretary of State, and his family. It is now the museum of the Harrison County Historical Society and contains collections of tools, antique furniture, and Indian artifacts. NR. Mar-Dec, Sa 2-4. 25¢ admission. (304) 842-3043.

While in the area, visit **Fort New Salem,** on the campus of Salem College, 12 miles W. in Salem. In twenty restored log cabins from all over the state, guides offer a living history program which describes pioneer life through crafts, music, and folklore. June-mid Dec. M-Sa 10-4, Su 1-5. $1.50 adults, 50¢ children. (304) 782-5245. ✔

Fairmont vicinity

PRICKETTS FORT STATE PARK, 5 miles N. of town off I-79 (exit 139), 1774. Situated on a knoll overlooking the Monongahela River, the original stockaded fort was built on land owned by Jacob Prickett, said to have been the first white settler in the county. Built as a defense against the Indians, the fort once contained cabins, shelters, storage areas, stables, and stock pens, but was dismantled late in the 18th century when the Indian threat was past. Now it has been carefully recreated by the Pricketts Fort Memorial Foundation, using old logs from other buildings in the area. A living history program on the premises vividly describes life in the 18th century. Open May-Sept, M-Sa 10-5, Su 12-6; April 15-May 1 and Oct, Sa-Su only. Donations accepted. (304) 363-3030. ★ ✔

Grafton

ANDREWS METHODIST CHURCH, 11 E. Main St., 1873. This church is known as the International Mother's Day Shrine, because Anna Jarvis, who taught Sunday school here and was the daughter of the minister, conceived the idea of dedicating a day to commemorating all mothers. Her missionary zeal resulted in a congressional resolution (1913) making the second Sunday in May a national holiday. NR. Open Apr-Oct, daily 9:30-12 and 1-4. Tours available (304) 265-1589.

GRAFTON NATIONAL CEMETERY, 431 Walnut St., 19th-20th centuries. Dedicated in 1868, this three-acre burial ground is the only national cemetery in the state. Private Thornbury Bailey Brown, the first Union soldier to be killed by a Confederate, is buried here along with hundreds of others who died defending the Union. Surrounded by a low stone wall, the rectangular cemetery is on three landscaped terraces connected by a graceful walkway. NR. Open daily 8-5. (304) 265-2044. ★

Morgantown

OLD STONE HOUSE, 313 Chestnut St., c. 1796. Built of sandstone, the two-story house is among the oldest buildings in the county and is one of the best extant examples of pioneer architecture. The house has served as a dwelling, tavern, pottery, church, tailor shop, and junk shop. Now it is a tearoom and a craft shop. NR. Open Jan-Feb, June-Aug, M-Sa 10-2; Mar-May, Sept-Dec, M-Sa 10-4. (304) 296-7825.

Visitors to the area may want to stop to see the stately 19th-century Second Empire buildings at **Woodburn Circle**, University Ave., on the West Virginia University Campus. Once there, don't miss **Stewart Hall** (19th century) which stands nearby. Some say it is the most significant example of the Richardsonian Romanesque style in the state. NR. (304) 293-0111.

Moundsville

GRAVE CREEK MOUND, Tomlinson and Ninth Sts., c. 500 B.C. 79 feet high, 900 feet in circumference, and 50 feet across the top, the Indian burial mound for which the town is named is the largest and oldest in the U.S. Archaeological excavations began on the Adena culture burial site in 1838. NR, NHL. Artifacts from the mound are now on display at the **Delf Norona Museum and Cultural Center**, 801 Jefferson Ave. Open all year M-F 10-4:30, Sa 12-5, Su 1-5. (304) 843-1440 or 1410.

Parkersburg vicinity

BLENNERHASSETT ISLAND HISTORICAL PARK, on the Ohio River about 2

Grafton National Cemetery

miles S. of town, Pre-Columbian-20th century. A wealthy Irish couple, Harman and Margaret Blennerhassett, fled their homeland for personal reasons (he was her uncle) and built a luxurious mansion with formal gardens on this secluded island. Blennerhassett was implicated in Aaron Burr's plan to carve out a new country in the West, and Harman and Margaret were forced to flee their island home when the Virginia militia, searching for Burr, invaded in 1806. Blennerhassett and Burr were both acquitted of treason charges, but their fortunes were ruined; and in 1811 the mansion accidentally burned to the ground. Blennerhassett Island is still being developed as a park. Activities now include a self-guided historical tour and active archaeological digs. Several trails and picnic areas have been established. NR. Catch the stern-wheeler *Centennial* for a ride to the island. It leaves from The Point, off WV 68, in downtown Parkersburg during Apr-May, Sept-Oct, Sa-Su at 1,2,3, and 4. Memorial Day-Labor Day, F-Su same hours. $2 adults, $1.50 children. (614) 423-7268. ✔

Philippi

PHILIPPI COVERED BRIDGE, Main St., over Tygart Valley River, 1852. Designed by Lemuel Chenoweth, this is one of the six remaining two-lane covered bridges in the U.S. and the longest still in use on a federal highway. Philippi was the scene of a small battle at the beginning of the Civil War, and the bridge was used by both Union and Confederate forces. NR.

Sistersville

SISTERSVILLE HISTORIC DISTRICT, from Chelsea to the Ohio River, between Catherine and Virginia Sts., 19th-early 20th centuries. Sistersville was laid out in 1815 by two sisters, Sarah and Delilah Wells, the daughters of the area's first settler, Charles Wells. At the turn of the century, black gold was discovered near this peaceful river town, and for a few years the economy boomed. Most of the 215 structures in the historic district are made of wood and were constructed between 1890 and 1915. Italianate dwellings abound, but fine examples of Gothic and Colonial Revival and Richarsonian Romanesque can also be seen. NR.

Weston and vicinity

JONATHAN BENNETT HOUSE, Court Ave., 1874-75. Jonathan Bennett, one of the area's best known political and business moguls, built this house late in life. The epitome of High-Victorian Italianate architecture, the seventeen-room mansion has been saved from alteration by a preservation clause in the deed. The 4½-story entrance tower with mansard roof stands between the main block of the building and the ell. The house is detailed with intricate millwork and elaborate pressed-tin ornamentation. Given to the people of Lewis County by Bennett's daughter-in-law in 1922, the mansion is now the Louis Bennett Library. NR. Open M-F 10-8, Sa 10-3. (304) 269-5151.

JACKSON'S MILL, E. of Jackson Mill on WV 1, 1837. Located on the site of Stonewall Jackson's grandfather's farm is a frame mill with all its gears and cogs and one original millstone still intact. The mill was operated until 1892. NR. Also on the site is the 19th-century McWhorter Cabin which houses a collection of period furniture and Civil War artifacts. Both buildings are now museums. Open June-Sept, M-Sa 10:30-5:30, Su 1:30-5:30. (304) 260-5100. ✔

WESTON STATE HOSPITAL (Trans-Allegheny Lunatic Asylum), River St., 1858-81. Said to be the largest handcut stone masonry building in the U.S., the hospital has a 1200-foot façade and was designed by Richard Snowden Andrews. Using blue sandstone from a nearby quarry, building was begun in 1858, but, delayed by the Civil War, it took over two decades to complete. The Gothic or "pointed-style" building looks much the same today as it did when it was completed in 1881. NR. Open for tours by appointment. (304) 269-1210.

Wheeling and vicinity

In Delaware language Wheeling means "the place of the skull." Story has it that early traders who ventured as far as "Scalp Creek" found a very explicit "No Trespassing" sign: a white man's head on a pole. Ebenezer Zane and his brothers were not scared off by that legend. They came to the area with their families around 1769 and founded a new settlement in the place they called "a vision of paradise." The Indians lived up to their reputation in the next few years, however, scalping a number of the men, women, and children living in the small settlement. A fort was built and used until after the Revolution when both the Indian and English threats were past.

door activities as well as a 200-room resort hotel. NR. Museum open M-Sa 9:30-5, Su 1-5. $2.50 adults, $2 senior citizens, children free. ✓

Wheeling's life as a modern trade center began in 1815 when Captain Henry Miller Shreve constructed a newfangled steamboat, *The George Washington.* Trade operations with New Orleans and other cities on the Ohio and Mississippi Rivers were vastly improved. By 1818 the National Pike between Cumberland, Maryland, and Wheeling was completed and this brought thousands of travelers on their way to the U.S. interior. In 1853, when the Baltimore & Ohio Railway was completed as far as Wheeling, population as well as commerce and industry increased dramatically.

OGLEBAY MANSION MUSEUM, N. of town on WV 88 in Oglebay Park, 1845. Once a brick farmhouse, this splendid mansion has grown up over the years. In 1901, Earl W. Oglebay, a wealthy industrialist from Cleveland, bought the house and made it a mansion. For four years architects and builders worked on the structure, expanding everywhere. They maintained the two-story composition but added rooms and wings and stylish Neo-classical details. Oglebay later gave the house and park to the city. The mansion has served as a museum of Wheeling's industrial, political, and social history since 1930. The collection includes Wheeling and Midwestern glass, Anglo-American china (1839-1912) and period rooms (1740-1850). The lovely 1,460-acre Oglebay Park offers all sorts of out-

SHEPHERD HALL (Monument Place), Monument Pl. and Kruger St., 1798. Moses Shepherd was builder/architect of this Georgian stone dwelling. Probably the oldest surviving house in Wheeling, it was once part of a plantation. Moses Shepherd was an industrialist and a bridge builder on the National Road who later became the city's mayor. The feminine wiles of his wife, Louise, were instrumental in convincing Henry Clay to run the National Road through Wheeling rather than through Wellsburg, the more direct

route—an important turn of events for Wheeling and a little coup for Louise. NR. Private, but visible from the street.

WHEELING HISTORIC DISTRICT, in

the downtown area, 19th-20th centuries. This is a fascinating place, especially for anyone interested in the evolution of commercial architecture from the early 19th century to the present. One has to be able to appreciate second-story design and detailing, however, since many of the older buildings suffer from 20th-century accretions at the street level. Still, fine examples of early Greek-Revival, Italianate, and turn-of-the-century Beaux Arts architecture abound. Most are constructed of brick or sandstone, and many have exterior appliques of stone, marble, or cast iron. Renovations in the district have been limited, for the most part, to the shops on Market St. facing the plaza that was once the locaiton of one of the town's markets. A walking tour of the area might include the following buildings:

Independence Hall (c. 1859), 1524 Market St., was once the customshouse, courthouse, and post office of Wheeling. The three-story Italianate building is made of gray sandstone and has tall round-arched windows. The state's declaration of independence from Virginia was written here in 1861. Independence Hall has been beautifully restored to its original appearance and contains collections of state artifacts and documents. NR. Open all year, Tu-F 9-5, Sa 1-3. (304) 233-1333.

Linsley Institute, 1413 Eoff St., 1859. A military academy turned medical clinic, this Neo-classical building is the site of the first capitol of West Virginia. NR. Private, but visible from the street. **Capitol Theater,** 1015 Main St., c. 1926. This wonderful building of late Beaux-Arts design was once a vaudeville theater and is now the city's main country and western music hall. NR. You may want to catch a show while you're in bluegrass country. (304) 233-5511.

WHEELING SUSPENSION BRIDGE, over the Ohio River at 10th St., 1849. The first structure to span the Ohio, the bridge was, at 1,010 feet across, the longest suspension bridge in the world upon its completion. The bridge, which was supported by sixty-foot high masonry towers and suspended with iron cables, collapsed in 1854. Rebuilding was completed in 1859, and the structure was not overhauled again for ninety-seven years. Today, it is believed to be the world's oldest suspension bridge. NR, NHL.

Historic Accommodations

An asterisk (*) indicates that meals are served.

Berkeley Springs

THE COUNTRY INN, 207 S. Washington St., 25411. (304) 258-2210. Open all year. Located in the center of town, this colonial-style inn is just steps away from the Berkeley Springs Spa. Aside from comfortable rooms, the inn offers excellent Southern food, and in summer guests may take their meals in the garden.*

Lewisburg

GENERAL LEWIS INN, 301 E. Washington St., 24901. (304) 645-2600. Open all year. Once a private dwelling, this charming building was constructed in 1834 and converted to an inn a century later. Today the General Lewis provides accommodations in antique-filled rooms as well as delicious Southern cooking.*

Sistersville

THE WELLS INN, 316 Charles St., on WV 2, 26175. (304) 652-3111. Open all year. Built by Ephraim Wells in 1894, this inn was a favorite resting place for those traveling by steamboat on the Ohio River. The inn was carefully restored and furnished with period pieces in the mid-1960s. NR.

White Sulphur Springs

THE GREENBRIER, US 60, 24986. (800) 624-6070. (See historical listing.) A world famous resort hotel, The Greenbrier provides luxurious accommodations, fine food, and a variety of activities which range from golf to ice-skating to rides in horse-drawn sleighs. NR, NHL.*

3. NORTH CAROLINA

FROM the Outer Banks to the Great Smokies, North Carolina enjoys an enviable reputation for its superb scenery and rich historical and cultural resources. The coastal region is dotted with cities and towns full of maritime flavor and history, places from which the products of the Piedmont—tobacco, cotton, marine supplies such as turpentine and pitch—were sent throughout the world. One hundred miles inland is the Piedmont plateau of extraordinarily rich farmland and fast-flowing streams perfectly suited for the purposes of industry. This central area has been at the crossroads of major military, political, and economic events since the Revolution. It is in the direct path of transportation and commerce between the Northeast and Southeast. Farther west is North Carolina's frontier region, cultivated in almost every respect but still wild enough in its mountain reaches to have attracted summer visitors for nearly 200 years. Western North Carolina is also Indian country, the ancestral home of several southeastern tribes. The tragic story of North Carolina's first settlers on Roanoke Island in the 1580s is told in the following pages. The colony established by Sir Walter Raleigh was only short-lived, having mysteriously disappeared from view by 1591. Today, at Manteo, Fort Raleigh has been rebuilt and visitors will find the location an ideal place from which to begin a journey into North Carolina's past which covers nearly 400 years, a period longer than that of Massachusetts or Virginia.

Nearly every coastal settlement prides itself on its well-preserved homes, churches, and other public buildings. Beaufort, Edenton, Bath, New Bern, and even a city as large as Wilmington are pleasant places to visit, and each offers its own unique blend of picturesque sights. The towns and cities of the Piedmont date primarily from the second half of the 18th century, and rose in prosperity during the 1800s. They range from such tiny towns as Hillsborough, used by English General Cornwallis as his military headquarters in 1781, to booming metropolitan centers such as Greensboro and Winston-Salem. Even here in the Piedmont, however, where scientific research is big business and "progress" a byword, there is a premium placed on saving the "old." Old Salem, the major Moravian settlement in Winston-Salem, is a pleasure to visit; so, too, are the various historical museums and houses in the state capital, Raleigh.

Visitors from throughout the eastern United States have traditionally enjoyed the resort centers of western North Carolina. Asheville, located not far from the Blue Ridge Parkway, has been a principal gateway for the area since the Civil War and is renowned for its splendid Biltmore family properties. Beyond Asheville to the north, south, and west are many small mountain communities—more active in the summer than any other season—where relaxation can be pursued at heights of more than 6,000 feet, the highest peaks in the East. An appreciation of what America must have been like before Europeans arrived to make history is not difficult to acquire in this naturally beautiful terrain.

Old Salem, Winston-Salem

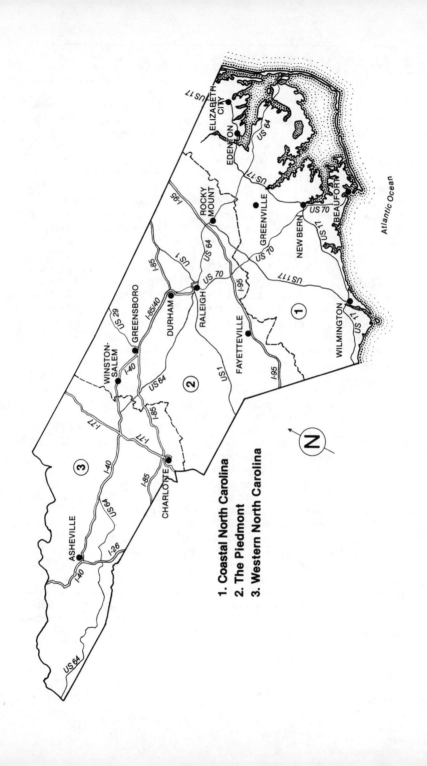

1. Coastal North Carolina
2. The Piedmont
3. Western North Carolina

Coastal North Carolina

North Carolina's coastal towns and cities are renowned for their distinguished architecture, attractive gardens, and picturesque harbors and inlets. Well-removed from the main flow of North-South interstate traffic, the easternmost portion of the state has escaped many of the worst effects of modern industrialization. The Outer Banks region, portions of which can be reached only by ferry, has been protected by the federal government, and its naturally beautiful landscape and indigenous wildlife should continue undisturbed. The port towns would not have developed as handsomely in the 18th and 19th centuries if they had not been linked to the interior, a land of plantations as well as more modest farms immediately west and in the central Piedmont. The merchants and shippers of such cities as Wilmington, New Bern, Edenton, and Beaufort prospered greatly from the maritime trade. The scene has been a great deal quieter in the 20th century, and this may be one reason why the inhabitants' coastal settlements live so much in the past, and enjoy doing so.

Bath

HISTORIC BATH STATE HISTORIC SITE, 14 miles SE of Washington on NC 92, 18th-early 19th centuries. One of North Carolina's earliest settlements (1705), the village of Bath has been preserved by the state, and many of its oldest buildings are open to the public. These include the **Palmer-Marsh House**

(1740), a two-story clapboard residence; the **Van Der Veer House** (1790), a frame building with a gambrel roof; and **St. Thomas Church** (c. 1734), the oldest extant North Carolina house of worship. These buildings are located along Main St., in what was the village's commercial center. Bath is situated along the Pamlico River and once served as a shipbuilding center and as the seat of Beaufort County. The story of the town's rise and decline in the 18th century is told in a film shown at the **Visitor Center.** Tours of the historic site leave from this point. NR, NHL. Open Tu-Sa 9-5, Su 1-5. (919) 923-3971.

Beaufort and vicinity

BEAUFORT HISTORICAL ASSOCIATION, the block formed by Front, Turner, Craven, and Ann Sts., mid 18th-mid 19th centuries. A tour of this beautifully situated and preserved town of old homes and public buildings should begin at the association's restored complex. A Reception Center for visitors is located at the **Josiah Bell House** (c. 1825), 138 Turner St., which is furnished with Victorian antiques. Within the same block are the tiny **Carteret County Courthouse** (1796), the **County Jail** (c. 1836), the **J. Pigott House** (c. 1830), and the **Apothecary Shop**

(c. 1859). Just across Turner St. is the **Joseph Bell House** (c. 1767), a handsome

frame residence painted conch red with white shutters. NR. These buildings are open M-Sa 9-5, Su 2-5. $2 adults and students, 50¢ children 8-12.
(919) 728-7647.

FORT MACON STATE PARK, 4 miles E. of Atlantic Beach at Bogue Pt., Bogue Island, 1826-34. The third fortification at this site, Fort Macon was built to protect Beaufort. It was an important Confederate outpost in the Civil War, and after it fell into Union hands in 1862, it served as a military prison for some years. Capt. William Tell Poussin is thought to have been the architect of the impressive brick and stone pentagonal fort. Stone jetties designed by Capt. Robert E. Lee in the 1840s helped to preserve the land area and have been augmented since that time. NR. Open daily 10-5. ★

HAMPTON MARINERS MUSEUM, 120 Turner St. This extension of the North Carolina State Museum of Natural History is located in the same block as the historical association complex. Both sea life and traditional marine activities are the subject of exhibits. There is also a boat-shop where old-fashioned wooden vessels are under construction. During the summer, there are special programs for children. Open M-F 9-5, Sa 10-5, Su 2-5. Free.
(919) 728-7317. ✔

If you have the time, don't limit your visit to Beaufort to only the relatively small area of local museum buildings. The historic center of this seafaring town, settled in the early 1700s and named for Henry Somerset, Duke of Beaufort, stretches for nearly nine blocks along Front and Ann Sts. The historical association can provide a walking tour guide to the many picturesque homes and other sites. Many of Beaufort's private homes, in fact, are open the last weekend in June each year, and details are available from the association. Across from the association buildings off Ann St. is the Old Burying Grounds (c. 1731), a romantic cemetery full of azaleas and shady trees.

Buxton

MUSEUM OF THE SEA, Cape Hatteras National Seashore, NC 12, Hatteras Island, 1870. The Cape Hatteras Lighthouse and keeper's dwellings are among this coastal barrier island's most durable and historic buildings. The National Park Service, which administers the region, opens the lighthouse to visitors during daylight hours all year. The tallest in North America, the tower is painted with a distinctive candy-striped pattern. Nearby is a self-guiding natural trail which traces life in the wetlands. Free.
(919) 473-2114. ✔

Creswell vicinity

SOMERSET PLACE STATE HISTORIC SITE, 9 miles S. of Creswell, Pettigrew State Park, c. 1820, 1830. Somerset Place is one of the most romantic and impressive ante-bellum plantations in North Carolina. From the time of the Civil War and the loss of slave labor, the estate sank into oblivion; since 1951, North Carolina has undertaken its restoration. The plantation was first laid out in the 1780s by Josiah Collins and named for his native Somerset-shire, England. By the time his grandson, Josiah Collins, III, began operating the estate in the 1820s, there were several thousand acres of land under cultivation, principally in corn. Three hundred Negroes provided the labor. One of the first estate houses is the two-story Colony House (c. 1820). This was superseded as the main residence in 1830 by a much larger 2½-story frame dwelling with full-length verandas that rise two stories. The State has restored and furnished this building with period pieces. Also visible are remains of two slave quarters, the hospital and chapel, and the overseer's house. NR. The plantation is open to visitors Tu-Sa 9-5, Su 1-5. Free.
(919) 797-4560.

Currie vicinity

MOORES CREEK NATIONAL MILITARY PARK, on NC 210, 1776. Not all colonists were wildly enthusiastic about the Revolutionary cause, and at Moores Creek Bridge on Feb. 27, 1776, 1,600 Scottish loyalists, among the early settlers in North Carolina, met a force of 1,000 patriots. The battle was small but significant and resulted in the total defeat of the British sympathizers and their leaders in the state. To learn more about the battle and to begin a tour of the site, stop first at the **Visitor Center** where there are interpretive exhibits. The National Park Service, which administers the battlefield, will direct you on a self-guided tour. NR. Open daily 8-5, summer 8-6. Free. (919) 283-5591. ★

Edenton

Once you have visited Edenton, you'll surely want to come back again. Beautifully situated on Edenton Bay, this community has gracefully safeguarded its historic character. Edenton was once a very important place — the earliest permanent settlement in the state, a bustling Colonial port, the home of such leading North Carolina Revolutionary statesmen as James Iredell, Samuel Johnston, Joseph Hewes, and Dr. Hugh Williamson. Some of the best old buildings have been preserved by Historic Edenton, Inc., and included among these are **Barker House** (1782, 19th century), a waterfront residence at the south end of Broad St., which is a house museum and serves as a **Visitor Center** for the historic district. A free audio-visual program on the area's sites is presented here, and a tour map is available. It is open for information and guided tours Tu-Sa 10-4:30, Su 2-5, and for information only on M 10-4:30. Free. (919) 482-3663. Admission for all of the following buildings on the Historic Edenton tour is $5 adults, $2 students. The hours are the same as for Barker House.

CHOWAN COUNTY COURTHOUSE, E. King St., 1767. This building is considered the finest Georgian structure in North Carolina and was the second building in Edenton to serve the purpose of county government. It is handsomely situated at the head of the village green. The courthouse was probably designed and built by Gilbert Leigh who is believed to have come from Williamsburg. The soft pink brick building has a projecting

pedimented center section and is crowned with a graceful two-story clock tower-cupola. NR, NHL.

CUPOLA HOUSE, 408 S. Broad St., c. 1725. Built for Richard Sanderson, this unusual clapboard frame home combines such 17th-century features as a second-floor overhang and a steeply pitched gable roof with Georgian details common during the mid-1700s. It is known that the building was remodeled at a later time for Francis Corbin who was serving as Lord Granville's land agent. The name of the building derives from the distinctive octagonal cupola with carved detailing. The Brooklyn Museum now possesses the interior paneling of the two major first floor rooms, this having been removed in 1918. But all of the fine woodwork has been expertly reproduced. NR.

ST. PAUL'S EPISCOPAL CHURCH, W. Church and Churton Sts., 1736-66. The second oldest Colonial church in the state, St. Paul's is unquestionably the first in beauty. The Flemish bond brickwork was admirably laid by talented masons. The box pews date from the 19th century as do the reconstructed side balconies. St. Paul's is still an active parish. NR.

JAMES IREDELL HOUSE, 107 E. Church St., c. 1776, c. 1816. Maintained by the state as an historic site, this home of a leading Revolutionary period patriot and associate justice of the U.S. Supreme Court is the most fascinating of the stops on an Edenton tour. In addition to the well-furnished clapboard frame dwelling, built in two sections at different times, there is on the same property a one-room school (1827), a carriage house, and a separate kitchen suitably supplied with antique cooking utensils. NR.

Elizabeth City vicinity

MUSEUM OF THE ALBEMARLE, 3 miles SW of Elizabeth City on US 17. Since the 18th century the Albemarle Sound region has been an important agriculture, small manufacturing, and shipping center, and Elizabeth City lies at the center of this activity. On display at the museum are lumbering items, duck carvings and decoys, Indian artifacts, and exhibits depicting old-time farming methods. Open Tu-Sa 9-5, Su 2-5. Free. (919) 335-1453. ✔

Fremont vicinity

CHARLES B. AYCOCK BIRTHPLACE, 6 miles from junction of US 117 and NC 1542, 1840. A typical 19th-century farmstead may tell us as much about the past as a splendid Georgian mansion. Aycock, governor of the state in the early 1900s, never forgot his humble beginnings and left his mark as an inspired champion of a free and quality education for all. His home and surrounding farm buildings are simple weatherboard frame structures. North Carolina has restored all of the buildings, including a separate kitchen,

corn barn, a large and a small smokehouse, and a stable. A schoolhouse (1879) was moved to this site in 1912. NR. Open Tu-Sa 9-5, Su 1-5. Free. (919) 242-5581. ✔

Kill Devil Hills

WRIGHT BROTHERS NATIONAL MEMORIAL, Cape Hatteras National Seashore, on Bypass US 158, midway between Kitty Hawk and Nags Head, 1900-1903. For over three years, Wilbur and Orville Wright trekked several times from their Dayton, Ohio, home to the Outer Banks to experiment with gliders and, finally, a machine-powered craft. On December 17, 1903 they achieved success — a flight of 120 feet which lasted 12 seconds. The Wright Monument Shaft, a 60-foot pylon, stands atop Kill Devil Hill where many of the glider experiments occurred. The National Park Service administers the site and has reconstructed the brothers' camp, which includes a hangar and workshop and living quarters. Also on display are replicas of the 1903 *Flyer,* and a 1902 glider model. NR. Open daily 8:30-4:30, summer 8-6:30. Free. (919) 473-2111. ✔

Kinston vicinity

CASWELL-NEUSE STATE HISTORIC SITE, 1 mile W. of Kinston on US 70A, 18th-19th centuries. There are two museums at this location, one situated near the family cemetery where North Carolina's first elected governor, Richard Caswell, is buried. His career as temporary governor (in 1776) through the Revolutionary period is traced in an audio-visual presentation. On the other side of the state-administered park rests the 500-ton hull of the Confederate States Navy gunboat *Neuse.* It had been abandoned in the Neuse River near Kinston in mid-March, 1865, when under attack by Northern forces. The *Neuse* was built as an ironclad ramming vessel, and was finally raised and transported to this site in 1963-64. Artifacts recovered from the ship are exhibited in a nearby Visitor Center, and an

audio-visual display retells her history.
Open Tu-Sa 9-5, Su 1-5. Free.
(919) 522-2091. ★

Manteo vicinity

FORT RALEIGH NATIONAL HIS-
TORIC SITE, 3 miles N. on US 64-264,
1585-91. There is no story in American
history more romantic or mysterious than
that of the "Lost Colony" established on
Roanoke Island. The first settlement was
made in 1585, and two years later, over
100 men, women, and children founded
what was to be a more permanent community on the north end of the island. This
is the birthplace of Virginia Dare, the first
child in the New World born of English
parents. The governor of the colony, John
White, appointed by Sir Walter Raleigh,
returned to England in 1587 for more pro-
visions, and by the time he could return
three years later, war with Spain having
disrupted all sea travel, there was no trace
of the colony's inhabitants. The only clue
to their whereabouts were the letters C R-
O A T O A N carved on a tree or post near
the entrance to a palisaded fort. It was
thought that they probably had been taken
or removed to Croatoan Island, an early
name for most of present-day Ocracoke
and part of Hatteras Island. But White was
prevented by bad weather and accidents
from pursuing this lead. Some historians
have speculated that members of the Lum-
bee Indian tribe of Robeson County are
descended from the original English colonists.

The Fort Raleigh site, administered by
the National Park Service, includes nearly
144 acres. After archaeological work in
1947-48, a fort built by explorer Ralph
Lane in 1585 was reconstructed. The exact
1587 village site is not known. A **Visitor
Center** features a film relating the moving
Fort Raleigh story and displays excavated
artifacts. NR. Open June 15-Labor Day,
daily 8:30-8:15; Labor Day-June 15, daily
9-5. Free. (919) 473-2116. ✔

Located adjacent to the site is the
Elizabethan Garden, a project of the
Garden Club of North Carolina. The 10½
acres include colorful and representative
plantings of the time of Queen Elizabeth I.

At the **Gate House Reception Center** are
displays of English portraits, heraldry, and
period furniture. Open Sept-May, daily
9-5; June-Aug, daily 9-8. $1.50 adults,
$1.35 seniors, free for children under 12.
(919) 473-3234.

Fort Raleigh is also the site of the outdoor drama, *The Lost Colony* by Paul
Green, presented each summer from mid-
May to late Aug. Call (919) 473-2127 for
information regarding hours and admission.

Murfreesboro

WILLIAM REA STORE, E. Williams St.,
c. 1790. The oldest brick commercial
building in North Carolina was built by a
wealthy Boston merchant trader. It has
been restored as a museum affiliated with
Chowan College. Along with displays of
Indian artifacts and antique agricultural
and carpentry tools are objects relating to
the inventor of the Gatling gun, Richard J.
Gatling. Woodwork saved from the nearby Gatling Plantation has been installed in
one room. NR. Open by appointment;
contact (919) 398-4886.

ROBERTS-VAUGHAN HOUSE, 116 E.
Main St., 1790, 1835. Murfreesboro's
Town Library and the Chamber of Commerce and Historical Association offices
are located in this building now known as
the **Village Center.** Originally a Federal
residence built by Benjamin Roberts, it
was given a Greek Revival portico by Col.
Uriah Vaughan in 1835. Much of the interior remains as originally built. NR.
Open M-Tu 9-5, W 9-4, Th-Sa 9-5. Free.
(919) 398-4886.

New Bern

One of North Carolina's most elegant and
picturesque small cities, New Bern was
founded in 1710 by German and Swiss settlers. The town, named after Berne,
Switzerland, became a busy seaport and,
just prior to the Revolution, became the
home of the royal governor and colonial
government.

TRYON PALACE RESTORATION
COMPLEX, 610 Pollock St., 1780s,

1952-59. The residence built by royal Governor William Tryon in 1767-70 burned to the ground in 1798 but it, as well as the kitchen wing which crumbled to pieces in the 1800s, have been completely reconstructed. The original plans of John Hawks, the architect who accompanied Gov. Tryon to America, were followed and Tryon's inventory of personal goods made possible an accurate furnishing of the 38-room mansion. During the 1770s it also served as the capitol of the colony. Everything graceful and elegant about the late Georgian period has been recreated in the imposing palace and all the rooms may be toured. Most of the furnishings are late 1800s English pieces although some objects made by American artisans are included. The grounds and gardens are laid out according to 18th-century English practice and are a pleasure to tour each season of the year. The palace complex is administered by the Tryon Palace Commission and the state. Open Tu-Sa 9:30-4, Su 1:30-4. $2 adults, $1 children and students. (919) 638-5109.

Also included on the palace grounds are two fine homes, the **Stevenson House** (c. 1805), built on one of the lots created after fire destroyed the mansion; and the **John Wright Stanly House** (1780s). Like many of New Bern's old homes, the Stevenson House is a Federal-style building built with the main entrance to one side. The interior layout follows the side hall arrangement. The rooms are furnished with Federal and Empire antiques. In contrast, the Stanly House is a typical center-hall Georgian and has a fine collection of high-style 18th-century furniture. Stanly House was the home of a prominent Revolutionary War patriot and maritime merchant. Washington really did stay here and is said to have enjoyed the visit. The building was relocated from another New Bern site. Both buildings, NR. Open same hours as Tryon Palace. Stevenson House: $1 adults, 50¢ students and children; Stanly House, $1.50 adults, 50¢ students and children. A combination ticket (including Tryon Palace) is available for $4 adults, $1.50 students. (919) 638-5109.

FIRST PRESBYTERIAN CHURCH, New St. between Middle and Hancock Sts., c. 1821. More like a New England meeting house than a Southern parish, the porticoed church has a high tower with an octagonal belfry. The builder, Uriah Sandy, may have been from the North. The interior has side galleries, which are reached by twin corner spiral stairways, and a raised pulpit. After a number of later 19th-century remodelings and additions, the building was extensively restored in 1934. NR. Open daily 9-4. (919) 637-3270.

While you are in the area, contact the New Bern Historical Society Foundation (638-8558) concerning the **Atmore-Oliver House** (c. 1790), 511 Broad St. It was built for Samuel Chapman, a Revolutionary War soldier and leading merchant. An appointment to visit this handsome frame house can be arranged. Nearby are the **Bryan House and Office** (c. 1804), 603-605 Pollock St; the **Jones-Jarvis House** (1810-16), 528 E. Front St.; and the **Eli Smallwood House** (c. 1810), 624 E. Front St. Each is a private residence, yet the elegant Federal architectural details can be enjoyed from the exterior. Each is also a typical New Bern side-hall plan house. Each, NR.

Newton Grove vicinity

BENTONVILLE BATTLEGROUND STATE HISTORIC SITE, off US 701, 1865. The Battle of Bentonville was fought here March 19-21, 1865, and was the last major Confederate offensive in the Civil War. Gen. William T. Sherman, on his march northward from Atlanta with some 30,000 Northern troops, engaged a force of 20,000 men led by Gen. Joseph E. Johnston. The battle was fought over an area of 6,000 acres, 51 of which have been preserved. After 30,000 more Union soldiers reached the Bentonville area, the Confederates began withdrawing, and, a month later, Johnston surrendered to Sherman. The frame **Harper House** (c. 1850) stands on the site of the fighting and served as a hospital for both Confederate and Union troops. The home of John Harper, a farmer and blacksmith, it is furnished as it would have been in 1865. There is also a **Visitor Center** located in the park which is administered by the state.

NR. Open Tu-Sa 9-5, Su 1-5. Free. (919) 594-0789. ★

Ocracoke Island

Ocracoke remains one of the most unspoiled regions of the Cape Hatteras chain of islands. It can only be reached by ferries from Hatteras Island or the mainland, and thus inhabitants have been able to fend off large-scale commercial intrusions. The only village is a tiny one and is where the 69-foot **Ocracoke Light Station** has stood since 1823. The oldest remaining lighthouse on the North Carolina coast, it was built by Noah Porter of Massachusetts to guard ships through the dangerous Ocracoke Inlet. Its light may be seen for 14 miles out to sea. The lighthouse is now maintained by the National Park Service as part of the Cape Hatteras National Seashore. NR. A **Visitor Center** offers interpretive exhibits on the history of the region. Open daily 9-5. (919) 473-2111. ✔

The ferry between Ocracoke Island and Hatteras Island is free and runs daily. Toll ferryboats operate between Ocracoke and Cedar Island (at the end of US 70) daily, and the ride takes approximately 2¼ hours. A second ferry service operates daily from Swanquarter (off US 264), and the run requires approximately two hours. Reservations are required for both lines. For further information regarding schedules and prices, call Ocracoke (919) 928-3841, Cedar Island (919) 225-3551, or Swanquarter (919) 926-1111. ✔

Across Ocracoke Inlet is the **deserted village of Portsmouth**. This northernmost section of Cape Lookout National Seashore can be reached by toll ferry from Ocracoke. Founded in the mid-1700s, the village was an important shipping port until the mid-19th century when ocean traffic started using the Hatteras Inlet further north. Now there are principally only the weathered remains of frame bungalows dating from the early 1900s, a Methodist church, and the former post office and general store along the narrow grass covered lanes. Some of the buildings that have survived the stormy winters are leased from the Cape Lookout National Seashore on a yearly basis as vacation retreats. NR. For information regarding ferry service to Portsmouth, call Ocracoke (919) 928-3841. ✔

Southport and vicinity

BRUNSWICK TOWN STATE HISTORIC SITE, E. of NC 133 N. of Southport, 1726-76, 1860s. Major archaeological work since the 1950s has uncovered one of the most interesting early North Carolina settlements. Founded in 1725, Brunswick was an important port until the Revolution. From 1765-70 it was the home of royal Governor William Tryon and thus the capital of the colony. The town suffered extensive damage in a raid by Spanish privateers in 1748, and the British burned down what was left of the village after most of its inhabitants fled to safer ground in nearby Wilmington in 1776. In 1842 it was possible for the owner of Orton Plantation, Frederick J. Hill, to buy the ruined town from the state for $4.25. It only came alive, albeit briefly, in 1861 when the state built **Fort Anderson** as a defense against a Federal attack of the Lower Cape Fear River coast. The site of the town and fort is now administered by the state, and the **Visitor Center** offers a 14-minute slide presentation on the history of Brunswick and the archaeological work undertaken there. NR. Open Tu-Sa, 9-5, Su 1-5. (919) 371-6613. ✔ ★

Among the most interesting aspects of a tour are the **St. Philip's Church** (1754-68) ruins. The massive brick walls of the church were incorporated into the earthworks of the Civil War fort and were excavated in 1966. It is now known that the parish was a very fashionable one. A large Palladian window opening dominates the east wall of the brick Georgian building.

Nearby are the enormous earthworks of **Fort Anderson,** mounds which sometimes reach 30 feet in height. The site of the barracks has also been uncovered. Little is left of **Russellborough House,** which was probably built in the early 1700s, and its later separate kitchen. This mansion, named for its first owner, Capt. John Russell of the *H.M.S. Scorpion,* became the official residence of Gov. Arthur

Dobbs and was then purchased, on his death, by Gov. William Tryon in 1765. It was burned and plundered by the British. The cellar foundations have been excavated.

North of the Brunswick site, and not included in the park, is **Orton Plantation** (c. 1735), at the junction of NC 1530 and 1529. It is one of the most frequently photographed of Southern ante-bellum mansions, with a great Doric portico. Although a private residence, Orton can be viewed easily from the paths which wind through the **Orton Plantation Gardens**. These are noted for their beautiful lawn and water scenes composed of azaleas and other flowering shrubs, magnolias, giant oaks, and lush beds of flowering plants. Open Mar-early Sept, daily 8-6; early Sept-Feb, daily 8-5. $3 adults, $1 for children 6-12; free for children under 6. (919) 371-6851.

FORT FISHER, off US 421, Kure Beach, 1862-65. Built for the defense of Wilmington during the Civil War, Fort Fisher is unusual in having been constructed principally of earth and sand. By 1865 the fort included more than a mile of sea defense and one-third mile of land protection. The palisaded fence which ran across the land face has been restored. The story of the building and final fall of Fort Fisher in January, 1865, is told at the **Visitor Center.** There are also displays of items recovered from sunken ships. NR, NHL. Open Tu-Sa 9-5, Su 1-5. Free. (919) 458-5538. Fort Fisher can be reached from Southport via a toll ferry. It runs daily, and information regarding cost and schedule can be obtained by calling (919) 726-6646. ★

SOUTHPORT HISTORIC DISTRICT, roughly bounded by Cape Fear River, Rhett, Bay, Short, and Brown Sts., 19th century. **Fort Johnston** was established here around 1750 on the waterfront at the end of Moore St. There is little left now of the early village and fort, but later Southport—mainly developed in the late 1800s as a resort and fishing village—has a sleepy, romantic appeal. All of the residential streets are lined with oaks trailing

Spanish moss and with modest frame houses built by local master carpenters. NR.

At the foot of Howe St. is moored the **Frying Pan Lightship** (1929), a 133-foot floating lighthouse. For 35 years the ship was anchored in the area off Frying Pan Shoals, about 35 miles from Southport. The lightship is equipped with two beacons which extend 65 feet above the water line, and was the first such vessel on the East Coast to be diesel-electric propelled. Permanent offshore structures, known as "Texas Towers," began to replace the ships in the 1960s, and in 1967 the retired vessel was presented to the city of Southport. It is open for viewing mid June-Labor Day, daily; May and Sept, weekends. Nominal admission fee. (919) 457-6911. ✓

Wilmington

North Carolina's leading port since the late 18th century, Wilmington is a prosperous and sophisticated city full of fine old homes and cultural institutions. There is little left of the 18th century, a series of fires in the 1800s having erased most of the traces of settlement. Founded in the 1730s, the city at first played second fiddle to more important Brunswick farther down the Cape Fear River. But Wilmington's geographical position was much superior, and, through a series of political maneuvers, aided by royal Governor Gabriel Johnston, the county seat was transferred from Brunswick in 1739. The name Wilmington was chosen in recognition of Gov. Johnston's sponsor and mentor, Spencer Compton, Earl of Wilmington. The city's merchants and traders first grew wealthy by supplying naval stores—tar, pith, rosin, and turpentine—and lumber. Later in the 1800s the processing and marketing of cotton became a principal activity. It is the city's maritime business, however, which has continued to provide so much of the region's vitality and wealth. Following World War II, the oldest parts of the city were beginning to be abandoned for greener suburban acres, but this flight away from the past has been checked by the vigorous efforts of such organizations as the Lower Cape Fear Historical Society and the Historic Wilmington Foundation. The **Historic Wilmington Tours** sponsored by these groups are an excellent way to begin a visit to the city. Five buildings are included on the daily self-guided driving or walking tour. These are held Feb-mid Dec, Tu-Sa 10-5, and begin at the Thalian Hall, N. 3rd and Princess Sts. $5 adults, $1 students 6-18. (919) 763-9328.

Thalian Hall (1858), also known as City Hall-Thalian Hall, was built, and is still in use, as a theater and city hall. The Thalian Association was founded in 1788 and is one of America's oldest dramatic groups. The hall has been renovated many times, but the essential form of the two-story stucco building is intact. A Mr. Thimble of New York, first name unknown, was the architect, although Wilmington's chief 19th-century builder, James F. Post, was probably resonsible for the final design of the Classical Revival building. NR.

The **Burgwin-Wright House and Garden** (1771), 224 Market St., is one of Wilmington's last remaining 18th-century properties. The Colonial Dames of America in the state of North Carolina have faithfully and carefully maintained the house as a museum since 1937. John Burgwin was the treasurer of the colony, and it was from him that Judge Joshua Grainger Wright purchased the building in 1799 following the Revolution and the return of Tory Burgwin from England. In April, 1781, the house served as Lord Cornwallis's headquarters. The graceful frame building is furnished throughout with 18th-century antiques. A three-story separate kitchen is located across an open courtyard. NR.

The **Zebulon Latimer House** (1852), 126 S. 3rd St., serves as the headquarters and museum of the **Lower Cape Fear Historical Society**. Latimer was a successful commission merchant, and his granite and stucco house, designed by James F. Post, is a very fancy Italianate mansion. The double parlor and double drawing rooms are two of the most handsome rooms to be toured; each is furnished with mid-Victorian furniture and decorative objects. NR.

The **Governor Edward Bishop Dudley Mansion** (c. 1825), 400 S. Front St., was greatly altered in the early 1900s, but it lost none of its charm. Originally, the main section was only two stories high, and the wings one story. The building now serves as the headquarters of the **Historic Wilmington Foundation** and is open as a house museum. NR.

St. John's Art Gallery (1804), 114 Orange St., is housed in the former Masonic lodge. Built of brick, laid in Flemish bond, it is a very late Georgian-style building. On permanent exhibition are fine collections of scent bottles, pottery, and paintings. NR.

As a major urban center, Wilmington is blessed with many cultural institutions which are open to the public. Among those of special interest to the historically-minded are the New Hanover County Museum, St. James Church, and the U.S.S. North Carolina.

NEW HANOVER COUNTY MUSEUM, 814 Market St. Costumes, photographs, and Victorian furniture from the lower Cape Fear River plantation country are among the museum's best collections. The Civil War is another area of interest, as the county was one of the last Confederate holdouts. Open Tu-Sa 9-5, Su 2-5. Free. (919) 763-0852.

ST. JAMES CHURCH, 1 S. Third St., 1839. Thomas U. Walter designed the notable stuccoed brick Gothic Revival church. It stands on the site of the original colonial building dating from 1751. A painting of Jesus wearing a crown of thorns, captured from Spanish pirates who attacked Brunswick in 1748, is found within. NR. (919) 763-1628.

Just up from St. James at the corner of Fifth and Market is the **First Baptist Church** (1859-70), built by James Post after a design by Samuel Sloan. NR. (919) 763-2647.

U.S.S. NORTH CAROLINA BATTLESHIP MEMORIAL, Cape Fear River on Eagles Island, 1941. The first modern battleship, nicknamed during World War II "The Showboat," is very much a dramatic memorial to the men and women who served in this global conflict. During the summer months there is a sound and light presentation of the history of the *North Carolina* which saw service in every major offensive engagement in the Pacific. The performance takes 70 minutes and begins each evening at 9. Visitors may tour the ship through the year. Winter: daily 8-sunset; summer: daily 8-8. $2.50 adults, $1 children 6-11, free for children under 6. Sound and light show, $1.50 adults, 75¢ children 6-11, free for children under 6. (919) 762-1829. ✓ ★

Windsor vicinity

HOPE PLANTATION, on NC 308 4 miles W. of US 13 and 17, 1803. This was the home of David Stone (1770-1810), U.S. congressman and senator, and gover-nor of the state. Built in a combination of the Georgian and Federal styles, the large two-story frame building has an impressive pedimented double-story portico. The interior has been furnished throughout with antiques of the period. The two most impressive rooms are the second-story drawing room and the library. The interior woodwork is original in all the rooms, as are the paint colors used throughout. NR. Open Tu-Sa 10-4, Su 2-5. $2 adults, 75¢ children. (919) 794-3140.

Historic Hope Foundation which administers the plantation house also maintains the **King House** (1763) restored on a nearby site. Built by William King, an early settler, it is one of only two surviving gambrel roof houses with brick end walls left in the state. NR. Inquire at Hope regarding admission.

The Piedmont

North Carolina's central agricultural and manufacturing region is among the wealthiest in the country. The land is extraordinarily fertile, and its productive use has led to the development of the textile and tobacco industries. Because of its abundant water resources, the area's manufacturing activity increased rapidly during the 1800s. Although the Moravians from Pennsylvania founded their city of Salem in the mid-1700s, much of the Piedmont remained undeveloped until after the Revolution. The establishment of Raleigh as the state capital in 1792, however, marked the beginning of expansion throughout the area.

Alamance and vicinity

ALAMANCE BATTLEGROUND STATE HISTORIC SITE, off NC 62, 1771. Back country farmers were in open rebellion against the provincial government in the late 1760s and early '70s, refusing to pay unjust taxes and fees. Two thousand of these men, called "Regulators," met their Waterloo along the Alamance Creek on May 11, 1771, against 1,000 well-equipped royal militiamen. The movement was crushed, but the cause came alive again in the Revolution. A tall granite **monument** marks the site of the two-hour engagement. The state administers the 40-acre park, including the log **Allen House** (1782), which is characteristic of the homes built by the first frontiersmen and was moved here from nearby Snow Hill in 1966 and restored. NR. Open Tu-Sa 9-5, Su 1-5. Free. (919) 227-4785. ★

ALAMANCE COUNTY HISTORICAL MUSEUM, S. of Alamance on NC 62, 1870s. The county's historical museum is located in the former home of the Holt family, pioneers in the textile industry which has dominated the Piedmont since the late 1800s. An Italianate frame building, it is named for L. Banks Holt, the second in a line of successful industrialists. The building is full of antiques and historical artifacts. NR. Open Tu-F 9-5, Sa 10:30-5, Su 1-5. Free. (919) 226-8254.

Chapel Hill

CHAPEL HILL HISTORIC DISTRICT,

Battle Park, E. Franklin and E. Rosemary Sts., and central campus of the University of North Carolina, 18th-20th centuries. Chapel Hill was chosen as the site of the country's first state university in 1792, and the school opened in 1795. It closed temporarily after the Civil War, but reopened by 1875. Among the notable early buildings still standing are **Old East** (1793), designed by James Patterson, with later additions by William Nichols and Alexander Jackson Davis. The brick building once contained the whole of the university; it now serves as a dormitory. The temple-form brick **Playmakers Theatre** (Smith

Hall) (1850) was first built as a combination library and social center. It is thought to have been designed by Davis. NR. For information regarding tours of the campus, contact (919) 966-3621.

Close to the campus is the **Chapel of the Cross** (1843-48), 304 E. Franklin St., as fine an example of a Gothic Revival building as you will find in North Carolina. There are corner turrets, pointed arched windows on the front and sides, and buttresses. An arcaded walkway leads to a later and larger chapel serving the university community. NR. Open 6 am-11 pm. (919) 929-2193.

Durham and vicinity

Once primarily known as the home of the American Tobacco Co., Durham is now well established as an educational and research center of the New South. The Collegiate Gothic campus of Duke University, built in the 1920s, is one of the most beautiful in the South. Within the Durham area are several outstanding historic sites

and restorations which are professionally administered:

DUKE UNIVERSITY, West Campus, 1925-30. Dominating the complex of native stone buildings is the **Duke Chapel** with its 210-foot tower. It contains a 50-bell carillon. It is open daily 8-11. Free. (919) 684-2572.

BENNETT PLACE STATE HISTORIC SITE, 4409 Bennett Memorial Rd., 1865. A one-story log farmhouse which stood at this location was the meeting place of Gen. Joseph E. Johnston of the Confederacy and Gen. William Tecumseh Sherman of the Union forces. Here on April 26, 1865, the documents of surrender which ended the Civil War in the Southeast were signed. The original house burned in 1921, but it has been reconstructed by the state. NR. Open Tu-Sa 10-5, Su 1-5. Free. (919) 383-4345. ★

DUKE HOMESTEAD AND TOBACCO FACTORY, ½ mile N. of Durham on Guess Rd. and E. of NC 1025, 1851. The simple clapboard frame building that was Washington Duke's home has been re-

stored and refurnished by the state as it would have looked in the 1870s. The founder of the American Tobacco Co. and his son originally used a small log building, now reconstructed on the site, as their first tobacco processing factory after the Civil War. The farm complex also includes other utilitarian buildings—a tobacco barn, well house, packhouse, and the third (1870) factory. The work that went into raising, harvesting, and processing tobacco for the market is explained at a modern **Visitor Center**. A color film, *Carolina Bright,* is also shown daily. NR, NHL. Open Tu-Sa 9-5, Su 1-5. Free. (919) 477-5498. ✔

Fayetteville

MARKET HOUSE, Market Sq., 1838. Market House is the focal point of downtown Fayetteville and is patterned after an 18th-century English town hall. The original 1780 building burned to the ground in 1831 and was reconstructed. The first floor is an open arcade where local farmers once sold meat and produce; the second level, intended to serve civic purposes, is now used for city offices. NR. Call (919) 483-1762 for information regarding admission hours.

Other noteworthy Fayetteville buildings include the **First Presbyterian Church** (1832), Ann and Bow Sts., a Federal-style brick edifice designed by A. J. Davis with a Tuscan portico and four-part steeple added by Hobart Upjohn in 1922. NR. Free. Open M-F 9-4. Free. (919) 483-0121. **St. John's Episcopal Church** (1833), Green St., is a distinctive Gothic Revival brick building of one story. The side lancet windows and front corner square towers surmounted by pinnacles are imaginative Gothic features. NR. (919) 483-7405.

Greensboro and vicinity

GREENSBORO HISTORICAL MUSEUM, 130 Summit Ave., 1895. The museum is located in the Romanesque Revival **First Presbyterian Church**. Some of the exhibits concern two of Greensboro's most famous citizens—Dolley Madison and the writer O. Henry (William Sydney Porter). There are also period rooms and a 19th-century village exhibit which includes a

reconstructed school, post office, law office, general store, firehouse, drugstore, and cobbler's shop. The museum, maintained jointly by the city and the historical society, also administers several historical properties, including the **Francis McNairy House** (1762), the **Christian Isley House** (1780), and the **Hockett Blacksmith Shop** (1830). The museum is open Tu-Sa 10-5, Su 2-5. Free. For further information on the historic properties, call (919) 373-2043. ✔

GUILFORD COURTHOUSE NATIONAL MILITARY PARK, New Garden Rd. and Old Battleground Rd., 1781. Lord General Charles Cornwallis was victorious at Guilford Courthouse on March 15, 1781, but within seven months his Southern campaign was brought to an end at Yorktown. The British were pitted against General Nathaniel Greene's colonial forces, and Cornwallis paid a heavy price for his victory, the loss of one-quarter of his troops. The National Park Service maintains a **Visitor Center** where an audio-visual program on the battle is offered daily. During summer weekends, there are demonstrations of 18th-century musket and cannon firing. Open June 15-Aug 15, daily 9:30-7; Aug. 15-June 15, daily 8:30-5. Free. (919) 288-1776. ✔ ★

Halifax

HISTORIC HALIFAX STATE HISTORIC SITE, US 301, 18th-19th centuries. By the time of the Civil War, Halifax had been largely abandoned. Ignored by the railroads, the Roanoke River Valley town fell into a deep sleep, only to be awakened in the 1950s by the state. Founded in 1757, it was one of the most important colonial and Revolutionary period settlements. The Fourth Provincial Congress met here in 1776 to adopt the Halifax Resolves which favored separation from Great Britain; later in the year the Fifth Provincial Congress gathered in Halifax to adopt the new state's first bill of rights and constitution.

Among the historic buildings which have been restored and can be visited in the village are the **Owens House** (1760), the home of a successful merchant; the

Constitution-Burgess House (1810), which once served as the law office and home of Thomas Burgess, and is so furnished today; the Clerk's Office (1832-33), built when Halifax was still the county seat to hold valuable court records; the Jail (1838), which replaced two earlier buildings that escaping prisoners burned to the ground; the Taproom (1770) and Eagle Tavern (1808), important social gathering places; and the Sally-Billy House (c. 1808), an elegant tripartite Federal-style plantation house.

Guided tours of the village begin at the Visitor Center, and here the development and decline of the community are traced in exhibits and an audio-visual presentation. NR. Open Tu-Sa 9-5, Su 1-5. (919) 583-7191.

High Point

HIGH POINT HISTORICAL SOCIETY, 1805 E. Lexington Ave., 1786. The society's museum, situated in the brick John and Phoebe Haley House, is one of several facilities administered by the organization which should engage the interest of the historically-minded. Exhibits pertaining to the development of High Point and the Piedmont include furnishings, textiles, tools, and various artifacts. The Haleys were among the many 18th-century Quaker settlers in the area. NR. The museum is open M-F 9-4:30, Sa-Su 1-5. (919) 885-6859.

Hillsborough

ORANGE COUNTY HISTORICAL MUSEUM, 106 E. King St., 1844. The Orange County Court House is the home of the museum and is an exceptionally handsome brick Greek Revival building with a Doric portico. The crafts of early settlers and fine domestic articles are displayed, including bedspreads and costumes, silver and china. NR. Open Tu-Su 1:30-4:30. (919) 732-2201.

Hillsborough is a charming town in which to stroll. Stop to see the Eagle Lodge (1823), 142 W. King St., a two-story square brick building which has served as a Masonic hall, lyceum, concert theater, and

Civil War hospital. St. Matthew's Episcopal Church and Churchyard (19th century), St. Mary's Rd., is an early example of Gothic Revival architecture with narrow pointed arches and a sharp spire. The Burwell School (early 19th century), N. Churton St., operated for twenty years as a Presbyterian boarding academy for young women. All are recognized National Register properties. Contact the Orange County Historical Museum for further information regarding accessibility at the previously given number or write to the museum, Hillsborough 27278.

Laurinburg

INDIAN MUSEUM OF THE CARO-LINAS, INC., 601 Turnpike Rd. North Carolina's native Americans have maintained a very visible presence in the state, and their history and that of tribes throughout the Southeast is traced in interpretive exhibits. The museum also sponsors formal educational programs with St. Andrews Presbyterian College and Pembroke State University. Open Tu 9-12 and 1-5, W-Su 1-5. Free. (919) 276-5880. ✔

Mount Gilead vicinity

TOWN CREEK INDIAN MOUND STATE HISTORIC SITE, 4½ miles SE of Mount Gilead on NC 73, c. 1550-1650. An Indian group related to the Creek nation of Alabama and Georgia migrated to the southern Piedmont in the 16th century

and built a ceremonial center above the junction of Town Creek and Little River. The site has been under excavation by state archaeologists since 1936, and a great deal has been learned of Creek religious and building practices. A ceremonial mound has been reconstructed with a temple structure at its summit. One example of a thatched burial hut has also been rebuilt. The entire complex was and is once again surrounded by a log palisade. A modern **Visitor Center** where the finds and the on-going research work are explained is located nearby. There are interpretive exhibits and a slide presentation. NR. Open Tu-Sa 9-5, Su 1-5. (919) 439-6802. ✔

Raleigh

"Raleigh is state government and state government is Raleigh. Both are more, but neither would be the same without the other." In this succinct manner, one North Carolina historian has explained the unique role of the capital city. Raleigh was founded in 1792 specifically as the center of state government because it lies literally in the middle of the state. Raleigh gradually grew out from the new capitol situated on a center square, now known as Capitol Sq. Most of Raleigh's historic buildings are situated in this area. A **Visitor Center,** located at 301 N. Blount St., offers information regarding the state buildings and other historic sites. It is open M-Sa 8:30-5:30, Su 1-8. (919) 733-3456.

CHRIST EPISCOPAL CHURCH, 120 E. Edenton St., 1848-52. Located on a corner of Capitol Sq. is one of Richard Upjohn's finest Gothic Revival churches, a one-story granite building with a freestanding tower that was added in 1861. The interior work is outstanding and includes an altar and reredos of Caen limestone installed in 1915. Hobart Upjohn, grandson of the first architect, designed a new chapel and parish house in 1921. NR. Open M-F 9-5. (919) 834-6259.

Close to the church and historically associated with it is the **State Bank of North Carolina** (1813), 11 New Bern Ave. A Federal building with classical columns, it remained a bank until the Civil War. Following that time until 1968, it served as a rectory for Christ Church. It has since been moved 100 feet southeast, where the North Carolina National Bank uses it as its downtown branch. NR.

MORDECAI HISTORIC PARK, 1 Mimosa St., c. 1785. **Mordecai House** is the oldest of the several buildings found in this complex. The oldest section of the country house was built for Henry Lane before the city was founded, and it has been enlarged several times. Moses Mordecai, Lane's son-in-law, arranged for a Greek Revival two-story addition and the raising of the original section to two stories from 1½. Also located within the park are the **Andrew Johnson birthplace** (c. 1808), where the 17th president of the United States was born in 1808, the son of a bank porter and church sexton; the **Old Raleigh Post Office,** the **Allen kitchen** (1842), and the **Badger/Iredell Law Office** (c. 1810). The Johnson homestead, a modest frame building, was moved to this site and has been restored and furnished with period antiques. NR. The park is open Oct-May, Tu-Th 10-1, Su 2-4; June-Sept, W 10-2, Su 2-4. Free. (919) 834-4844.

NORTH CAROLINA EXECUTIVE MANSION, 210 N. Blount St., 1883-91. The home of the governor is a sprawling Queen Anne building with many projecting bays and steep gable roofs. The brick building, with sandstone trim, has the customary two parlors, a dining room, library, and ballroom on the first floor; the second story is the private quarters of the state's first family. NR. Open for tours Mar-May, Tu-F 10:30 and 1:30; Sept-Nov, Tu-F 10. Free (919) 733-3456.

NORTH CAROLINA MUSEUM OF HISTORY, 109 E. Jones St. The general history museum ranks with the best in the country, and the exhibits cover the full spectrum of cultural materials—furnishings, costumes and uniforms, photographs, industrial artifacts, archaeological artifacts, guns and other military objects, textiles, paintings, and graphics. The state's division of archives and history, administrator of an impressive array of historic properties throughout the state, is also located here. Open Tu-Sa 9-5, Su 1-6. Free. (919) 733-3894.

NORTH CAROLINA STATE CAPITOL, Capitol Sq., 1833-40. The state's first capitol burned to the ground in 1831, and the New York firm of Town and Davis was chosen to design the new edifice. It is an exceptionally fine Greek Revival building of locally quarried granite, basically cruciform in plan with Doric-columned porticos on the west and east ends. At the center rises a great copper-covered dome. A new legislative building was added to the capitol complex in recent years, and now the old capitol functions primarily as a museum. The legislative chambers have been restored to their early appearance. NR. Open M-Sa 8:30-5:30, Su 1-6. Free. (919) 733-4994.

Sanford vicinity

HOUSE IN THE HORSESHOE STATE HISTORIC SITE (Alston House), SE of Glendon on NC 1624, c. 1772. Located above a sharp bend in the Deep River, this typical 18th-century plantation house is set amidst country gardens. The scene was a great deal more fractious in 1781 when the owner, Col. Phillip Alston, a dedicated Revolutionary, and his small force engaged a larger unit of Tories and lost. The house was damaged, but the skirmish did not involve too much human or property damage. In the early 1800s the plantation of some 2,500 acres became the property of Gov. Benjamin Williams, and until the Civil War it was an important cotton-producing farm worked by about 50 slaves. In the 1950s the property was purchased and restored by the Moore County Historical Association and is now administered by the state. The interior appointments are very fine, and the rooms have been furnished with late colonial and early Federal antiques. NR. Open Tu-Sa 9-5, Su 1-5. Free. (919) 947-2051. ★

Tarboro

THE PENDER MUSEUM (Walston-Bulluck House), 1018 St. Andrews St., 19th century. The one-story frame farmhouse which houses the museum is very much like those built through eastern North Carolina in the early 1800s. The Edgecombe County Historical Society has furnished it with 19th-century North Carolina pieces and accessories. NR. Open 1st Su of each month 2-5; Nov-Su before Christmas, W-Sa 10-5, Su 2-5. (919) 823-7380.

Wadesboro

BOGGAN-HAMMOND HOUSE (c. 1787) and **ALEXANDER LITTLE WING** (1839), 210 Wade St. The oldest house in Wadesboro was built by Patrick Boggan, a Revolutionary War captain and co-founder of the town. Prior to the Revolution, he had been one of the leading members of the group known as the Regulators who were opposed to the colonial administration. The Federal-style house was added on to by Alexander Little, but these two parts have been separated and restored by the Anson County Historical Society and serve as museum buildings. Furnished with period furniture, the museum features exhibits on county history. NR. Open Su 3-5. $1 adults, 25¢ children. (704) 694-2090.

Winston-Salem and vicinity

Two important elements in American culture developed in this prosperous western Piedmont community: the development of a major center of Moravian culture during the mid- to late-1700s in the village of Salem, and nearly 100 years later, the founding of the tobacco manufacturing town of Winston. Winston-Salem, formally brought together as one city in 1913, has become much more than a religious settlement and industrial center, but these activities are deeply imbedded in the cultural and economic life of the city today. The visitor can tour a number of buildings and museums which reflect the twin historical concerns. It is perhaps fitting that the name Salem, selected by Count Zinzendorf, should mean "peace," and that Winston was named for Major Joseph Winston, the military hero of a bloody Revolutionary War battle—King's Mountain, fought in 1780 on the North Carolina/South Carolina border.

HISTORIC BETHABARA, 2147 Bethabara Rd., 1753-mid-19th century. Betha-bara, located N. of the main part of the city along NC 67, was the first Moravian settlement in the area and was meant only as a temporary facility until Salem proper was completed. The name of the community means "House of Passage," and, by 1772 when Salem was ready for occupation, most of the Moravian settlers—who moved south from Bethlehem, Pa.—abandoned Bethabara. Enough remained behind, however, to maintain a separate village, and the buildings which today make up the Historic Bethabara Park date from after 1772. Beginning in the 1950s, the Moravian church reacquired the land encompassing the old village, and the city administers the park. The most important building is the **Gemein Haus** (1788), the community's church and parsonage, with a distinctive octagonal bell tower. The two other surviving Moravian buildings are the **Potter's House** (1782), a Flemish-bond brick building which was first used by a dyer, Johannes Shaub, and then potters Gottlob Krause and John Butner; and the **Brewer's House** (1803), a stuccoed brick structure which housed a distillery operated by Hermonn and Elizabeth Buttner. **God's Acre,** the earliest of the Moravian cemeteries, overlooks the village from a wooded hill. Archaeological investigation has been pursued for the past thirty years, and a number of interesting sites, including the original **1756 fort,** have been documented. The fort itself has been reconstructed on the basis of this work. NR. Open Easter-Nov, M-F 9:30-4:30, Sa-Su 1:30-4:30. Free. (919) 924-8191.

OLD SALEM, the area bounded by Old Salem Rd., and Church, Race, and Bank Sts., c. 1770. The restored village of Salem is alive in a way that puts most historical museum villages to shame. Not a recreation or an assemblage of disparate buildings moved from other sites, Old Salem has the integrity and spirit of well-documented history. Associated with the village is the South's leading institution devoted to the study and display of the decorative arts, the Museum of Early Southern Decorative Arts (MESDA). Tours of the village begin at the **Reception Center,** off Academy St. and Old Salem Rd. One can purchase a

combination ticket, which includes MESDA, $8 adults, $4 children 6-14, or a ticket for the nine restored buildings, $6 adults, $3 children 6-14. Tickets to individual buildings are also available. Open M-Sa 9:30-4:30, Su 1:30-4:30. (919) 723-3688. ↙

The nine buildings included in the tour are the **Single Brothers House** (1769, 1786), **Miksch Tobacco Shop** (1771), **Winkler Bakery** (1800), **Boys School** (1794), **Market-Fire House** (1803), **John Vogler House** (1819), **Salem Tavern** (1784), **Schultz Shoemaker Shop** (1827), and **Vierling House** (1802). The Boys School is the home of the **Wachovia Museum** where the early history of the area is documented; and the Salem Tavern, the first brick building in the community, houses other museum exhibits. Authentic furnishings and early Moravian artifacts are found in all of the buildings. Each of the structures is located on Main St. NR, NHL.

MESDA, 924 S. Main St., is devoted to furniture, ceramics, textiles, metalwares, as well as such fine objects as paintings and prints produced in all of the South prior to 1820. There are fifteen meticulously furnished period rooms to tour. Open M-Sa 10:30-5, Su 1:30-4:30.

Just on the other side of the restored village is the campus of **Salem College,** Church St., founded in 1772 for the education of women. Campus tours may be arranged by calling (919) 721-2600.

REYNOLDA HISTORIC DISTRICT, Reynolda Rd., 1913-17. The founder of Reynolds Tobacco, Richard Joshua Reynolds, created a model farm community on his 1,000-acre estate. The 178 acres which remain, and now constitute an historic district, include the mansion house, extensive gardens, a Presbyterian church, and a 13½-acre village which once housed many of the estate's employees. A number of the estate's buildings were designed by Charles B. Kenn; the gardens were the work of Thomas W. Sears.

The creation of the Reynolda complex reflected, in part, the desire of Reynolds' wife, Katharine Smith, to establish a progressive rural community where pioneering work in agriculture and education would serve to uplift the whole Piedmont region. Schools were established for black and white children in the picturesque village, and various farming techniques were explored. Although the estate has been broken down into various independent units, the spirit in which it was created is still very much alive.

Three hundred acres were donated by the Reynolds to become the new campus for **Wake Forest University,** and the building program was completed in 1956. Reynolda House has become an art museum. The 125-acre gardens and nature preserve is administered by Wake Forest. Various local horticultural societies, environmental groups, and Reynolds family charities have aided with the restoration of the formal plantings, greenhouses, woodland, and open fields. The village was also given to Wake Forest, and in the past few years its buildings have been successfully adapted as rental housing units, offices, studios, and shops.

Reynolda House, the family mansion, is a Colonial Revival building known by the family as "The Bungalow." Since 1964 it has housed an exceptional collection of American paintings dating back to the 18th century, as well as ceramics and costumes. It is open Tu-Sa and holidays 9:30-4:30, Su 1:30-4:30. $3 adults, $2 senior citizens, $1 students. (919) 725-5325. The adjoining Reynolda Gardens are also open to the public with admission to the museum.

SAWTOOTH BUILDING (Shamrock Mills), SW cor. Marshall and 3rd Sts., 1911. The first home of the Hanes Hosiery Mills Co., originally known as Shamrock Knitting Mills, has been imaginatively adapted as an art center and restaurant. The name *Sawtooth* derives from the jagged roof construction which allowed for the placement of six-foot skylights in each of seven sections. The form made the best possible use of natural light and was first employed in England in 1854. NR. Open M-F 9 am-10 pm; Sa-Su 1-5. (919) 725-2361.

Western North Carolina

Western North Carolina is another country. In longitude it extends as far west as Columbus, Ohio. Nearly 600 miles separate Murphy in Cherokee County from Nag's Head along the Outer Banks. When the sun is setting in the old capital of New Bern, the residents of Asheville can enjoy nearly another hour of daylight. The western portion of the state is mountainous rather than hilly, as in the Piedmont, or a flat expanse, as on the coast. The historical contrasts are nearly as great as the geographic. As North Carolina's last settled region, the west remained frontier territory much longer. Even today, many of the communities of the area west of the Catawba River or I-77 seem to be removed 75 or 100 years in time. The isolation imposed by the mountains—the Brushy, Blue Ridge, Great Smoky, Snowbird, Nantahala, Bald, which are part of the Appalachian family—has slowed the spread of plastic modernity. This is also Indian territory, and, although many were driven to the West, a sizeable community remains to guard its traditional homeland.

Asheville

Asheville has been a famous summer resort town since the mid-1800s. Situated between the Blue Ridge and Great Smoky Mountains, this principal city of western North Carolina is a natural gathering spot for tourists. Many are as attracted by the famous former residents of the town as they are by the splendid climate and striking vistas. George Washington Vanderbilt (1862-1914) is the best known of Ashevillians, and the estate he left behind is considered the greatest in America. Thomas Wolfe lived in much humbler surroundings, but his novels, especially *Look Homeward Angel,* which is set in Asheville, have already endured several generations of readers.

BILTMORE ESTATE, 1 Biltmore Plaza, 1890-95. G. W. Vanderbilt, the grandson of the "Commodore" who made a fortune steamship lines and railroads during the mid-1800s, created an estate of 125,000 acres. Of this vast wooded barony, some 10,000 acres remain, the majority of the land having been donated for such uses as the Pisgah National Forest and the Blue Ridge Parkway. Biltmore House, a grand French chateau in the style of Francis I, is as impressive as the setting. The carved limestone mansion took five years to complete and was designed throughout by the master Beaux Arts architect Richard Morris Hunt. Of the 250 rooms, 55 are open to the public. The 35-acre formal gardens which surround the house were designed by Frederick Law Olmsted, and these, too, can be toured. NR, NHL. Open daily 9-5. $7 adults, $5 children. (704) 274-1776.

BILTMORE HOMESPUN SHOPS, Grovewood Rd., adjacent to Grove Park Inn, 1917. Mrs. George Vanderbilt supported the work of local craftsmen and in 1901 established a school and business known as Biltmore Industries in which young men and women could profit from professional training and the sale of their work, particularly in the areas of woodworking and weaving. The program was a great success, and in 1917 Mrs. Vanderbilt, occupied with wartime charity work, sold the operation to Fred L. Seely, a builder and owner of the Grove Park Inn. He was responsible for erecting the cottage-like buildings, some of which continue to serve as studios for weaving homespun. NR. Open M-Sa 9-5; summer, also Su 1-6. Free. (704) 253-7651.

BILTMORE VILLAGE, roughly bounded by All Souls Crescent, Lodge, and Brook Sts., 1896-1910. The romantic English-style manorial village planned by Vanderbilt's architect, Richard Morris Hunt, is no longer a cohesive unit, but many picturesque buildings remain. Principal among them is the Romanesque style **All Souls Church.** When it was consecrated in 1896, Vanderbilt arrived in his private railroad car from New York with the rector of St. Bartholomew's, New York City, in tow. The opalescent glass windows, designed and made by Maitland Armstrong, are considered outstanding. Other buildings which remain from the original model village include sixteen half-timbered **cottages** (c. 1900-1910), designed by Hunt's successor on the overall Biltmore project, Richard Sharp Smith, and the timbered private **railway station** designed by Hunt. NR.

THOMAS WOLFE MEMORIAL, 48 Spruce St., 1883. Wolfe's early years were spent in Asheville, the "Altamont" of *Look Homeward Angel,* and the rambling Queen Anne boarding house which his mother, Julia, acquired in 1906 is furnished as he knew it. "The Old Kentucky Home" was its formal name and Wolfe called it "Dixieland" in his writings. Since his father, W. O. Wolfe, refused to join the family enterprise and remained at the former residence on Woodfin St., the household could not have been a very happy one. Wolfe, however, drew from his experiences there some of his very best writing. NR, NHL. Open Tu-Sa 9-5, Su 1-5. $1 adults, 50¢ children. (704) 253-8304.

Belmont

BELMONT ABBEY CATHEDRAL, on NC 2093, 1892-94. The late Gothic Revival brick abbey is one of the most prominent Roman Catholic centers in the country. The building is exceptional for its use of such architectural elements as pointed-arch tracery windows, buttresses, and pinnacles. It is on the site of **Belmont Abbey College** (1876), a pioneer Catholic religious institution. NR. Open daily. (704) 825-3711.

Not far from Belmont is the **St. Joseph's Catholic Church** (1844), junction of NC 273 and 1918, Mountain Island. It was founded by Irish immigrants who had arrived to work the gold mines of the western Piedmont in the early 1800s. It has been extensively restored. NR.

Charlotte

Charlotte is a very busy commercial center, and little is left of the early city which was founded in 1768. A branch of the U.S. Mint was established here in 1837, and the building is now the home of the art museum. When the mint was located in Charlotte, the town was at the center of the gold mining region of Mecklenburg and Cabarrus counties.

THE MINT MUSEUM OF ART, 501 Hempstead Pl., 1835. Originally located downtown, the Neo-classical building designed by William Strickland was dismantled and moved to a residential section of town in the 1930s. The exhibits are devoted primarily to the fine and decorative arts, but the story of mining operations in the Piedmont and the production of gold coins is also told. Open Tu-F 10-5, Sa-Su 2-5. Free. (704) 334-9723.

THE MINT MUSEUM OF HISTORY, 3500 Shamrock Dr. The development of Charlotte and neighboring counties is traced in displays at the historical museum. These include furniture, decorative objects, and costumes which originated or were used in the area. Behind the museum building is the stone **Hezekiah Alexander House** (1774), where antiques are displayed in period room settings, dating as late as 1801. Alexander moved to Charlotte from Maryland in the mid-1700s, and his house closely resembles those built in the Mid-Atlantic states at the time. He became a prosperous farmer and helped to frame North Carolina's first constitution. NR. Museum hours are Tu-F 10-5, Sa-Su 2-5. Free. Alexander House hours are Sept-May, Sa-Su 2-4; June-Aug, Sa-Su 2-5. $1 adults, 50¢ children. (704) 568-1774.

Cherokee and vicinity

GREAT SMOKY MOUNTAINS NATIONAL PARK, Oconaluftee Visitor Center, Newfound Gap Rd. and Blue Ridge Pkwy., north of Cherokee. Most of the national park lies within Tennessee. The **Visitor Center** is located at the entrance to North Carolina and the Cherokee Indian Reservation. Exhibits on the park as well as on the archaeological work that has been done in the region for many years are found at the center. Adjacent to it is the **Pioneer Farmstead,** where the life of an early frontier family has been recreated. Up the Newfound Gap Rd. is the **Mingus Mill,** a water-powered operation where corn and wheat are ground. The mill is open mid Apr-Oct. The center and Pioneer Farmstead can be visited June-Labor Day, daily 9-7; Labor Day-mid June, daily 8-4. Free. (704) 497-9146. ✔

MUSEUM OF THE CHEROKEE INDIAN, US 441. The Eastern Band of the Cherokee Indian Nation maintains this museum devoted to tribal history. Artifacts and relics are displayed alongside portraits and documents. Nearby is the largest Indian reservation in the Eastern U.S., a homeland for the members of this ancient society, so many of whom were forced into exile in Oklahoma in the 19th century. Open mid June-Sept, M-Sa 9-8, Su 9-5:30; Oct-mid June, daily 9-5:30. $2.50 adults, $1.25 children 6-13. (704) 497-3481.

Claremont vicinity

BUNKER HILL COVERED BRIDGE, 2 miles E. of Claremont on US 70, 1900. One of four remaining covered bridges in the state, Bunker Hill extends 80 feet across Lyle's Creek. The sides are covered with board-and-batten siding and the gable roof is of tin. It is now maintained by the Catawba County Historical Association with help from the state. NR. ✔

Cullowhee

MOUNTAIN HERITAGE CENTER, Western Carolina Univ. The special history of this far-western Carolina territory is traced in the collections and exhibits of the museum. The folklore of generations of mountain dwellers who have lived so far removed from urban culture is examined in lectures, films, and educational programs. Artifacts of the early frontier settlers are on display. Open M-F 8:30-4:30. Free. (704) 293-9685. ✔

Dallas

DALLAS HISTORIC DISTRICT, bounded by Holland, Main, Gaston, and Trade Sts., 19th century. Time has dealt kindly with Victorian Dallas, once the Gaston County seat (1847-1909). The county Art and History Museum is housed in the Old

Gaston County Courthouse (1848, rebuilt 1875) on Court Sq. Within the Greek Revival landmark are exhibits relating to the region's history, particularly the textile industry. Other buildings of interest are the **Hoffman Hotel** (1852), once the largest mid-19th-century hotel in the state; and the **Dallas Depot** (1901). Both of these buildings are maintained by the historical society. The museum is open Tu-F 10-5, Sa 10-2, Su 2-5. Free. (704) 922-8361.

Flat Rock

CARL SANDBURG HOME NATIONAL HISTORIC SITE, ¼ mile W. of Flat Rock off Little River Rd., 1838. The 240-acre farm which Sandburg and his wife Paula, the sister of photographer Edward Steichen, purchased in 1945 remained their home until 1967. It was a perfect setting for the Pulitzer Prize biographer and poet who so expertly portrayed the American past. The house and complex of farm buildings are now maintained by the National Park Service just as the Sandburgs left them. The property, known also as Connemara Farm, was built as the summer home of Christopher Gustavus Memminger of Charleston, S.C., first secretary of the treasury for the Confederacy. Guided tours of the house, which contains all of the author's personal and literary effects, are given, and visitors are free to explore the other buildings of the farm complex. NR. Open daily 9-5. Free. (704) 693-4178.

Hickory

MAPLE GROVE (c. 1875), 542 2nd St. NE, and PROPST HOUSE (1881), Shuford Memorial Garden. Hickory craftsmen have been producing fine furniture for American homes since the 19th century, and similar talent was shown by local house carpenters. Two of the best examples of Victorian carpentry have been preserved by the Hickory Landmarks Society. Maple Grove was built for Adolphus Lafayette Shuford, a town official, and originally consisted of what is now an ell. The house was enlarged with a two-story addition that has a double-level porch extending nearly the full length of the façade.

Both levels have artfully patterned scroll balustrades. The Propst House is a highly ornamental Second Empire cottage believed to have been built by its first owner, J. Summie Propst, a contractor-carpenter. Both buildings are furnished with Victorian furniture. NR. Open Apr-Oct, Su 2-5; other times by appointment. Each museum $1 adults, 50¢ students, free for children under 12. (704) 327-3612.

Newton and vicinity

CATAWBA COUNTY HISTORICAL MUSEUM, 1716 S. College Dr., 19th century. Fourteen and a half acres of the former John Ervin plantation serve as the historical complex of the society. The galleries in the main house include exhibits on the history of the Catawba Valley. Also on the grounds are four log cabins spanning over 100 years in time: the **Barringer Cabin** (1759), furnished as a colonial kitchen; the **Waugh Cabin** (1839), fitted for spinning and weaving; the **Little Cabin** (1859), furnished as a store; and the **Yount Cabin** (1870), a working blacksmith shop. An extensive agricultural collection is housed in a recent building. Open Tu-Su 1-5. Free. (704) 465-0383. ✔

OLD ST. PAUL'S CHURCH, 1½ miles W. of Newton at junction of NC 1149 and 1164, 1808. The simple log church, sided with weatherboards, is thought to be one of the oldest in western North Carolina. It replaced an even older building, and many of the logs came from that structure. Henry Cline was the chief carpenter for the combined Lutheran and German Reformed congregation. The interior walls and ceiling are finished with wide vertical beaded sheathing; a gallery extends around three sides. Almost untouched by time, the church is no longer used by today's congregation, which erected a modern building across the road. NR. Open Apr-Oct, Su 1-5. Free. (704) 464-3853.

Old Fort vicinity

CARSON HOUSE, E. of Pleasant Gardens on US 70, c. 1810. Col. John Carson first built a single-room log dwelling; by the mid-1800s this had expanded into the substantial dwelling seen today. A two-story veranda with tapered wooden pillars extends across the façade. In 1843 the home served temporarily as the courthouse of newly-formed McDowell County. Now it holds a fine collection of pioneer artifacts, including quilts and coverlets, clocks, period furniture, and musical instruments. NR. Open May-Oct, M-F 10-5, Sa-Su 2-5. $1 adults, 50¢ children, 25¢ children under 12. (704) 724-4640.

Pineville vicinity

JAMES K. POLK MEMORIAL STATE HISTORIC SITE, S. of Pineville off US 521, 1968. The log birthplace of the 11th president of the United States has been reconstructed on this site. Born in 1795, he spent only eleven years here before moving with his family to Tennessee. Polk's accomplishments during his one term as president (1845-49) are often overlooked, but were significant. His role in the acquisition of the California territory and the settlement of the Oregon border dispute with Great Britain are among the highlights of his career, which is traced in the exhibits housed in the **Visitor Center.** The birthplace is furnished as it might have been in the first years of the 1800s. Open Tu-Sa 9-5, Su 1-5. Free. (704) 889-7145.

Salisbury and vicinity

SALISBURY HISTORIC DISTRICT, roughly bounded by Jackson, Innis, Caldwell, Marsh, Church, E. Bank, Lee, and Liberty Sts., 18th-early 19th centuries. Salisbury retains a great deal of its heritage, and its historical properties reflect diverse social and historical interest. The former **Rowan County Courthouse** (1857), 200 N. Main St., is now the Community Building. It is a noble stuccoed brick Greek Revival building with a Doric portico. The **Maxwell Chambers House** (1819), 116 S. Jackson St., is a two-story Federal town house which serves as the Rowan Museum with period rooms covering the years from the late 1700s to the early 1900s. It is open during the winter months, Tu-Su 2-5; and in summer, W, Sa-Su 2-5. Free. (704) 633-5946.

OLD STONE HOUSE (Michael Braun

House), NW of Granite Quarry off US 52, 1766. Considered the oldest remaining dwelling in Rowan County, the Braun House reflects 18th-century Pennsylvania-German building techniques. The two-story granite building has a one-story frame kitchen wing. It has been restored and furnished by the Rowan Museum. Open Sa-Su 2-5. 50¢ adults, 10¢ children. (704) 633-5946.

Stansfield vicinity

REED GOLD MINE, Reed Mine Rd., off US 601 and NC 200, 1799. Gold was discovered at this site on John Reed's farm in 1799, eventually touching off America's first gold rush. For three years the find went undiscovered, and the original 28-pound nugget found by Reed's son, Conrad, in Little Meadow Creek was used as a doorstop. A jeweler in Fayetteville recognized its value in 1802, and the story spread and spread. Mining began in other areas of the state as well, and, until the California gold rush, over a million dollars worth of the precious metal a year were recovered. Underground mining finally ceased at the Reed site in 1912. The remains of the mine complex include several open pits, a large stone chimney, and crushing machinery. The state assumed ownership of the property in 1971. In the **Visitor Center** a film describing the development of the mine and the processes that were used to recover gold is shown. There is also a guided tour of a restored section of the underground works. NR, NHL. Open Tu-Sa 9-5, Su 1-5. Free. (704) 786-8337. ✔

Statesville vicinity

FORT DOBBS, Fort Dobbs Rd., 1756. Built as North Carolina's chief defense post during the French and Indian War, Fort Dobbs was completely abandoned by 1764. The French never appeared, but the Cherokees attacked once in 1760 and again the following year, the second time losing not only lives but their land for 50 or more miles to the west. Named for royal governor Arthur Dobbs, the fort was never more than a temporary garrison, albeit an important one. Excavation to date by the state has unearthed the fort's moat, cellar, magazine area, and well. The main building was probably a combination barracks-blockhouse similar to those found on the New England frontier during the colonial period. Exhibits in the **Visitor Center** cover the civilian and military history of the outpost. NR. Open Tu-Sa 9-5, Su 1-5. Free. (704) 873-5866. ★

Weaverille vicinity

ZEBULON B. VANCE BIRTHPLACE, off US 19-23 and 5 miles E. on Reems Creek Rd., 1795. The Vance family homestead, probably settled between 1785-90, has been expertly reconstructed by the state. Zeb Vance was the most famous of those born and raised here. His service to the state as governor from 1862-65 earned him the admiration of many; he served again as governor in 1877-79 and then began a long and distinguished career in the U.S. Senate which ended only with his death in 1894. The homestead is a rustic two-story log house of yellow pine and has been furnished in a fashion representative of the period 1790-1840. Six outbuildings, typical of those to be found on a frontier country farm, have also been rebuilt. Nearby is a **Visitor Center** where Vance's career is documented in exhibits. Open Tu-Sa 9-5, Su 1-5. (704) 645-6706.

Historic Accommodations

An asterisk (*) indicates that meals are served.

Asheville

FLINT STREET INN, 116 Flint St., 28801. (704) 253-6723. Open all year. The Eva Clark House, built in 1915, has been recently renovated as a bed-and-breakfast accommodation. It is located in Asheville's Montford Historic District. NR.

GROVE PARK INN AND COUNTRY CLUB, 290 Macon Ave., 28804. (704) 252-2711. Open all year. Pharmaceutical manufacturer E. W. Grove built up this rustic resort complex in the early 1900s. Situated next to the Biltmore Homespun Shops (see historical entry), the inn is a most pleasant, picturesque place to stay.*

Blowing Rock

GREEN PARK INN, US 321 Bypass, 28605. (704) 295-3141. Open mid Apr-Oct. Established in 1882, the Green Park is a superbly maintained late-Victorian mountain retreat. The rooms are mainly furnished in a modern manner, but the public areas still have original period pieces.*

Burnsville

THE NU-WRAY INN, Town Sq., 28714. (704) 682-2329. Open May-Dec. The Wray family has been operating an inn at this location since the mid-1800s. Their inn prides itself on a fine collection of antiques and a tradition of Southern home-style cooking.*

Cashiers

HIGH HAMPTON INN AND COUNTRY CLUB, NC 107, 28717. (704) 743-2411. Open May-Oct, Dec-Mar. The Hampton family of South Carolina owned the 2,600-acre property until the late 1800s; their summer house burned in 1932. Although the present inn dates only from the 1930s, its style is more late-Victorian than it is 20th-century. *

Clemmons

TANGLEWOOD MANOR HOUSE, Tanglewood Park, 27012. (919) 766-6461. Open all year. The main house of the former William Reynolds estate was built in 1859 and is one of several accommodations for guests. Forsyth County administers the huge park which also includes a racetrack, golf courses, and other recreational facilities.

Ellerbe

ELLERBE SPRINGS CAMP GROUND, 1 mile N. of Ellerbe on US 220 and junction of NC 73, 28338. (919) 652-5600. Open all year. This extraordinary vacation complex, of which the late-Victorian Ellerbe Springs Hotel is the crowning glory, was founded in the 1850s by Col. W. T. Ellerbe. The main building has been converted to a restaurant; nearby are fully-equipped camping facilities. NR. *

Flat Rock

WOODFIELD INN, Flat Rock 28731. (919) 828-0333. Open June-mid Nov. For 150 years Flat Rock has been a gracious resort community for guests escaping the heat of summer. The Woodfield dates from the mid-1800s and was originally known as the Farmer Hotel.

Hillsborough

COLONIAL INN, 159 W. King St., 27278. (919) 732-2461. Open all year. In a town noted for its historical pleasures, the Colonial is a fitting place to stay. Part of the white clapboard building dates from the mid-1700s; General Cornwallis is known to have stayed here in 1781. *

Pinehurst

PINEHURST HOTEL AND COUNTRY CLUB, NC 5, 28374. (800) 334-9560. Open mid Mar-late May, and early Sept-mid Nov. One of the South's most noted resorts, the Pinehurst complex dates from the 1890s. A drive through the grounds, laid out by Frederick Law Olmsted, is a must; a stay at the resort is highly recommended if the pocketbook will allow. NR.*

4. SOUTH CAROLINA

IN the 16th century both the Spanish and French attempted to establish settlements on South Carolina's sandy shores, but it was not until 1670 that a permanent colony was founded. In 1663 Charles II of England granted the Province of Carolina to eight Lords Proprietor. The community's "Fundamental Constitutions" were written by the renowned political philosopher John Locke, and one of the Lords Proprietor, Anthony Ashley Cooper, Earl of Shaftesbury. The precepts of this constitution were essentially feudal and required the existence of a nobility. Though America's first and only aristocracy lasted for less than half a century, it set the tone for South Carolina's development by encouraging the plantation system and condoning the ownership of slaves. Religious toleration was practised in the new colony, and persecuted peoples from all over Europe flocked to Charleston. The city grew quickly; within a century of its founding, it was widely known as one of America's wealthiest and most refined communities.

South Carolina's geography is varied and beautiful; it ranges from the lofty peaks and deep valleys of the Blue Ridge Mountains in the northwest to the rolling terrain of the Piedmont province which sinks into the coastal plain of the Low Country. Many of the state's most successful plantations were operated in the coastal area where the ground is flat and even, and the soil near the region's many rivers is rich and fertile. Aristocratic planters and their families lived on enormous cotton plantations, while new arrivals headed for the hills and established small farms and industrial communities. By 1790, eighty percent of South Carolina's white population lived in the Piedmont and the Upcountry, and they demanded with vigor that the capital be moved from Charleston to Columbia, a new town laid out within three miles of the geographic center of the state. South Carolinians were both vocal and independent, and they participated enthusiastically in the bellicose moments of America's history. Over 140 Revolutionary battles were fought on this state's soil, and many were won by poorly armed and trained backcountry men. Less than a century after winning independence from Britain, South Carolinians were up in arms once again. Ardently in favor of Southern independence, the state was the first to pass the Ordinance of Secession. And it was in Charleston Harbor that Civil War hostilities began: in April, 1861, Confederate troops fired on Union forces at Fort Sumter. Four years later, General Sherman and his troops roamed the state, laying waste to cities and towns and destroying numerous landmarks. Fortunately, Charleston and Beaufort were not put to the torch, and in other places the flames were put out before they incinerated the buildings which comprise South Carolina's architectural legacy.

For the convenience of the traveler, the state's historic highlights have been broken down into three sections: (1) the Low Country, which includes Charleston, Beaufort, and the region on the southeastern coastal plain; (2) the Piedmont, the central region of the state including Columbia, the capital; (3) the Upcountry, the tiny region in the northwest where the Blue Ridge Mountains begin to rise and fold and livelihoods are eked out on small rustic farms in the midst of dramatic scenery.

St. John's Lutheran Church, Charleston

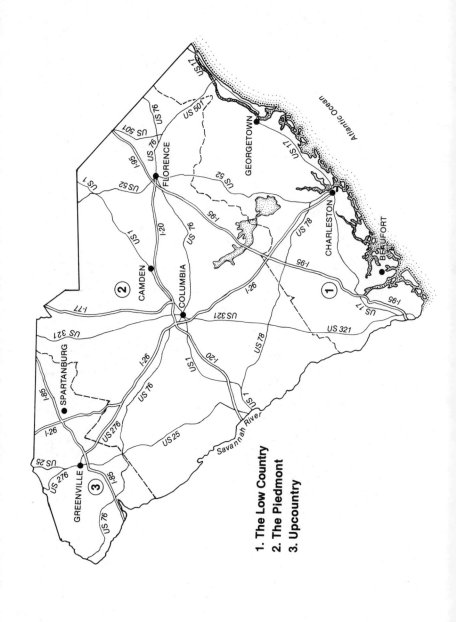

1. The Low Country
2. The Piedmont
3. Upcountry

The Low Country

The region of the state where Europeans first settled and the site of South Carolina's best-known historical attractions, the Low Country is traditionally and thoroughly Southern. Greek Revival plantations and handsome Georgian town houses are almost commonplace. Colonial churches, colorful gardens, and moss-clad oaks add to the picturesque quality of the region. The traveler wandering from town to town along the Low Country's sandy shores and winding rivers will find a wealth of historic attractions to explore.

Beaufort

A small group of French pioneers established the first Protestant colony on the continent near here in 1562, but Beaufort was not officially founded and laid out until 1710. A picturesque old port town, Beaufort has been beautifully preserved; its gracious mansions and other historic buildings reflect the opulence of the town's ante-bellum era. Town houses are surrounded by peaceful gardens and front narrow streets shaded by palmettos and moss-draped oaks. Most of the buildings in Beaufort's **Historic District,** between Boundary, Hamar, and Bladen Sts. and the river, date from the early 18th to the mid-19th century, and this entire section of town has been designated a National Historic Landmark. The mansions speak of the resplendent era prior to the Civil War when enormous fortunes were made, first in rice and indigo and then in the production of Sea Island cotton. Tours of many of these ante-bellum residences are offered each Spring. For further information, write Historic Beaufort Foundation, Box 11, 29902, or call (802) 524-6334.

THE BEAUFORT COUNTY MUSEUM, 713 Craven. This museum offers good collections of historic and prehistoric artifacts, including Indian pottery, Civil War relics, and memorabilia from county plantations. Open M-F 10-12 and 2-5, Sa 10-12. Free. (803) 524-4444.

GEORGE ELLIOTT HOUSE MUSEUM, corner of Bay and Charles Sts., c. 1840. A well-preserved Greek Revival structure built by George Elliott, the house later belonged to W.J. Jenkins, a wealthy doctor. During the Civil War, Northern forces put Jenkins out and used it as an Army hospital. The elaborate detail work on the interior survived intact and is worthy of special note; the exquisite ceilings and rococo plasterwork were executed by Italian craftsmen. NR. Open all year, M-F 11-3. $2 adults, $1 children under 18. (803) 524-8450.

ST. HELENA'S EPISCOPAL CHURCH, 507 New Castle St., c. 1724. One of the oldest functioning churches in America, St. Helena's is now well into its third century. The church has been twice enlarged since its original construction, but the northeast corner remains as it was in 1724, and bricks from the original walls were used in the expansions. During the Civil War, the building was converted to an army hospital, and the gravestones from the churchyard were brought in and used as operating tables. In the cemetery are buried many soldiers who died in the Revolutionary and Civil Wars. NR. Open M-Sa 8-6. Free. (803) 524-7595.

JOHN MARK VERDIER HOUSE, 801 Bay St., c. 1790. Built for John Mark Verdier, a wealthy Beaufort merchant, this two-story Federal frame house reflects the Adam style in its concern with symmetry and balance. Above the raised tabby foundation rises the pillared and pedimented double portico entrance with a balconied upper story. Handcarved mantels grace the living and dining rooms; dividing these two rooms, a delicately worked stairway leads to the second floor. Following the Civil War, during which this house served as a headquarters for Union forces, it was used for many purposes and never properly kept up. It was not until a group of citizens banded together in recognition of this landmark's historical significance that restoration was begun. Today the Verdier home represents, both in structure and ornamental detail, the Federal period during which its wealthiest inhabitants flourished. NR. Open Mar-mid Dec, Th-Sa 11-3. $1.50 adults, 75¢ children. (803) 524-6334.

Beaufort vicinity

HUNTING ISLAND LIGHTHOUSE, 17 miles SE of Beaufort on US 21 in Hunting Island State Park, 1875. Designed by the U.S. Coast Guard, this towering 136-foot lighthouse is built of cast-iron plates. The circular balcony at the top is surmounted by a polygonal monitor. The original complex included a keeper's dwelling, oil house, and other buildings, and the light served as a guide to vessels on the sea route between Charleston and Savannah. In 1933, the structure was acquired by the state for use as an observation tower for visitors to Hunting Island, and a landmark for sailors on the Intracoastal Waterway. NR. Open all year, dawn to dusk. Oct-Mar, Free; Apr-Sept, $1 per car. (803) 838-2011. ✔

PARRIS ISLAND HISTORIC DISTRICT, 10 miles S. of Beaufort on Parris Island off SC 281, 19th-20th centuries. Foremost among the historic sites at this military installation are the remains of the **Parris Island Drydock** (1891-93). The largest known wooden drydock ever constructed in America, this enormous structure was used to remove boats from the water and completely expose their hulls for cleaning or repair. Another notable site is the **Commanding General's Quarters** (1891-95). This enormous Victorian house provides ample living space (twenty-seven rooms) for the man in charge. The **Visitor Center** is located in Building 283, and a **museum** with exhibitions of photographs, uniforms, and weapons from the Civil War to Viet Nam can be found in the **War Memorial Building.** Open Su-F 8-4:30; Sa 9-4:30. Free. (803) 525-2951 or 3771. ★

Also on Parris Island, though not within the historic district, is the site of **Charles Forte.** Established in 1562 by Jean Ribaut for Admiral Coligny, it was the first French stronghold in America. Today all that remains is the tall and sturdy stone marker set up by Ribaut. NR.

Charleston

Charleston's unique and delightful ambience is derived in part from the rich blend of its many European traditions with its more exotic African and Caribbean heritage. In 1670, the first English colonists arrived on the white sandy shores of the new Province of Carolina. The 160 settlers founded a community on Albemarle Point, three miles away from the present city. They called their settlement Charles Town in honor of Charles II. In 1680 the settlers moved to Oyster Point, a safe and strategic spot located between the Ashley and Cooper Rivers. The new Charles Town grew quickly, and with its fine harbor and good bay a booming trade was soon established with England and the West Indies. In the century before the Revolution, Charleston established itself as the largest and wealthiest city south of Philadelphia. Today, its relaxed and peaceful atmosphere, elegant homes, and beautiful waterfront combine to make it one of the most visited cities in all the South. The **Visitor Information Center** is located in the Arch Building, 85 Calhoun St., 29402. (803) 722-8338. Many guided tours of the city are available, one of the most pleasant of which is the **Carriage Tour from the Battery.** Horse-and mule-drawn carriages are available daily from 9-5 at the foot of Meeting St. $6 adults, $4 children under 12. Each spring from mid-March to mid-April, many of the city's fine colonial and ante-bellum residences are opened to the public during the **Festival of Houses.** For further details, write Historic Charleston Foundation, 51 Meeting St., 29401, or call (803) 723-1623. The Preservation Society also sponsors **House & Garden Tours** for three weeks in October. Write Box 502, 29402, or call (803) 722-4630.

BETH ELOHIM SYNAGOGUE, 90 Hasell St., 1841. A fine example of Greek Revival architecture, this is the second oldest synagogue in the United States. The stuccoed brick walls have been painted white and scored to give the appearance of

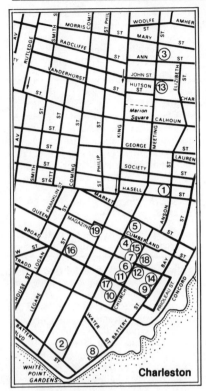

Charleston

Courtesy of Charleston Trident Chamber of Commerce and Charleston County Park Recreation and Tourist Commission

1. Beth Elohim Synagogue
2. Calhoun Mansion
3. Charleston Museum
4. Circular Congregational Church
5. Confederate Museum
6. Dock Street Theatre
7. The Thoms Elfe Workshop
8. Edmondston-Alston House
9. Exchange and Provost
10. Heyward-Washington House
11. Hunley Museum
12. Huguenot Church
13. The Joseph Manigault House
14. Old Slave Mart Museum
15. Powder Magazine
16. St. John's Lutheran Church
17. St. Michael's Episcopal Church
18. St. Philip's Episcopal Church
19. Unitarian Church

stone. Jews, as well as other persecuted peoples, found the Carolinas a haven for religious dissenters and began to arrive here soon after the first settlers. A congregation was formed by the mid-18th century, and within fifty years a synagogue was constructed, though it was destroyed by fire in 1838 and the present structure is therefore the second building to stand on this site. NR. Open for regular services. (803) 723-1090.

MILES BREWTON HOUSE, 27 King St., 1765-69. Well known as an excellent example of a Charleston "double house," this lovely Georgian residence has symmetrical rooms off a central hall. Designed by builder/architect Ezra Waite, the dwelling is beautifully proportioned and features a richly embellished double portico. Because of its ample size and lavishly decorated interior, the house was twice occupied by members of the military: General Sir Henry Clinton used it as his headquarters during the Revolution, and Union Generals George Meade and John Hatch stayed here when Charleston was occupied in 1865. The house is private but visible from the street. NR, NHL.

CALHOUN MANSION, 16 Meeting St., c. 1876. A colossal structure that could house a family of giants, this residence has 24,000 feet of floor space, fourteen-foot ceilings, and a dome above the stairwell which reaches seventy-five feet above ground. George Walton Williams built this oversized mansion and had the rooms embellished with intricate plaster and wood moldings and magnificent chandeliers. Open Mar-Nov, daily 10-4; Dec-Feb, daily 10-3. $2 adults, $1 children. (803) 577-9863 or 8205.

CHARLESTON MUSEUM, 360 Meeting St. Founded in 1773, the Charleston Museum is the oldest in the United States. Now housed in a brand new $6 million complex, collections include furniture, textiles, decorative arts, and natural history with a special emphasis on the Southeast. Open daily 9-5. County residents $1 adults, 50¢ children. Others $1.50 adults, 50¢ children. (803) 722-2996.

CIRCULAR CONGREGATIONAL CHURCH, 150 Meeting St., 1891. Now an essentially rectangular structure, the church takes its name from an earlier building, designed by Charleston-born architect Robert Mills, which burned in 1861. The adjacent **parish house** survived

the fire and is Mills's work. The temple-style parish house sits on a high cellar with arched entrances on both the basement and first floor levels. Curving cast-iron stairs lead to the portico on the main floor. NR, NHL. Church open for regular services. (803) 723-9261.

Unitarian Church, 8 Archdale St., 1772-87. Originally the Second Independent or Congregational Church, this lovely structure became the place of worship of the Unitarians after they divided from the Trinitarian Congregationalists in 1817. In 1852, the building was extensively remodeled, using plans by architect Francis Lee which were based on the chapel of Henry VII in London's Westminster Abbey. NR, NHL. Open for regular services. (803) 723-5295.

CONFEDERATE MUSEUM, 188 Meeting St., 1841. The Daughters of the Confederacy have been operating a museum in the old Market Hall since 1898. On view are flags, uniforms, weapons, and other mementos of the War for Southern Independence. This Greek Revival building was designed by Edward

Brickell White and constructed in 1841. The temple-style building sits on a raised basement, and steps on each side lead up to a monumental Doric portico. NR. Open Tu, Th 2-4, Sa 12-5. $1 adults, 25¢ children. (803) 723-1541. ★

DOCK STREET THEATRE (Planter's Hotel), 135 Church St., c. 1809. A reconstruction of a Georgian-style theatre and a renovation of an ante-bellum hotel, this three-story brick structure is used as a showplace for the performing arts today. The ornate iron balcony above the main entrance is original, but the interior woodwork was taken from other houses of the period. NR. Open M-F 10-6. Free. (803) 723-5648.

EDMONDSTON-ALSTON HOUSE, 21 E. Battery, c. 1828. Charles Edmondston built this wonderful three-story house with a gallery on every floor and a view of the harbor. Colonel William Alston bought it a decade later and furnished it in the fashionable Greek Revival style. Many of his furnishings, documents, and books are on view. Operated by The Historic Charleston Foundation. Open M-Sa 10-5, Su 2-5. $2.50 admission. Combination ticket with Nathaniel Russell House $4. (803) 722-7171.

THE THOMAS ELFE WORKSHOP, 54 Queen St., c. 1760. This restored building is furnished with reproductions of 18th-century pieces and with ceramics excavated on the site. Exhibitions include a collection of cabinetmaking tools in honor of Thomas Elfe who was one of Charleston's best cabinetmakers. Open M-F 10-5, Sa 10-1. $2 adults, $1 children. (803) 722-2130.

EXCHANGE AND PROVOST, 122 E. Bay St., 1767-71. This stately Georgian brick structure has been used for everything from a dungeon to a market to a meeting place for the state legislature. The building has been restored and is now a museum. NR. Open all year, Tu-Sa 9-4:30, Su 12:30-4:30. Nominal fee. (803) 792-5020.

FARMERS' AND EXCHANGE BANK, 14 E. Bay St., c. 1853. Edward Jones and

Francis Lee were the architects of this exotic-looking two-story brownstone and brick building. The English predilection for Moorish and Indian design had considerable influence on the plans for this building. NR, NHL. Private, but visible from the street.

FORT SUMTER, on a man-made island at the mouth of Charleston Harbor, 1829-60. Fort Sumter is one in a chain of coastal defenses built by the U.S. Government after the War of 1812. Begun in 1829, the five-sided brick fort was still not complete when the Confederates opened fire on Union troops occupying the fort on April 12, 1861. The mortar shell which exploded over fort Sumter marked the beginning of the Civil War. The Confederates won the first battle and held the citadel for almost four years. In the end, however, the walls of Fort Sumter, which had once been five feet thick, were reduced to rubble. NR. Open summer, daily 9-6; winter, daily 9-5. Free. (803) 883-3123. Accessible only by private boat or tour boat. **Fort Sumter Tour,** Municipal Yacht Basin, 29401, can arrange group tours. $4.50 adults, $2.50 children. (803) 722-1691. ★ ✔

FORT MOULTRIE, 1214 Middle St. on Sullivan's Island, 10 miles E. of Charleston off SC 703, has been modernized four times since it was first constructed prior to the Revolution. Built to protect Charleston Harbor, it served in four wars, the last of

which was World War II. Visitors to the fort will find vestiges of each period of military occupation. NR. Open summer, daily 9-6; winter, daily 9-5. Free. (803) 883-3123. ★ ✔

THE HEYWARD-WASHINGTON HOUSE, 87 Church St., 1772. The Charleston Museum operates this rather severe-looking three-story Georgian brick house. Built by a wealthy planter named Daniel Heyward, the house was inherited by his son, Thomas, a signer of the Declaration of Independence. George Washington stayed here in 1791. The house and kitchen building have been beautifully restored and furnished with Charleston antiques. NR, NHL. Open daily 10-5. $2.50 adults, $1 juniors. Combination ticket with Manigault House. $4 adults, $2 juniors. (803) 722-2996.

Down the street at #76 is the mid-18th-century house in which DuBose Heyward lived from 1919 to 1924. Heyward is best known for his novel *Porgy,* which was later set to music by George Gershwin and became America's first folk opera, *Porgy and Bess.* NR. Private, but visible from the street.

HUGUENOT CHURCH, 136 Church St., 1844-45. Designed by Edward Brickell White in the Gothic Revival style, this is the fourth church to stand on this site. A large number of French Huguenots were forced to flee their homeland to avoid religious persecution, and many arrived in South Carolina soon after the colony was founded. Many Huguenots lived on plantations by the banks of the Cooper River, and, as they traveled by boat, services were scheduled to allow them to come to church and return home on the ebb and flow of the tide. NR. Open for special occasions. (803) 723-3235.

HUNLEY MUSEUM, 50 Broad St., 1798. Originally the Citizens and Southern National Bank building, this two-story brick structure is a fine example of Federal commercial architecture. The carved woodwork, black and white tile floors, and cluster columns inside are worthy of special note. The museum's exhibitions include a replica of the Confederate submarine *Hunley* and Civil War relics. NR. Open M-Sa 10-5, Su 2-5. Free. (803) 722-2996. ★ ✔

THE JOSEPH MANIGAULT HOUSE, 350 Meeting St., 1803. Designed by architect/planter Gabriel Manigault for his brother Joseph, this house is one of the finest examples of Federal architecture in America. The elegant three-story brick structure has a bowed side section and bowed side and rear porticos as well as a two-story entrance porch. Operated by the Charleston Museum, the house has been furnished with period pieces made in Charleston. The formal garden in back is planted with shrubs and flowers appropriate to the period. NR, NHL. Open daily 10-5. $2.50 adults, $1 juniors. Combination tickets with Heyward-Washington House $4 adults, $2 juniors. (803) 722-2996.

OLD SLAVE MART MUSEUM, 6 Chalmers St., 1853. Thomas Ryan and James Marsh designed this brick and stucco two-story building once used as the office of an auctioneer who dealt in slaves. Since 1938, the structure has been used as a museum of black history, and exhibitions include objects made by slaves, relics of plantation life, and African arts and crafts. NR. Open M-Sa 10-4:30, Su 2-5. Closed Jan and Sept. $1.50 adults, 50¢ children 8-12, children under 8 free. (803) 722-0079.

POWDER MAGAZINE, 79 Cumberland St., 1703-13. The South Carolina Society of the Colonial Dames of America have their headquarters in this one-story stuccoed brick structure. With walls thirty-two inches thick, the building was used to store gunpowder until the end of the Revolution. Today it is a museum filled with artifacts from the Province of Carolina. NR. Open M-F 9:30-4; closed Sept. $1 adults, 50¢ students. (803) 722-3767.

NATHANIEL RUSSELL HOUSE, 51 Meeting St., c. 1809. The outstanding architectural feature of this three-story Federal brick house, built by one of Charleston's wealthiest merchants, is the flying staircase which seems to float from floor to floor. With its spacious rooms, polygonal bay, and lovely period furnishings, the house should not be missed. Operated by The Historic Charleston Foundation. NR. Open M-Sa 10-5, Su 2-5. $2.50 admission. Combination ticket with Edmondston-Alston House $4. (803) 723-1623.

ST. JOHN'S LUTHERAN CHURCH, Clifford and Archdale, 1817. Henry Melchior Muhlenburg, the man often referred to as the "father of Lutheranism in America," established Charleston's Lutheran congregation in 1742. A dignified Greek Revival structure, it is the second church to stand on this site. Open for regular services. (803) 723-2426.

ST. MICHAEL'S EPISCOPAL CHURCH, 80 Meeting St., 1752-61. A superb Georgian building with a two-story Doric portico, this is the oldest ecclesiastical structure in Charleston. Built of brick, stuccoed, and ornamented with balustrades, pilasters, cornices, and a stunning tower, the church is attributed to builder Samuel Cardy. NR, NHL. Open for regular services. (803) 723-0603.

ST. PHILIP'S EPISCOPAL CHURCH, 146 Church St., c. 1835. The third church built to house the state's oldest congregation (est. 1681), this stuccoed brick one-story building has an octagonal spire and a four-columned Tuscan portico. In the churchyard are the tombstones of several noteworthy figures, including John Calhoun, a vice-president of the U.S., and DuBose Heyward, author of *Porgy*. NR, NHL. Open for regular services. (803) 722-7734.

Charleston vicinity

CHARLES TOWNE LANDING, on SC 171 between I-26 and US 17, Pre-Columbian-20th century. Early Woodland Period Indians lived on this site around 500 B.C. They were followed by the Province of Carolina's first white settlers who arrived here two thousand years later. For the decade from 1670 to 1680, eighty houses and a fort stood on this site, but, when the community moved to its new location, the settlement deteriorated. Today the area is a state park with a zoo, botanical gardens, and replicas of a 17th-century boat, and a colonial garden and dwellings. Archaeological excavations on the site were begun by U.S.C. in 1969. NR. Open in summer, daily 9-6; winter, daily 9-5. $3 adults, $1.50 senior citizens, $1 students 6-14, under 5 free. (803) 556-4450. ✔

DRAYTON HALL, 12 miles NW of Charleston on SC 61, 1738-42. A fine example of Palladian symmetry and proportion, Drayton Hall has changed little since its construction by John Drayton in the colonial era. One of the most beautiful mansions on the Ashley River, the house is widely known for its exceptional ornamented ceiling, carved woodwork, and sumptuous entrance hall. Still without such amenities of the 20th century as running water, electricity, or central heat, this residence provides an unusual opportunity to observe an unmodified 18th-century dwelling. NR, NHL. Open daily 9-4. $3 adults, $2 students. (803) 766-0188 or 1219.

MAGNOLIA PLANTATION AND GARDENS, 10 miles NW of Charleston on SC 61, 17th century. Begun by the Drayton family when they arrived in the area in 1672, the gardens did not grow to their present size until the mid-19th century, when a tubercular Reverend John Drayton was advised by his doctor to pursue gardening and landscaping. This he did with a vengeance, and today the fifty acres of informally landscaped garden feature 250 varieties of Azalea Indica and 900 varieties of Camellia Japonica. Other highlights include a 125-acre waterfowl refuge, a horticulture maze, herb garden, walking and biking trails on 500 acres, a petting zoo and small horse ranch. The Victorian plantation house is the third to have stood on the site and was constructed in 1873. NR. Open daily 8-dusk. $5 adults, $4 teens, $3 children. (803) 571-1266 or 845-5230. ✔

If time allows, stop by **St. Andrews Episcopal Church,** 5 miles NW of Charleston on SC 61, 1764. This unusual one-story church, built in the shape of a Latin cross, was used as an office by the colonial government. NR. Open for regular services. (803) 763-8772.

MIDDLETON PLACE, 14 miles NW of Charleston on SC 61, 1755. One of the most famous estates of its era, Middleton Place was built by Henry Middleton, the president of the first Continental Congress. Only the south flanker of the enormous plantation house has survived (the rest was burned by Union troops), but this has been beautifully restored and furnished with period pieces. With its ornamental butterfly lakes, grandes alées, and wide terraces leading down to the Ashley River, this was one of the first landscaped gardens in America. Today not only the house and gardens, but the plantation barnyard—complete with demonstrations of blacksmithing, carpentry, tanning, shinglemaking, and other crafts necessary to life on a colonial rice plantation—are open to the public. NR, NHL. Open daily 9-5. $6 adults, $3 children 4-12, children under 4 free. (803) 556-6020. ✔

Frogmore vicinity

PENN CENTER HISTORIC DISTRICT, S. of Frogmore on SC 37 on St. Helena Island, mid 19th-20th centuries. The oldest structure in this interesting collection of brick and frame buildings is **Brick Church**, 1855. The two-story building has a gabled roof, corbeled cornice, and a blind lunette. Situated between the pseudo-pilasters of its façade, recessed windows look out onto the district. NR. Open for regular services. (803) 838-3033. Also located in this historic area is the **Penn Center** (1862), Lands End Rd., the first school for free blacks built in the South. It served the community not only as an educational institution, but also as a health clinic, farm bureau, and repository for the preservation of Gullah heritage and history unique to St. Helena Island. Gullah is a dialect used by blacks from Georgetown to the Georgia coast and was widely spoken by African slaves on the coastal plantations. (*Porgy*, DuBose Heyward's novel of 1925, was written in Gullah dialect.) The school was closed in 1948, but the campus still serves the community, and a cultural center/museum containing exhibits concerning the life styles on the Carolina Sea Islands is open to the public year 'round. NR, NHL. M-F 8:30-5; other times by appointment. Free. (803) 838-2432.

Georgetown

GEORGETOWN HISTORIC DISTRICT, on the N. side of the Sampit River, 18th and 19th centuries. Much remains of Georgetown's rich historical past: close to thirty 18th-century buildings and almost twenty ante-bellum structures grace the wide and deeply shaded boulevards which meander through the heart of Georgetown's historic section. The buildings document the city's architectural heritage and range from colonial rusticity to luxurious mansions. NR. The oldest of this city's buildings is the **Allston-Read House**, 405 Front St., c. 1737. A simple colonial dwelling, it has unusual slant-hinges which provide self-closing doors. NR. Private, but visible from the street.

Among other interesting Georgetown buildings are:

Harold Kaminski House, 1003 Front St., 1760. This charming colonial dwelling houses a fine collection of 18th- and 19th-century antiques. NR. Open Tu-F 10-4. $2 adults, $1.50 children. (803) 546-4358.

Old Market Building, Front and Screven Sts., c. 1842. A two-story rectangular brick structure with a low gabled roof and projecting clock tower, this building has served over the years as a market, jail, police department, and printing shop. It presently contains the delightful **Rice Museum** which exhibits maps and other memorabilia relating to the rice industry on which the town's economy was based. NR. Open May-Sept, M-F 9:30-4:30, Sa-Su 10-4:30; Oct-Apr, M-F 9:30-4:30, Sa 10-1. $1 adults, students and children free. (803) 546-7432.

Prince George, Winyah, Church and Cemetery, Broad and Highmarket Sts., 18th century. Although the church was not built until 1750, the parish was formed in 1721. Made of brick, the building is basically rectangular in shape, with a semicircular apse at the east end and a vestibule at the west which is highlighted by a majestic square tower with a belfry, dome, and cross. Unusual Jacobean gables embellish the church. NR. Open all year 8-5. Free. (803) 546-4358.

Georgetown vicinity

BROOKGREEN GARDENS, 18 miles NE of Georgetown on US 17, 18th-20th centuries. Brookgreen Plantation, established in 1790 by William Allston, was situated where the present sculpture garden stands. Today, nothing is left of the original buildings, and the 1600-acre property is covered with a lush profusion of semi-tropical plants, forests of pine and hardwood, marshes, lily ponds, and developed gardens. Brookgreen Gardens is dedicated to preservation of flora and fauna peculiar to the southeastern states and to the exhibition of 19th- and 20th-century American sculpture. NR. Open

daily 9:30-4:45. $2 adults, 50¢ children. (803) 237-4218.

HOPSEWEE PLANTATION, 12 miles S. of Georgetown on US 17, 1735-40. Thomas Lynch, Jr., a signer of the Declaration of Independence, was born on this plantation overlooking the picturesque North Santee River. The 2½-story frame house reflects West Indian influence in its double-tiered piazza and hipped roof, mingled with more traditional colonial and Georgian elements. The architecture of this house is typical of that of South Carolina Low Country manors. NR, NHL. Open all year, daily 8-dusk. $2.50 adults, $1 children. (803) 546-7891.

Goose Creek vicinity

ST. JAMES CHURCH, stands just to the S. of Goose Creek on SC 61, 1708-19. One of the best known of South Carolina's early churches, it is a beautifully restored and unusual stuccoed brick structure. The extraordinary west door is surmounted by a frieze embellished with triglyph and metope reliefs in the form of flaming hearts. Though the church is rarely open, it is well worth the trip just to see the highly unusual exterior. NR, NHL.

McClellanville vicinity

HAMPTON PLANTATION HOUSE, 2 miles W. of US 17, 8 miles N. of town, 1735. This 2½-story frame house combines both Georgian and Federal elements. Originally only six rooms, the house was enlarged in 1760, and the portico was added in 1791. Hampton is best known as the ancestral home of Archibald Rutledge, the late poet laureate of South Carolina. NR, NHL. Open Sa-Su 1-5; other times by appointment. Free. (803) 758-3622.

ST. JAMES EPISCOPAL CHURCH, SANTEE, off US 17, W. on SC 857 for 1½ miles, S. on a dirt road, 1768. After just over two miles on this pastoral dirt road, one will find the St. James Church, Santee. Built to serve planters during the months spent on the plantation, this is an excellent example of South Carolina's innovative 18th-century vernacular architecture. With its pedimented portico supported by columns of molded bricks, this is one of South Carolina's gems and a place for intrepid seekers of historic sites to discover. NR, NHL. Special services at noon on Easter and the Su closest to 15 October. Open daily.

Mount Pleasant

BOONE HALL PLANTATION, off US 17, 8 miles N. of Charleston, c. 1750. Captain Thomas Boone planted the oak trees which still line the drive leading to this mansion in 1743. Today visitors may tour the first floor of the plantation house, the building in which cotton was ginned, and the nine brick slave cabins. Open mid Mar-Aug, M-Sa 8:30-6:30, Su 1-6:30; Sept-mid Mar, M-Sa 9-5, Su 1-5. $3.75 adults, 50¢ children. (803) 884-4371.

MOUNT PLEASANT HISTORIC DISTRICT, bounded by Charleston Harbor, Shem Creek, Royal Ave., and McConts Dr., 18th-20th centuries. Planters and their families came to this peaceful resort town by the seaside to spend the summer. Settled just as the Revolutionary War broke out, the town was first occupied by the Americans and later by the British. Today this historic community features numerous one-story summer cottages as well as larger 19th-century residences executed in Greek Revival and Gothic Revival styles. NR.

Also of interest is the **Patriots Point Naval and Maritime Museum,** Patriots Point. This fascinating museum is housed on the aircraft carrier, *USS Yorktown.* Visitors can also board the world's first nuclear-powered merchant ship and a World War II submarine. Open daily 9-6. (803) 884-2727. ★ ✔

St. George vicinity

INDIAN FIELDS METHODIST CAMP-GROUND, 4 miles NE of St. George on SC 73, 1848. Built to accommodate the large crowds of Methodist converts which flocked here to hear the word of evangelists, the campground retains its original layout: ninety-nine identical cabins surround a pavilion which served as a tabernacle. The huge impact of 19th-century evangelism is evidenced by the fact that the campground is still used for its original purpose. NR. Private, but visible from the road.

Summerville and vicinity

SUMMERVILLE HISTORIC DISTRICT, roughly bounded by S. Railroad Ave., Magnolia and Main Sts., and the town boundary, 19th-20th centuries. Appropriately named, this town was developed as a summer resort for Low Country planters and their families and later became popular with city dwellers and northerners. The historic district has retained its 19th-century ambience and boasts numerous structures from the last century. Today, wonderful houses decorated with gingerbread and complemented with whimsical gazebos can be found throughout this charming town. NR.

OLD DORCHESTER, in Dorchester State Park, 6 miles S. of Summerville on SC 642, 17th and 18th centuries. Situated on the banks of the Ashley River are the ruins of the village of Dorchester, a town which was established by Congregationalists from Massachusetts in 1695 and was once a major trading center. Abandoned after the Revolutionary War, the buildings deteriorated, and today the ruins at the site

include the tower of **St. George Church** (1753) and the ruins of a **fort** constructed in 1755. Also on the site is an **outdoor museum** with interpretive exhibits concerning the town. NR. Open dawn to dusk. Free. (803) 873-1740.

Walterboro

WALTERBORO HISTORIC DISTRICT, bounded by Carn and Black Sts. and Rivers and Memorial Aves., 19th-20th centuries. The buildings in this district represent a fascinating pastiche of architectural periods and styles, ranging from simple bungalows to elaborate Gothic Revival homes. A substantial number of summer houses, built in the first decades of the 19th century, remain in fine condition. A particularly elegant expression of a two-story frame summer cottage with a sweeping veranda may be seen in the **O.T. Canady House** (c. 1890), 109 Carn St. The house features turned veranda posts, an applique frieze, and a bracketed extension cornice. Private, but visible from the street. If time allows, be sure to see the **Colleton County Jail** (1855), Jeffries Blvd. A two-story stuccoed brick Gothic Revival building, it is designed, appropriately, in the manner of a miniature castle. The **Colleton County Courthouse** (c. 1820), corner of Hampton and Jeffries Sts., is attributed to Robert Mills. Housed in the stuccoed brick one-story Greek Revival building is the **Colleton County Cultural Complex,** which displays collections of arts and crafts as well as local historical artifacts. NR. Open M-F 8-5. Free. (803) 549-2621. Walking and driving tour maps of the historic district are available from the Walterboro-Colleton Chamber of Commerce, 213 Jeffries Blvd., 29488. (803) 549-1132.

The Piedmont

The enormous central section of South Carolina which lies between the coastal plain and the Appalachians is known as the Piedmont. With a landscape of rolling hills, gentle valleys, and pellucid streams, this region has attracted settlers since the early 18th century. Today travelers tend to shoot through this area en route to the coast or points south, but there is much to see in picturesque horse-country towns like Aiken or Camden and in the more polished and planned capital, Columbia.

Aiken and vicinity

AIKEN COUNTY HISTORICAL MUSEUM, 226 Chesterfield, 1923. Housed in the old jail and an 1880 one-room school-house, this museum exhibits collections of state memorabilia, including Civil War relics and Indian artifacts. Open M, W, F 10-4. Free. (803) 649-4658.

REDCLIFFE, 15 miles SE off US 78 in the Beech Island vicinity, 1857. When this two-story Greek Revival frame house was finished, James Henry Hammond (its builder) was just beginning his term in the U.S. Senate. He had previously served as South Carolina's governor and as a U.S. congressman. The mansion now contains some of the Hammond family's belongings, as well as collections of antiques and art. NR. Open Sa 10-3, Su 12-3. $1 admission. (803) 827-1473.

Bennettsville

JENNINGS-BROWN HOUSE, 121 S. Marlboro, c. 1826. The only surviving house in town built before 1850, it is now being restored by the Marlboro County Historical Museum, which is located next door. The spacious ante-bellum home, with its intricate interior woodwork, was Union General F. P. Blair's headquarters in March, 1865. Visitors may want to see how the restoration is progressing. NR. Open M-F 9-5, Su 2:30-5:30. $1 adults, 50¢ students, children free. (803) 479-7748.

The **historical museum** at 119 S. Marlboro contains collections of ante-bellum antiques made in the South as well as local memorabilia from prehistoric times through World War II. Open M 2-5, Tu-F 9-5, Su 2:30-5:30. Free. (803) 479-4521.

Bethany vicinity

KINGS MOUNTAIN NATIONAL MILITARY PARK, NW of town on SC 161, 1780. This lovely hill is part of a spur of the Blue Ridge Mountains and the site of a Revolutionary War battle which marked the beginning of the end for Britain's last campaign of the war. Encamped on Kings Mountain, Major Patrick Ferguson and 1,100 redcoats were attacked and defeated by furious "overmountain" settlers. Today the park has a **Visitor Center** which offers interpretive exhibits and collections of military artifacts. NR. Open Labor Day-Memorial Day, daily 9-5; Memorial Day-Labor Day, daily 9-6. Free. (803) 936-7508. ★

Camden

Best known today for its horse races and bridle tracks, Camden is the oldest inland city in the state. A dignified and gracious town, with wide tree-shaded avenues and 178 acres of green parks, it was founded in 1733 and saw action during the Revolution and the Civil War. Many of the town's more historic residences were destroyed in a fire in 1813, but Greek Revival and Victorian-era dwellings of all sizes may be seen in this dignified and historic municipality. A number of buildings in town were designed by Robert Mills, the man from Charleston who later served as Architect of Public Buildings in Washington. The most notable of these is the **Bethesda Presbyterian Church** (1820), 502 De Kalb St. NR. The Greek Revival brick church is open to the public M-F 9-4:30, Sa 9-1. (803) 432-4593.

HISTORIC CAMDEN, S. Broad St. a group of citizens began this effort at interpreting Camden's 18th-century history in the 1960s, and today their project has blossomed into a full-fledged museum complex. Several colonial and ante-bellum structures from the Camden vicinity have been dismantled and reconstructed on the site, and other buildings have been recreated using old records. In addition to the buildings are a craftshop, a children's farmyard, a hiking trail, and archaeological areas. Open winter, Tu-F 10-4, Sa 10-5, Su 1-5; summer, Tu-F 10-5, Sa 10-5, Su 1-5. $1 adults, 50¢ children. (803) 432-9841. ✔

Columbia

The capital of South Carolina since 1786, Columbia was laid out for that purpose when farmers from the Upcountry demanded a more centrally-located legislative center than Charleston. Most of Columbia's beautiful ante-bellum structures were lost on February 17th and 18th, 1865, when, after the city had surrendered, General Sherman and his troops occupied Columbia and put it to the torch. Eighty-four blocks and over 1,300 buildings were reduced to smoking rubble. Nonetheless, visitors will find a surprising number of buildings of historic interest in South Carolina's capital city.

FIRST BAPTIST CHURCH, 1306 Hampton St., 1856. As there was not enough room in the State House, this one-story Greek Revival church was the place where the South Carolina Secession Convention held its first meeting. Story has it that when Union troops began to burn the town in 1865, they wanted to be sure to get the church where the convention was held. When the soldiers arrived at the door, the sexton told them they'd made a mistake. It was the Methodist church down the street that they were looking for. An effective fib. NR. Open M-F 8:30-4:30. (803) 256-4251.

FIRST PRESBYTERIAN CHURCH, 1324 Marion St., 1854. The second church to be constructed on this site, the English-Gothic structure was built for Columbia's oldest organized congregation. Woodrow Wilson's parents worshipped here and are buried in the cemetery. NR. Open M-F 8:30-5, Sa 8:30-12. (803) 799-9062.

FORT JACKSON MUSEUM, Fort Jackson, at the edge of the city on US 1 and US 76. In **building 4442,** at one of the largest Army traning camps in America, the visitor will find exhibitions concerning local and world military history, including mementos of the life of Andrew Jackson. Open all year, Tu-Su 1-4. Free. (803) 751-7419 or 7355. ★

GOVERNOR'S MANSION, 800 Richland St., 1855. Once part of a military school which burned in 1865, this elegant residence is furnished with antiques and houses a collection of art concerned with the history of South Carolina. Open Tu-Th 9:30-4 by appointment. Grounds open 9:30-5:30 without appointment. Free. (803) 758-3452.

The state also administers the **Boylston House,** 829 Richland St., 1830. This fine Greek Revival frame house is best known for its boxwood gardens which are open to the public by appointment. NR. (803) 758-3452.

HAMPTON-PRESTON HOUSE, 1615 Blanding St., 1818. This spacious 2½-story stuccoed brick house was designed by Zachariah Philips and occupied by Wade Hampton I, II, and III. Restored to the period 1835-55, the house contains many of the Hamptons's possessions and reflects the decorating style of Wade Hampton I's daughter, Caroline. NR. Open Tu-Sa 10-4, Su 2-5. $1.50 adults, 75¢ students, children under 6 free. (803) 252-7742.

MANN-SIMONS COTTAGE, 1403 Richland St., c. 1850. A black woman who bought her way to freedom, Celia Mann built this Columbia cottage, and she and her descendants lived here for over a century. After the Civil War, she organized the First Calvary Baptist Church and held services in the raised basement of her 1½-story home. Today the house is furnished in the style of the 1880s. NR. Open Tu-F 9-4, Sa-Su 2-5. $1.00 adults, 50¢ children. (803) 252-1450.

ROBERT MILLS HOUSE, 1616 Blanding St., 1823. This handsome house, one of the few dwellings designed by Robert Mills, is a fine example of his interpretation of the Greek Revival style. At one time the building housed the Columbia Theological Seminary. Today it has been restored for use as a museum and furnished with period pieces. NR, NHL. Open Tu-Sa 10-4, Su 2-5. $2 adults, $1 students, children under 6 free. (803) 252-7742.

SOUTH CAROLINA DEPARTMENT OF ARCHIVES AND HISTORY, 1430 Senate St. Situated close to the State House, this is the building those interested in the written history of South Carolina should visit. The people at the Archives mount interesting exhibits of books and papers, and the collection includes over 12,500 cubic feet of archival manuscripts. Open M-Sa 9-9, Su 1-9. Free. (803) 758-5816.

SOUTH CAROLINA STATE HOUSE, Main St., 1855. John Niernsee based his plans for this beautiful state capitol on the Capitol in Washington. The Civil War and Reconstruction slowed the building of the important edifice, and Niernsee died be-

fore its completion. In 1900, another architect, Frank Milburn, was hired to oversee the project. He changed Niernsee's plans, adding the central dome and cupola rather than the intended tower. The brass stars on the outer walls of the building mark the spots where Sherman's troops damaged the structure when shelling the city in 1865. Open M-F 9-5. Free. (803) 758-3208.

TRINITY CATHEDRAL, 1100 Sumter St., c. 1845. Edward Brickell White drew the plans for this towered and pinnacled Gothic Revival church. Worthy of special note is the marble baptismal font, designed by Hiram Powers, and the hand carved choir stalls. In 1977, this church was designated the Cathedral Parish of the Episcopal Diocese of Upper South Carolina. NR. Open M-Sa 9-5. Free. (803) 771-7300.

UNIVERSITY OF SOUTH CAROLINA HORSESHOE (Old Campus), Sumter St. between Pendleton and Green Sts., 19th century. Chartered in 1801 as South Carolina College, the institution did not open until 1805 when **Rutledge College** was completed. Designed by Robert Mills, this was the first building on campus. As the college grew, more buildings were erected including the **South Caroliniana Library** (1840), also by Robert Mills, which is thought to be the first separate college library building in America. The brick wall surrounding the Horseshoe was constructed in 1835 to separate town from gown and keep obnoxious students out of trouble with the police. NR, NHL. The campus is a fine place for a stroll at any time of day. U.S.C.'s **McKissick Museum** can be found at the eastern end of the Horseshoe. Here visitors will find world famous collections of silver, gemstones, dolls, Art Nouveau objets d'art, and pottery. Open M-F 9-4, Su 1-5, during spring and fall semesters. Free. (803) 777-7251.

WOODROW WILSON BOYHOOD HOME, 1705 Hampton St., 1872. This should actually be called Woodrow Wilson's Teen Home as he spent only three years here (1872-75) from the age of sixteen to nineteen. Nonetheless, the Italianate frame house was built by Wilson's father, Joseph Ruggles Wilson, a professor at the Columbia Theological Seminary. Today the 2-story structure has been restored to its 19th-century appearance and is appointed with period pieces and original Wilson family furniture. Worthy of note are the mantels which look like marble and are actually painted iron. NR. Open Tu-Sa 10-4, Su 2-5. $1.50 adults, 75¢ students, children under 6 free. (803) 252-7742.

Edgefield and vicinity

Laid out around the courthouse square in 1787, the town of Edgefield still retains its 19th-century ambience and about forty buldings of that period. **Oakley Park** (1835), Columbia Rd., was a plantation house owned by General Martin W. Gary; after the Civil War, the Red Shirts were organized here to help with reconstruction in South Carolina. Today the house is a shrine of the United Daughters of the Confederacy, who have furnished it with period antiques and exhibits of Civil War relics. NR. Open M, T, F 10-4. Free.

In the 19th century, Pottersville in Edgefield County was an important pottery-producing center. Today the **Pottersville Museum,** housed in the 1820 Pottersville Kitchen, 1 mile N. of Edgefield on US 25, exhibits examples of stoneware produced in this area between 1810-70. Open M-Sa 9-6. Free. (803) 637-3333.

Lexington

LEXINGTON COUNTY MUSEUM, 230 Fox St. In several historic houses in this interesting museum complex can be seen living history demonstrations illustrating life in the 18th and 19th centuries. Houses date from 1771 to 1850 and contain collections of furniture made in Lexington County, antique dolls, Indian artifacts, textiles, spinning wheels, and farm implements. Open Tu-Sa 10-4, Su 1-4. $1 adults, 50¢ children. (803) 356-8369. ✔

McConnells

BRATTONSVILLE HISTORIC DISTRICT, CR 165, 18th-19th centuries. In this small complex, the visitor can see the development of modest residential architecture in York County from 1776 to 1855. The oldest house belonged to Colonel William Bratton and was originally a one-room log cabin that was later enlarged. **The Homestead** was built around 1830 by Col. Bratton's son and is Greek Revival in style. The two-story brick dwelling has elements of Jeffersonian Classicism. Known as the **Brick House,** it was built for use as girls' school and general store. Also on the property are a doctor's office and a brick slaves' quarters. NR. The buildings have been restored and are open to the public Tu, Th 10-4, Su 2-4; other times by appointment. $1.50 adults, 50¢ students. (803) 684-2327.

Ninety Six

OLD NINETY SIX NATIONAL HISTORIC SITE, 2 miles S. of Ninety Six between SC 248 and 27, 18th century. A thriving commercial and governmental center once stood on this site. During the Revolution, the town was occupied by the British and heavily fortified. Today little remains but earthworks, bricks, and a strip of road. Nevertheless, the National Park Service has established a **Visitor Center** in an 1810 log cabin at the site. Inside, visitors will discover displays concerning pioneer life, the French and Indian War, and the Revolution. NR. Open daily 8-5. Free. (803) 543-4068. ★

Sumter and vicinity

MUSEUM-ARCHIVES OF THE SUMTER COUNTY HISTORICAL SOCIETY, 122 N. Washington St., 1845. The three-story brick house now contains a museum with collections of antique dolls, toys, furniture, and farm and household implements. Archives include the complete South Carolina census rolls and an excellent collection of genealogical files. Open W-Su 2-5. Free. (803) 775-0908.

STATEBURG HISTORIC DISTRICT, 1 mile N. of US 76-378 on SC 261, 12 miles W of Sumter, 18th-20th centuries. Named Stateburg because General Thomas Sumter intended it to be South Carolina's capital, this is now an area characterized by farms and ante-bellum structures. Of note are the **Borough House Plantation** (c. 1758) and the **Holy Cross Episcopal Church** (c. 1850) which stand on SC 261 across from one another. The house and its outbuildings form the largest pise-de-tere (rammed earth) complex in this country. The first successful operation on a cancerous jawbone was performed by a resident of this house, Dr. William Anderson, in 1829. Private. The one-story Holy Cross Episcopal Church is also constructed of pise-de-terre though it is stuccoed. Designed by Edward C. Jones, the Gothic Revival structure has a towering spire and pointed windows and doors. The stained glass windows over the altar and at the entrance were based on designs by Viollet-le-Duc. NR, NHL.

Union and vicinity

EPISCOPAL CHURCH OF THE NATIVITY, Church and Pinckney Sts., 1855. This one-story granite Gothic Revival building features three Tiffany windows and a marble font designed by Hiram Powers. NR.

ROSE HILL STATE PARK, 9 miles SW of town off US 176, 1828-32. This lovely three-story stuccoed brick house was built for William Gist, who was state governor in 1860 when South Carolina became the first state to secede from the Union. The stucco and the two-story piazzas on the back and front façades were added after 1860. NR. Grounds open daily, dawn to dusk; house Sa-Su 1-5, and by appointment. Free. (803) 758-3622.

Winnsboro

FAIRFIELD COUNTY MUSEUM, 231 S. Congress St., 1830. Housed in the three-story Federal brick Ketchin Building, the museum offers interesting exhibits of pioneer and ante-bellum memorabilia and furnishings as well as Indian artifacts. NR. Open M, W, F 10:30-12:30 and 1:30-4:30. Free. (803) 635-9811.

Upcountry

Always looking to the west, hardy and adventurous pioneers were attracted to this area by the dramatic landscapes and relative freedom of this hilly and untamed area. Traces of early settlements are few and far between but, with the help of a few well-preserved cabins and churches, it is not difficult to imagine the trials and rewards of pioneer living in this beautiful western province.

Chesnee vicinity

COWPENS NATIONAL BATTLEFIELD, 2 miles E. of town at junction of SC 11 and 110, 1781. On January 17, 1781, Revolutionary General Daniel Morgan deployed his bedraggled and untested forces in the area around what was known as Hannah's Cowpens. When British Lieutenant-Colonel Banastre Tarleton arrived at the pasture, American troops were ready. The British suffered terrible losses, and the Americans celebrated their second victory in three months (see Kings Mountain). NR. The **Visitor Center** is the best place to begin a tour of the battleground. Open daily 9-5, later in summer. Free. (803)461-2828. ★

Clemson

FORT HILL (John C. Calhoun House), Clemson University Campus, 1803. John C. Calhoun, whose illustrious career in politics included positions as secretary of state, vice president, secretary of war, and senator, lived here from 1825 until 1850. The estate was inherited by his son-in-law, Thomas Clemson, who willed it to South Carolina for use as the **Clemson Agricultural College.** Today the house is a muse-

um containing original family furnishings and memorabilia. NR, NHL. Open Tu-Sa 10-12 and 1-5:30, Su 2-6. Free. (803) 656-2475,

Also on campus is colonial **Hanover House** (1714-16). The 1½-story building with a gambrel roof and pedimented dormers was built by a French Huguenot named Paul de St. Julien. Today the house contains a collection of antique furnishings. NR. Same hours as above. Free. (803) 656-2061.

Pendleton and vicinity

A picturesque Upcountry area, Pendleton as well as much of the surrounding countryside in Anderson, Oconee, and Pickens counties is replete with sites of historic interest. It has been said that Pendleton is to this region what Charleston and Beaufort are to the Low Country, and it is certainly

true that the magnificent landscapes in the northwest edge of South Carolina make it a place to explore. The **Pendleton District Historical and Recreational Commission,** 125 E. Queen St., functions as the area's Visitor Center and supplies the traveler with maps and information. Located in the 1850 **Hunter's Store,** the commission also offers a regional photo collection and historical artifacts from the tri-county area. Open M-F 9-4:30, other times by appointment. (803) 646-3782.

ASHTABULA, 1¼ miles NE of town off SC 88, 1828. This almost-square plantation house with Greek Revival elements is exemplary of Low Country architecture in the Upcountry. The two-story frame dwelling, with a hipped roof and a widow's walk, is connected to a smaller two-story brick building which served as the servants' quarters and kitchen. Today this house has been restored and furnished with period antiques by the Foundation for Historic Restoration in the Pendleton Area. NR.

The Foundation has also restored and furnished **Woodburn** (early 19th century), Woodburn Rd., to the period. Built for Charles Cotesworth Pinckney, the house is typical of summer residences: its spacious rooms, wide veranda, and many windows and doors keep the house cool and the air circulating freely. NR. Both houses are open Apr-Oct, Su 2-6, other times by appointment. $1 adults, 50¢ children 2-14. (803) 646-3442.

OLD STONE CHURCH, 1½ miles N. of town off US 76, 1797-1802. This pioneer-era church is constructed of fieldstone and is 1½-stories high with a gabled roof. The building retains its modest original interior. Visitors will find hand-hewn ceiling beams and wooden benches and pulpit. In the adjacent cemetery are the gravestones of many of the area's early leaders. NR.

Pickens

PICKENS COUNTY HISTORICAL MUSEUM, corner of Johnson and Pendleton Sts., 1903. Located in the old county jail, the museum contains local memorabilia, Indian artifacts, and pioneer relics. The two-story brick structure served as a jail and a home for the sheriff and his family from 1903 to 1975. NR. Open M, F 2-5, W 9-12, Th 1-4. Free. (803) 878-4965.

Spartanburg and vicinity

THE PRICE HOUSE, junction of CR 86, 199, 200, c. 1800. This 2½-story house made of brick laid in Flemish bond was constructed by Thomas Price and used as a "home of entertaining." Travelers stopped here for rest and a repast. NR. Today the house has been restored and is open to the public Tu-Sa 11-5, Su 2-5. $2 adults, $1 children. (803) 476-2483.

SPARTANBURG COUNTY REGIONAL MUSEUM, 501 Otis Blvd.. A museum of local history, its collections include Indian artifacts, antique dolls, quilts, and General Daniel Morgan's rifle. Open June-mid Sept, Tu-Sa 10-12 and 3-5; mid Sept-May, Tu-Sa 10-12 and 3-5, Su 3-5. Free. (803) 585-2441.

WALNUT GROVE PLANTATION, 8 miles SE of town, about 1 mile E. of junction of US 221 an I-26, c. 1765. Charles Moore, a pioneer of Scottish-Irish origin, moved to South Carolina from Pennsylvania in 1763 when he received a land grant from George III. This modest two-story log and clapboard house reflects the influences of both Pennsylvanian and local architectural styles. It served as home to Moore and his descendants for almost two centuries. Today the house and its outbuildings have been carefully restored, and visitors to the complex will be free to explore the furnished Moore House and kitchen as well as a schoolroom, blacksmith shop, and smokehouse. NR. Open Apr-Sept, Tu-Sa 11-5, Su 2-5; other times by appointment. $2.50 adults, $1.50 children under 18. (803) 576-6456.

Historic Accommodations

An asterisk (*) indicates that meals are served.

Beaufort

BAY STREET INN, 601 Bay St., 29902. (803) 524-7720. Open all year. Housed in an ante-bellum mansion in the midst of Beaufort's historic district, the inn offers rooms with views of the river. Included in the charge are breakfast in the morning, bicycles for touring during the day, and sherry and fruit at night. NR.

Charleston

BATTERY CARRIAGE HOUSE, 20 South Battery, 29401. (803) 723-9881. Open all year. Housed in an 1845 mansion, this gracious inn with colorful gardens and a view of the harbor offers fine accommodations and the ambience of ante-bellum Charleston. NR.

ELLIOTT HOUSE INN, 78 Queen St., 29401. (803) 723-1855. Open all year. Every guest room in this pleasant inn is furnished with antique pieces. And if breakfast in bed is a luxury you enjoy, it is offered here; otherwise guests take their breakfasts in the charming courtyard. NR.

TWO MEETING STREET INN, 2 Meeting St., 29401. (803) 723-7322. Open all year. This stately Queen Anne mansion was built following the earthquake which devastated Charleston in 1886. Today the galleried house has been converted for use as an inn and offers eight pleasant rooms furnished with family antiques. NR.

SWORD GATE INN, 11 Tradd St., 29401. (803) 723-8518. Open all year. Each of the guest rooms in the Sword Gate is simply but elegantly appointed in its own distinctive style. Each day fresh flowers are placed in the rooms. A hearty Southern breakfast is served to guests in the cozily-furnished old kitchen. NR.

VENDUE INN, 19 Vendue Range, 29401. (803) 577-7970. Open all year. The casual observer might never know that this handsome inn, located one block from the waterfront, was once a warehouse. Today each of the guest rooms is furnished with antique pieces. Thoughtful touches include the breakfast served each morning and the wine and cheese available in the courtyard in the afternoons. NR.

5. GEORGIA

THE largest state in the Southeast, Georgia epitomizes much of the old and the new South for many Americans. The gracious cities of Savannah, Augusta, Athens, Macon, Milledgeville, and countless smaller towns of considerable charm, cast a picturesque image which is as true as life itself. Although General William Tecumseh Sherman marched and burned his way through Georgia during the Civil War, his lieutenants must have tired from setting the torch to Atlanta for they left a great deal of ante-bellum Georgia unscathed.

Savannah lies along what is called the "Colonial coast." It was here that Gen. James Edward Oglethorpe founded the colony of Georgia in 1733. His plan for the city, incorporating a number of public squares, is still very much intact in the oldest part of town that comprises one of America's largest historic districts. After San Francisco and Boston, Savannah is clearly one of the most pleasant cities in North America to visit. It is liberally endowed with fine accommodations and restaurants.

Savannah is an excellent introduction to historic Georgia, but to experience the true Deep South flavor of the state, a visit to the region west and northwest of Savannah is often recommended, and with good reason. Such small towns as Madison and Washington offer especially rewarding experiences for the historically-minded traveler, as do Athens and Augusta. Athens, the home of the University of Georgia, brings together the best of academic and ante-bellum architecture.

For many Georgia visitors, the Atlanta area may be the only stop that time allows. While there is much to be explored in the city itself, it is not difficult to escape to the nearby countryside, to towns such as Roswell and Oxford. Here it seems that time has stood still, at least during recent times when Atlanta became so fashionably modern.

Other areas of the state which remain in part delightfully old-fashioned are the southwest, now better known as "Plains" country; the north, a region of national forests, small villages, and mountain resorts; and the coastal area stretching from Savannah to Cumberland Island on the Florida state line and west to the Okefenokee Swamp. Each of these sections has its special traditions and historic attractions well worth exploring.

Gordon-Banks House, Newnan

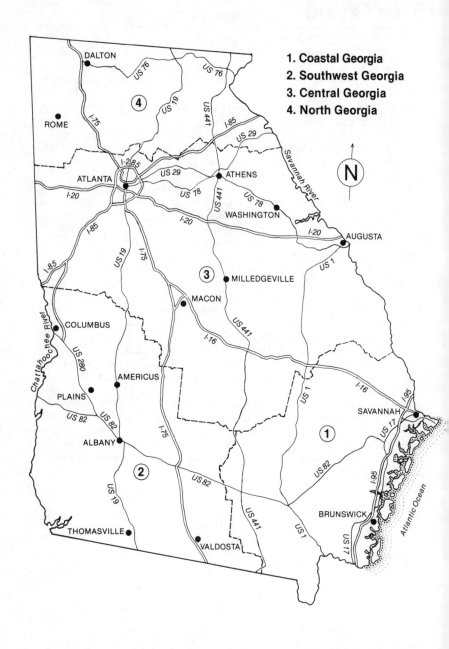

1. Coastal Georgia
2. Southwest Georgia
3. Central Georgia
4. North Georgia

Coastal Georgia

A visit to Georgia ideally begins along the coast where the state was first settled. Gen. James Oglethorpe founded Savannah in 1733, but, for at least 200 years, Spanish explorers attempted to establish colonies on the islands which dot the coastline. Very little is left to see from this early colonial period or from that which followed the first English settlement, but, almost since the Revolution, the residents of the coastal area have prided themselves on preserving the best of the past. Savannah is today one of the loveliest cities in America largely because its Federal and Greek Revival buildings and public squares and avenues have been so well taken care of within a 2½-mile square historic district. As one follows the coast to the south toward Darien, Brunswick and the Golden Isles, and St. Mary's, other attractive and historic sights come into view.

Brunswick and the Golden Isles

During the 19th century Brunswick was a serious rival to Savannah as Georgia's leading port city, but today it is a much quieter place. The Spanish are known to have settled here prior to the establishment of an English town in 1771, named in honor of King George III of the House of Brunswick. There is little of the 18th century left in Brunswick or the surrounding territory. The historical buildings and sites are largely Victorian or were built in the early 1900s. Brunswick's modern-day reputation is principally that of the gateway city to two of the Golden Isles — Jekyll Island and St. Simons Island — reached via causeways across the Marshes of Glynn. These are tidewater flats, the largest on the East Coast, and there is an Overlook Park located along US 17 where the view is unobstructed.

Brunswick and vicinity

JAMES OGLETHORPE MONUMENT, Queen's Sq. The founder of the Georgia colony in 1733 is honored here in the center of what is known as Old Towne, the downtown area roughly bounded by First, Bay, New Bay, H, and Cochran Sts. The old city was laid out with neighborhood squares in the manner of Savannah. A driving tour map which pinpoints the interesting Victorian buildings can be purchased at the Old City Hall, Newcastle St.

HOFWYL-BROADFIELD PLANTATION, N. of Brunswick on US 17, mid-1800s. The frame plantation house offers the public an interesting view of what domestic life was like for the wealthy rice growers of the region. The plantation, in existence from the 18th century, is now maintained by the state. The furnishings of the two-story dwelling date from 1830-1972, most being of the ante-bellum period. NR. Open Tu-Sa 9-5, Su 2-5:30. Free. (912) 264-9263.

Jekyll Island

MILLIONAIRES' VILLAGE (Jekyll Island Club), between Riverview Dr. and Old Village Blvd., 19th-20th centuries. Members of some of America's wealthiest late 19th-century industrial families joined together in 1886 and bought Jekyll Island as their private retreat. Here the Rockefellers, McCormicks, Goodyears, Pulitzers, and others could gambole away the winter months. A spacious clubhouse was built, as well as a number of private villas, and Faith Chapel. Life remained much the same until World War II, when the presence of enemy ships off the coast caused President Roosevelt to order the evacuation of the island. Following the war, the club did not reopen and the state of Georgia purchased the island. Group tours of the village leave the Macy Cottage (1896) at 375 Riverview Dr. Among the other buildings which can be visited are: Rockefeller Cottage (1892), the former home of William Rockefeller; Goodyear Cottage (1902), built for Frank Henry Goodyear; Mistletoe Cottage (1901); Crane Cottage (1916), the home of

Richard Teller Crane; **Faith Chapel** (1903); and the **Jekyll Clubhouse Library** (1888). NR. Tours are held M-Sa 10, 12, and 2; Su 1 and 3. $3 adults, $2 students 10-18, free for children under 10. (912) 635-2727.

Very little remains of the home of the earliest inhabitants of the island. The two-story **Horton House,** Main Rd., was built of tabby — a concrete-like substance made of shells, lime, and sand — before 1742 for Maj. William Horton. NR.

St. Simons Island

FORT FREDERICA NATIONAL MONUMENT, off Country Rd., 1736-46. From 1736 until the mid-1700s the fort and community of Frederica was among the most important on the Georgia coast. The fort was established to protect English settlers on the island and mainland from the Spanish and was manned by a regiment of 650 British soldiers, who were indispensable during the 1739-48 Anglo-Spanish conflict. The last major battle, victorious for the British, took place on July 7, 1742, farther south on the island at **Bloody Marsh,** Frederica Rd. From that time until Florida was ceded to Britain in 1763, a military presence was needed, but the Spanish were no longer a real threat. The town which grew up around the fort steadily declined in population, and, after 1763, was practically deserted. The National Park Service administers the 250-acre site and has not attempted to reconstruct any of the buildings. It has very carefully tended the ruins of the fort, however, and has overseen the careful excavation of the romantic, great oak-shaded location. One can tour the grounds, walking down the remnants of Frederica's Broad St. past the foundations of the John Calwell and Hawkins-Davidson houses, the barracks tower, and on to the site of the fort. A **Visitor Center** is located near the entrance to the monument. NR. Open winter months daily 8-5; summer months, daily 8-6. Free. (912) 638-3639. ★

ST. SIMONS LIGHTHOUSE and LIGHTHOUSE KEEPER'S BUILDING, 600

Beachview Dr., 1868-72. A lighthouse has stood at this spot since 1802, the first having been destroyed by the Confederates in 1862. Its 102-foot replacement was automated in 1964. Right next door is the eclectic keeper's residence designed by Charles B. Cluskey. It was built for two keepers and their families and now houses the **Museum of Coastal History,** which treats all aspects of the history of the Georgia coast. The museum is maintained by the Coastal Georgia Historical Society. NR. Open Tu-Sa 1-4, Su 1:30-4; June-Labor Day, Tu-Sa 10-5, Su 1:30-5. Free. (912) 638-4666.

Darien vicinity

FORT KING GEORGE STATE HISTORIC SITE, 1½ miles E. of US 17, 1721. The site of the oldest British fortress on the Georgia coast is now maintained by the state. A modern **museum** contains artifacts of both the Indian and Spanish who preceded the British at the location on Altamaha River delta. Exhibited are reproductions of the uniforms worn and weapons used by the British troops who were garrisoned here until 1727. Nothing remains of the fort, but, through archaeological investigation, much of its early history has been pieced together. NR. Open Tu-Sa 9-5, Su 2-5:30. Free. (912) 437-4770. ★

Fargo vicinity

STEPHEN C. FOSTER STATE PARK, 18 miles NE of Fargo on Jones Island via GA 177. Okefenokee Swamp is Georgia's greatest natural historical wonder, and the park lies at the western entrance. Foster's beloved Suwannee River flows through the tract. There is an excellent museum here where the history of lumbering and turpentining in the region is explained along with the story of its natural life. Open Tu-Sa 9-5, Su 2-5:30. Free. (912) 637-5274.

Midway and vicinity

MIDWAY CONGREGATIONAL CHURCH, junction US 17 and GA 38, 1792. The 1½-story meeting house might well have been built in New England, so close is its style to the typical early 19th-century steepled church of Connecticut or Massachusetts. The building is frame with clapboarding, and inside, little changed over time, is a U-shaped gallery and the original box pews. This building replaced the 1756 church, burned by the British during the Revolution along with much of the rest of the village. Midway was settled by two families of a band of Dorchester, Massachusetts, Puritan missionaries to the Indians. Among the notable parishioners were two signers of the Declaration of Independence, Lyman Hall and Button Gwinnett. NR.

Located right next door is the **Midway Museum** (1959), a reproduction of a vernacular 18th-century cottage. It is filled with furniture, artifacts, and documents from the 1700s to the mid-1800s. Open Tu-Sa 10-4, Su 2-4. Free. (912) 884-5837.

SUNBURY HISTORIC SITE (Fort Morris), approximately 10 miles E. of Midway off GA 38, mid-18th century. Fort Morris was founded to protect the now abandoned port of Sunbury during the Revolution. It commanded a site overlooking the Midway River, and, in the first engagement in 1778, the Americans were successful. A year later, however, they had to surrender. The remains of the earthwork fortifications can be seen. The story of Fort Morris and the lost city of Sunbury is told in

exhibits at the **Visitor Center**. NR. Open Tu-Sa 9-5, Su 2-5:30. (912) 884-5999. ★

Richmond Hill vicinity

FORT McALLISTER HISTORIC SITE, 10 miles E. of I-95 on GA Spur 144, 1861-64. The earthwork fortification, built to protect Savannah's southern flank, withstood much bombardment from Northern ships prior to its fall in December, 1864, to Gen. William Tecumseh Sherman's land forces. The fort was erected along the south bank of the Great Ogeechee River and consisted of five irregular sides with large earthern mounds known as "bombproofs." Troops ate and slept within these enclosures. The protective walls and bombproofs have been restored and can be viewed by visitors. NR. Open Tu-Sa 9-5:30, Su 2-5:30. Free. (912) 727-2339. ✔ ★

St. Mary's and vicinity

ST. MARY'S HISTORIC DISTRICT, roughly bounded by Waterfront Rd., Norris and Alexander Sts., and Oak Grove Cemetery, late 18th-early 20th centuries. This early port town on the Florida border lies along the St. Mary's River. It is a very pleasant town in which to stroll, especially along the old waterfront area. **Orange Hall** (c. 1846), 311 Osborne St., is the most notable building in town, a fine Greek Revival temple with a Doric portico. Among the offices located here is the **Chamber of Commerce,** where information about tours of the St. Mary's area is available. Open Th-M 1-4:30. (912) 882-4000.

CUMBERLAND ISLAND NATIONAL SEASHORE, NE of St. Mary's, 16th-20th centuries. Protection of the 16-mile island was assumed by the National Park Service in 1972, not too late to safeguard the historic area's abundant natural resources. Cumberland Island can be reached only by ferry from St. Mary's, a 45-minute trip. The Spanish built a fort on the island that they called San Pedro as early as 1566; Gen. James Oglethorpe renamed the island Cumberland after the Duke of Cumberland in 1736 and built two forts—St. Andrews and Prince William. Today the only historic buildings remaining are the ruins of **Dungeness,** a mansion built in the 1780s and destroyed by fire after the Civil War; a second winter retreat built in 1881 by Andrew Carnegie's brother, Thomas, and named **Carnegie Dungeness;** and the **Greyfield Inn** (see accommodations). A **Visitor Center** for the park is located on the mainland 1 block W. of where GA 40 dead-ends at the St. Mary's River. Reservations for the ferry and ranger-guided tours of the historic and natural areas can be made here. Open daily 8:15-4:30. (912) 882-4335. ✔

Savannah

Founded in 1733 Georgia's oldest settlement, Savannah, remains the state's most picturesque and pleasant city. It is said that more than 1,000 buildings have been restored to new life in the past twenty-five years. Most of these are located in the **central historic district,** among the largest officially designated landmark areas in the country. Included in this district, bounded by E. Broad, Gwinnett, W. Broad Sts., and the Savannah River, are tree-shaded squares and fine Georgian, Federal, Greek Revival, and Gothic Revival homes and public buildings. South of this area is Savannah's officially designated **Victorian historic district.** Primarily residential, it is now receiving the kind of careful attention paid to the old downtown. Here are to be found large picturesque frame buildings built along Queen Anne lines and brick row houses of a much simpler design.

Savannah has profited from good urban planning since its founding. Gen. James Oglethorpe established the city on a high bluff overlooking the river which forms the boundary with South Carolina. Col. William Bull, one of his aides, was responsible for carrying out Oglethorpe's grid plan of squares and compact neighborhoods surrounding them. To a remarkable degree, the basic scheme is still in place today making the center city a particularly pleasant area in which to walk or bicycle.

Information about the city is most easily secured at the **Chamber of Commerce and Visitors Center,** 301 W. Broad St., (912) 233-3167, housed in the former Central of Georgia Railroad Station (1860-76). Material available here will aid the visitor in planning his own self-guided tour of the city. More formal excursions are offered by several organizations. The **Historic Savannah Foundation,** William Scarborough House, 41 W. Broad St., (912) 233-7703, offers an "Historic District Tour" and a "Low Country Tour," featuring sights on the outskirts of town. A Black Heritage Trail Tour is sponsored by the **Association for the Study of Afro-American Life and History,** and includes Savannah's oldest black residential neighborhood—Yamacraw—where many free blacks lived prior to Emancipation, and other sites. For information regarding this tour, contact W. W. Law at (912) 233-2027. **The Savannah Carriage Co.,** 230 Vernonburg Ave., (912) 236-6756, provides horse-drawn vehicles for tours of the old city. Bicycles can be rented at the DeSoto Hilton or the Hyatt Regency.

CHRIST CHURCH, 28 Bull St., 1837. The Episcopal parish was the first (1733) to be established in the state. The present brick Greek Revival building with an Ionic portico was gutted by fire in 1897 and completely rebuilt the following year. The first church building on the site was erected c. 1750, and a second was built in 1811. One of the early preachers was John Wesley, resident in Savannah in 1736-37. NR. Open M, W-F 9-4. (912) 232-4131.

COTTON EXCHANGE, 100 E. Bay St., 1887. The center of the 19th-century trade in cotton has been considerably refurbished. The exchange, designed by William G. Preston, is in the midst of the Factors Row area, where farmers delivered their bales for inspection and purchase by the city's merchants. All of the commercial comings and goings were facilitated by an unusual system of below-ground passageways and iron bridges over the dray ways. The exchange and neighboring buildings appear from Bay St. to be only two-stories high. From River St., alongside the water-

Courtesy Savannah Area Convention & Visitors Bureau

Savannah

1. Visitors Centers
2. Christ Church
3. Cotton Exchange
4. Customs Houses
5. Scarbrough House
6. First African Baptist Church
7. Nathaniel Greene Monument

8. Davenport House
9. Owens-Thomas House
10. Telfair Academy
11. Juliette Grodon Low Birthplace
12. Independent Presbyterian Church
13. Green-Meldrim House
14. Andrew Low House

way and promenade, they extend as many as five stories. This area of warehouses now consists of largely commercial buildings—smart shops and restaurants where

one can easily wile away a pleasant afternoon. The exchange has been converted to offices and is most interesting from the outside.

CUSTOMS HOUSE, 1-3 E. Bay St., 1848-53. The most important public building in Savannah, the monumental granite Customs House stands on the site of Gen. Oglethorpe's headquarters. The portico is supported by monumental Corinthian columns of the design known in the South as "Tower-of-the-Winds." The customary classical acanthus leaves and scrolls of the capitals were replaced with tobacco leaves, a fitting alteration considering the importance of tobacco to the area's shipping community. The lobby is especially noteworthy as it features a central flight of marble stairs that divides into a dramatic double flight. John S. Norris of New York was the architect of the building. NR. The Customs House is open during regular office hours. (912) 944-4264.

ISAIAH DAVENPORT HOUSE, 324 E. State St. on Columbia Sq., 1815. Visitors to Savannah today would find nothing but another dreary parking lot on this site if the Historic Savannah Foundation had not formed to save Davenport House in 1955 and, subsequently, other important buildings. A master builder from Rhode Island, Davenport made his career in Savannah between 1799 and 1827. The Federal-style mansion with brownstone trim is now one of the house museums maintained by the Foundation. Beautifully furnished with Chippendale, Hepplewhite, and Sheraton furniture, it is a joy to visit. The ornamental plaster cornices, open-well stairway, and unusual center hall are among the notable features. NR. Open M-Sa 10-4:30, Su 1:30-4:30. $1.50 adults, 75¢ students 10-17, free for children under 10. Included on HSF tour. (912) 236-8097.

FIRST AFRICAN BAPTIST CHURCH, 23 Montgomery St., 1859-61, 1888. Both this church, built by members, and neighboring First Bryan Baptist Church, owe their existence to a black congregation founded in 1788 at Brampton Plantation in the Savannah area, the earliest known black parish. First African was originally a brick Federal building, but has undergone significant changes, including the addition of a tower. The interior features a three-sided gallery supported by Corinthian columns and late stained glass windows which probably replaced clear glass. There is a museum at 13 Montgomery St. in which exhibits and taped recordings trace the history of the congregation. NR. Open W and F 11-2, and by appointment. (912) 233-6597.

NATHANIEL GREENE MONUMENT, Johnson Sq., 1825-30. The square is the first public park that one encounters along Bull St. when leaving the waterfront area. Greene's Revolutionary War campaign through the South is credited for the successful conclusion of the American cause. He died in 1785 at Mulberry Grove near Savannah. His monument, a 50-foot marble obelisk, was designed by William Strickland, and the cornerstone was laid by Lafayette in 1825. Greene's remains were reinterred beneath the monument in 1902.

GEORGIA HISTORICAL SOCIETY, Hodgson Hall, 501 Whitaker St., 1874-75. Founded in 1839, the society possesses what is the most valuable collection of historical materials in the state. On display are prints, photographs, paintings, and artifacts relating to Georgia's development as a colony and state. Hodgson Hall was designed by Detlef Lienau. NR. Open M-F 10-6, Sa 9:30-1. Free. (912) 944-2128.

GREEN-MELDRIM HOUSE, Macon and Bull Sts., 1850-61. Considered one of the finest Gothic Revival houses in America, the home now serves as the parish house for St. John's Episcopal Church. It was built for a wealthy English cotton merchant, Charles Green, and probably was designed by John Norris. Judge Peter Meldrim was a later owner. What sets this residence apart from most others is the especially fine workmanship inside and out. Many of the building materials were brought from England and the Continent. The center hall with its freestanding marble stairway and the first-floor rooms with elaborate decorative plasterwork cornices and medallions, black walnut woodwork, marble fireplaces, tile floors, silver-plated hardware, and gold-leaf pier and mantel mirrors are worthy of a prince's palace. At the invitation of Green, the residence became the headquarters of Gen. William Tecumseh Sherman after the city fell to the North in December, 1864. The west wing, containing the former kitchens, servants' quarters, and stable, were converted for the use of the church. NR. Open Tu, Th-Sa 10-4. $2 donation. (912) 232-1251.

INDEPENDENT PRESBYTERIAN CHURCH, Oglethorpe Ave. and Bull St., 1819, 1890. The first frame home of Savannah's leading Presbyterian congregation burned to the ground in 1889 and was replaced by this exact granite replica. It is an impressive Federal building with a Doric portico, designed originally by John Holden Greene. There is an interior gallery or three sides and an oval domed ceiling supported by four Corinthian columns. In 1885 Woodrow Wilson was married in the original church to Ellen Axson, granddaughter of the minister.

JULIETTE GORDON LOW BIRTHPLACE, 142 Bull St., 1818-21. The founder of the Girl Scouts of America was born here in 1860. Designed by English-trained architect William Jay, the home had been built for James M. Wayne, mayor of the city. The third floor was added in 1886 and tends to give the building a top-heavy appearance, but other details of the town house are exceptionally well executed. The principal rooms have black marble fireplaces and elaborate plasterwork decoration and woodwork. The building has been restored to the 1870s period and

Green-Meldrim House

is furnished with many original Low family pieces. NR, NHL. Open M-Tu, Th-Sa 10-4, Su 2-4:30. $1 Girl Scout adults, $1.75 regular adults, 50¢ Girl Scouts under 18, 75¢ regular students/children 12-17, free for children under 6. (912) 233-4501. ✔

ANDREW LOW HOUSE, 329 Abercorn St., 1849. Now the headquarters of the Georgia Colonial Dames, the Low House was where Mrs. Low organized the first Girl Scout troop. John Norris is thought to be the man who designed the brick home for Low, a wealthy cotton merchant. Robert E. Lee and William Makepeace Thackeray were among the Lowses' better known guests. Basically Italianate in style, the building is simply but handsomely composed inside and out. The Colonial Dames embarked on a very ambitious refurbishing project in 1978 to return the interiors to the period of the 1840s. Open daily 10:30-4:30. $2 adults, $1 students, 75¢ children under 12 and Girl Scouts of all ages. (912) 233-6854.

MICKVE ISRAEL TEMPLE, 20 E. Gordon St., 1876-78. The oldest Jewish congregation in the South dates back to 1733 when a company of Sephardic and Ashkenazic Jews arrived from London. The temple is unusual in having been built in the Gothic Revival style with pointed-arch windows. Henry G. Harrison and J. D. Foley were the architects. A museum housed here contains the oldest Torah in America and various records from the Colonial and Federal periods, including letters from Presidents Washington, Jefferson, and Madison to the congregation. Tours, M, Tu, and Th 10-12. Free. (912) 233-1547.

OWEN-THOMAS HOUSE, 124 Abercorn St., 1816-19. Designed by William Jay while he was residing in England, this is a transplanted English Regency town house. The interiors of the stuccoed brick mansion are exquisite in their Neoclassical detailing. The drawing room, with a white marble mantel, flat domical ceiling, and intricate plasterwork, is one of the most beautiful interiors in America. A parterre garden to the rear of the house is illustrative of 1820 landscaping effects and plant materials. The house was built for Richard Richardson, a cotton merchant and banker, and was purchased in 1830 by George Welchman Owens, one-time mayor of Savannah and a U.S. congressman. It descended in the Owens family to Margaret Thomas, who bequeathed the property to the Telfair Academy in 1951. NR, NHL. Open Tu-Sa 10-5, Su-M 2-5. $2 adults, $1 students, 50¢ children 6-12, free for children under 6. (912) 233-9743.

WILLIAM SCARBROUGH HOUSE, 41 W. Broad St., 1818-19, c. 1835-45. Another of William Jay's refined Regency designs, Scarbrough House is a most appropriate home for the Historic Savannah Foundation. The monumental stuccoed brick town house was built for Scarbrough, a cotton merchant and financier of the *U.S.S. Savannah,* the first transatlantic steamship. Recent restoration has removed some of the later 19th-century changes such as a third floor. One need go no further than the entrance hall, a two-story atrium, to appreciate Jay's design. A large ballroom and two parlors are on the first floor. From 1872 until the 1950s, the building served as the West Broad Street School, Savannah's first black public school. Restoration work is on-going, and there are changing displays treating Savannah's history, architecture, and decorative arts tradition. Open M-W, F-Sa 10-4. $1.50 adults, 75¢ students 10-17, free for children under 10. (912) 233-7787.

TELFAIR ACADEMY OF ARTS AND SCIENCES, 121 Barnard St., 1818, 1883. Architect William Jay built an English Regency mansion for Alexander Telfair, son of a governor and Revolutionary patriot, on the site of Government House, the royal governor's home. In 1875 the house was given by Alexander's sister, Mary, as a public museum; a Sculpture Gallery and Rotunda was designed by Detlev Lienau and added in 1883. Telfair family furnishings are on view in the elegantly proportioned and decorated rooms. The museum's holdings are also strong in the area of 18th- and 19th-century European and American painters. NR, NHL. Open Tu-Sa 10-5, Su 2-5. $2 adults, $1 students and children 12 and over, 50¢ senior citizens and children under 12, free for children under 6. (912) 232-1177.

Savannah vicinity

BETHESDA HOME FOR BOYS (Cunningham Historic Center), S. of Savannah at Ferguson Ave. and Bethesda Rd., 1740. George Whitefield, the English evangelist, preached throughout the colonies with intermittent trips back to England. His most enduring memorial is the orphanage, the oldest continuously operating facility in America, with its own 500-acre campus. The complex now consists of 18 buildings dating from the 1870s to the present. Whitefield memorabilia and artifacts relating to the colony's early history are on display at the historic center. Visitors can also tour the beautiful grounds and stop by the Federal brick **Whitefield Memorial Chapel** (1925). NR. Open M-F 10-4. Free. (912) 355-0905.

FORT JACKSON, Island Expwy, 3 miles E. of Savannah on the Savannah River, 19th century. The brick and stone fort now appears much as it did in the 1850s. It was first garrisoned during the War of 1812 and was used during the Civil War for the defense of Savannah. The fort is now administered by the Coastal Heritage Society, and on display are objects relating to the military history of the area. NR. Open summer, daily 9-5; winter, Tu-Su 10-5. $1.50 adults, 75¢ students, retired persons, and military personnel. (912) 232-3945. ★

FORT PULASKI, 17 miles E. of Savannah, Cockspur Island, 1829-47. After the War of 1812, Fort Pulaski, named for the

Fort Pulaski

Polish hero of the Revolution, was built by the Federal government. It was not actively used until the Civil War when Confederate troops seized the fort in 1861. Over a year later Federal soldiers began their bombardment of the brick masonry fortification and were victorious. The National Park Service now maintains the fort and has reconstructed or restored some of the key sections, incuding the brick walk around the fort. The **Visitor Center** is where one begins a tour of the important military complex. NR. Open July-Sept 2, daily 8:30-6:45; Sept 3-June, daily 8:30-5:30. $1 per car. (912) 786-5787. 🚶 ★

WORMSLOE PLANTATION, 7 miles SE of Savannah on Skidaway Rd., 18th-20th centuries. From 1756 until 1974 the plantation granted to the Noble Jones family by royal charter was passed down from generation to generation. Much of the land was presented in 1975 to the Georgia Heritage Trust. The complex includes a small museum and the ruins of the original fortified "tabby" house—built of crushed shell, lime, and sand by Jones. Earthworks thrown up by Confederate troops who unsuccessfully attempted to hold off Union seizure of the estate are visible. The setting is very beautiful and has been landscaped over the years in an impressive manner. NR. Open Tu-Sa 9-5, Su 2-5:30. Free. (912) 352-2548.

Springfield vicinity

EBENEZER TOWNSITE AND JERUSALEM LUTHERAN CHURCH, E. of Springfield on GA 275 at Savannah River, 1736. German Protestant settlers from the territory comprising the Archbishopric of Salzburg were among the first immigrants to the Georgia colony. The Salzburgers first settled NW of Savannah; today only their church and cemetery remain. **Jerusalem Church** (1767-69) is a lovely brick meeting house and is the only remaining 18th-century public building in Georgia. The Georgia Salzburger Society administers a small museum on the site where there are exhibits on old and new Ebenezer. NR. Open Su 3-5. Call (912) 355-1825 for information.

Waycross vicinity

OKEFENOKEE HERITAGE CENTER, 2 miles W. of Waycross on US 82. All roads and rail lines in southeast Georgia seem to come together at Waycross, a town just north of the **Okefenokee Swamp and National Wildlife Refuge and Wilderness Area.** Transportation history and the story of the development of the region's rich natural resources are told at the center. On display is a 1912 train with a steam engine and tender, two baggage cars, a postal car, passenger car, and caboose. Open M-F 9-5, Sa-Su 2-4. $1 adults, 50¢ children. (912) 285-4260.

Southwest Georgia

Reporters no longer crowd the cafes and motels of Americus seeking out a story in nearby Plains. Brother Billy's gas station has been sold, and except for the Secret Service contingent that watches over the welfare of the former First Family, nothing out of the ordinary seems to be occuring in Plains. Peace and quiet have settled over the town, making it all the better for a visit. With the spotlight off Plains, it is also possible to see that there are other places within the region worthy of the traveler seeking a respite from turnpike driving and eight-lane food—towns like Columbus and Thomasville, where there is a gracious mix of ante-bellum charm and Victorian elegance. Then, too, there are other small towns like Plains—towns like Lumpkin and Tifton, where the rich agricultural history of the region is still celebrated.

Albany

THRONATEESKA HERITAGE FOUN-

DATION, 100 Roosevelt Ave., 1910. Albany's history and science organization is housed in a former train depot. The McIntosh Indian collection of arrowheads and other artifacts is on display along with costumes and pioneer tools. The organization also maintains the **Smith House** (1860), Albany's first brick residence; the **Jarrard House** (1840); and the **Hilman kitchen** (1850). Museum open Tu-F 9-5, Sa 2-5. Free. For information regarding the museum and the properties, contact the foundation at (912) 432-6955.

Andersonville and vicinity

ANDERSONVILLE OLD-TIME FARM AREA/MUSEUM AND WELCOME CENTER (Confederate Village), GA 49. The 300 residents of Andersonville began restoring their historic village in 1973. The main attraction is the **pioneer farm complex**, which includes a log cabin, barn, farm animals, sugar cane mill, and country store. A turn-of-the-century depot houses the **historical museum** and **visitors center.** Civil War artifacts and local historical materials are on display. Open daily 9-5. (912) 924-2558. ✔

ANDERSONVILLE NATIONAL HISTORIC SITE, 1 mile E. of Andersonville on GA 49, 1864-65. The site of the infamous Civil War prison, where nearly 13,000 Northern soliders died, includes the site of the stockade, the fortifications surrounding it, and the right-of-way to the Andersonville railroad station. Nearby is the **Andersonville National Cemetery,** the cemetery sexton's residence (1872), and the chapel (1908). Andersonville was chosen as the location of the prison because of its convenience along a railroad supply line, but too many prisoners (at one time, 33,000) were crowded into the stockade, where too little food and clothing reached them. At the **Visitor Center** one can learn more about this tragic landmark and similar, but less dramatic, sites in other Civil War-torn states, North and South. The 201-acre site is maintained by the National Park Service. NR. Open

June-Aug, daily 8-7; Sept-May, daily 8-5. (912) 924-0343. ★

Columbus

Once known as the "Lowell of the South" because of its giant textile mills, Columbus has emerged in the late 20th century as a major New South industrial and commercial center. It has not entirely lost its 19th-century character, however. Columbus is still a city of tree-lined streets, pleasant parks, and a multitude of fountains, so many, in fact, that it has earned the title of Fountain City. Situated along the Chattahoochee River, the city has since its founding in 1828 been in a superb position to ship its manufactured goods south via the river to the Gulf of Mexico. The Chattahoochee Promenade along the historic waterfront ties together various local points of interest, including the **Ironworks,** 801 Front Ave. The old industrial complex, organized in 1853, has been skillfully transformed into a convention and trade center.

CONFEDERATE NAVAL MUSEUM, 202 4th St. The most impressive remains on view at the museum are two Confederate gunboats, the CSS *Muscogee,* and ironclad ram designed for coastal defense, and the CSS *Chattahoochee,* a three-masted sailing veseel. They were sunk in the river during a Federal raid on Columbus in April 1865, and parts were recovered nearly 100 years later. Other exhibits pertain to the Confederate Navy and Marine Corps. NR. Open Tu-Sa 10-5, Su 2-5. Free. (404) 327-9798. ✔ ★

PEMBERTON HOUSE, 11 7th St., 19th century. This was the home of Dr. John Styth Pemberton from 1855 to 1860, when he developed the first Coca-Cola formula. A pharmacist, he formulated many of his patent medicines in the kitchen of an outbuilding adjoining the simple clapboard cottage. Pemberton House is one of several properties maintained by the Historic Columbus Foundation. NR. Open M-F 9:30-4:30. The building is part of the official two-hour **Heritage Tour** which leaves from the **Georgia Welcome Center,** Victory Dr. at the junction of US 27 and 280. (404) 577-7455. $5 adults, $2.50 servicemen and students 6-12, free for children under 6. Individual tours can also be arranged by contacting the Historic Columbus Foundation, 700 Broadway, 31906, (404) 322-0756.

Other buildings included on the tour are **Rankin House** (c. 1860), 1440 2nd Ave., a Greek Revival mansion designed by Lawrence Wimberly Wall for James A. Rankin, a wealthy planter; **Illges** (c. 1850), 1428 2nd Ave., a stuccoed brick Greek Revival house with a monumental Corinthian portico (the house was bought by Abraham Illges in 1877, and he engaged an Italian artist to fresco the ceilings of the first-floor rooms with designs of angels and cupids); and the **Walker-Peters-Langdon House** (1828), 716 Broadway, a Federal cottage that may be the oldest house in town and which is now restored and furnished with period antiques. All NR.

SPRINGER OPERA HOUSE, 105 10th St., 1871. Nearly every important name in the American theater of the past 100 years has appeared at the Springer. The three-story brick building was restored in the 1960s and is a delight to visit. In addition to the orchestra level, there are two balconies and three tiers of boxes. The opera house is included in the Heritage Tour and is open for performances Sept-May. (404) 324-1100.

Columbus vicinity

NATIONAL INFANTRY MUSEUM, U.S. Army Infantry Center, Fort Benning. The fort was established in October, 1918, to meet the need of trained replacements for the American Expeditionary Force in Europe. Since that time, Fort Benning has only grown larger. The collection of firearms in this military museum is extensive. There are also Indian and early military artifacts on display and an excellent photographic archives. Open Tu-F 10-4:30, Sa-Su 12:30-4:30. Free. (404) 544-4762. ★

Irwinville vicinity

JEFFERSON DAVIS MEMORIAL

PARK, approximately 1½ miles N. of Irwinville, 1865. The place where the President of the Confederacy was captured by Union troops on May 10, 1865 is now administered as a 12-acre park by Irwin County. A month after General Lee surrendered at Appomattox, Davis, his wife, Postmaster-General John Reagan, and a small contingent of soldiers were attempting to escape across south-central Georgia. Two Union regiments closed in on the party. The present tract of land includes woods and swamps and is the site of a museum, caretaker's house, and small pavilion. NR. Open daily 9-5. (912) 831-2335. ★

Lumpkin and vicinity

BEDINGFIELD INN, Cotton St., c. 1838. The Stewart County Historical Commission has restored and furnished this crossroad inn. It was built for Brian N. Bedingfield, a doctor and merchant, and was a popular stagecoach stop between Columbus and Fort Gaines. Also on the site are a detached kitchen, a log house, and a period garden. NR. Open during the summer, daily 1-5; other months, Sa-Su 1-5. $1 adults, 50¢ children. (912) 838-4945.

WESTVILLE HISTORIC HANDICRAFTS, ½ mile S. of Lumpkin County Rd. Buildings dating before the 1850s have been relocated in this living history village. It is a center for the practice and demonstration of old-time craft skills such as smithing, weaving, potting, quilt-making, and other domestic projects such as candle- and soap-making. There are over 25 commercial, residential, and agricultural buildings to tour. Open M-Sa 10-5, Su 1-5. $3 adults, $2 senior citizens and students, free for preschoolers. (912) 838-6310. ✔

Plains

Plains is a much quieter place now that Jimmy and Rosalynn Carter are back home. And it is a more pleasant place to visit than when reporters outnumbered townspeople. Plains is located along US 280, 8 miles W. of Americus. The home of the former president and that of his mother, Miss Lillian, are very private enclaves, but you can easily visit other sites on foot or take the **Carter Country Trolley Tour.** Information regarding tours of the Plains area can be secured from the Chamber of Commerce, 105 S. Dudley St., 31780, (912) 924-2646.

Thomasville and vicinity

LAPHAM-PATTERSON HOUSE, 626 N. Dawson St., c. 1884. A highly ornamental Queen Anne residence, the Lapham-Patterson House is now owned by the state and open for tours. It was built by Chicago merchant Charles W. Lapham as a resort home. This is but one of many homes built by wealthy Northerners who

began coming to Thomasville in the late 19th century. NR. Open Tu-Sa 9-5, Su 2-5:30. Free. (912) 226-0425.

Other Thomasville homes are included in a two-hour **Plantation Tour** which leaves from the Chamber of Commerce office, 401 S. Broad St., M-Sa. Among the properties are **Greenwood Plantation** (1826), **Boxhall Plantation,** and **Millpond Plantation** (c. 1905). For further information, contact the Chamber at Box 560, Thomasville 31702, or call (912) 226-9600.

Tifton

GEORGIA AGRIRAMA—THE STATE MUSEUM OF AGRICULTURE, I-75 exit 20 at 8th St. Over 25 historic buildings have been carefully restored to the period of the late 1800s, including a typical farmhouse, log cabin, gristmill, printing office, railroad depot, doctor's office, church, commissary, and other interesting shops. Very much a part of the scene are mules and milk cows, pigs and chickens. You can visit a smokehouse where ham and bacon are being cured, watch a demonstration of a steam-powered cotton gin, and observe the workings of a turpentine distillery. Open winter months, M-Sa 9-5, Su 12:30-5; summer months, daily 9-6. $2.50 adults, $1 children 6-11, free for children under 5. (912) 386-3344.

Central Georgia

The heart of Georgia is the most Southern and traditional of the state's regions. Here there is no stigma to "living in the past." The Colonial Revival style of architecture which so swept other areas of the country had little or no impact here. Residents of Macon, Milledgeville, Augusta, and Athens just kept building in the antebellum Greek Revival style, even to the point of adding a columned portico to a bungalow. Atlanta is the exception, and has been since its founding as a transportation center and the state capital in the mid-1800s. Yet even here, amid the glittering glass skyscrapers, there is an emphasis

on the romantic past. Throughout the area, the attention given to such small but significant aspects of a cultivated life—furnishings, gardens, stylish homes, and public buildings—can be seen in numerous private and public homes which are opened with pride to visitors.

Athens

Founded in 1801 as the home of the University of Georgia (originally named Franklin College), Athens remains a cultivated, patrician town. Now, as in the past, Athens attracts an unusually high number of visitors to its campus, antebellum homes, and public buildings. Industry thrived here in the 19th century—textile mills, machine shops, agricultural products. One of the old textile mills from the 1850s, at Baldwin and William Sts., has been converted into a commercial complex of shops, a restaurant, and tavern. It is indicative of the imaginative approach taken to historic preservation in the city.

CHURCH-WADDEL-BRUMBY HOUSE, 280 E. Dougherty St., 1820. Now the **Athens Welcome Center,** the clapboard frame Federal residence is believed to be the oldest house in town. It was built for Alonzo Church, later president of the university, and within the year was sold to the Rev. Moses Waddel, university president 1820-29. After 1839 it became the property of Mrs. Stephen Harris whose descendants were the Brumby family. **"Athens of Old" tours** begin here, and information on fifty local historic sites is available. NR. Open M-Sa 9-5, Su 2-5. (404) 546-1805.

GARDEN CLUB OF GEORGIA MUSEUM-HEADQUARTERS HOUSE (Founder's Memorial Garden), 325 S. Lumpkin St., 1857. Built on the university campus as a home for professors, Headquarters House has been used for many purposes. The Ladies Garden Club of Athens was founded here in 1891, the first in America, and the 2½-acre garden is maintained by the university and the organization. The two-story brick house is furnished throughout with 18th- and 19th-century antiques. NR. Open M-F 9-12 and 1-4. (404) 542-3631.

OLD NORTH CAMPUS, UNIVERSITY OF GEORGIA, bounded by Broad, Lumpkin, and Jackson Sts., 19th century. Entry to this oldest part of the state university campus is through **The Arch** (1858), an iron archway cast at the Athens Foundry. The buildings are arranged around two quadrangles and include a variety of different 19th-century styles. The most venerable of the structures is the **Old College** (1801-1805), a three-story brick building with granite trim. Other especially handsome buildings are the Greek Revival **Phi Kappa Hall** (1836); the **Chapel** (1832), with a six-column Doric portico;

Demosnian Hall (1824), a two-story stuccoed brick structure with a second-floor Palladian window; and the **Gov. Wilson Lumpkin House** (Rock House) (1842-44), a stone residence built for the former governor (1831-35) which has served as a dormitory, classroom building, and library. NR. Tours of the campus can be arranged at the Athens Welcome Center (Church-Waddel-Brumby House).

TAYLOR-GRADY HOUSE, 634 Prince Ave., 1839. The thirteen Doric columns which wrap around this Greek Revival residence are said to represent the thirteen original colonies. Gen. Robert Taylor, cotton merchant and planter, built the house as a summer residence. William S. Grady bought the building in 1863, and his son, Henry, rose to fame as the managing editor of the **Atlanta Constitution** in the 1880s. The Taylor-Grady House is owned by the city and leased by the Athens Junior Assembly which has seen to the building's restoration and period furnishings. NR. Open M, W, F 10-2, Su 2-5. (404) 549-8688.

Atlanta

Atlanta is now so identified with the New South of multinational corporations and sleek modernity that it may come as a surprise to some readers to learn that, yes, there is something of the past left to be enjoyed in town. A great deal of the old downtown has been leveled to make way for convention-goers and bankers, but even in this artificial civic showcase there is a residue of the blue denim, tobacco-chawing Atlanta of bygone days, of the bedraggled Scarlett trying to make do with a set of draperies for a ballgown. Atlanta was named in 1845 after a railroad, the Western and Atlantic, and prospered as a transportation center both before and after the Civil War. The forty-day siege of the city known as the Battle of Atlanta, from July to September, 1864, destroyed most of the city. Within a short time, however, rebuilding began, and in 1868, Atlanta became the state capital.

ATLANTA HISTORICAL SOCIETY, 3101 Andrews Dr., N.W. The historical complex maintained by the society is among the most ambitious and impressive in the country. The headquarters is located at **Walter McElreath Hall,** and here the society exhibits art and artifacts relating to the history of the Atlanta region. The society's collections are especially strong in memorabilia of *Gone With the Wind* author Margaret Mitchell, early 19th-century furniture and tools, and Civil War artifacts. The society's gallery is open Tu-Sa 10:30-4:30, Su 2-4:30.

Two museum houses are situated on the 25-acre historical society complex: the **Tullie Smith House** (c. 1835-40), and the **Swan House** (1928). No two properties could be quite so dissimilar. The Smith frame farmhouse was moved to this site with its detached kitchen from DeKalb County in 1969. It is one of the oldest houses in the Atlanta area. It was first the home of Robert H. Smith, a North Carolina native; Tullie Smith, his great-granddaughter lived here until 1967. Other antebellum log buildings—a barn, double corncrib, smokehouse, and slave cabin—stand nearby. Mr. and Mrs. Edward Inman had the Swan House designed by Philip T. Shutze and lived there until 1965. It is a residence of great elegance and reflects an eclectic love of European Neoclassicism. Like many great houses built during the 1920s, Swan House is a mixture of the refined and the flamboyant. The figure of the swan, an obvious symbolic favorite of the Inmans, is to be found incorporated in architectural decoration and furnishings. Both homes are NR. Open Tu-Sa 10:30-4:30, Su 2-4:30. $2 single admission, $3 for joint ticket. (404) 261-1837.

CYCLORAMA, Cherokee Ave., Grant Park, 1885-87. What better way to learn about the 1864 Battle of Atlanta? The Cyclorama has just been restored. It is an enormous painting, 50 feet in height and 400 feet in circumference, weighing 18,000 pounds. Ten German artists produced the rendering in the studios of the American Cyclorama Co. in Milwaukee, Wisconsin. It was first displayed in Detroit in 1887 and then was moved to other cities before being presented to the city of Atlanta in 1897. It is housed in its own granite and marble building. NR. Open daily 9-5. $3 adults, $1.50 for children 16 and under. (404) 658-7625. ✔ ★

FOX THEATER, 660 Peachtree St., NE, 1927. If time allows, catch a show, any show at the Fox so that you can tour one of America's most colorful movie palaces. It was built as a Shrine mosque but, under movie magnate William Fox, it prospered as popular theater. Moorish motifs are incorpated just about everywhere—from the exterior cream and red striped brick walls, towers, and minarets to the interior decorative ceiling effects and rhinestone curtains. The Fox is now ued as a concert hall and for plays and ballet. For information regarding programs, call (404) 881-1977.

GEORGIA STATE CAPITOL, Capitol Sq., 1889. Constructed of Georgia marble and Indiana limestone, the capitol is a Beaux Arts palace of monumental proportions. The building rises in tiers like a wed-

ding cake with a gold-leaf dome topping off the whole structure at 237 feet. The firm of Edbrooke and Burnham was responsible for the design. One can visit the **Hall of Fame** and the **Hall of Flags.** The **State Museum of Science and Industry** is housed on the 4th floor. The Senate and House chambers, each oak-paneled, are located in separate wings. NR. Open M-F 8-5. (404) 656-2846.

MARTIN LUTHER KING, JR., HISTORIC DISTRICT, bounded roughly by Irwin, Randolph, Edgewood, Jackson, and Auburn Aves., 19th-20th centuries. The area in which the famous civil rights leader was born and often preached during his ministry can be toured, beginning at **Ebenezer Baptist Church,** 413 Auburn Ave. Adjoining the building is the gravesite. King's **childhood home,** 501 Auburn Ave., is a two-story frame Queen Anne building. NR. The home is open M-F 9:30-5:30, Sa-Su 9:30-4. $1 adults, 50¢ senior citizens and students 6-12, free for children under 6. The church is open M-Sa 11-4:30. Donation requested. (404) 524-1956.

UNDERGROUND ATLANTA, 84 Old Pryor St., SW, late 19th-20th centuries. Atlanta's old railroad district, first formed in the mid-1800s around the east-west line of the Western and Atlantic Railroad, has been buried over the years under viaducts crisscrossing in almost every direction. The two-block area which once contained the city's major hotels and commercial warehouses has been reclaimed since 1968 in a major restoration effort. Many of the brick buildings have cast-iron columns and other forms of decoration. Underground Atlanta is basically an entertainment center of specialty shops, restaurants, and nightclubs with late-Victorian period appearance. NR. The establishments are generally open daily noon to midnight. ✔

WREN'S NEST (Joel Chandler Harris House), 1050 Gordon St., SW, 1881-1908. Children everywhere love Harris's "Uncle Remus" characters and stories. Their parents are likely to remember Walt Disney's *Song of the South,* the 1946 movie based on the Uncle Remus tales and

the film's theme song, "Zip-a-Dee-Doo-Dah." Harris was obviously fond of birds as his frame home was named for a wren who settled down to raise a family in his mail box; the gentle writer would not disturb the animal and simply erected another box for the postman. The house, with a fanciful veranda across the front and one side, is maintained as a museum and contains many original objects associated with the writer. NR. Open M-Sa 9:30-5, Su 1:30-4:30. (404) 753-8535. ✔

Augusta

Augusta is one of the most pleasant of Georgia's cities. Superbly situated along the Savannah River in the lower Piedmont, it was settled first as a trading post and fort in 1735 and named for Princess Augusta, mother of George III of England. Tradition is taken seriously in Augusta, and since the colonial period considerable attention has been given to the outward symbols of propriety and culture in the city's homes, churches, and public buildings. There are so many landmarks in the Augusta area, in fact, that several days may be required to fully appreciate them. **Augusta Heritage Trust** and **Historic Augusta** are the two leading preservation organizations in the city and are housed in the **First Christian Church parsonage** (1876), 629 Greene St. The Trust will provide information on walking tours of the old downtown as well as the nearby Summerville area. Open M-F 9-4:30. (404) 733-6768.

AUGUSTA-RICHMOND COUNTY MUSEUM, 540 Telfair St. 1802. The museum building served originally as the Academy of Richmond County, the oldest educational institution in the state and founded in the 1790s. A fine collection of early American objects, costumes, and military items is located here. The style of the stuccoed brick building is Gothic Revival with exterior parapets and porches with Tudor arches. It is thought that these elements were executed in 1856-57 during renovations, and research is continuing into whether the building was originally Federal in style. NR. Open Tu-F 11-5, Sa 1-5, Su 2-5. Free. (404) 722-8454.

Administered by the museum is the nearby **Brahe House** (1846), 456 Telfair St. It is still a private residence, but the owner kindly opens her home by appointment. The frame Greek Revival cottage was built by Frederick Adolphus Brahe, a silversmith. NR. Contact the museum for information regarding tours.

FIRST PRESBYTERIAN CHURCH, 7th and Telfair Sts., 1808. Robert Mills was the architect of this stuccoed brick church, which still has its original box pews. The building was considerably remodeled in 1892 to conform with the Romanesque Revival style. In 1861, during the pastorate of the Rev. R. W. Wilson, father of Woodrow Wilson, the Presbyterian Church in the U.S. (Southern Presbyterian) was organized here. Open for regular services. (404) 724-1864.

The **manse**, where Woodrow Wilson lived from 1858-70, is located at 419 7th St. and was built c. 1840. It is a substantial two-story brick building with a rear two-story kitchen and servant's wing. Private, but may be viewed easily from the street. NR.

EZEKIEL HARRIS HOUSE (Mackay House), 1822 Broad St., c. 1797. The home of tobacco merchant Harris was restored in the 1960s as a house museum with relics from the Revolution included in the furnishings. A Revolutionary War battle was fought on the grounds in September 1780, in which the American forces were defeated. NR. The museum is open by appointment through the Augusta Heritage Trust. Free. (404) 733-6768.

GERTRUDE HERBERT MEMORIAL INSTITUTE OF ART, 506 Telfair St., 1818. The Nicholas Ware House or Ware's Folly, so-named because the owner — mayor of Augusta and a U.S. senator — lavished $40,000 on it, now serves as Augusta's art museum. The two-story frame house was built over a high brick basement. Most unusual is the three-story bowed entrance portico with twin sets of steps leading up each side. Equally dramatic are such interior elements as an elliptical flying stairway, ornamental woodwork, and ornate fanlights. NR. Open Tu-F 10-12 and 1-4, Sa 4-6. (404) 722-5495.

MEADOW GARDEN, 1230 Nelson St., 1791. George Walton, one of Georgia's signers of the Declaration of Independence, lived in the older part of this house. The first section (SW) was attached to an early 19th-century building c. 1900. Both have been expertly restored and furnished by the DAR. Walton family antiques are on display along with other period furnishings. NR. Open M-F 10-4. (404) 724-4174.

SUMMERVILLE HISTORIC DISTRICT, W. of downtown Augusta along and off Walton Way, 19th-20th centuries. The name of the district was adopted because early Augustans came here to spend the summer in an attempt to escape the town's intermittent outbreaks of malaria. The first families to avail themselves of the cooler climes were the wealthy, and they built lovely Federal and Greek Revival 1½-story cottages. George Walton was one of the first (see Meadow Garden), and he sold off lots to others. Typical of the seasonal residences is the **Carnes cottage** (c. 1816), 914 Milledge Rd., visible from the road. Gradually larger homes were built and used as permanent residences. The **Artemas Gould House** (1856), 828 Milledge Rd., is a handsome example of the Italianate style with overhanging eaves, an octagonal cupola, and a hipped roof. It has recently been converted to a condominium. From 1890 through the 1920s, many lavish mansions were built throughout the area. Fruitlands, the Augusta National Golf Club, borders the district. NR.

Crawfordsville

LIBERTY HALL, Alexander H. Stephens Memorial Park, US 278, c. 1830. A two-story frame house was the home of Stephens, vice president of the Confederate States of America. Next door is the **Confederate Museum** where Civil War arms and memorabilia are on display. Stephen's grave is located on the property. NR. Open Tu-Sa 9-5, Su 2-5:30. Free. (404) 456-2221.

Juliette vicinity

JARRELL PLANTATION, 6 miles E. of East Juliette off Dames Ferry Rd., 19th-20th centuries. The state has wisely preserved this agricultural complex as a typical Middle Georgia farm. The original dwelling (1847), built by John Jarrell, is still standing along with many other structures dating from the 1890s through the 1930s, including a smokehouse, chicken house, two wheat houses, a barn, and blacksmith's and carpenter's shops. South of the house is a mill complex containing a gin house, sawmill, engine house, and a boiler used for caning sugar. NR. Open Tu-Sa 9-5, Su 2-5:30. (912) 986-5172. ↙

Kennesaw

BIG SHANTY MUSEUM, 2829 Cherokee St. Buster Keaton's 1926 film classic, *The General*, made the story of the Civil War locomotive chase world-famous. And at the museum, the eight-wheel American-type steam locomotive is given an honored place. A civilian, James J. Andrews, and nineten Northern soldiers kidnapped *The General* and three boxcars and chugged their way north toward the Union line. They hoped, of course, to cut off rail communication with Atlanta, a main Southern supply depot. The chase began in Kennesaw and the pursuit party consisted of three locomotives, a push car, and soldiers on foot. Finally, after a run of 87 miles, *The General* ran out of steam and was abandoned, and the plucky Northern raiders were captured. NR. Open daily 9:30-6. $1 adults, 50¢ children 10-16, free for children under 10. (404) 427-2117.

La Grange

BELLEVUE (Benjamin Harvey Hill House), 204 Ben Hill St., 1835-55. Hill, a noted orator, served in the state legislature and the U.S. Congress as representative and senator. His handsome Greek Revival frame mansion with fluted Ionic columns has been restored and furnished as a house museum. The rooms are immense, and the ornamental plaster cornices are widely admired for their beauty. La Grange is one of the most charming of small Georgia towns, and although only Bellevue is open on a regular basis, a drive through the old residential streets such as Broad and Vernon can be very rewarding. La Grange was named after the French estate of the Marquis de Lafayette soon after he made his triumphal 1824 American tour. NR. Bellevue is open during the winter, Tu-Sa 10-12 and 2-5; summer, Tu-Sa 10-12 and 2-6, Su 2-6. (404) 884-1832.

Macon and vicinity

Macon lies at the very center of Georgia on each side of the Ocmulgee River. It became a prosperous manufacturing and transportation center within 20 years of its founding in 1818. The town was named for Nathaniel Macon, a North Carolina Revolutionary War hero and later a U.S. congressman and senator. During the Civil War it was an important Confederate supply center, and gold for the Southern cause was stored in the Hay House, one of several residential museums that can be toured. The **Middle Georgia Historical Society,** located in the Sidney Lanier Cottage, 935 High St., sponsors 2½-hour tours of historic Macon, Tu-Sa 10:30 and Su 2. $6.50 adults, $3 children under 12. For further information contact the society at the above address, Macon 31201, or at (912) 743-3851.

FORT BENJAMIN HAWKINS, US 80 E. (Emery Hwy). The blockhouse of the fort established in the Macon area in 1806 by the federal government has been reconstructed on its original site. The reproduction is based on careful archaeological investigations. Benjamin Hawkins was a North Carolina planter, Indian agent, and U.S. senator who negotiated important treaties with the Indians. NR. Open Apr-Oct, Su 2-6; other times by appointment. Admission, 25¢ for adults, and students, free for preschoolers. (912) 742-2627.

THE HAY HOUSE (Johnston-Hay House), 934 Georgia Ave., 1855-60. Splendiferous seems the only word appropriate for the 24-room Italiante mansion built for jeweler William B. Johnston and designed by the New York City firm of T. Thomas and Sons. You know from the exterior that this is one of America's great homes. A sweeping flight of marble steps leads to an open balustraded porch which extends across the front; atop the low hip roof, set off by scroll-type brackets, is a bulbous octagonal cupola. Nothing, however, quite prepares you for entering the magnificent marble-floored central hall with its open-well three-flight stairway. On one landing appears to be a niche; it is actually a cleverly camouflaged door leading to a secret chamber. Legend has it that over $3 million worth of Confederate gold was stored here during the Civil War. The architectural interior appointments are splendid to behold as are the furnishings brought from throughout the world. The house is adminstered by the Georgia Trust for Historic Preservation. NR. Open Tu-Sa 10:30-4:30, Su 2-4. $3 adults, $1.50 students, $1 children 1-12. (912) 742-8155.

SIDNEY LANIER COTTAGE, 935 High St., c. 1840. The birthplace of Georgia's greatest poet is well maintained by the Middle Georgia Historical Society. His poetic career began only in the last years of his life, brought to a tragic end at age 39. Material about Lanier is displayed along with furnishings appropriate to the period of his life, 1841-81. The building, originally Gothic Revival in style, has been remodeled twice. NR. Open M-F 9-5. $1 adults and students, free for children under 5. (912) 743-3851.

OLD CANNONBALL HOUSE, 856 Mulberry St., 1853. Nearly every Atlantic coast state has a "cannonball" house, a building that was pierced with some sort of projectile in either the Revolutionary or Civil War. Georgia is no exception. The United Daughters of the Confederacy guard the ball which landed in the front hallway during the Battle of Dunlap Hill in July, 1864. The building is a handsome Greek Revival residence with a striking two-story Ionic portico. The home was built for Judge Asa Hall. NR. Open Tu-F 10:30-1 and 2:30-5, Sa-Su 1-4. (912) 743-8407.

OCMULGEE NATIONAL MONU-
MENT, 1207 Emery Hwy., 1250-1821.
The National Park Service administers one
of the most important prehistoric sites in
the Eastern United States, probably first
settled by the Swift Creek Indians, and, in
1690, by the ancestors of the present-day
Creek Indian tribe. The burial mounds of
the early Creeks are preserved exactly as
they were found. The Park Service has reconstructed the ceremonial **Earthlodge,**
and the floor of the council chamber
within dates to the 11th century. The
visitor will find the story of the development of the Ocmulgee site well chronicled
at the **Visitor Center** museum; tours of the
Earthlodge leave from here. NR. Open
daily 9-5. Free. (912) 742-0447.

Madison

MADISON HISTORIC DISTRICT,
roughly bounded on both sides by US 129-
441 and US 278 at GA 83, 19th century.
Madison, deep in the heart of Dixie, revels
in the past and has nearly thrity-five landmarks to enjoy. Many of its period homes
are located along Dixie Ave. Three of the
best are the **Nathan Bennett House** (1850),
Bonar Hall (1832, 1880), and **Thurleston**
(1818, 1848). General Sherman's Federal
troops occupied the city in 1864, and he
was argued out of setting fire to it. Most of
the ante-bellum homes are private, but can
be toured during **Tours of Homes** events in
May and December each year. For information regarding the tours, contact the
Morgan County Historical Society, 277 S.
Main, Madison 30650, (404) 342-4743.

Marietta vicinity

KENNESAW MOUNTAIN NATIONAL
BATTLEFIELD PARK, Jct. Stilesboro
Rd. and Old US 41, 2 miles N. of Mariet-
ta, 11864. The battle fought between
Union forces led by General William T.
Sherman and Confederate troops under
the command of Joseph E. Johnston in
June, 1864, was decisive in preparing the
siege and fall of Atlanta. The Southern army of 50,000 men was victorious against
nearly double that many Northern
soldiers, but Confederates were forced to
abandon their Kennesaw Mountain

stronghold. A tour map is available at the
Visitor Center. The 15-minute slide program and exhibits at the center provide a
useful orientation to the rugged site. There
are also exhibits and interpretive markers
placed in significant locations. **Kolb Farm,**
an 1836 farmhouse, is where the fighting
first broke out and is in a separate section
of the park along GA 120; signs point the
way. NR. Open Labor Day-May, daily
8:30-5; June-Labor Day, daily 8:30-7.
(404) 427-4686. ★

Milledgeville

MILLEDGEVILLE HISTORIC DIS-
TRICT, bounded by Irwin, Thomas, and
Warren Sts., and Fishing Creek, 19th century. Milledgeville served as capital of the
state from 1806 to 1867, having been laid
out in 1803 for this purpose. The original
Gothic Revival **statehouse** (1807) was
damaged by fire in 1941, but a reconstruction is in place at 201 E. Greene St. It is
now part of Georgia Military College, and
contains a small museum. The **Old Governor's Mansion** (1838), 120 S. Clark St.,
was home for ten Georgia governors. A
classic stuccoed brick Greek Revival
building, it was restored in 1967 and is
open as a museum with period rooms Tu-
Sa 9-5, Su 2-5. (912) 453-4545.

Oxford

OXFORD HISTORIC DISTRICT, Oxford College of Emory University and the
residential district centered around Wesley
St., mid-late 19th century. If you've had it
with ultra-modern Atlanta, escape to rural
Newton County and the village of Oxford,
where there is a wonderful mix of Federal,
Greek Revival, and later Victorian-period
buildings. **Old Emory Church,** (1841) W.
side of Wesley St. between W. Clarke and
W. Soule Sts., is one of the important landmarks, It is a handsome Greek Revival
clapboard building and is arranged inside
with a gallery on three sides. Two buildings on the Emory-at-Oxford campus (the
main seat of the university now being
located in Atlanta) are delightful Greek
Revival temples: the **Few Literary Society
Hall** (1852) and the **Phi Gamma Literary
Society Hall** (1852). NR. Private, but may
be viewed easily from the street.

Roswell

ROSWELL HISTORIC DISTRICT, 1837-20th century. Roswell is an extraordinary town. Founded by Roswell King as a model community, it has somehow survived in relatively good shape in the 1980s. King and his son, Barrington, invited only their cultivated friends to settle along the beautiful lands near the Chattahoochee River. Most of the homes are still private, but one, **Bulloch Hall** (c. 1840), 180 Bulloch Ave., is open as a museum. It was designed by Willis Ball for Maj. James Stephens Bulloch and patterned after the Parthenon. It has been lovingly maintained in its original form. The father of President Theodore Roosevelt, Theodore, Sr., married Maj. Bulloch's daughter, Martha, in the house. It is open W 10-4 and at other times by appointment. Other Greek Revival homes, still private but visible from the street, are **Barrington Hall** (1839-42), the residence of Barrington King and also designed by Ball; **Mimosa Hall** (1847), 123 Bulloch Ave., a third Ball design; and **Lewis House** (Holly Hill) (1840-45), 632 Mimosa Blvd., built by Barrington King for Robert A. Lewis, a Savannah cotton broker. NR.

STONE MOUNTAIN PARK, 16 miles E. of Atlanta on US 78. The ante-bellum complex of buildings in the 3,200-acre park comprise the most "historical" of the attractions to be seen here. Nineteen buildings of various types were moved here to form what is called a plantation. The history of each building is documented and, unlike some other collections of transplanted buildings, there has been no attempt to "dress" them alike in the same colors and materials. Among the noteworthy buildings to be visited are the **"Overseer's House"** (c. 1845) from Allen Plantation, near Kingston; the **"Big House"** (1840s), moved here from Dickey; and the **Thornton House** (c. 1790). All of the buildings are well furnished with appropriate period pieces. The Plantation is open during the summer months, daily 10-9; winter, daily 10-5:30. $2 adults, $1 children. (404) 469-9831.

Warm Springs

WARM SPRINGS HISTORIC DISTRICT, S. of GA 194 and W. of GA 85W, 19th-20th centuries. The state now administers the site of President Franklin D. Roosevelt's cottage, the **Little White House,** and the complex of other buildings in the health resort. Roosevelt began coming to Warm Springs in 1924 and found that the waters were especially therapeutic in treating the paralysis caused by polio. Two years later he bought up 1,200 acres, including the grounds of the spa, and the Warm Springs Foundation was established. Roosevelt's Little White House was built in 1932 and today is furnished exactly as it was on April 12, 1945, the day on which he died in the cottage. Since that time a museum, formerly a summer residence (c. 1900), has been opened, and here a 12-minute documentary film, "A Warm Springs Memoir of Franklin D. Roosevelt" is shown to visitors. Other buildings which may be toured are the **Guest House** (1833), and the **servant's**

Little White House

quarters. NR, NHL. Open Sept-May, daily 9-5; June-Aug, 9-6. $3 adults, $1.50 children 6-12, free for children under 6. (404) 655-3511.

Washington and vicinity

THE CALLAWAY PLANTATION, 5 miles W. of Washington on US 78, 18th-19th centuries. The centerpiece of the Callaway family farm is a two-story brick Greek Revival mansion. The plantation was held by descendants of John Callaway, granted the land in 1785, until being donated to the town of Washington in 1963. The main house, built c. 1869, is furnished with a varied collection of antique pieces. Visitors can also view the much simpler Parker Callaway frame homestead (c. 1817); a hewn log kitchen which may have served as the first home (c. 1785); and various outbuildings. NR. Open Apr 15-Oct 15, M-Sa 10-5, Su 2-5. Free. (404) 678-7060.

ROBERT TOOMBS HOUSE, 216 E. Robert Toombs Ave., c. 1797, c. 1819, c. 1837. Toombs served as a U.S congressman and senator before the Civil War, and, following a brief stint as secretary of state of the Confederacy, assumed the rank of general in the Confederate Army. His home, now a state historic site, was built in several stages, the last major change being the addition of a Greek Revival façade. NR. It is open by appointment only while restoration of the building is underway. Free. Contact (404) 678-2226 for further information.

WASHINGTON-WILKES HISTORICAL MUSEUM, 308 E. Robert Toombs Ave.,

c. 1835, 1857. The original frame house built by Albert Gallatin Semmes was greatly enlarged in the 1850s by a new owner, Samuel Barnett. The city of Washington acquired the property in the 1950s, and restoration of the house was undertaken by the Georgia Historical Commission. There are period rooms on the main floor—a double parlor, dining room, and bedroom—furnished in the style of the mid-1800s, and exhibits on the second floor, including many Civil War artifacts. NR. Open Tu-Sa 9-1 and 1:45-5, Su 2-5:30. (404) 678-2105.

Washington, the first town in the country to be named for the first President, has a number of outstanding ante-bellum residences which are open to the public on special occasions. Notable among the homes are the **Tupper-Barnett House** (c. 1832, 1860), 101 W. Robert Toombs Ave.; and the **Campbell-Jordan House** (c. 1808-1810, 1841), 208 Liberty St. A tour brochure, including these homes and thirty-eight others, is available from the **Chamber of Commerce,** located on the city square (P.O. Box 661, Washington 30673). It is open M-Tu, Th-F 8:30-12. (404) 678-2013.

Watkinsville

EAGLE TAVERN, US 441, c. 1820. The simple frame building was originally a four-room tavern and store. It was extensively restored by the state in the 1950s and now serves as a museum, visitor center, and chamber of commerce. The furnishings are appropriate for such a frontier inn. NR. Open M-F 9-5. (404) 769-5197.

North Georgia

North Georgia is the state's frontier country, a mountainous area of small villages, backwoods camps and farms, and national forests. The region shares with western North Carolina and eastern Tennessee what might be termed the "log cabin" tradition. While stills are unlikely to be encountered along the dirt roads, revenue

agents are not encouraged to vacation here. The style of living, despite rural electrification and modern educational facilities, is plain and still reflective of an earlier, individualistic America. Gold was discovered in the hills of Lumpkin County in the 1820s, and the rush for land spelled the end of Indian occupation throughout the region. Some of the most important historic sites are devoted to the telling of the story of these most individualistic first Americans, both before and after white settlement.

Calhoun vicinity

NEW ECHOTA, NE of Calhoun on GA 225, 1825-28. New Echota briefly served as the capital of the Cherokee nation. Only one building, that serving as the 1827 home of missionary Samuel Worcester, has survived. The state has been reconstructing the most important of the buildings, including the **Supreme Court Building** and **Print Shop**. The village is where Sequoyah developed his Cherokee alphabet, utilized in the publication of the only Indian newspaper in America, the *Cherokee Phoenix*. Moved to this site is the **Vann Tavern,** an early enterprise of the Vann family, among the most prosperous of the Cherokees. The discovery of gold in the north Georgia hills in 1828 sealed the fate of the Cherokee nation, and in the late 1830s the long trek west to Oklahoma began for the majority of the tribe. NR, NHL. Open Tu-Sa 9-5, Su 2-5:30. Guided tours, 9:30, 11, 1:30, 3. $1 adults, 50¢ children 12-17, free for children under 12. (404) 629-8151.

Cartersville vicinity

ETOWAH MOUNDS ARCHAEOLOGI-CAL AREA, 3 miles S. of Cartersville on GA 61, c. 1350. Several thousand Etowah Indians once lived in a fortified village along the Etowah River. Here they built log homes and earth mounds; three of the latter still exist. Archaeological investigation was begun by the Smithsonian Institution in the 1880s and has continued over the years by the Georgia Historical Commission. A museum on the site exhibits many of the valuable findings—sculptural figures, jewelry, pottery, implements. NR, NHL. Open Tu-Sa 9-5, Su 2-5:30. Free. (404) 382-2704.

Chatsworth vicinity

VANN HOUSE, US 76 and GA 225, 1805. Half-Cherokee James Clement Vann built this sophisticated Federal brick mansion and here entertained such dignitaries as President James Monroe and John C. Calhoun, secretary of war, in 1818. The house stood at the center of a great plantation worked by black slaves. The building is distinguished by a narrow two-story front portico and the fine architectural details of the main rooms. It is maintained as a state historic site, and is furnished with period and reproduction pieces. NR. Open during winter months, Tu-Sa 9-5, Su 2-5; in summer, a half-hour longer each day. Free. (404) 695-2598.

Chickamauga

CHICKAMAUGA-CHATTANOOGA NATIONAL MILITARY PARK, US 27, 1863. The mountainous terrain was unlikely ground for a major Civil War battle, but it was here that the Confederates gained their last significant victory. The park, the nation's oldest and largest military reserve, is situated in both Tennessee and Georgia, but the Battle of Chickamauga was fought entirely within Georgia on Sept. 18-20, 1863. Commanding the Southern troops was Gen. Braxton Bragg; in charge of the Northern forces was Gen. William S. Rosecrans. Rosecrans and half his army were forced to flee back to the safety of Chattanooga, and Gen. George H. Thomas assumed the difficult defense at Chickamauga. Casualties on both sides totaled more than 34,000 men, with about 4,000 fatalities. The Park Service has established a **Visitor Center** near the N. entrance to the battlefield. In addition to an instructive audio-visual presentation explaining the battle, there are exhibits and a display of some 355 military arms. A seven-mile auto tour through the park is recommended for visitors. This is covered in a brochure available at the center. NR. Open daily 8-5. Free. (404) 866-9241. ★

Dahlonega

DAHLONEGA COURTHOUSE GOLD MUSEUM, 1-A Public Sq., 1838. When

gold was discovered five miles S. of Dahlonega in Auraria in 1828, Lumpkin County quadrupled in population. A permanent county seat was needed and Dahlonega—the English equivalent of a Cherokee word meaning "precious yellow"—was established. The gold museum occupies what was the county courthouse and is a two-story brick building with a Tuscan portico. At one time a branch of the U.S. Mint was also situated in Dahlonega, but by 1861 it was closed down. Gold mining continued, but at a greatly reduced rate. The museum exhibits colorfully tell the story of the gold rush days. Open Tu-Sa 9-5, Su 2-5:30. Free. (404) 864-2257.

Rome and vicinity

CHIEFTAINS, 80 Chatillon Rd., c. 1792, c. 1837, 1923. Major Ridge, first name unknown, was an important leader of the Cherokees in the early 1800s. His two-story log home, now buried within a Georgian Revival structure, was the center of much economic and political activity. Seeing the future all too clearly, Ridge signed the Treaty of New Echota which called for the Indians to move west to new land in Oklahoma. Whether there was a real choice to be made or not, Ridge's decision was despised by the majority of the Cherokees. He and his son, John, were murdered by vengeful survivors of the Trail of Tears in Oklahoma in 1839. NR, NHL. Open Tu-F 11-4, Su 2-5. (404) 291-9494.

THE BERRY SCHOOLS, N. of Rome on US 27, 20th century. Martha Berry was born into a wealthy Rome area family and began working with uneducated, economically-deprived children and adults of the north Georgia mountains around the turn of the century. Her energy never flagged for forty years, and she attracted to her social causes such enthusiastic backers as Andrew Carnegie, Theodore Roosevelt, Woodrow Wilson, Henry Ford, and Eleanor Roosevelt. The Berry Schools—Berry College and Berry Academy—are the outgrowth of the pioneer institutions which provided an almost totally free education to many thousands of persons. NR. Two special buildings honor her dedication and achievements, **Oak Hill** (1847), the antebellum plantation home of the Berrys; and the **Martha Berry Museum** (1972), where there are exhibits and a visitor information and reception center for the Berry educational complex. Both buildings are located across from the campus on US 27 and are open M-Sa 10-5, Su 2-5. Free. (404) 234-4465.

Rossville

JOHN ROSS HOUSE, Lake Ave. and Spring St., c. 1830. Ross, a Cherokee chief, strongly opposed signing the Treaty of New Echota which led to the tragic trek to Oklahoma in the late 1830s. His two-story log home is furnished with Ross family possessions. It is only fitting that they should have been returned to Georgia. Despite his opposition to the move, Ross led his tribe west. There he was instrumental in creating a stronger Cherokee nation from the survivors. NR, NHL. Open June-Aug, daily 2-5; spring and fall months, Sa-Su 2-6. (404) 866-3748.

Toccoa vicinity

TRAVELER'S REST, 6 miles E. of Toccoa on US 123, late 18th-early 19th centuries. Known also as Jarrett Manor, Traveler's Rest started out as the home of Jesse Walton, a Revolutionary War soldier and Indian fighter. It was built as a fortress, and observation holes for spotting Indians can be seen in the gables. Devereaux Jarrett bought the property in the 1830s and expanded the main house, opening it up as an inn, trading post, and post office. It became a favorite stopping place for travelers between Charleston and Chattanooga. The state now administers the site and has undertaken the building's restoration. NR, NHL. Open Tu-Sa 9-5, Su 2-5:30. (404) 886-2256.

Historic Accommodations

An asterisk (*) indicates that meals are served.

Atlanta

ATLANTA BILTMORE HOTEL, 817 W. Peachtree St., 30308. (404) 881-9500. Open all year. The neo-Georgian red brick building is an Atlanta landmark and a classic reminder that hotels need not be wrapped in tinted glass to attract guests. The elegant, comfortable Biltmore, built in 1923-24, is a welcome exception to the sterile local hotel scene. NR.*

Augusta

TELFAIR INN, 349 Telfair St., 30901. (404) 724-3315. Open all year. Six renovated Victorian homes, dating from 1860-90, make up the inn complex. The buildings are located right in the middle of Augusta's historic district. NR.

Columbus

DE LOFFRE HOUSE, 812 Broadway, 31901. (404) 324-1144. Open all year. A frame Italianate mansion built in 1863 is a pleasant alternative to the usual type of accommodations found in southwest Georgia. The inn is conveniently located in the historic district of town. NR.

Cumberland Island

GREYFIELD INN, Drawer B, Fernandina Beach, FL 32034. (904) 356-9509. Open all year. The Greyfield is the last of the Carnegie family properties and was built in 1902. It is still privately held, and provides a unique vacation retreat. Special boat service is provided daily except Saturday from Fernandina Beach.

Savannah

BALLASTONE INN, 14 E. Oglethorpe Ave., 31401. (912) 236-1484. Open all year. A former private residence built c. 1835 and redesigned in the 1890s, the Ballastone is a gracious, well-furnished inn. Its garden courtyard is especially inviting. NR.

FOLEY HOUSE INN, 14 W. Hull St., 31401. (912) 232-6622. Located on Chippewa Sq., the inn is situated in a handsome brick town house dating from 1896. NR.

SHERATON SAVANNAH INN AND COUNTRY CLUB, 612 Wilmington Island Rd., 31404. (912) 897-1612. Open all year. Built in the early 1930s, this very handsome resort complex SE of the city on Wilmington Island recalls a more relaxed era than the present. Savannah's main historic attractions are only fifteen minutes away. *

ELIZA THOMPSON HOUSE, 5 W. Jones St., 31401. (912) 236-3620. Open all year. The 1847 town house is a pleasant place to stay when touring Savannah. The rooms are well furnished with period pieces, and a fountained courtyard is a perfect setting for a leisurely breakfast. NR.

JOHN WESLEY HOTEL, 29 Abercorn St., 31402. (912) 232-7121. Open all year. Opened as the Hotel Collins in 1913, the six-story Wesley is now the city's oldest. John Wesley preached the Gospel and lived on this site in the 1730s. The hotel is located on pleasant Reynolds Sq. NR.

Thomasville

SUSINA PLANTATION INN, Meridian Rd., 31792. (912) 377-9644. Open Aug. 15-June 15. Ante-bellum hospitality is available in abundance at the plantation house built by James J. Blackshear in 1841. In an area noted for its handsome porticoed homes, Susina Plantation is especially fine. The estate comprises some 115 acres of woods and fields. NR.

6. FLORIDA

PONCE de Leon discovered the tropical peninsula of Florida during the Feast of the Flowers (Pascua Florida) in 1513. Although he was not successful in his quest for the Fountain of Youth, he was soon followed by a series of Spanish conquistadors who believed that Florida would yield the same wealth of precious metals as the countries of Mexico and Peru to the south. The French soon developed an interest in the territory as well, as did the English, and it was 1821 before Florida was officially ceded to the United States.

Florida's long history has left her with a legacy of diverse and fascinating buildings and relics. St. Augustine, on Florida's East Coast, is America's oldest continuously-occupied European city. Founded by Mendez de Aviles in 1565, the city has retained a distinctly Spanish flavor.

Henry Morrison Flagler is largely responsible for turning Florida into the tourist attraction that it became in the late 19th and early 20th centuries and remains today. He extended the railroad from Jacksonville to Key West and built luxurious resort hotels at every east coast town that caught his fancy. He had a competitor on the west coast in Henry Plant, but Plant's projects were smaller in number, though the buildings were every bit as grand. Florida became a retreat for millionaires and celebrities at the turn of the century; in the state's Gilded Age of the '20s, the allure of warm blue waters, brilliant sunshine, and swaying palms attracted the middle classes as well.

Today Florida has the largest population of any of the southeastern states. Tourism, of course, is the state's largest industry, and though the beaches cover more than 8,400 miles of coastline, they are not the only attraction. The Mediterranean-style hotels constructed by Plant and Flagler, E. W. Merrick's Coral Gables, and even the later Art Deco buildings of Miami Beach are all historic precursors of modern-day fantasy towns like Orlando's Disney World.

For the traveler's convenience, Florida has been divided into four sections. South Florida includes the Keys, Miami, and Palm Beach, as well as the southern coastal regions—both Atlantic and Gulf—south of Lake Okeechobee. The Atlantic Coast covers much of the central peninsula and the eastern coast north of Lake Okeechobee. The Gulf Coast includes Tampa and St. Petersburg and stretches south to Sarasota and north to Dixie County. West Florida is the state's panhandle, where both the capital, Tallahassee, and the thriving port of Pensacola are located.

McAneeny-Howerdd House, Palm Beach

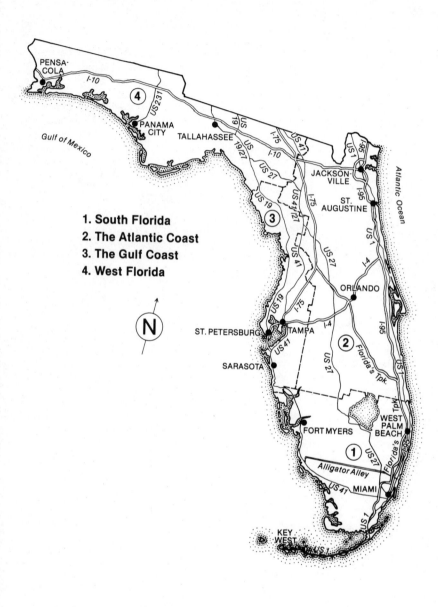

PENSA-
COLA

I-10

US 231

4

Panama
City

Gulf of Mexico

TALLAHASSEE

US 19

US 19/27

I-75

US 41

I-10

US 27

US 19

US 41/27

US 41

I-75

US 27

JACKSON-
VILLE

I-95

US 1

ST.
AUGUSTINE

US 1

I-4

Atlantic Ocean

1. South Florida
2. The Atlantic Coast
3. The Gulf Coast
4. West Florida

3

N

ORLANDO

US 19

I-75

I-4

I-95

ST. PETERSBURG

TAMPA

US 41

SARASOTA

I-4

2

US 27

Florida's Tpk.

FORT MYERS

WEST
PALM
BEACH

I-95

1

US 27

Florida's Tpk.

Alligator Alley

US 41

MIAMI

US 1

KEY
WEST

US 1

The first settlers of Florida's southernmost reaches were fishermen, fortune-hunters, and pirates, drawn to the area by the coral reefs which attracted plentiful sea life — and which also meant death for unwary sea captains who ventured too close. By the early 20th century, the names of South Florida's major cities — Miami, Palm Beach, Key West — immediately suggested wealth, opulence, and leisure; for the major resorts were designed and built for the very rich by the very rich. The exclusive preserves have all but vanished, however, as millions of Americans have discovered the temperate climate and have settled in for the winter, or, in retirement, have come to live here year-round.

Coral Gables

Coral Gables is a fantasy city, the product of one man's dream. In 1911, George Merrick began to enlarge a plantation begun by his father in 1898; within ten years he had amassed nearly 2,000 acres and planned a new city surrounded by massive walls with elaborately-designed gates, the whole reminiscent of an ancient Spanish town. With the help of a team of architects whom he sent to the Mediterranean for inspiration, Merrick had the town laid out and was selling lots by November of 1921. Today Coral Gables is one of Greater Miami's ritziest municipalities. One of the four grand gateways into the walled city is **Douglas Entrance** (La Puerta del Sol), at the junction of Douglas Rd. and 8th St. SW. Built in 1925, the stone and stucco gate sports a forty-foot curved archway and a ninety-foot belfried tower. Surrounded by shaded terraces, ornamented balconies, winding stairs, and cloistered walls, the gateway area contains numerous small businesses and shops. NR.

CORAL GABLES CITY HALL, 405 Biltmore Way, 1927. Stop here for a map of the city, which will outline a walking tour; signs around town will also help you find your way. And for the ambitious, a 20-mile marked bicycle tour starts at Cartagena Plaza. The city hall is a limestone and stucco three-story building designed by two of Merrick's leading architects, Phineas Paist and Denman Fink. NR. Open during business hours. Free. (305) 442-6445.

CORAL GABLES CONGREGATIONAL CHURCH, 3010 De Soto Blvd., 1924-5. The first church completed in the new city, Coral Gables Congregational is a masonry and stucco building with a heavily-sculptured main entrance (facing Malaga Blvd.). The original furnishings are still in place, as are the iron lighting fixtures Merrick purchased in Spain and donated to the church. NR. (305) 448-7421.

VENETIAN POOL AND CASINO, 2701 De Soto Blvd., 1924. "The world's most beautiful swimming hole" was transformed from the quarry where coral for the city's buildings was obtained. Fink and Paist designed the pool to resemble a Venetian lagoon, with arcades, loggias, patios, and fountains surrounding it. NR. Open June-Aug, M-F 10:30-7:45, Sa, Su 10-4:45; Sept-May, daily 10-4:45. $1.30 adults, 50¢ children 2-12. (305) 442-6483. ✓

Fort Lauderdale

DISCOVERY CENTER, 231 SW 2nd Ave. Antique household furnishings, looms, cording and spinning equipment, and a variety of natural science exhibits are on display here; the complex includes two early Florida buildings, the **New River Inn** (1905) and the **King Cromartie House** (1907). Open Tu-Su 10-5. $1 admission. (305) 462-4115.

GOLD COAST RAILROAD, 3389 SW 9th Ave. A four-mile train ride will delight the kids; there's an old passenger car full of railroad mementoes; and best of all, the *Ferdinand Magellan* (1928), the luxuriously-appointed bullet-proof, private Pullman car used by Presidents

Franklin Roosevelt, Truman, and Eisenhower until the first Air Force One replaced it. NR. Open Su 1-5. $3 adults, $1.50 children 3-12. (305) 524-5339. ✔

Fort Myers and vicinity

EDISON WINTER HOME AND MUSEUM, 2350 McGregor Blvd., c. 1884. Thomas Alva Edison and his wife spent nearly fifty winters in this prefabricated house, which was built in Maine and shipped to Florida by boat. An adjacent museum exhibits many of Edison's inventions, along with some of the family's personal belongings. Open M-Sa 9-4, Su 12:30-4. $2.50 adults, $1 children. (813) 334-3614.

KORESHAN STATE HISTORIC SITE, off US 41. In 1894 a community called Estero was established on the banks of the Estero River near Fort Myers. The founder, a Chicago visionary named Cyrus Reed Teed, believed that Estero would become a great city and that the religion he and his followers preached would spread around the world. Obviously, he was wrong. Today the buildings and grounds are under restoration; park rangers conduct tours of the settlement. Open daily 9 - dusk. Free. (813) 992-0311.

Key Biscayne

CAPE FLORIDA LIGHTHOUSE, 1200 S. Crandon Blvd., 1825, 1846, 1855. In July, 1836, during the Second Seminole War, Assistant Keeper John W. B. Thompson and his helper barricaded themselves within this circular brick lighthouse; hostile Indians then set it afire, but a Navy schooner came to the rescue just in time. The lighthouse was not rebuilt until 1846, when the Indian threat had abated; it was then in use until the late 1870s. NR. Open daily 9-5. 50¢ admission. (305) 361-5811.

Key Largo vicinity

JOHN PENNEKAMP CORAL REEF STATE PARK, US 1, 17th-19th centuries. This state reserve, named for a Miami newspaper editor active in the conservation of natural properties in Florida, was the first underseas park in the continental United States. Along the reef and on the flats, under the turtle grass and sand, lie an unknown number of possible archaeological sites, including several shipwrecks, making the area a mecca for snorklers and skin-divers. Those less athletically-inclined can take a glass-bottomed boat trip for an additional fee. NR. Open daily 9-dusk. Nominal admission. (305) 451-1621. ✔

Key West

It is thought that pirates began to use Key West as a haven in the 18th century, lying in wait for ships to be wrecked on the treacherous reefs, and pouncing on the wreckage to hunt for salvage. In 1822, the year after Florida received territorial status, the army was sent to clean up the island, and settlers soon followed, most lured by the riches they were sure the shipwrecks contained. By 1870, Key West was the largest city in Flroida. Although that is no longer true, the community still has somewhat of an offbeat reputation, with a citizenry composed mainly of artists, writers, and fishermen. Much is being done to restore old houses and hotels to their mid-19th century condition, and Key West is variously called "the Hamptons of the South," and "the Last Resort," since it is located at the tip of Florida, only 90 miles from Cuba.

EAST MARTELLO GALLERY AND MUSEUM, S. Roosevelt Blvd., 1862. A martello is a fortified tower built to serve as the outworks to a main fortification. An art gallery and museum is now housed in one of a pair of such structures begun during the Civil War, but never completed and never armed. Collections include antique clocks, watches, arms, paintings by local artists, and historic artifacts. NR. Open daily 9:30-5. $1.50 adults, 25¢ children 7-16. (305) 296-3913.

FORT ZACHARY TAYLOR, west end of the island off US 1, 1844-46. Fort Taylor was a bastion of Union strength in the South during the Civil War: the thick trapezoid formed by its brick walls was virtually impregnable. Within the grounds of the fort is the **Little White House** (quarters

A), a clapboard dwelling dating from the 1890s, which was President Truman's favorite vacation home. NR, NHL. Access to the fort is limited: call (305) 294-2354 for information. ★

KEY WEST HISTORIC DISTRICT, bounded roughly by White, Angela, Windsor, Passover, Thomas, and Whitehead Sts. and the Gulf, 19th-20th centuries. The historic district is famous for its "Conch" houses, named for their builders rather than for their style. (Early settlers were fond of conch, the ubiquitous shellfish used in soups, fritters, and a variety of other dishes.) The homes are beautifully crafted of Pensacola pine, cedar, cypress, juniper, and mahogany. Wide verandas with slender columns, louvered shutters, lacy wood trim, and delicately-carved balustrades are common in these sturdy dwellings, built to withstand high winds and torrential rains.

The Audubon House and Gardens, Whitehead and Greene Sts., 1831. In the 1830s John James Audubon visited the owner of this lovely frame house while he was studying and painting tropical birds. The house has been restored and is furnished with antiques, as well as a valuable four-volume set of the original Audubon Double Elephant Folio. Open daily 9-12, 1-5. $1.50 adults, 50¢ children. (305) 294-2116.

Ernest Hemingway Home and Museum, 907 Whitehead St., 1851. Hemingway and his wife Pauline bought this large, two-story native stone house in 1931 and lived here until 1940. The novelist wrote

two of his most famous works here: *Death in the Afternoon* and *To Have and Have Not.* Much of the furniture the Hemingways purchased for their Key West home is on display, as well as mementoes the author picked up on his world travels. NR, NHL. Open daily 9-5. $1.50 adults, $1 students, 50¢ children. (305) 294-1575.

The Oldest House Museum, 322 Duval St., 1829. Sea captain Francis Watlington was the original owner of this lovely conch house; it is furnished with antiques, and the kids will enjoy the early toys and games on display. NR. Open Th-T 10-4. $1.75 adults, 50¢ children. (305) 294-9502. ✓

The Old Key West Historic Center, 512 Greene St. Exhibits in this museum complex are housed in three buildings: the **Cuban Coffee Mill** (1899), and two 1870s **conch houses.** There's something of interest here to almost everyone; the collections range from rocks and minerals to an aviary and an insect collection. Open June-Oct, M-Sa 9-5. $1 adults, 50¢ children. (305) 294-2587.

Lighthouse Military Museum, 938 Whitehead St., 1847. This circular lighthouse was in use from its construction until the late 1960s; today the keeper's cottage and part of the tower house a military museum, which includes a Japanese two-man submarine captured at Pearl Harbor and a TF-9 Cougar airplane once used by the Navy's Blue Angels acrobatic team. The view from the top of the tower is worth the trip. Open all year, daily 9:30-5. $1.50 adults, 50¢ children. (305) 294-0012.

Key West vicinity

FORT JEFFERSON, 68 miles W. in the Gulf of Mexico, 19th century. The largest in a chain of seacoast defenses erected in the 1800s, Fort Jefferson was built to protect commercial ships en route from the Mississippi to Europe. Initially slaves were used to construct the eight-foot-thick walls, but were replaced after the Civil War with Union deserters imprisoned on the coral reef. The fort is part of a national park. Guided tours of the fort are given by park rangers. NR. Open daily dawn-dusk. Free. Information about boats to the park is available through the Key West Chamber of Commerce, Old Mallory Square, 33040. (305) 294-2587. ★

Miami

Entrepreneur Henry Flagler pushed his East Coast Railroad south to what is now Miami in 1896; at the time, the area was settled only by a few farmers and fishermen. The razzle-dazzle reputation the city enjoys today wasn't born until the 1920s, when the American upper classes suddenly discovered the joys of the tropics in winter. A building boom followed, and today the area attracts nearly 14 million sun-worshipers every year. Although the beaches, discos, and hotels are the main attractions in the greater Miami area, there are a number of historic sites to visit.

THE BARNACLE (Ralph Munroe House), 3485 Main Hwy., Coconut Grove, 1891. Commodore Munroe was one of the first settlers in the Miami area and was enthusiastic about the climate and the opportunities it afforded. His two-story frame house was adapted to the climate, with a concrete-block ground floor, wide airy veranda, and large windows to attract the breeze off the nearby bay. NR. Open W-Su 9-4.

HISTORICAL MUSEUM OF SOUTHERN FLORIDA, 3280 S. Miami Ave., Bldg. B. Seminole Indian artifacts, relics from underwater explorations, and historical displays relating to the south Florida area and the Caribbean explain the Sunshine State's development. Open M-Sa 9-5, Su 12:30-5. Free. (305) 854-3289.

VILLA VIZCAYA, 3251 S. Miami Ave., 1914-16. Industrialist James Deering, co-

founder of International Harvester, lived in splendor at this fantastic 70-room Italian Renaissance mansion, surrounded by priceless antiques and decorative arts. Many of the furnishings and much of the interior woodwork were imported from European palaces; Deering hired landscape architect Diego Suarez to design 36 acres of extravagant gardens, fountains, and pools. Operated by the state. NR. Open daily 10-5. $3.75 adults, $2 students ($2 admission to gardens only). (305) 579-2708.

Miami Beach

MIAMI BEACH ARCHITECTURAL DISTRICT, bounded by 6th St. Alton Rd., Lincoln Rd., and the Atlantic Ocean, 1920-45. "Old Miami," as it is popularly known, is the country's youngest historic district and contains the largest concentration of '20s and '30s Art Deco architecture

in America. Anyone with a taste for streamlined curves, ribbon windows, and geometric appliques will enjoy a ramble through the resort town's oldest section. Miami Beach is an island: eight miles long, and from one to three miles wide, it is linked to the city of Miami by causeways across Biscayne Bay. During the 1920s, its population grew from under a thousand residents to more than ten times that

number, as affluent sun-seekers built enormous Mediterranean-style mansions, developers erected elaborate Spanish Revival hotels, and businessmen opened tony Art Moderne shops and restaurants. The **Miami Design Preservation League,** 1630 Euclid Ave., offers information on tours of the district. NR. (305) 672-1836.

North Miami Beach

OLD SPANISH MONASTERY (Monastery of St. Bernard de Clairvaux), 16711 W. Dixie Hwy. This antique Cistercian monastery was built in Segovia in 1141; many centuries later, it was dismantled and shipped to the United States by William Randolph Hearst, but it was not reconstructed in the North Miami area until 1952, some years after Hearst's death. Reconstruction was completed using the early 20th century plans and much of the 12th-century stone and tile. The monastery complex includes a refectory, cloister, and chapter house, and is now an art museum. NR. Open M-Sa 10-5, Su 12-5. $3 adults, 75¢ children 6-12. (305) 945-1462.

Palm Beach

Nicknamed "the Nice of the United States," Palm Beach has been through the same sort of transition as its French sister resort in the last few decades: once the exclusive preserve of the very rich, it now attracts admirers of wealth and glitter by the busload. Originally the island on which Palm Beach is situated was a 14-mile stretch of sand. In 1878, a ship was wrecked just offshore, and her cargo of coconuts washed onto the beach and took hold. The shade of the palms provided the ideal atmosphere for the affluent resort developed by railroad magnate Henry Flagler at the turn of the century (see Flagler Museum, following). Today companies such as Elizabeth Arden, Cartier, Gucci, Chanel, Saks, and Yves Saint Laurent run branch offices on **Worth Ave.,** the luxurious shopping area begun in the early decades of the century, whose buildings are a mix of Spanish Colonial, Romanesque, and Moorish styles.

THE HENRY MORRISON FLAGLER MUSEUM, Whitehall Way, 1901. Henry M. Flagler, co-founder of Standard Oil, built a rail line from Jacksonville to Miami in the 1890s and initiated the development of coastal resorts. He must have had a special fondness for Palm Beach, for it was here that he spent $4 million on an opulent fifty-five room winter mansion for his wife, Mary Kenan. Today the house is a museum, featuring lavishly-decorated period rooms and special collections of porcelain, paintings, silver, and glass. Flagler's private railroad car, *Rambler,* is on the property and can also be toured. NR. Open Tu-Sa 10-5, Su 12-5. $3 adults, $1 children. (305) 655-2833. ✔

Stuart

HOUSE OF REFUGE AT GILBERT'S BAR INLET, Hutchinson Island, 1876. During the 19th century ten houses of refuge were built on Florida's east coast to accommodate shipwreck victims; this 1½-story frame dwelling is the only one that remains. Exhibits of Florida maritime history are housed here. NR. Open daily 1-5 (closed M June-Oct). 50¢ adults, 25¢ children. (305) 287-1088.

While you're in the area, stop off at the **Elliott Museum,** 825 NE Ocean Blvd. The museum's collection includes painting and sculpture, as well as Seminole Indian artifacts, antique autos, and early furnishings. Open daily 1-5. $1 adults, 50¢ children 6-13. (305) 225-1961.

The Atlantic Coast

Florida's east coast and surrounding areas contain both the state's youngest and oldest attractions. By far the most popular is Disney World and its new offshoot, Epcot Center; the oldest European sites are to be found in St. Augustine, settled in the 16th century, whose venerable houses and fortifications date from the early 1700s.

Bunnell vicinity

BULOW PLANTATION RUINS, 9 miles SE off Kings Rd., 19th century. Charles Bulow established a sugar cane and cotton plantation on 4,000 acres in 1821; it was developed into a prosperous enterprise, but was destroyed in 1836 during the Seminole wars. Operated by the state, the plantation today includes the ruins of the main house, the slave quarters, remnants of Bulow's sugar mill and springhouse, and a number of wells established on the grounds. A **visitor center** displays historic exhibits. NR. Open daily 9-5. Free. (904) 439-2219.

Bushnell vicinity

DADE BATTLEFIELD, 1 mile W. off US 301, 1835. The Second Seminole War began here just after Christmas in 1835, when Indian forces ambushed a column of Federal troops in retaliation for the government's plan to relocate the tribe west of the Mississippi. Only 3 soldiers of the 108-man force survived. A museum on the site contains Indian artifacts and 19th-century military equipment. NR. Open daily 9-5. (904) 793-4781. ★

Daytona Beach

MARY McLEOD BETHUNE HOUSE, Bethune-Cookman College Campus, 640 2nd Ave., 1920s. This 2½-story clapboard dwelling was the home of Mary McLeod Bethune, a founder of the college and a leading spokeswoman for the concerns of black Americans. Mrs. Bethune saw education as the route to black freedom and started her first school, the Daytona Normal and Industrial Institute for Negro Girls, in 1904. Her home is operated as a museum: many of her personal belongings and furnishings are on display. NR. NHL. Open daily 9-5. Donations accepted. (904) 252-3519.

HALIFAX HISTORICAL MUSEUM, 128 Orange Ave. Early photographs, documents, Indian artifacts, mementoes of local families, Civil War relics, and antique dolls are among the items displayed here. Open Tu-Sa 10-4, Su 1-4. Nominal admission. (904) 255-6976.

Fernandina Beach

FORT CLINCH STATE PARK, 2601 Atlantic Ave., 19th century. Amelia Island, whose northern end commands the entrance to St. Mary's River and Cumberland Sound, was early recognized as strategically important: the flags of eight nations have flown over it since the 18th century, and it was under Union control during the Civil War. The pentagonal brick and cement structure has been restored; park rangers dressed as Union soldiers demonstrate 19th-century chores, and an interpretive center just outside the fort houses exhibits. NR. Open daily 9-5. 25¢ adults. (904) 261-4212. ★ ✔

The downtown area of Fernandina Beach has been designated an **historic district**: the community flourished in the period following the Civil War, and many fine Queen Anne and Italianate residences remain. NR.

Fort George Island

KINGSLEY PLANTATION STATE HISTORIC SITE, Fort George inlet, 18th-19th centuries. Kingsley Plantation was founded in 1791 by John McQueen, who was given the island by the King of Spain. The estate was owned by Florida legislator Zephaniah Kingsley from 1817 to 1836. His plantation is one of the few remaining in the state; the complex includes a barn, carriage house, slave cabins, and two main plantation houses, both with tabby foundations and frame upper stories. NR. Open daily 8-5. 50¢ adults. (904) 251-3522.

Hawthorne vicinity

MARJORIE KINNAN RAWLINGS HOUSE, S. of Cross Creek on FL 325., late 19th century. Typical of central Florida "cracker" farmhouses of the period, the Rawlings House is a sprawling frame building with three separate units connected by wide porches. Mrs. Rawlings purchased the house in 1928; while living here, she wrote her Pulitzer-Prize-winning novel, *The Yearling*. Many of her furnishings remain. NR. Open W-Su 9-5. Admission 50¢. (904) 466-3672.

Jacksonville

One of the largest cities in Florida, Jacksonville was once just a convenient cattle ford on the St. Johns River. When the British ruled the area, the town that grew up at the curve in the river was called Cowford; after the United States took possession, the village was renamed for Andrew Jackson. Described as the "working son in the Florida family of playboys," Jacksonville today is a thoroughly modern city.

FORT CAROLINE NATIONAL MEMORIAL, 12713 Ft. Caroline Rd., 1564-5. The struggle between France and Spain for supremacy in southeastern North America began and virtually ended here. When Fort Caroline was founded, there was no other European colony on the North American continent this side of Mexico, and France hoped this colony would establish her claim in the New World. But a Spanish armada under Pedro Menendez de Aviles, founder of St.

Augustine, captured the fort within a year. Reconstruction of Fort Caroline was based on a 16th-century sketch; a **visitor center** exhibits Indian relics, armor, spears, guns, and jewelry found at the site during excavations. NR. Open daily 9-5. Free. (904) 641-7111. ★

JACKSONVILLE MUSEUM OF ARTS AND SCIENCES, 1025 Gulf Life Dr. Exhibits here include 19th and 20th-century antique and ethnic dolls, Indian artifacts, folk art, and old clothing. Skywatchers will want to plan a visit to the planetarium. Open Oct-Aug, Tu-F 11-5, Su 1-5. Museum: free. Planetarium: $1 adults, 75¢ children. (904) 396-7062. ✓

Orlando

ORANGE COUNTY HISTORICAL COMMISSION, 812 E. Rollins St. Local furniture, Indian artifacts, models of early forts, a frontier saloon, a Victorian parlor, and a blacksmith shop are among the displays administered by the county. Open Tu-F 10-4, Sa-Su 2-5. Free. (305) 898-8320.

PINE CASTLE CENTER OF THE ARTS, 5903 Randolph St. Antique tools, clothing, and other pioneer relics are housed in a turn-of-the-century Florida "cracker" house, two smaller houses, and a gazebo set on four acres of grounds. Special workshops and seasonal cultural events are held here. Open M-F 9-5. Free. (305) 855-7461.

Ormond Beach vicinity

TOMOKA STATE PARK, 2 miles N. via Old Dixie Hwy., 16th-17th centuries. The remains of the Timucuan Indian village of Nocoroco are located at this state park and were first described by a Spaniard in the early 1600s. Excavations have uncovered a number of artifacts, some of which are displayed at a small museum. NR. Open W-Su 9-5. 25¢ admission. (904) 677-3931.

St. Augustine

St. Augustine is the oldest continuously-occupied city in the United States: the Spanish made several attempts to occupy the area in the early 1500s, as did the French. In 1565 Don Pedro Menendez de Aviles, on instructions from King Philip II, successfully established a permanent settlement, which Spain held continuously,

Hotel Ponce de Leon

except for twenty years of British rule in the 18th century, until 1821.

The palm thatch huts erected by the Spanish colonists in the first century of settlement were leveled during an English attack in the early 1700s; when the town was rebuilt, more durable stone (coquina) and wood were used, and many of these early houses remain today.

Much of central St. Augustine has been designated an historic district and a National Historic Landmark: the area bounded by Castillo de San Marcos, St. Francis and Cordova Sts., and Mantanzas Bay contains many venerable buildings dating from the 17th-19th centuries. The street plan established in 1598 remains virtually unchanged. Narrow residential thoroughfares surround a central plaza, where the government buildings and the **Cathedral of St. Augustine** are located. The façade of the present cathedral, on Cathedral St. opposite the plaza, dates from 1797; the balance was rebuilt from a design by James Renwick in the 1880s after a fire had damaged much of the building. NR, NHL.

Like Palm Beach and Miami, St. Augustine was transformed into a popular winter resort at the end of the 19th century by Henry Flagler, who built two enormous resort hotels here, both now adapted for new uses (see following).

The historic attractions listed are by no means all-inclusive; they have been selected because of their importance to the city as well as for their authenticity. Stop in first at the **Visitors Information Center,** 10 Castillo Dr., for a map and detailed information about specific sites. Open daily 8-5:30. Free. (904) 829-5681.

CASTILLO DE SAN MARCOS NATIONAL MONUMENT, 1 Castillo Dr., 1672-96. Castillo de San Marcos, the northernmost outpost of the Spanish empire in the New World, was established as a permanent defense against foreign settlement and as protection for coastal shipping. Spanish forays against the Carolinas and Georgia began here, and it was the target of at least six major raids by the English, as well as by marauding pirates and Indians. After Florida was ceded to the

United States in 1821, the fort served as a military prison.

Its walls are thirty feet high, and in places as much as thirteen feet thick. Housed within them is a federally-administered **museum,** which exhibits Indian and Spanish artifacts, antique artillery pieces, and other objects relating to the fort, the oldest such structure in the United States. NR. Open late Oct-late Apr 8:30-5:15, otherwise 9-5:45. 50¢ admission. (904) 829-6506. ★

FLAGLER COLLEGE, King St. The main building of this small college is the former **Hotel Ponce de Leon** (1888), one of two grand luxury hotels designed by Carrère and Hastings for Henry Flagler. The round-arched coquina and concrete structure, decorated with tiles, mosaics, and Tiffany glass, can be toured. NR. (904) 829-6481.

LIGHTNER MUSEUM, City Hall Museum Complex, King St., 1889. The central building of this large complex is the former **Alcazar Hotel,** the second constructed through the efforts of Henry Flagler. Also designed by Carrère and Hastings, the Alcazar is a fabulous 300-room Spanish Renaissance building; its fountains and gardens have been restored, and the museum contains a fine

St. Augustine Historic District

collection of 19th-century decorative arts. NR. Open daily 9-5. $2 adults, 75¢ children over 12. (904) 829-9677.

OLDEST HOUSE AND TOVAR HOUSE, 14 St. Francis St., 18th century. The oldest house in St. Augustine is a Spanish colonial structure of coquina and wood built shortly after the siege of 1702. The adjacent **Tovar House** (c. 1760) contains exhibitions of Spanish glass, tiles, ceramics, maps, and an interpretive show on early architecture; the Oldest House is furnished with period antiques. NR, NHL. Open daily 9-5. $1.25 adults, 50¢ children 6-18. (904) 829-9624.

SAN AGUSTIN ANTIGUO, St. George St. and environs. The Historic St. Augustine Preservation Board has undertaken restoration of more than forty buildings on St. George St. and neighboring blocks. Most are early Spanish houses, dating from the 18th and early 19th centuries. A general admission ticket, available at **Ribera House,** 22 George St. or **Sanchez de Ortigosa House,** St. George and Cuna Sts., includes eight historic buildings, where cooking, silver working, candlemaking, dyeing, spinning, and weaving are demonstrated. Open daily 9-5:15. $2 adults, 75¢ children 8-18, group rates. (904) 824-3355.

Also within the preservation area is the **Old Wooden Schoolhouse,** 14 St. George St. (c. 1760). Made of cedar and cypress, it is the oldest wooden building in the city. Open daily 9-5. $1 adults, 50¢ children 6-11. (904) 824-3355.

St. Augustine vicinity

FORT MATANZAS NATIONAL MONUMENT, 15 miles S., 1 Castillo Dr., Rattlesnake Island, 17th-18th centuries. Originally built of wood in the 1560s, this coquina tower was part of the defense system built by the Spanish to warn St. Augustine inhabitants of approaching ships. Accessible only by boat (there is daily ferry service), Fort Matanzas is part of a 300-acre federal preserve. NR. Open all year, daily 8:30-5:30. Free. (904) 829-6506. ★

Sebastian vicinity

SPANISH FLEET SURVIVORS AND SALVORS CAMPSITE, between Sebastian and Sebastian Inlet, 1715. Fifteen-hundred survivors of a Spanish merchant fleet wrecked in a hurricane camped here; and the area was the base for later Spanish salvage efforts. Excavations in the 1960s uncovered part of the treasure lost in the wreck, along with earlier Indian artifacts: some of the booty is displayed in a museum at the site. NR. Open W-Su 9-5. 50¢ admission. (305) 589-3754.

The Gulf Coast

Florida's west coast is best known for two of the state's largest cities, Tampa and St. Petersburg, which together with their surrounding bedroom communities, form one of the country's most popular vacation and retirement spots. Colonized later than the east, the Gulf Coast soon made up for lost time: railroads linked the area to northern climes in the late 19th century, and wealthy entrepreneurs built lavish hotels to attract vacationers eager to escape the winter's chill.

Bradenton

DE SOTO NATIONAL MEMORIAL, 75th St. NW. In 1537 Hernando de Soto received a grant from the Spanish crown to "conquer, pacify, and populate" the North American continent. Two years later, he landed near Tampa Bay and began his expedition inland. De Soto and his men ranged as far north as Tennessee and west to the Mississippi River, where the explorer died in 1542. De Soto Memorial

Park commemorates the 16th-century trek; employees in period costume demonstrate food preparation and the use of early weapons like the crossbow, and explain the hardships encountered by the Spanish soldiers. NR. **Visitors Center** open daily 8-5. Demonstrations given Dec-Apr, daily 9:30-5. Free. (813) 792-0458.
✔

SOUTH FLORIDA MUSEUM AND BISHOP PLANETARIUM, 201 10th St. W. Models of 16th-century Spanish buildings, local Indian artifacts, early surgical and medical instruments, old guns, dolls, fans, clocks, musical instruments, period costumes—these exhibits and many more help to explain Florida's early history. Open Tu-F 10-5, Sa, Su 1-5. $2.50 adults, $2 senior citizens, $1.50 students. (813) 746-4131.
✔

Cedar Key

CEDAR KEY STATE MUSEUM, Museum Dr. Exhibits depicting the colorful history of the Cedar Key area, first settled in the 1840s, are housed in this museum and visitor center. Once a thriving port from which lumber, cotton, and naval stores were shipped overseas, Cedar Key is now a small commerical fishing center and a charming place for a stroll: many of its early 20th-century buildings are perched on stilts for protection against severe Gulf storms. Open daily 9-5. 25¢ admission. (904) 543-5350.

Crystal River vicinity

CRYSTAL RIVER INDIAN MOUNDS, 2 miles NW via US 19-98, pre-Columbian.

Archaeologists have discovered indications that Indian tribes occupied this area for some 1,600 years, from 200 B.C. to 1400 A.D. Temple mounds, burial mounds, and middens (refuse mounds) have been unearthed; a **visitor center** houses many of the artifacts excavated during recent digs. NR. Open daily 9-5. 25¢ admission. (904) 795-3817.

YULEE SUGAR MILL RUINS, 7 miles S. via US 19 on FL 490, 19th century. From 1851 to 1864, this 5,100-acre tract of land was the site of a thriving sugar plantation. During the Civil War, Federal troops burned the main house; although the mill escaped destruction, it was never operated again. Interpretive signs throughout the area, which is now a state park, explain how the plantation was operated. Much of the early machinery has been restored, and several original structures remain. NR. Open daily 9-sunset. Nominal admission. (904) 795-3817.

Dade City

PIONEER FLORIDA MUSEUM, US 301. Exhibits depict the family life of early Florida residents; the museum administers two restored 19th-century buildings: a schoolhouse and a church. Craft demonstrations are held periodically. Open Tu-Su 1-5. $1 adults, 50¢ children. (904) 567-0262.

Ellenton

THE JUDAH P. BENJAMIN CONFEDERATE MEMORIAL AT GAMBLE PLANTATION, US 301, 1845-50. A rare survival, this two-story ante-bellum plan-

tation house was once the center of a 3,500-acre estate on the Manatee River and was one of the most successful sugar farms in the state. Confederate Secretary of State Benjamin is said to have hidden here before making his escape to England in May, 1865. Furnished with period antiques, the brick and tabby house is operated by the United Daughters of the Confederacy. NR. Open daily 9-5. 50¢ admission. (813) 722-1017.

Largo

PINELLAS COUNTY HERITAGE PARK, 11909 125th St. N. This lovely park contains a number of historic buildings, along with a museum displaying photographs, primitive paintings, early furnishings, and musical instruments. A costumed guide leads the way down old brick paths lined by palmettos and pines to the **House of Seven Gables** (1907), **Plant-Summer House** (1896), **Lowe Barn** (1912), **Coachman-McMullen Log House** (1856), and several early 20th-century buildings arrayed within the park's twenty-one acres. Open Tu-Sa 10-4. Free. (813) 462-3474. ✔

St. Petersburg

There were settlements in the St. Petersburg area as early as the 1840s, but it wasn't until the end of the century that a permanent community began to thrive here, when railroad magnate Peter Demens completed a rail line to the community and named it for his native Russian birthplace. Today St. Petersburg and neighboring St. Petersburg Beach are sprawling, busy communities, attractive both to retirees and to younger residents who appreciate the wonderful climate (the local newspaper is given away free on sunless days) and the business opportunities of nearby Tampa and other communities.

HAAS MUSEUM, 3511 2nd Ave. S. The St. Petersburg Historical Society museum complex contains an old-time barber shop, blacksmith's shop, and kitchen, as well as two early Florida dwellings, **Lowe House** (1850), a cypress and pine cottage, and the

Grace Turner House, a 1920 Florida bungalow completely furnished with beautiful antiques. Open Oct-Aug, Tu-Su 1-5. $1 adults, 25¢ children under 12. (813) 894-1401. ✔

THE ST. PETERSBURG MUSEUM, 335 2nd Ave. NE. More than 10,000 objects relating to St. Petersburg and Tampa Bay history are displayed at this modern museum facility: 19th-century furnishings, an ancient cypress canoe, maps, land-grant documents, Indian artifacts, and even an Egyptian mummy. Open M-Sa 11-5, Su 1-5. 75¢ adults, 25¢ children over 4. (813) 894-1052.

Sarasota

THE RINGLING MUSEUMS, US 41. Circus czar John Ringling left his beautifully-landscaped 68-acre estate to the state of Florida on his death in 1936. The crowning jewel of this popular museum complex is **Ca'd'Zan,** an opulent 30-room mansion built by Ringling in 1925. Marble floors, Venetian glass windows, handwrought iron work, gold plumbing fixtures, priceless antiques — all of the trappings Ringling collected on his world tours — remain as he left them.

The **John and Mable Ringling Museum of Art** houses masterpieces by Rubens and other early European artists; the museum building is an Italian-style villa employing marble, sculpture, and decorative accents shipped from Italy. **The Museum of the Circus** has an extensive collection of memorabilia from the "Greatest Show on Earth," including programs, posters, calliopes, wagons, and a "Back Yard" exhibit which depicts life in a typical circus camp.

A year-round program of films, plays, lectures, and musical performances is given at the **Asolo Theatre,** which incorporates much of the original 1798 interior of Queen Catherine Cornaro's castle from Asola, Italy. The Ringling Museums are open M-F 9am - 10pm; Sa 9-5, Su 11-6. $3.50 adults, children under 12 free. (813) 355-5101. ✔

Tampa

The first Spaniards sailed into Tampa Bay in 1528, but it was nearly three hundred years before the area was permanently settled, since the local Indians were said to be "too tough to conquer and too stubborn to convert." The first plantation was built by entrepreneur Robert Hackley in 1823; for the next sixty years Tampa remained a tiny outpost in the wilds of Florida's west coast. In 1883, Henry B. Plant began the development of Port Tampa, investing millions of dollars in buildings and railroads, which attracted thousands of new residents. Today Tampa is Florida's third largest city and the center of Gulf Coast commerce.

TAMPA THEATER AND OFFICE BUILDING, 711 Franklin St., 1925. This 10-story Italian Renaissance Revival building is famous for its million-dollar vaudeville and movie palace. Built during Florida's land boom, the theater is embellished with romantic balconies and towers, colonnades, niches with Greek and Roman-style sculpture, and other adornments. Recently restored, the theater is now used for special musical performances and other productions. NR. (813) 223-8981.

UNIVERSITY OF TAMPA, 401 W. Kennedy Blvd., 1888-91. It would be hard to miss the University's crowning glory: an extraordinary Moorish-style five-story landmark embellished with thirteen silver minarets. Built as the **Tampa Bay Hotel** for Henry Plant, who was attempting to outdo his east coast rival, Henry Flagler, the spectacular building features ornately-carved verandas, cavernous public rooms, and hundreds of exotic decorative touches. The 500-room hotel was so vast that rickshaws were used to transport guests down the long halls. The rickshaws are gone, but reminders of the Tampa Bay's heyday can be seen in the hotel's south wing, now operated as the **Henry B. Plant Museum.** Its collection includes many of the hotel's original Asian and European furnishings. NR. Open Tu-Sa 10-4. Free. (813) 253-8861, ext. 400.

YBOR CITY, roughly bounded by Columbus Dr., 5th and Nebraska Aves., and 22nd St., 19th-20th centuries. In 1886, Vincente Martinez Ybor purchased forty acres of land in what is now central Tampa and relocated his cigar factory, complete with a group of trained workers, from its original site in Key West. Most of the state's other cigar makers soon followed suit, and the area around Ybor's factory developed into a Latin Quarter, with a population of more than 30,000 residents, most Cubans who emigrated here to escape the despotism of their homeland. Although a misguided 1960s redevelopment project destroyed many buildings, a number still remain, and restoration has converted several, such as the three large factories at **Ybor Square,** into shops and restaurants. NR.

The **Ybor City State Museum,** 1818 9th Ave., is housed in the renovated Ferlita Bakery. This is a good place to see exhibits explaining the development of the area and of the cigar industry which fostered it. NR. Open daily 9-12, 1-5. 50¢ admission. (813) 247-6323.

Tarpon Springs

TARPON SPRINGS SPONGE EXCHANGE, Dodecanese St., 1908. Tarpon Springs was founded in the 1870s by Greek immigrants who recognized that the Gulf waters offered an opportunity to use their native sponge-diving skills. The Sponge Exchange, located opposite the docks where spongers' boats are still moored, is a one-story stuccoed complex of buildings.

Tarpon Springs Sponge Exchange

The courtyards they enclose are still used for sponge auctions and social gatherings. NR. A **museum** at the docks offers a film on the art of sponge diving, along with displays of industry relics. Open daily 10-5:30. $1 adults, 50¢ children 4-11. (813) 937-4111. ✔

Zephyrhills vicinity

FORT FOSTER, 9 miles S. via FL 156, 1836. Fort Foster was erected during the Second Seminole War, primarily for use as a supply depot. The square log stockade has been carefully reconstructed by the Florida Parks Service, which now administers a living history program depicting daily life at the fort in the 19th century. A **museum** near the site offers interpretive exhibits. NR. Open F-Su. $1 adults, 50¢ children 6-12. (813) 986-1020. ★ ✔

West Florida

Florida's Panhandle was settled far later than other regions of the state; early Spanish exporers landed at what is now Pensacola in the 1600s, but were not able to maintain permanent settlements in the area because of hostile Indian tribes and French incursions.

Remnants of some early fortifications remain, but most of western Florida's historic sites date from the 1800s, when permanent communities at last grew and flourished. One of the most noteworthy is in Pensacola, in whose Plaza Ferdinand VII (Palafox St.) the Florida territory was ceded to the United States by the Spanish in 1821.

Apalachicola

JOHN GORRIE STATE MUSEUM, Ave. C. and 6th St. Dr. John Gorrie produced the first air conditioner in 1845—an ice machine he used to cool the rooms of yellow fever victims. Floridians have been blessing his invention ever since. A replica of Gorrie's first cooling machine is

Plaza Ferdinand VII, Pensacola

displayed here, along with other mementoes of local history. Open daily 8-5. 25¢ admission. (904) 653-9347.

Panama City

THE JUNIOR MUSEUM OF BAY COUNTY, 1731 Jinks Ave. Exhibits devoted to pioneer Florida life and natural history include a log cabin, smokehouse, barn, gristmill, and cane mill. A raised walkway leads through a swamp where reptiles and other denizens lurk; mounted African animal trophies are less threatening. Open M-Sa 9-4, Su 2-4. Free. (904) 785-8722. ✔

Pensacola

20th-century Pensacola is an important industrial port best known as the home of a large naval air station. Remnants of the city's earlier history are numerous; most are located within the confines of the city's historic district (which see) or on the naval base itself.

PENSACOLA HISTORICAL MUSEUM, 405 S. Adams St. Housed in the Gothic Revival **Old Christ Church** (c. 1830) is a broad collection of historical artifacts, including clothing, silver, Indian relics, household items, and early glass negatives. NR. Open M-Sa 9-4:30. Free. (904) 443-1559.

PENSACOLA HISTORIC DISTRICT, bounded by Chase St., 9th Ave., Palafox St., and the Bay, 19th century. Within the confines of this large residential and commercial district are dozens of 19th-century buildings representing a wide variety of architectural styles. Attractions open to the public include:

Buccaneer Schooner, Municipal Wharf, early 20th century. Two-masted wooden vessels such as this, carrying a crew of fifteen or so, often made month-long trips to exotic destinations like the Yucatan Peninsula. Operated by the Historic Pensacola Preservation Board. NR. Open M-Sa 10-4:30, Su 1-4:30. Donations accepted. (904) 434-1042. ✔

Clara Barkley Dorr House, 311 S. Adams St., 1871. This lovely Classical Revival frame house has been carefully restored and furnished with antiques of the Victorian age. Open M-Sa 10-2, Su 1-2. Donations accepted. (904) 434-1042.

The **Lavalle House,** 203 E. Church St. (c. 1810), is one of the earliest surviving dwellings in town, a Gulf Coast cottage furnished with period antiques and decorative arts. NR. Open M-Sa 10-4:30, Su 1-4:30. Free. (904) 434-1042. Two other early Gulf Coast houses are located nearby; both have been restored and refurbished. The **Quina House,** 204 Alcaniz St., dates from 1810. Open mid May-mid Oct, daily 1-4. Donations accepted. (904) 432-4184. The **Walton House,** 221 E. Zaragoza St. (c. 1815), is also open mid May-mid Oct, Tu-Su 1-4. 50¢ admission. (904) 434-1042.

West Florida Museum of History, 200 E. Zaragoza St., is housed in two 1880s warehouses. Its myriad exhibits depict the history of the Gulf Coast. NR. Open M-Sa 10-4:30; Su 1-4:30. Donations accepted. (904) 432-6717.

PENSACOLA NAVAL AIR STATION HISTORIC DISTRICT, 19th-20th centuries. Attracted by the area's protected deep-water port, the Navy began constructing wooden ships here in 1826. Largely destroyed by the Confederate Army in 1862 the shipyard was not reopened until 1914, when the Navy's first Naval Aeronautic Station was established here. The **Naval Aviation Museum,** Radford Blvd. and Hovey Rd., is a good first stop for information about the base. Open daily 9-5. Free. (904) 452-3604.

Fort San Carlos de Barranca within the Air Station Historic District, is the site of a Spanish fort built in 1698 and destroyed by the French in 1719. The ruins of a later brick fortification remain. Also of historic interest is the **Pensacola Lighthouse and Keeper's Quarters.** Built in 1859, the conical brick tower is still in operation. NR, NHL. ★ ✔

Pensacola Beach vicinity

FORT PICKENS, S. via FL 399 to Ft. Pickens Rd., 1834. Built to protect Pensacola Harbor, this pentagonal brick fort has walls forty feet high and twelve feet thick; it remained in Federal possession throughout the Civil War and was afterwards used as a prison. One of its most famous inmates, Apache Chief Geronimo, was held here in 1886. A museum interprets the fort's colorful history. NR. Open daily 8-sunset. $1 per car. (904) 932-5018. ★

Perry

FOREST CAPITAL STATE MUSEUM, 204 Forest Park Dr. Timber is Florida's third largest industry, producing nearly $4 billion in annual revenues. Interpretive exhibits about the industry are located here, as well as a reconstructed North Florida "cracker" homestead which depicts early pioneer life. Open daily 9-5. Nominal admission. (904) 584-3227.

Port St. Joe

CONSTITUTIONAL CONVENTION STATE MUSEUM, 200 Allen Memorial Way. Florida's first constitution was drafted in what was then the town of St. Joseph in late 1838. At the time, St. Joseph had a population of 6,000, and was a thriving commercial center. A severe yellow fever epidemic in 1841, followed shortly thereafter by a devasting hurricane, destroyed St. Joseph; Port St. Joe was founded at the turn of the century. The museum, which interprets Port St. Joe's shadowed history, is open M-Sa 9-5, Su 1-5. 50¢ admission. (904) 229-8029.

St. Marks

SAN MARCOS DE APALACHE STATE HISTORIC SITE, FL 363, 17th century. The first wooden fort was built here at the confluence of the St. Marks and Wakulla Rivers in 1679 by order of the Spanish governor of Florida. Rebuilt once in wood, and then in stone, it changed hands several times before Florida was ceded to the United States in 1821. Some of the stone ruins are visible; a visitor center contains exhibitions interpreting the fort's history: Andrew Jackson's capture of Fort San Marcos in 1818 was instrumental in Florida's acquisition by the United States. NR, NHL. Open daily 9-5. 25¢ admission. (904) 925-6216. ★

Sumatra vicinity

FORT GADSDEN HISTORIC MEMORIAL, 6 miles SW via FL 65, 18th century. Built on Prospect Bluff overlooking the Apalachicola River, Fort Gadsden was constructed by the British in an effort to control river traffic; it was destroyed when the magazine exploded, but rebuilt in 1818 under orders from General Andrew Jackson. Only the earthen outlines of the two forts remain; a miniature replica has been built on the site, and interpretive displays are located in kiosks around the park. NR. Open 8-sunset. Free. (904) 670-8988. ★

Tallahassee

Spanish explorers visited the Tallahassee area in the 1500s; Franciscan missionaries established a settlement here about a century later, but it was totally destroyed during Queen Anne's War. A permanent settlement was begun in 1824, when Tallahassee was selected as the capital of the brand-new state of Florida. Within a year there were fifty houses, several stores, a church, and a school, but for the next century Tallahassee remained a quiet town whose economy was based on cotton and tobacco from nearby plantations. Many residences and public buildings constructed in the mid-19th century have been restored; brochures delineating walking tours are available at the Brokaw-McDougall House or The Columns (see following).

BROKAW-MCDOUGALL HOUSE, 329 N. Meridian, 1856. Peres Bonney Brokaw, a successful livery stable owner and local politician originally from New Jersey, built this graceful Classical Revival home for his family, paying as much attention to the design and planting of the grounds as he did to the interior plan and finishing. The Brokaw-McDougall House is now operated by the Historic Tallahassee Preservation Board, which has restored both house and grounds to reflect their original appearance. NR. Open M-F 8-5. Nominal admission. (904) 488-3901.

THE COLUMNS, 100 N. Duval St., c. 1830. The Tallahassee Area Chamber of Commerce moved and restored this lovely Jeffersonian Classical brick residence in the 1970s, furnishing it with appropriate antiques, and making it headquarters for historic tours of the city. NR. Open M-F 9-5. Free. (904) 224-8116.

MUSEUM OF FLORIDA HISTORY, R.A. Gray Building, S. Bronough St. Exhibits depicting Florida's history, from prehistoric times to the present, are located in a new modern facility. Among the artifacts on view are extensive collections of Spanish treasures recovered from coastal wrecks. Open M-Sa 9-4:30, Su 1-4:30. Free. (904) 488-1484.

OLD FLORIDA STATE CAPITOL, S. Monroe St., 19th-20th centuries. Barely rescued from the bulldozer, Florida's old capitol has recently been replaced by a new facility, but the old building has received a multi-million-dollar facelift. The three-story Neo-classical Revival landmark was constructed in 1845; additions were made in 1902; the renovation has restored the building to its turn-of-the-century appearance. Operated by the Historic Tallahassee Preservation Board. NR. (904) 488-3901.

TALLAHASSEE JUNIOR MUSEUM, 3945 Museum Dr. A restored 1880s Florida "cracker" homestead is the centerpiece of this living history museum, whose extensive grounds also include a

Old Florida State Capitol

reconstructed Indian village, a church, and a schoolhouse. Demonstrations of pioneer crafts are given. Open Tu-Sa 9-5, Su 2-5. $2 adults, $1 children 4-18. (904) 576-1636. ✔

White Springs

STEPHEN FOSTER STATE FOLK CULTURE CENTER, off US 41 and FL 136. Though "America's Troubador" Stephen Foster never saw the Suwannee River, he made its name familiar to millions through his song, "Old Folks at Home," which has been adopted as Florida's state song. In recognition of its composer, the state administers exhibits explaining the composer's life and works, including such classics as "Oh! Susanna," "My Old Kentucky Home," and "Jeannie with the Light Brown Hair." A carillon tower peals out Foster's music hourly; guided tours of the center and boat tours of the Suwannee River are given. Open daily 8-sunset. Free. (904) 397-2733.

Historic Accommodations

An asterisk (*) indicates that meals are served.

Captiva Island

CASA MARINA RESORT, Reynolds St., 33040. (305) 296-3535. Open all year. Railroad tycoon Henry Morrison Flagler built the opulent Spanish Renaissance-style Casa Marina in 1912; the intricate paneling, piazzas, and arched windows have been meticulously restored. *

SOUTH SEAS PLANTATION, Box 194, 33924. (813) 472-5111. Open all year. This large, luxurious resort hotel was once part of a successful plantation, begun in 1856. Surrounded by more than 300 acres of lovely tropical vegetation, the South Seas is located at the tip of beautiful Captiva Island. *

Key West

JASMINE GYPSY, 817 Fleming St., 33040. (305) 294-5734. Open all year. Located within the Key West Historic District, the Jasmine Gypsy is one of the lacy, ethereal-looking, but substantial conch houses for which the Keys are famous. NR.

Miami Beach

There are a number of wonderful Art Moderne hotels within Miami Beach's Historic District; contact the Miami Design Preservation League, 1630 Euclid Ave., 33480, for information. (305) 672-1836.

Palm Beach

THE BREAKERS, S. County Rd., 33480. (305) 655-6611. Open all year. Built in 1925, this magnificent Classical Revival hotel features coffered ceilings and rich Flemish tapestries in its public rooms. NR. *

St. Augustine

ST. FRANCIS INN, 279 St. George St., 32084. (904) 824-6068. The white stuccoed walls of the St. Francis were raised in 1791 by Gaspar Garcia; the landmark, located within St. Augustine's historic district, became a boarding house in the late 19th century. NR.

St. Petersburg Beach

DON CESAR BEACH RESORT, 3400 Gulf Blvd., 33706. (813) 360-1881. Open all year. The flamboyant, turreted pink Don Cesar was built by entrepreneur Thomas J. Rowe at the height of Florida's real estate boom in 1928. It remains one of the country's best resort hotels; try for a room with a view of the surf. NR. *

7. ALABAMA

In 1507 a map of the world by a young German geographer/cartographer named Martin Waldseemüller was published at Saint Dié; he called the land mass on the other side of the Atlantic "America" in honor of Amerigo Vespucci. The maps spread through Europe, and the name was soon popularly known. On that very early map was the outline of Mobile Bay. Many Europeans explored this area in the 16th century, but the first permanent colonies were founded by the French in the early 1700s, first at Dauphin Island and then at Mobile. In 1812, there were still relatively few pioneers living in Alabama; ninety percent of the land was owned by Indians. But, in 1814, at the Battle of Horseshoe Bend, the Indians lost 20 million acres. Five years later, Alabama became the twenty-second state to join the Union. The cotton boom followed; by the mid-19th century this was the leading cotton producing state in America. The glorious period before the onset of civil strife was exceedingly brief. In the first days of 1861, Alabama became the fourth state to secede from the Union. Jefferson Davis was elected president of the Confederacy in Montgomery; and in April, the order to fire on Fort Sumter was sent from that city. Alabama experienced the losses of war: of its white population approximately one-fifth was sent to the front; later, many of its lovely buildings were destroyed by Union troops.

In the century following the war, black history began to be made in Alabama. Tuskegee, the well-known institution for the education of the black population, was opened by Booker T. Washington who was later joined in his efforts by the renowned scientist, George Washington Carver. In the 1950s, Martin Luther King, the inspired pastor who led the crusade for civil rights, spent six years at the Dexter Avenue Church in Montgomery and spoke at meetings and rallies all over the state.

The word Alabama is derived from the Choctaw Indian word for "thicket clearers." And though the state has been industrialized in some sections, it has remained relatively undeveloped; as one drives through the forested countryside, the state's name will seem particularly appropriate. There are over twenty-two types of oaks in Alabama, where streets shaded with that tree are a commonplace. And sites of cultural and historic interest abound: the traveler will find numerous examples of ante-bellum mansions, colonial forts, and ancient Indian mounds.

In the following pages, the state has been divided into three regions: Southern Alabama includes Mobile and Eufaula as well as several smaller municipalities; Central Alabama includes Montgomery, Selma, and other historic towns in this fertile region; Northern Alabama includes sites in the Tennessee River Valley and the more industrialized region around Birmingham.

Oakleigh, Mobile

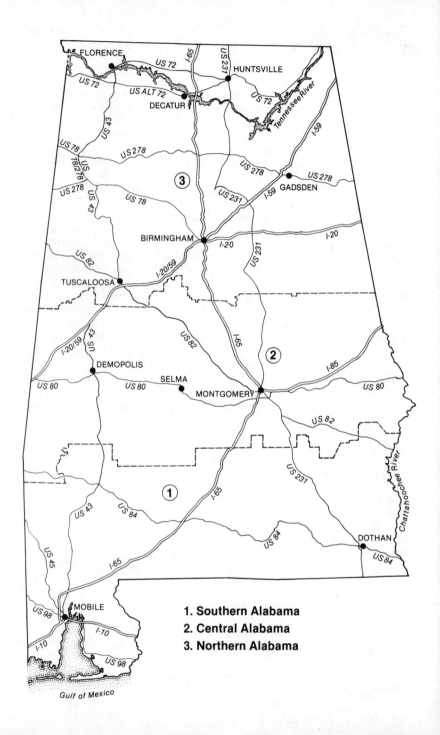

1. Southern Alabama
2. Central Alabama
3. Northern Alabama

Southern Alabama

This semi-tropical region was the first area of Alabama to be settled by Europeans. Finding the sandy soil and exceptionally long growing season suitable to their needs, the French settled along the coast and then in Mobile, where vestiges of their refined tastes are hinted at in the decorative iron fancywork and the azaleas which they imported to this part of the world. Life here is languid and leisurely, and travelers will find that the ante-bellum heritage of the little towns and larger cities has been lovingly preserved.

Dauphin Island

FORT GAINES, E. end of the island off AL 163, 19th century. Designed by Joseph Totten and begun in 1818, this pentagonal fortification was altered in 1854. The 24-foot-high brick walls encompass two guardhouses, a storehouse, parade ground, barracks, and tunnels. Along with Fort Morgan, Fort Gaines served to guard the entrance to Mobile Bay. A **Confederate Museum** houses war artifacts and interpretive exhibits. NR. Open June-Sept, daily 8-8; Oct-May, daily 9-5. $1 adults, 50¢ children under 12. (205) 861-6992. ★

Enterprise

BOLL WEEVIL MONUMENT, Main and College Sts., 1919. In 1915 and 1916 disaster struck Enterprise in the form of the cotton-eating insect known as the boll weevil. Over two-thirds of the crops were destroyed, and from this calamity farmers in the area learned that agricultural diversity was the answer to their problem. Economic recovery followed almost immediately, and this region of Alabama is now the nation's greatest peanut-producing area. New prosperity led citizen R.O. Fleming to conceive of the Boll Weevil Monument, the world's only monument to an insect. The cast-lead statue of a three-foot female figure on a graduated base in the middle of a concrete pool was erected only four years after disaster first struck. In 1949, an aluminum boll weevil was placed in the cast-lead arms. NR.

Eufaula

The Lower Creek Indians settled at this lovely spot above the Chattahoochee River by 1733. White pioneers arrived less than a century later and claimed the site as their own. The settlers farmed the rich lands by the river; by the mid-19th century many residents were wealthy cotton planters. Rather than build mansions on their plantations, the farmers of the Eufaula area chose to build them in town; most of the historic structures were erected before the Civil War, though the visitor will find a number of lavish Victorian mansions. Fortunately, the Civil War ended just before Union troops reached town. Today Eufaula has the largest **historic district** in Alabama. Walking and driving tour maps, as well as information about the annual Spring Pilgrimage, are available from the Chamber of Commerce, located in **Sheppard Cottage** (1837), 504 E. Barbour St. This one-story home is the oldest surviving building in town. Open during regular business hours. Free. (205) 687-3879 or 6664.

FENDALL HALL, 917 W. Barbour St., 1854. This Italianate building, crowned with a widow's walk, was used as a hospital for Confederate soldiers during the Civil War. The house is best known for its lavish interior: the floor hall is black and white Italian marble; the dining and drawing rooms feature gold-leaf ceiling medallions and beautiful stencilled walls and doors painted by a French artist. The house is now being restored as a museum by the Alabama Historical Commission. Open by appointment. (205) 832-6621.

SHORTER MANSION, 340 N. Eufaula Ave., 1906. Eli Shorter and his wife Wileyna Lamar financed the construction of this extraordinary Neo-classical Revival mansion. The elegant exterior, with its Corinthian columns and ornamental frieze, is matched by the beautifully refurbished interior. Open M-Sa 10-4, Su 1-4. $2 adults, 50¢ children under 12. (205) 687-3793.

THE TAVERN, 105 Front St., 1836. This wonderful frame building was constructed by Edward Williams high on a bluff overlooking the Chattahoochee River. Steamboat passengers rested and dined here when Eufaula was a small trading center. Later, the inn was used as a church, a dwelling, and a Confederate hospital. Open M-Tu, Th-F 9-5, W 9-12. Free. (205) 687-4451.

WELLBORN HOUSE, 630 E. Broad St., c. 1837. Built for Dr. Levi Wellborn, this frame residence introduced the Greek Revival style to town. The house is now a museum of fine art administered by the Eufaula Arts Council. Open M-F 8-5. Free. (205) 687-9775 or 6631.

Gasque vicinity

FORT MORGAN, at the western terminus of AL 180, 1833-34. Constructed along the lines of an Italian fort designed by Michelangelo in the 16th century, this five-point-star-shaped citadel was built to guard the entrance to Mobile Bay. Though it came under attack by Admiral David Farragut and his troops during the Civil War, it is still in excellent condition. During the battle which resulted in Union control of Mobile Bay in August, 1864, Farragut gave the memorable order, "Damn the torpedoes, full steam ahead." Fort Morgan Museum offers exhibits of weapons, flags, Indian artifacts, and war mementos. NR, NHL. The park is open daily 8-sunset. $1 adults, children free. (205) 540-7125. Museum open winter, daily 8-5; summer, daily 8-6. Free. (205) 540-7127. ★

Mobile

One of the oldest communities in America, Mobile was founded in 1702 by Jean Baptiste le Moyne, Sieur de Bienville. He called his little colony Fort Louis de la Mobile, honoring both the Sun King in France and the Mauvilla Indians who had inhabited this plain at the mouth of the Mobile River long before the arrival of the Europeans. The French stay was relatively short: sixty-one years after the colony was founded, they were driven out by the Spanish. Mobile developed slowly; in 1803 the town had only 810 inhabitants. Finally, in 1813, the American flag was raised over Mobile, and the city began to expand. By the beginning of the Civil War, the community numbered almost 15,000 people, and, as Alabama's only port town, it became extremely prosperous. During World War II, the rapid growth of industry led to the destruction of many of Mobile's early buildings. Several have survived, however, and today one can still discover Greek Revival mansions surrounded by magnolias, dogwoods, and azaleas in the midst of a modern metropolis. For further information about walking and driving tours, write the Mobile Historic Development Commission, P.O. Box 1827, 36633, or call (205) 438-7281.

CARLEN HOUSE, 54 S. Carlen St., c. 1843. A vegetable farmer who sold his produce in Mobile's market, Michael Carlen bought three acres of land almost three miles from the city in 1842. He constructed this well-made 1½-story frame "Creole cottage" soon after he purchased the land. Over the years the city has spread, and the cottage is now on the campus of Murphy High School. The city owns the building and has furnished it with appropriate period pieces. NR. Open Tu-Sa 10-5, Su 1-5. Free. (205) 438-7569.

CATHEDRAL OF THE IMMACULATE CONCEPTION, 4 S. Claiborne St., c. 1835. An Italian Renaissance-style minor basilica, this beautiful building was designed by architect Claude Beroujon; the portico was added in 1874 and the towers in 1890. Noteworthy are the German stained-glass windows and the bronze canopy above the altar. NR. Open during daylight hours. Free. (205) 432-6684.

FORT CONDÉ, 150 S. Royal St., 1717. During excavations in the 1960s, the foundations of this fort, which was originally constructed by Jean Baptiste le Moyne, Sieur de Bienville, were discovered. The first masonry fort on the Gulf Coast when it was built at the beginning of the 18th century, it was reconstructed in the 1970s at great expense to the city. The fort is now manned by guides in French period costumes, and reproductions of 18th-century weapons are on display. NR. Open daily 9-5. $2 adults, $1 children.
(205) 438-7304. ★
 Adjacent to the fort is the **Condé-Charlotte House** (1822-24), 104 Theatre St. This two-story brick dwelling was built by John Kirkbride in 1845 on the founda-

tions of the earlier city jail building. A house museum run by the National Society of Colonial Dames, it features rooms furnished in the style of each of the nationalities that occupied Mobile. NR. Open Tu-Sa 10-4, Su by appointment. $1.50 adults, 50¢ children.
(205) 432-4722.

GOVERNMENT STREET PRESBYTERIAN CHURCH, 300 Government St., 1836. Constructed at a cost of $60,000, this porticoed building, designed by New Orleans architects James Gallier and Charles Dakin, is one of Alabama's finest Greek Revival edifices. NR. Open Sundays. (205) 432-1749.

MOBILE CITY HALL, 11 S. Royal St., c. 1856. This Italianate building has the distinction of being one of the few extant structures in America designed to house both a city hall and market. Today the market has moved elsewhere and the building is used for municipal offices. Open daily 8-5. Free. (205) 438-7411.

MUSEUM OF THE CITY OF MOBILE (Bernstein-Bush House), 355 Government St., 1872. This gracious Italianate structure was designed by James Hutchisson. Today it is a museum which houses relics of Mobile's colonial days as well as the world's second-largest collection of Boehm porcelains. NR. Open Tu-Sa 10-5, Su 1-5. Free. (205) 438-7569.

OAKLEIGH, 350 Oakleigh St., c. 1831. James Roper, a wealthy Mobile merchant, designed and built this handsome Greek Revival house. The "T" shape and raised basement are common features of houses built in semi-tropical climates; such a plan admits good light and provides the best ventilation possible. The beautiful curving exterior staircase, connecting the ground level to the first floor, is an extraordinary feature. Today the headquarters of the Historic Mobile Preservation Society, the house has been furnished with fine period pieces. NR. Open M-Sa 10-4, Su 2-4. $2 adults, $1 students 12-18, 50¢ children under 12. (205) 432-1281.

PHOENIX FIRE MUSEUM, 203 S. Claiborne St., 1859. In 1964, when the wrecker's ball threatened this wonderful two-story brick firehouse, with an octagonal cupola and iron balustrades, the city moved it to its present location. It is now a museum containing a good collection of fire-fighting mementos and equipment, including an 1819 steam fire engine. Open Tu-Sa 10-5, Su 1-5. Free. (205) 433-5343.

RICHARDS HOUSE, 256 N. Joachim St., c. 1860. Built by Charles G. Richards, a river boat captain from Maine, this delightful house is best known for its fanciful cast-iron gallery and fence which feature representations of the four seasons. Inside, the marble mantels, bronze and brass chandeliers, and cranberry-colored Bohemian glass panels are worthy of note. Now run by the D.A.R., the house boasts a colorful and fragrant garden with plantings which include azaleas, camellias, and sweet olive. NR. Open Tu-Sa 10-4, Su 1-4. $1 adults, 50¢ children. (205) 438-7320.

USS ALABAMA BATTLESHIP, Battleship Parkway. This WW II battleship is now a monument to the citizens of Alabama who served in the war effort. Also on view is the 1942 submarine, *USS Drum,* as well as army and marine weapons and equipment. Open daily 8-sunset. $2.50 adults, $1 children 6-11, under 6 free. (205) 433-2703. ★ ✔

Theodore

BELLINGRATH GARDENS AND HOME, off US 90 and I-10, 20th century. Situated on a bluff overlooking the Isle-aux-Oies River are seventy-five acres of gloriously planted and landscaped gardens on the grounds of this 1,000-acre estate. Flowers are in bloom during every season, and Spanish moss hangs from the

numerous oak trees which surround the mansion. The gardens are based on designs from the Orient to Italy and plantings include azaleas, poinsettias, roses, crysanthemums, and camellias. The inside of the Mediterranean-style house is almost as opulent as the gardens which surround it. Every room features antique furniture and pieces from Mrs. Walter D. Bellingrath's collections of silver, china, and porcelain. Gardens open daily 7-dusk. $3 adults, $1.50 children 6-12, under 6 free. House open daily 8:30-5. $3.75 additional. (205) 973-2217.

Troy

PIKE PIONEER MUSEUM, off U.S. 231 N. of town. This collection of reconstructed pioneer buildings and artifacts is a treat for anyone interested in the life style of Americans living on the frontier. The collection includes such objects as a horse-drawn hearse, hand-pegged pie safes, and relics concerning tenant farming in Alabama. Open M-Sa 10-5, Su 1-5. $1 adults, 50¢ students. (205) 566-6158.

Central Alabama

Much of Alabama's central region lies in the richly fertile area known as the black belt. Demopolis, Eutaw, and Montgomery grew to be rich and beautiful during the cotton boom prior to the Civil War.

In these towns stand many of the state's most opulent mansions and public buildings; most were constructed by wealthy plantation owners. Today this is still an important agricultural region, and the cities and hamlets alike have retained their ante-bellum charm.

Dadeville vicinity

HORSESHOE BEND NATIONAL MILITARY PARK, 12 miles N. of town on AL 49, 1814. Situated at a bend in the Tallapoosa River, this park commemorates a battle which ended the Creek Indian War (1813-14). Major General Andrew Jackson led the Tennessee militia against the "Red Sticks"; in the end, the Indians were forced to give up over 20 million acres. Jackson's reputation as an "Indian fighter" was made. Today there is a **Visitor Center** in this 2,040-acre park which houses a museum with interpretive exhibits concerning the battle. NR. Park open daily 8-dusk. Visitor Center daily 8-4:30. (205) 234-7111, 329-9905. ★

Demopolis

After Napoleon was defeated at Waterloo, Louis XVIII ran hundreds of the Emperor's liegemen out of the country. Many of them came to America and, once here, formed a society known as "French Emigrants for the Cultivation of Vine and Olive." They convinced the U.S. government to allocate land to their cause, and before long these effete courtiers were in the process of establishing an agricultural experiment in the fertile land near the confluence of the Tombigbee and Black Warrior Rivers. They called their town Demopolis, meaning city of the people. The French settlers were overcome by the hardships of pioneer life, and many soon deserted their new home high on picturesque chalk bluffs overlooking the river for the comforts of more settled regions. Some years later, American settlers from Northern states came and established cotton plantations in this area. The Americans knew what to expect, and before long they prospered. The lovely Greek Revival and Victorian homes which remain in the area attest to the 19th-century affluence of this charming river town.

BLUFF HALL, 405 N. Commissioners Ave., 1832-late 1840s. Built for lawyer-planter Francis Strother Lyon, this stuccoed brick house reflects the changing tastes of the first half of the 19th century. Though the residence was originally built as a Federal-style town house, the columned portico, rear wing, and Corinthian columns and neo-classical plasterwork inside, were added to make the house conform to the whims of Greek Revival fashion. Now administered by the Marengo County Historical Society, the house has beautifully appointed period rooms and a fine collection of antique clothing. NR. Open Tu-Sa 10-5, Su 2-5. $2 adults, 50¢ children. (205) 289-1666.

GAINESWOOD, 805 S. Cedar St., 1842-60. This may be the most lavish ante-bellum mansion in the state, and it is, perhaps, the best one open as a museum. Built and designed by the original owner, Nathan Bryan Whitfield, the house reflects a desire to create the most outstanding Greek Revival house in the state. Whitfield claimed that the drawing room was "the most splendid in Alabama." Notable are the incredibly elaborate plasterwork, the elegant furnishings, and the domes with lantern skylights in the parlor and dining room. NR. Open M -Sa 8-5, Su 1-5. $2 adults, $1 students, 50¢ children under 12. (205) 289-4846.

While you're in town, you may want to stop at the **Confederate Park,** bounded by Main, Capitol, Walnut, and Washington Sts., which displays such refined features as a goldfish pond, gazebo, and fountain, and a variety of flowering trees and shrubs. Planned as the town square in 1819, it is one of Alabama's oldest. NR.

Eutaw

KIRKWOOD, 111 Kirkwood Dr., 1857-60. Built by planter Foster M. Kirksey, this Greek Revival mansion features an exceptional full Ionic portico with a second-story balcony. The house has been extensively restored and is situated in the center of a lovely seven-acre garden. NR. Open by appointment. $2 admission. (205) 372-9009.

Also of interest are two of the town's handsome Greek Revival public buildings: **The**

First Presbyterian Church (1851), Main
St., and the **Greene County Courthouse**
(1869), Courthouse Sq. The small columns on the courthouse are said to
evidence the diminishing affection for that
popular mid-19th century architectural
mode. NR. The church is open for regular
services. (205) 372-3367. The courthouse
is open during business hours. (205)
372-3598.

Greensboro

MAGNOLIA GROVE, 1002 Hobson St.,
1835. A two-story stuccoed-brick Greek
Revival temple-style home, this was the
birthplace of the Spanish-American War
hero, Richmond Pearson Hobson. The
dwelling's front façade features a six-
columned Doric portico with an intricate
wrought-iron balustrade ornamenting the
second-floor gallery. The museum in the
building is operated by the Alabama
Historical Commission and offers a collection of memorabilia about Hobson and
mementos from his foreign exploits. NR.
Open Th, Sa, Su 2-5. $1.50 adults, 75¢
students. (205) 624-8618.

Montgomery

Situated in the heart of Alabama's black
belt, Montgomery was founded in 1817 by
a native of Long Island named Andrew
Dexter. Dexter called his settlement
New Philadelphia, and it retained that
name for two years. Located beside the
deep and navigable Alabama River, on
some of the richest soil in the country, with
coal and iron fields to the north, and pine
forests to the south, Montgomery was
bound to become an industrial city. By the
middle of the 19th century, four railroad
lines converged at this point. Montgomery
serves as the state capital and bears the
distinction of having been the first capital
of the Confederacy. The fateful telegram
carrying the order to "fire on Fort Sumter"
was sent from the new capital in 1861,
touching off Civil War violence. And
though Union troops did occupy this town
in 1865, it was not destroyed and still retains much of its ante-bellum heritage and
charm. For further information, walking

and driving tour maps, and state literature,
stop by the Montgomery Area Chamber of
Commerce, 41 Commerce St. Open M-F
8:30-5. (205) 834-5200.

ALABAMA STATE CAPITOL, Bain-
bridge St. at Dexter Ave., 1851. This
Greek Revival building, which served as
the first capitol of the Confederacy, was
designed by Barachias Holt. The Corin-
thian-columned structure has had many
additions, including three wings, two of
which (north and south) were designed by
McKim, Mead and White. Of note are the
murals in the rotunda and the six-pointed
star at the top of the steps of the west portico which marks the spot where Jefferson
Davis stood when he was sworn in as president. NR, NHL. Open daily 8-5. Free.
(205) 832-6011.

DEXTER AVENUE BAPTIST CHURCH,
454 Dexter Ave., 1878. Martin Luther
King was pastor at this simple brick church
from 1954 until 1960 when he moved to
Atlanta. It was here that King launched the
Montgomery Bus Boycott in 1955-56,
which eventually gave rise to the national
civil rights movement. NR, NHL. Open
for regular services. (205) 263-3970.

Enthusiasm for King's ideas was not
universal, and you can still see the scars left
by a bomb thrown at the **Pastorium**
(1912), 309 Jackson St., where King and
his family lived. The house is located in a
black neighborhood known as Centennial
Hill and is a one-story frame cottage
typical of dwellings available to blacks at
that time. NR.

FIRST WHITE HOUSE OF THE CON-
FEDERACY, 644 Washington Ave.,

c. 1825. With its many-bracketed cornice, rear veranda, and lacy woodwork, this building was the home of Jefferson Davis, the first and only president of the Confederacy, from March until May of 1861. Many of Davis's belongings, as well as Civil War memorabilia and period furnishings, are displayed in this house museum. NR. Open M-F 8-5, Sa-Su 8-11:30 and 12:30-5. Donations accepted. (205) 832-5269.

GOVERNOR'S MANSION, 1142 S. Perry St., 1907-8. Designed by Montgomery architect Weatherly Carter, this Neo-classical Revival house is furnished with reproductions of Victorian furniture made in Alabama and hung with chandeliers from a hotel in New Orleans. Open Tu, Th 10:30-12:30 and 2-4. Free. (205) 834-3022.

MURPHY HOUSE, 22 Bibb St., 1851. An enterprising Scot named John Murphy built this handsome Greek Revival home. Of note is the portico with fluted Corinthian columns and marble floor. The house is made of brick, but is stuccoed and scored to resemble stone. NR. Open M-F 8-5. Free. (205) 264-3491.

ORDEMAN-SHAW HISTORIC DISTRICT, 220 N. Hull at Jefferson, mid-19th century. Operated by the Landmarks Foundation of Montgomery, this complex consists of over a dozen restored and reconstructed 19th-century buildings, including a barn, doctor's office, church, grange hall, slave quarters, and a number of residences. The Visitor Center is located in the Lucas Tavern (c. 1819); it is said that Lafayette stopped here. The Italianate Ordeman-Shaw House (c. 1850), 310 N. Hull St., is perhaps the most distinctive building in the district and was built by architect/engineer Charles Ordeman. All of the structures in the complex are furnished with appropriate period pieces and are open to the public. NR. M-Sa 9:30-4, Su 1:30-4. $2.50 adults, 75¢ children. (205) 265-1731 or 7886.

ST. JOHN'S EPISCOPAL CHURCH, 113 Madison Ave., 1855. Designed from plans by architects Frank Wills and Henry Dudley, this Gothic Revival church has an octagonal spire, beautiful stained-glass windows, and an unusual stenciled ceiling. Jefferson Davis once sat in one of the carved oak pews. NR. Open daily by appointment with the church office. Free. (205) 262-1937.

Moundville

MOUND STATE PARK, AL 69. One of the most important mound sites in all the South, this area was inhabited by Indians of the Mississippi culture from 1200-1400 A.D. Today over forty "platform" mounds which once held dwellings and ceremonial structures remain. These have been excavated, and many of the artifacts recovered are on view in a museum building. NR, NHL. Open daily 9-5. $2 adults, $1 children. (205) 371-2572.

Selma and vicinity

Situated in the center of Alabama's black belt, on a bluff overlooking the Alabama River, Selma is the seat of Dallas County and a farming and industrial town. Selma was on the map as early as 1732 and was then known as Ecor Bienville. The town remained insignificant as it was overshadowed by nearby Cahawba. When Cahawba was wiped out by repeated floods and the trials of the Civil War, Selma began to prosper. During the war, a foundry and arsenal in Selma supplied ammunition to Confederate troops, and when Union forces reached town, much of the city was burned. Selma recovered quickly, becoming in time a thriving industrial town. An annual pilgrimage to the city's older homes and buildings takes place each spring. For further information call (205) 872-8713.

BROWN CHAPEL AFRICAN METHODIST EPISCOPAL CHURCH, 410 Martin Luther King, Jr. St., 1908. On January 2, 1965, in this rose-windowed Byzantine and Romanesque Revival church, Martin Luther King spoke to 700 people about the issue of civil rights and the campaign sponsored by the Southern Christian Leadership Conference to gain equal voting rights. NR. Open by appointment. (205) 874-9420.

Half a block away, in the **First Baptist Church,** supporters of the civil rights movement gathered regularly to talk with Dr. King, Ralph Abernathy, and other members of the SCLC. Constructed by black builder/architect Dave West in 1894, this church was badly damaged by a tornado in 1979. The congregation is attempting to restore it. NR. (205) 874-6665.

JOHN TYLER MORGAN HOUSE, 719 Tremont St., c. 1859. An ardent secessionist and brigadier general in the Confederate Army, Morgan was later elected to the U.S. Senate. His two-story brick house with full porch and French windows is now run by the Selma-Dallas County Historic Preservation Society. NR. Open by appointment. (205) 872-6489.

OLD CAHAWBA, 11 miles SW of Selma, off AL 22. This picturesque site at the confluence of the Cahaba and Alabama Rivers seemed a fine place for the Dallas County seat when the county was created in 1818. Cahawba became the first state capital two years later and expanded quickly until 1826, when a flood destroyed most of the town. Although the capital was moved to Tuscaloosa, many townspeople persevered and Cahawba recovered and became an important port town. Floods struck again in 1865 and 1866, and the county seat, along with most of the population, moved to higher ground. Today, little remains of the town but romantic columns, overgrown ruins, and gravestones. Plans are in the works to restore the historic district, but at the moment you will find interpretive markers at the site. NR. Open daily sunrise to sunset. Free. For further information call the Selma Chamber of Commerce. (205) 875-7421.

ST. PAUL'S EPISCOPAL CHURCH, 210 Lauderdale St., 1871-74. This brick Gothic Revival church, with a four-stage belltower and original stained-glass Tiffany windows, was designed by Richard Upjohn and his son Richard. NR. Open by appointment. (205) 874-8421.

JOSEPH T. SMITHERMAN HISTORIC BUILDING, 109 Union St., c. 1848. This handsome three-story brick building, with four monumental Ionic columns and ornamental balustrades, was built by the Free and Accepted Masons as a school for orphans and the children of indigent Masons. During the Civil War, it served as a Confederate hospital, eventually becoming headquarters for Dallas County officials. After 1904, it was once again a school and then a hospital. In 1960, it was vacated and stood empty for almost ten years until Mayor Smitherton took an interest in the ante-bellum structure. It has been extensively restored and today houses a collection of local mementos, including Civil War and Indian artifacts, antique furnishings, and collections of stamps, glass, and coins. Open M-F 9-4, Su 2-4. Free. (205) 872-8713.

STURDIVANT HALL, 713 Mabry St., 1853. Robert E. Lee's cousin Thomas was the architect of this fine Greek Revival building with Italianate elements. Two stories high, with a bracketed cupola and thirty-foot columns, this mansion was built for city council member Col. Edward T. Watts. The city of Selma bought the building in 1957, funded in large part by

Carnegie Hall, Tuskegee Institute

Robert Sturdivant who had provided in his will for a museum for the city. The Sturdivants' own collection of Victorian, Chippendale, and Hepplewhite furniture, as well as rugs, china, silver, and paintings, now belongs to the museum. The cast-iron balustrades and interior woodwork and plasterwork are extraordinary. NR. Open Tu-Sa 9-4, Su 2-4. $2 adults, $1 students, children free. (205) 872-1377.

Tuskegee

TUSKEGEE INSTITUTE NATIONAL HISTORIC SITE, off AL 126, 1881. Booker T. Washington, born a slave, founded this college for the education of blacks. His objectives were to train his students to educate others, to teach them his version of morality and cleanliness, and to prepare them for the "real world" with occupational skills. Supported by philanthropists from all over the country, Tuskegee prospered and has contributed to the education of blacks for just over a century. George Washington Carver, the renowned scientist, came to work there in 1896. He stayed for forty-seven years, and a museum in his honor has been established at the college. A tour of the college should begin at the **Visitor Center,** located on campus in the ante-bellum mansion, **Grey Columns.** NR, NHL. Open daily 9-5. Free. Phone (205) 727-8335 for tours and 727-6390 for information about the site.

Northern Alabama

Both heavily industrialized and extremely rural, this area of contrasts is known for its varied landscapes and magnificent river; the Tennessee traverses the northern part of Alabama, entering in the northeast and flowing into Tennessee in the northwest. Travelers to this area will not find the mansions which are so common in the fertile regions to the south; instead they will discover Alabama's pioneer heritage, its early public buildings, and the vestiges of its 19th-century iron and steel industries.

Anniston

ST. MICHAEL AND ALL ANGELS EPISCOPAL CHURCH, 18th St. and Cobb Ave., 1888-90. In 1872 Samuel Noble and General Alfred Tyler formed the Woodstock Iron Company and laid out a little industrial town around it. Many of the laborers who came to the model community were of British extraction and the Anglican faith. Though one church was built, it could not accommodate everyone, and one of Noble's civic-minded nephews commissioned this extraordinary ecclesiastical structure in 1887. Designed by William Hulsey Wood and executed by a team of master craftsmen, the complex,

which included a community center, school, and free clinic, was completed at a cost of $250,000. A double hammer beam ceiling is embellished with the carved heads of angels on each of the major beams; the heads are turned so that each angel has a view of the altar. One of the stained-glass windows was made by Tiffany and the floors are Alabama marble. The altar is Italian Carrara marble and the reredos (the ornamental screen to the rear of the altar) consists of five brick towers covered with alabaster and crowned with angels. One of the finest examples of church architecture in Alabama, it is open to the public every day of the year. NR. Open daily 9-4. Free. (205) 237-6766.

Another local building of interest is **The Noble Cottage** (1887), 900 Leighton St. Designed by L.B. Wheeler, an architect influenced by the designs of both Henry Hobson Richardson and Stanford White, this structure is rubble on the first story and shingled on the second. Much of the interior woodwork has survived; the building has been carefully restored and is now an architect's office. NR. Open daily 8-5. Free. (205) 237-9846.

Ashland

CLAY COUNTY COURTHOUSE, Courthouse Sq., 1906. This wonderful Renaissance Revival building, with porticos, parapets, swags and cartouches, was designed by C.W. Carlton. The brick and stone structure has a dome and a cupola. NR. Open M-F 8-5. Free. (205) 354-7926.

Birmingham

A pioneer named John Jones passed into this valley at the southern end of the Appalachian mountains in 1813. Before long a town named Elyton was established in what is now Birmingham's West End. Indians called "Red Sticks" by the pioneers because they painted their faces red also inhabited this fertile area near the Warrior River. When the settlers discovered that the pigment was made of a substance which came from nearby Red Mountain, they did not understand its worth. In 1860, the value of this region's hematite iron ore began to be recognized, and by the time of the Civil War there was a small blast furnace in town producing arms and ammunition for the Confederacy. In the late 19th century, the manufacturing town of Birmingham grew at a prodigious rate. Named for the British industrial center, Birmingham recognizes its place as Alabama's largest and most industrialized city and calls itself "the Pittsburgh of the South."

ARLINGTON ANTE-BELLUM HOME AND GARDENS, 331 Cotton Ave., 1822, 1842. The oldest surviving structure in Birmingham, the west wing of this building was originally a four-room house. The east wing of the two-story frame structure was added later by William Mudd. Today the Greek Revival house is a museum with well-appointed period rooms. NR. Open Tu-Sa 9-5, Su 1-6. $2 adults, $1 students 12-18, 75¢ children under 12, children under 4 free. (205) 780-5656.

VULCAN, Vulcan Park, US 31, 1904. Named for the Roman god of fire and metalworking, this statue was created by Italian sculptor Giuseppe Moretti for the Louisiana Purchase Exhibition in St.

Louis. Now billed as the "world's largest iron man," the statue weighs 120,000 pounds and stands 55 feet tall. A monument to local industry, the sculpture is made of Birmingham iron and was cast in local foundries. An observation deck at the base of the tower affords a lovely view of the valley; the deck is reached by glass-enclosed elevator. NR. The six-acre Vulcan Park in which the statue is located is open daily 8:30 am-10 pm. $1 admission, children under 8 free. (205) 254-2628.

Bridgeport vicinity

RUSSELL CAVE NATIONAL MONUMENT, 8 miles W. of town on US 72, 7000 B.C.-500 B.C. Twelve feet under the present floor of this enormous cave near the edge of the Tennessee River Valley, archaeologists have found evidence of Indians who lived here as much as 9,000 years ago. Today there are interpretive displays at the site which include collections of the spearheads and prehistoric cooking utensils discovered during excavations. NR. Open daily 8-5. Free. (205) 495-2672. ✓

Cullman and vicinity

CULLMAN COUNTY MUSEUM, 211 Second Ave. NE. After the people of the town of Cullman celebrated their centennial in 1973, they decided to build a facsimile of the house which had once belonged to the village founder, a German

immigrant named Col. John G. Cullman. The original had been destroyed in a fire in 1912. Today this "Swiss Victorian" house contains a collection of county memorabilia. Open M-W, F 9-12 and 1-4:30, Th 2-4:30, Sa-Su 1:30-4:30. $1 adults, 50¢ children. (205) 739-1258.

Nine miles west of Cullman on US 278 is **Clarkson Covered Bridge**, Alabama's longest construction of this type. Built in 1908 and restored in 1973-74, the 275-foot-long structure spans Crooked Creek. Today the bridge is closed to vehicles, but the traveler can park the car and walk across.

Decatur

OLD STATE BANK, Bank and Wilson Sts., 1833. Five stone Doric columns support the portico of Alabama's oldest bank building. One of five structures in town left standing after the devastations of the Civil War, this attractive brick structure is being restored to its original condition. The old vault is still in the basement. NR. Open by appointment. Free. (205) 353-5319.

Florence

W.C. HANDY RESTORED BIRTHPLACE AND MUSEUM, 620 W. College St., 1845. The "father of the blues," W.C. Handy, was born in this one-room log cabin in 1873. Today it is a museum containing mementos of Handy's life. Open Tu-Sa 9-12 and 1-4. $1 adults, 25¢ children. (205) 764-4661.

POPE'S TAVERN, 203 Hermitage Dr., 1811. Florence's oldest surviving structure, this building was used first as a tavern and then as a hospital during the Civil War. Andrew Jackson stopped here in 1814 during one of his trips through Alabama. Today the brick building with its wide veranda is used as a museum and contains a good collection of colonial furnishings. Open Tu-Sa 9-12 and 1-4. $1 adults, 25¢ children. (205) 766-2662.

Gadsden

PIONEER MUSEUM, Noccalula Rd. in

the Noccalula Botanical Gardens, 18th century. This collection of hand-hewn log buildings was originally constructed around 1777 in Lawrenceburg, Tennessee. They have since been reassembled at this site and contain a good collection of pioneer furniture. Open daily 8-sunset. $1.50 adults, 50¢ children. (205) 543-7412.

Huntsville

BURRITT MUSEUM, 3101 Burritt Dr. SE, 1935. Dr. William Burritt built this unusual eleven-room stone house in the shape of a Maltese cross and later willed it to the city for use as a house museum. Collections include Indian artifacts and historic mementos. In the 167-acre park in which the house stands are reconstructed log homesteads, a blacksmith shop, smokehouses, and a church. Open Apr-Oct, Tu-Su 12-6; Mar-Nov, Tu-Su 12-5. Donations accepted. (205) 536-2882.

TWICKENHAM HISTORIC DISTRICT, bounded roughly by Clinton and Hermitage Aves., and Madison and California Sts., 19th-20th centuries. Many stately mansions line the streets of Huntsville's peaceful residential section. A mélange of styles—Federal, Greek Revival, Italianate, Gothic Revival, Eastlake, and Queen Anne—reflect the long period of prosperity in Huntsville. NR. Also of interest is the **Episcopal Church of the Nativity** (c. 1858), 212 Eustis Ave. New York architects Frank Wills and Henry Dudley designed this one-story brick Gothic Revival church. NR. Open for regular services. (205) 533-2455.

While you're touring the streets of the district, look in at **The Weeden House** (1819), 300 Gates Ave. This dignified two-story brick Federal house is operated by the Twickenham Historic Preservation District Association as a museum and is open by appointment. NR. $2 adults, $1 children. (205) 533-1450.

McCalla

IRON AND STEEL MUSEUM OF ALABAMA, Tannehill State Park, off I-20. A memorial to the pioneers of the iron and steel industries, this park features exhibits of 19th-century forging and casting implements and the ruins of pre-Civil War furnaces, as well as a group of restored buildings (1820-1900) known as the **Tannehill Rural Village Complex.** Open Tu-Sa 10-5, Su 2-5. 25¢ admission, under 6 free. (205) 477-6101.

Tuscaloosa

The University of Alabama is situated in this peaceful town beside the Black Warrior River. Settled in 1816 and named Tuscaloosa after an Indian chief defeated by De Soto in the 16th century, the city became the state capital in 1826. For twenty years Tuscaloosa was the hub of Alabama social and commercial life. Clothing, plows, hats, and paper were produced here, and the fertile fields just outside town contributed to the area's prosperity. When the capital was moved to Montgomery, Tuscaloosa adjusted to a quieter existence. Though Union soldiers burned many of the town's ante-bellum buildings, there are still a number of fine examples of Greek Revival architecture gracing the oak-shaded streets.

BATTLE-FRIEDMAN HOUSE, 1010 Greensboro Ave., 1835. Built by Alfred Battle, this two-story T-shaped house has walls eighteen inches thick. The full-width portico features a marble floor and square columns two stories high. The Friedman family acquired this house in 1875 and lived here until it was willed to the city. The grounds are beautifully laid out with period gardens. NR. Open Tu-F 10-12 and 1-4, Sa-Su 1-4. $1 adults, 50¢ children. (205) 758-6138.

THE OLD TAVERN, W. end of Broad St. at 28th Ave. in Capitol Park, 1827. When Tuscaloosa became the capital, an enterprising man named William Dunton took the opportunity to build a tavern. The two-story brick building with a second-story gallery reflects the influence of French immigrants who populated the area. The tavern has been used as a dwelling and is now a museum administered by the Tuscaloosa County Preservation Society. Collections include period furnishings and mementos of Alabama folklore. NR.

Open Tu-F 10-12 and 1-4. $1 adults, 50¢ children. (205) 758-8163.

STRICKLAND HOUSE, 2900 6th St., 1820. A small cottage constructed of hand-hewn boards and held together with wooden pegs and square nails, this is thought to be the oldest building in town. The original wide pine flooring, as well as the shutters and window panes, have survived. The structure has been carefully restored by the Tuscaloosa County Preservation Society and is now used as offices. NR. Open M-F 8:30-12. Free. (205) 758-2238.

UNIVERSITY OF ALABAMA, off University Blvd., between Thomas St. and Third Ave., 1819. Only four buildings were left on campus after the devastation wrought by the Civil War. The **Gorgas House** (1829), Colonial Dr., was designed by the English architect William Nichols and built of brick supposedly used as ballast in English ships making the trip to America to collect cotton. The modest two-story house is Federal in style and features such architectural details as a twisting exterior staircase leading to the second-story portico. The structure was the home of University President, Josiah Gorgas and his son, Dr. William Gorgas, who is famed for his work eradicating yellow fever during the building of the Panama Canal. Today the building is a museum with collections of historical artifacts. Open M-Sa 10-12 and 2-5, Su 3-5.

Free. (205) 348-5906. The Greek Revival **Old Observatory** (1844), just behind the Gorgas House, and the **Round House** (1860), near the Gorgas Library, are two of the other buildings to have survived the war. The fourth extant ante-bellum structure is the fully articulated Greek Revival **President's Mansion** (1841), University Blvd. Also designed by William Nichols, this three-story building has balustrades, a third-story balcony constructed of wrought iron, and a portico featuring massive Ionic columns. NR. Open by appointment. (205) 348-5378.

Tuscumbia

IVY GREEN (Helen Keller Birthplace), 300 W. North Common, 1820. Every American knows the story of Helen Keller and Annie Sullivan, about how the teacher from Boston's Perkins Institute taught the obstreperous deaf and blind child to communicate. At the age of 22, Helen Keller published her autobiography, *The Story of My Life;* two years later she graduated from Radcliffe with honors. In 1968, at the age of 88, she died after a full life devoted to the aid of the handicapped. Today the 1½-story frame Keller family house and a one-story cottage known as Helen Keller's birthplace are open to the public. They contain period furnishings and memorabilia from Keller's life. NR. M-Sa 8:30-4:30, Su 1-4:30. $1.50 adults, 50¢ children 6-11, children under 6 free. (205) 383-4066. ✔

Historic Accommodations

An asterisk (*) indicates that meals are served.

Mobile

MALAGA INN, 359 Church St., 36602. (205) 438-4701. Open all year. Two adjacent 1860s town houses now form the lovely Malaga Inn. Named for the Spanish city, the hotel is furnished in a combination of Mediterranean and 19th-century styles. Excellent food is served in El Restaurante, and the quiet, verdant courtyard provides a relaxing spot for guests. NR.*

Montgomery

SHERATON RIVERFRONT STA-TION, 200 Coosa St., 36104. (205) 834-4300. Open all year. An imaginative re-use of Montgomery's superb Victorian Gothic and Romanesque Revival Union Railroad Station, this 1897-98 building by Benjamin Bosworth Smith has been transformed into an exciting hotel. A number of restaurants provide excellent food. NR.*

8. MISSISSIPPI

THE lyrical name of the river and the state is thought to have derived from either the Choctaw word for "beyond age" or Illinoian for "great water." Hernando de Soto was the first European to discover this area, having spent several months here in an unsuccessful quest for gold in 1540-41. In the 1680s, this temperate land inhabited by friendly Indians was claimed for Louis XIV of France by Sieur de la Salle. The first permanent settlement was formed near Biloxi in 1699; the area remained in French hands, as part of the Louisiana territory, until 1763 when it was appropriated by the British. During the Revolution, the Spanish took advantage of British weakness and captured Natchez and the surrounding area. Within two decades, the Americans had staked their claim, and Mississippi was, at least in name, a U.S. territory.

By the late 18th century, settlers were generally of Scottish and Irish origin and came South from colonies on the eastern seaboard. It seems likely that many of them used the **Natchez Trace** to come into the territory. The Trace was a network of trails, running from Nashville to Natchez, which had been developed over the years by the Choctaw and Natchez Indians. Later the trail became an important route for explorers, merchants, and pioneers. By 1800, when mail began to be carried by this route, the postmaster general complained that it could be delivered only "at great expense to the public on account of the badness of the road which is said to be no other than an Indian footpath very devious and narrow." In the following year, Thomas Jefferson set the Army to work clearing the Trace, but little progress was made; eventually funds from Congress were given to the postmaster general so that he might contract free-lance road builders. With the advent of steamboats on the Mississippi, the Trace became obsolete; after a time, it all but disappeared. Today, Natchez Trace is part of the National Park System, and a new, modern highway is being built along virtually the same 450-mile-long route through Mississippi, Alabama, and Tennessee. For further information, contact the **Parkway Headquarters and Visitor Center,** 5 miles N. of Tupelo at the junction of US 45 and the Natchez Trace National Parkway. A museum is located in the visitor center. Open daily 8-5. Free. (601) 842-1572.

Mississippi suffered much violence and hardship during the Civil War, and, though the extent of destruction was almost ruinous, the state's restrained yet opulent ante-bellum past has survived in the old plantations and town houses gracing the streets of Vicksburg and Natchez and other more rural towns. The people of Mississippi are very proud of their Southern heritage; almost every city which has any buildings of historic interest opens them to the public during the traditional Pilgrimages. Usually sponsored by local garden clubs or historical societies, these gala events offer the tourist a chance to visit the houses which epitomize the Old South.

Riverview, Columbus

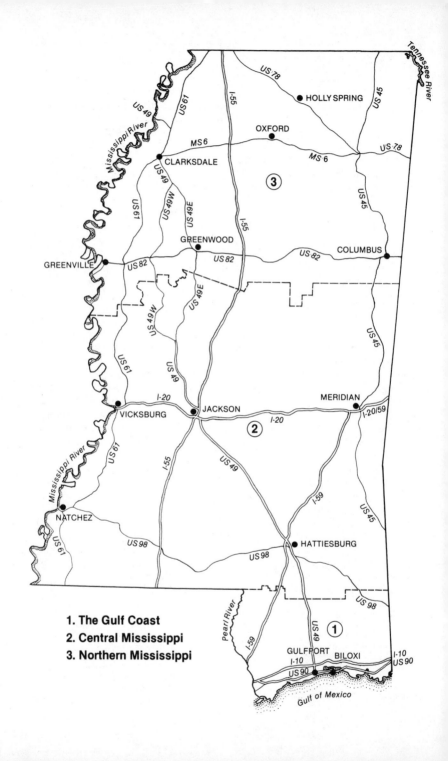

1. The Gulf Coast
2. Central Mississippi
3. Northern Mississippi

The Gulf Coast

Settlers along Mississippi's Gulf Coast have depended on the ocean's bounty for survival since the first French pioneers arrived in this region in 1699. With its sandy soil and long-leaf pine forests, the coastal plain has never been suitable for agriculture, but the semi-tropical climate, the moss-laden oaks, and the colorful profusion of azaleas, poinsettias, and camellias have made it a popular spot for those attracted to peaceful coastal areas. Almost all of the seaside communities have their own annual pilgrimages, but the **Gulf Coast Pilgrimage** which occurs in May guides tourists to structures ranging from ante-bellum homes to space technology laboratories in towns from Pascagoula to Bay St. Louis. Call or write the Biloxi Chamber of Commerce for further information. (See Biloxi for address and telephone number.)

Biloxi

The city of Biloxi was founded in 1721 and has grown at a slow and steady pace ever since. Though the Spanish and British both claimed it, Biloxi remained essentially French until 1798 when Mississippi came under U.S. dominion. With its wonderful seafood and miles of sandy white beaches, Biloxi has been a popular resort since the 1840s. For a driving tour map and information concerning the Spring Pilgrimage, stop by the Chamber of Commerce, 1036 Fred Haise Blvd. (601) 374-2717.

BEAUVOIR, 200 W. Beach Blvd., c. 1852. Jefferson Davis, the only president of the Confederacy, spent the last twelve years of his life in this one-story cottage. Politicians have published their versions of history since the dawn of the printed word, and Davis was no exception; in the study building outside the house, he wrote *The Rise and Fall of the Confederacy* (1881). Tour the grounds, the library, and the house. Collections include Civil War artifacts and some of Davis's furnishings and mementos. NR. Open daily 8:30-5. $3.25 adults, $2 senior citizens, $1.25 children. (601) 388-1313.

BILOXI GARDEN CENTER (OLD BRICK HOUSE), 410 E. Bayview Ave., early 19th century. This 1½-story brick house, with a shed porch and double front door, is thought to be the oldest surviving building in Biloxi. Mayor John Henley lived here during the Civil War. NR. Open by appointment. Nominal admission. (601) 432-5836.

BILOXI LIGHTHOUSE, on US 90 at Porter Ave., 1848. The first cast-iron lighthouse in the South, this sixty-five-foot tower offers a spectacular view of the coastline. The people of Biloxi painted the

Beauvoir

white tower black after Lincoln's assassination. Today it is white again and is open Sa 9-5 and by appointment. Free. (601) 374-2717 or 4355.

CREOLE COTTAGE, 216 Lameuse St., c. 1836. Now a museum and the headquarters of the Biloxi Art and History Authority, this building was the first free library in the state. The museum's collection includes local memorabilia and furnishings. Open M-F 8-5; other times by appointment. Free. (601) 374-8600.

MAGNOLIA HOTEL, 137 Magnolia St., 1847. This 2½-story frame structure with plastered exterior walls is thought to be the oldest surviving hotel on the Mississippi Gulf Coast. Today the hotel is used as a museum which houses a gallery of Southern art and exhibitions of local artifacts. NR. Tu-Sa 11-4; other times by appointment. Free. (601) 435-7762.

TULLIS-TOLEDANO MANOR, 947 E. Beach Blvd., 1856-57. This 2½-story Greek Revival mansion was built as a holiday retreat for Spanish-Creole businessman Cristoval Toledano and his wife, Matilda Pradat. Note the spiral stairs which wind around a tapered tree trunk which serves as the newel post. NR. Open M-F 1-5, and by appointment. $1 donation. (601) 436-4236.

Gulfport vicinity

FORT MASSACHUSETTS, S. of Gulfport on Ship Island, c. 1859-63. The U.S. Army Corps of Engineers was stationed here when the Civil War began. The Mississippi militia had no trouble capturing the D-shaped coastal defense, for the walls were unfortified and only six feet high. Later the Union recaptured the fort and raised the walls another twelve feet. After the war, Fort Massachusetts served as a Federal prison. NR. Open all year, sunrise to sunset. Ship Island is accessible by boat only. **Tours** may be arranged at the Buena Vista Hotel, US 90. May-Sept, daily 9 and 2:30; Apr, M-F 2:30, Sa-Su 9 and 2:30. The round trip takes four hours. $8 adults, $4 children 4-12, children under 3 free. (601) 432-2197. ★ ✔

For information concerning Gulfport's **Spring Pilgrimage,** contact the Chamber of Commerce, Drawer FF, 39501. (601) 863-2933.

Pascagoula

OLD SPANISH FORT, 4602 Fort St., 18th century. Regardless of its name, it is thought that this building may be part of a fort complex constructed by the French upon the arrival of 300 settlers here in

Parham-Katz House, Scenic Drive Historic District

1721. The citadel was later occupied by conquering Spaniards. The one-story rectangular edifice is frame with tabby (shell, sand, and lime) fill. One of the oldest structures in Mississippi, it is now a museum containing collections of Indian, military, and archaeological artifacts, and handmade furniture. NR. Open F-W 10-4. $1 adults, 50¢ children. (601) 769-1505. ★

For information concerning Pascagoula's **Spring Pilgrimage**, contact the Chamber of Commerce, Drawer P, 39567. (601) 762-3391.

Pass Christian

SCENIC DRIVE HISTORIC DISTRICT, off US 90, 19th and 20th centuries. Ten miles west of Gulfport lies this charming 19th-century summer resort; one of the beachfront streets, Scenic Drive, is an oak-lined avenue ornamented with spectacular summer "cottages" in styles ranging from Greek Revival and Queen Anne to Colonial Revival. Though the mansions are private, a drive along Scenic Drive is recommended. NR. Some of the historic homes are open to the public during the **Spring Pilgrimage**. Write or call the Chamber of Commerce for further information. Box 307, 39571. (601) 452-2252.

Central Mississippi

Greek Revival houses, which are the hallmark of the Deep South, abound in Central Mississippi. The fertile land of the Delta area, which encompasses the region around the Mississippi and the Yazoo Rivers, provided the state with abundant crops of cotton, its largest source of income. Natchez, one time shipping and cotton capital of the area, is one of the South's most extraordinary cities. Wealthy merchants and plantation owners built extravagant town houses in this community. Today, Mississippi's central region is characterized by charming ante-bellum river towns: some are virtually ghost towns as a result of the Civil War or the caprices of the meandering Mississippi, and others, like Jackson, the state capital, are active commercial and tourist centers, rich in the remnants of history.

Church Hill

CHRIST CHURCH, MS 533, 1858. Designed by a little-known Natchez architect, J. E. Smith, this stuccoed brick structure exhibits impressive handling of the Gothic form. The Gothic Revival frame building, which crowns a hill in rural Jefferson County, is now a dark gray but was once salmon colored. The original painted pews, wonderful hammer-beam ceiling, chairs, and marble font are all original. The pipe organ, which is said to have been

imported from Scotland, is also original and remains in the church even though it no longer makes music. NR. Open by appointment. (601) 442-6538.

Fayette vicinity

SPRINGFIELD PLANTATION, 8 miles W. on MS 553, 1786-90. This 2½-story brick manor house was built by Thomas Marston Green Jr., a wealthy Virginian, when this part of Mississippi was still considered West Florida and was under Spanish dominion. The house was the first in the area to have a two-story porch with a colonnade across the entire façade. Worthy of note are the original woodwork and mantels. Some of the doors, windows, and hardware have survived the last two centuries and are still in place. Andrew Jackson and Rachel Robards were married here in August, 1791. NR. Open daily 10:30-5:30. $3 adults, $2 children, children under 1 free. (601) 786-3802.

Jackson

A French-Canadian trader noted that this splendid site beside the Pearl River would be an ideal spot for a new trading post. A town was established here in 1821, but the inhabitants focused on government rather than commerce. By the beginning of 1822, the state's legislature was meeting in

Jackson. The Old Capitol was completed in 1839, and twenty-two years later the Secession Convention was held in that building. In 1863, Generals Sherman and Grant defeated the Confederates in the Battle of Jackson; Sherman and his troops entered the capital in the afternoon of May 14 and were instructed to "destroy the railroads, bridges, factories, arsenals, and everything valuable." For a time the capital was known as "Chimneyville," perhaps because chimneys were the only structures left standing. Jackson was soon rebuilt, however, and today there is much to see in this handsome and dignified city.

GOVERNOR'S MANSION, 316 E. Capitol St., 1839-41. A handsome Greek Revival building, designed by William Nichols, the mansion was originally square shaped; a porte cochere and a two-story rear wing were added in 1908-09. The structure's most outstanding feature is the two-story semi-elliptical Corinthian portico. NR. Open Tu-F 9:30-11:30. Free. (601) 354-7650.

MANSHIP HOUSE, 420 E. Fortification St., c. 1857. This one-story frame house, with fancy lace woodwork dripping from the eaves and intricately designed iron balustrades on the porches was built by a talented craftsman, Charles Henry Manship, who served as mayor of Jackson during the Civil War. Manship owned a wallpaper and paint shop, and the paper which now hangs in the house is a reproduction of some that he may have designed. The house has been restored in recent years and contains some of the original furnishings and woodwork. One of the few extant ex-

amples of a Gothic Revival dwelling in Mississippi, the Manship house should not be missed. NR. Tours begin at the Visitor Center next door, which contains exhibits concerning the Manship family and a collection of 19th-century decorative arts. Open Tu-Sa 9-4, Su 1-4. Free. (601) 961-4274.

MISSISSIPPI MILITARY MUSEUM, 120 N. State St., 1939. Housed in the War Memorial Building, the museum's exhibits include artifacts from the Spanish-American War through Vietnam. Uniforms, weapons, flags, photos, and a model of the USS Mississippi may be seen here. Open M-F 9-4:30. Free. (601) 354-7207. ⚓ ★

MISSISSIPPI STATE HISTORICAL MUSEUM, N. State and Capitol Sts., 1839. Architect William Nichols used all three classical orders in the design of this 3-story brick and stone Greek Revival structure, which served for many years as the Capitol Building. In 1959, restoration work was begun on the deteriorating structure, and in 1961 the Old Capitol was opened to the public as a history museum affiliated with the Dept. of Archives and History, 100 S.

State St. The museum's collection includes state memorabilia, archaeological artifacts, and a Mississippi Hall of Fame which features oil portraits of prominent citizens. NR. Open M-F 8-5, Sa 9:30-4:30, Su 12:30-4:30. Free. (601) 354-6222.

THE OAKS, 823 N. Jefferson St., c. 1856.

A Greek Revival dwelling constructed of hand-hewn timbers, this one-story house was built by James Boyd, a three-term mayor of Jackson. The dwelling now serves as a museum of local history, administered by the Colonial Dames of America, and is furnished with period pieces. NR. Open Tu-Su 10-5. $1.50 adults, 75¢ students, 25¢ children. (601) 353-9339.

STATE CAPITOL, Mississippi St., between N. President and N. West Sts., 1903. This dignified building is typical of Beaux-Arts Classicism and is based on the Capitol in Washington, D.C. Constructed of granite and limestone, the Capitol has a four-story central block crowned by a dome surmounted by a lantern and an eagle. Those not familiar with the national Capitol may be interested in seeing this one, and those who know the building in Washington will find a comparison interesting. NR. Open M-F 8-5. Free. (601) 354-7294.

Lorman and vicinity

ALCORN STATE UNIVERSITY, off MS 552 in Alcorn, 19th and 20th centuries. Founded in 1871, Alcorn was the first land-grant school for blacks in this country; Hiram Revels, America's first black senator, was chosen as the school's initial president. The most significant of the historic buildings on campus is **Oakland Chapel** (c. 1838). Bought by the state at the time of the school's founding, this distinguished Greek Revival structure has a clock tower and a Tuscan portico with five unfluted columns. The monumental front steps were donated to the college after Windsor Mansion (which see) burned in 1890. NR. Open by appointment. Free. (601) 877-3711 ext. 116.

ROSSWOOD PLANTATION, off US 61, E. of Lorman, 1857. The owners of this extraordinary Greek Revival house open it to the public seven months a year. Designed by architect David Shroder, the 2½-story residence still stands in a lovely 100-acre plantation setting and is furnished with American and European antiques. NR. Open Mar-Nov, M-Sa 10-5, Su 12:30-6. $3 adults, $2 children. (601) 437-4215.

Visitors to this area may want to stop in at the **Old Country Store** (1875), US. 61 in Lorman. The store has been in operation ever since it opened over a century ago; a **museum** on the premises contains memorabilia from the store's early years. Open Mar-Nov 15, M-Sa 10-5, Su 12:30-6. $3 adults, $2 children. (601) 437-3661.

Meridian

HIGHLAND PARK, bounded by 13th and 19th Sts. and 37th and 47th Aves., 20th century. In the first years after the park's completion in 1913, visitors arrived by trolley at the concrete streetcar platform which served as the main entrance. From here they could wander through thirty-two landscaped acres and admire the park's many delightful features, among which were a gazebo, a lagoon, a footbridge, and a wonderful 1909 **Dentzel carousel** with twenty-eight hand-carved

animals and two chariots. One of only two surviving carousels made by the Dentzel Co. of Germantown, Pennsylvania, the merry-go-round features three tiers of original paintings of the Middle East and Europe that conceal the mechanical equipment. The snowflake-patterned mosaic floor of the carousel building remains intact. NR. ✔

Also in the park is the **Jimmie Rodgers Museum,** which honors the Meridian-born "father of country music" and houses some of his possessions as well as a 1917 Baldwin steam engine. Open M-Sa 10-4, Su 1-5. $2 adults, under 10 free. (601) 483-5202. ✔

MERREHOPE, 905 31st Ave., 1856, 1904. Extensive additions have been made to the original ante-bellum frame dwelling; just after the turn of the century the house grew into a twenty-six-room Colonial Revival mansion. A monumental portico, with huge Ionic columns resting on six-foot plinths, adorns two sides of the residence. Today Merrehope is a museum furnished with Empire-style pieces. NR. Open M-Sa 9-4, Su 1-5. $2 adults, 50¢ children. (601) 483-8439.

Natchez

La Salle and Tonti explored this splendid spot on high bluffs overlooking the Mississippi River in 1662. The first settlers arrived in 1716; with their leader, Le Moyne de Bienville, they built a fort and named it for Rosalie, Duchess of Ponchartrain. Later the fort was occupied by the British and Spanish, and finally, in 1798, by the Americans. In 1803 Natchez was incorporated; during the first half of the 19th century, the town experienced an unparalled economic boom as Natchez grew into one of the busiest cotton markets in the world. The city's 500 ante-bellum houses, peaceful and deeply-shaded streets, and leisurely atmosphere attract sightseers from all over the world.

The **Natchez-Adams County Chamber of Commerce,** 300 N. Commerce St., offers walking tour maps of the city and a list of the historic houses open to the public. Open during regular business hours. (601) 445-4611. The official **Tour and Tourist**

Headquarters is housed in the Gay '90s Building, 410 N. Commerce St. Tickets to many of the mansions open to the public must be purchased here. During the **Spring and Fall Pilgrimages,** guided tours of the historic houses may be arranged, or visitors can pick up maps and tour the mansions on their own. Of the thirty residences open during the pilgrimages in March and October, a guided tour will include three to six and will take 2 to 2½ hours. For further information write the Tour and Tourist Headquarters, Box 347, 39120, or call (800) 647-6742 or (601) 446-6631.

AUBURN, Duncan Park, 1812. A fine example of Neo-classicism with Palladian elements, designed and built by architect Levi Weeks, this two-story brick house has a full Ionic pedimented portico and a balustraded balcony on the upper level. The dwelling's spiral staircase and finely carved woodwork are extraordinary. Called "the handsomest house about Natchez...a perfect castle" in 1820, Auburn became a paradigm for many of Natchez's other elegant homes. The wings were added after 1820. Today, the Town and Country Garden Club has its headquarters in the mansion. NR, NHL. Open daily 9:30-5. $3.50 adults, $1 students, children under 10 free. (601)442-5981.

THE BRIARS, The Briars Rd., 1818. Planned and built in the vernacular "undercut" form found only in the Mississippi Valley, the house is designed to provide good circulation and increased comfort in the near-tropical heat and humidity of this area. The "undercut" style is characterized by front and rear galleries built as an integral part of the long, thin house. The Briars, with its fine proportions and beautiful Federal woodwork, is the best surviving expression of this form in Mississippi. It was the scene of the marriage of Jefferson Davis and Varina Howell in 1845. This house, which stands on a bluff and has a commanding view of the Mississippi, has been restored and furnished with 19th-century antiques. NR. Open daily 9:30-5. $4.50 adults, $2 students 10-19, children under 10 free. (601) 442-7210.

CONNELLY'S TAVERN, N. Canal and Jefferson Sts., c. 1798. Built on Ellicott's Hill overlooking the Mississippi, this two-story building, with a double balustraded porch, was built while the Spanish still occupied Natchez. Now owned by the Natchez Garden Club, the tavern is appointed with appropriate period pieces. NR, NHL. Open daily 9-5. $3 adults, $1.25 students 10-18, children under 10 free. (601) 442-2011.

DUNLEITH, 84 Homochitto St., c. 1855. Confederate General Charles C. Dahlgren built this monumental 2½-story Greek Revival mansion. The building's most extraordinary feature is the Tuscan portico which completely surrounds the house and is supported by a single row of columns. The stuccoed brick edifice is painted white on the exterior and has richly carved white carrara marble mantels and ornate plaster ceiling medallions inside. NR, NHL. Open daily 9-5. $4 adults, $2 students under 18, children under 10 free. (601) 446-6631.

GRAND VILLAGE OF THE NATCHEZ INDIANS, 400 Jefferson Davis Blvd., c. 1600-1700. The Suns, or chiefs, of the Natchez nation lived at this site when the first Europeans arrived in this area. The Natchez were wiped out by the French in 1730 in retaliation for a massacre at Fort Rosalie, but several of their ceremonial and dwelling mounds are still extant. The Temple Mound was excavated in 1930 and 1960: glass bottles, knives, brass beads, a pistol, and other objects of European origin were buried with the Indians. Today the site is open to the public and a **Visitor Center** offers interpretive exhibits. NR, NHL. Open M-Sa 9-5, Su 1:30-5. Free. (601) 446-6502. ✔

KING'S TAVERN, 611 Jefferson St., c. 1789. Situated at the end of the Natchez Trace, which runs from Nashville to Natchez, King's Tavern is thought to be the oldest building in the area. Today the two-story brick and frame house has been restored by the Pilgrimage Garden Club and is once again being used as a restaurant. NR. Known as the **Post House**, it is open M-F 11-10, Sa 11-11 as well as Su 11-11 during Pilgrimages. (601) 442-1881.

LONGWOOD (Nutt's Folly), Lower Woodville Rd., 1860-62. Elaborate and fanciful, this three-story octagonal dwelling with crowning sixteen-sided windowed drum and silver onion dome, was designed by Philadelphia architect, Samuel Sloan, for a wealthy Natchez planter, Haller Nutt. The exterior shows both Moorish and Italian influences in its wealth of architectural detailing, though most of the interior, never completed, is just an empty shell. The Nutt family lived on the completed ground floor of the house until 1968 when the building and original furnishings were given to the Pilgrimage Garden Club by the McAdams Foundation. The Club has left the brick and frame structure incomplete as a monument to the effect of the Civil War on Southern plantation economy. NR, NHL. Open daily 9-5. By tour only during Pilgrimages. $3.50 adults, $1 children under 18. (601) 446-6631 or (800) 647-6742.

MELROSE, Melrose Ave., c. 1845. This complex of buildings which includes not only the main house, but also a separate two-story brick kitchen, servants quarters, privies, octagonal latticed cisterns, carriage house, stable, dairy barn and dairy, is an excellent example of an ante-bellum residential grouping. The design and construction of the two-story brick mansion is thought to have been executed by Captain Thomas Rose and features a tetrastyle Doric portico with an intricate iron balustrade enclosing the second-story balcony. The complex is extraordinarily well-preserved. NR, NHL. Open daily 9-5. $5 adults, $1 children 4-18, children under 4 free. Tickets available at the house. (800) 647-6742 or (601) 446-6631.

ROSALIE, 100 Orleans St., c. 1820-23. Peter Little of Pittsburgh, Pennsylvania, built this 2½-story Neo-classical house for himself and his family. It is said that the plans were drawn by his brother-in-law, James Griffin, a Baltimore architect. Worthy of note is the elegant open-well stair with its scrolled step-ends and newel in the shape of a column. In 1858, several stylish rococo details, such as the fancy arched marble mantels surmounted by elaborate cartouches in the double parlors, were added. Little named the house Rosalie for the 18th-century French fort of the same name. Ulysses S. Grant stayed here after the fall of Vicksburg in July, 1863. The Mississippi chapter of the D.A.R. bought the house in 1938 and has used it as its state shrine ever since. NR. Open daily 9-5. $3 adults, $1 students 10-18, children under 10 free. Hours and admission vary during Pilgrimages. (601) 445-4555.

STANTON HALL, 401 High St., 1851-57. One of the biggest and the best of

Natchez's ante-bellum houses, this gorgeous white Greek Revival mansion was built for a wealthy cotton broker named Frederick Stanton. Designed and built by Captain Thomas Rose, the two-story house features a pedimented portico with intricate iron lacework balustrades. Original chandeliers, French mirrors, marble mantels, and Sheffield hardware grace the elaborate interior. The house is crowned by a belvedere with a bracketed cornice and arched windows. Administered by the Pilgrimage Garden Club, the house is now a museum. NR, NHL. Open daily 9-5. $3.50 adults, $1 children under 18. (601) 446-6631.

Port Gibson vicinity

GRAND GULF MILITARY PARK, 10 miles NW of town off US 61, 19th century. Grand Gulf was once a booming port town

on the Mississippi, but what the river giveth, she also taketh away; between 1855 and 1860, fifty-five of seventy-six city blocks were claimed by floods. What was left of the town was destroyed during the Civil War, as Confederate troops twice occupied this site and fought extended battles with Union troops here in 1862 and '63. Today one can visit the surviving fortifications of Fort Cobun and Fort Wade, the Grand Gulf cemetery, a reconstructed sawmill, and a museum of Civil War relics located in the park's **Visitor Center.** NR. Open M-Sa 8-5, Su 10-6. Donations accepted. (601) 437-5911. ★ ✔

THE RUINS OF WINDSOR, 12 miles SW of town on MS 522, 1859-61. One of the most lavish of the Mississippi Valley ante-bellum plantations, this splendid 2½-story house was once surrounded by a portico supported by twenty-nine columns each thirty feet tall. The Corinthian columns with intricate cast-iron capitals were based on those of the Pantheon in Rome. The house was built for Smith Coffee Daniell II by 600 slaves and at a cost of $175,000. So extravagant a project must have had a directing architect, but his name is unknown. General Grant is said to have found it the most beautiful home in the Mississippi Valley and spared it from burning. However, the magnificent house went up in smoke in an accidental fire in 1890; all that is now left at the site are some of the columns which serve as a poignant reminder of Windsor's former grandeur. One set of iron steps are now at Alcorn State University. Administered by the Claiborne County Chamber of Commerce, the site is open daily. Free. (601) 437-4351.

Vaughan

CASEY JONES MUSEUM, 1 Main St., 1900. This museum of railroad memorabilia is housed in the Pickens, Mississippi, railroad depot. The state moved the station from Pickens to Vaughan—only ¾ of a mile from the spot where Casey Jones wrecked his train—before opening it as a museum in honor of this American folk hero. So whether you know T. Laurence Seibert's ballad, or Carl Sandburg's poem, or the Grateful Dead tune, a stop at the town where Casey Jones ran the *Cannonball Express* into a freight train in 1900 and "hurtled himself to death and immortality" is recommended. Of special interest is an exhibit of the marks which hobos left on fences to communicate to others how they had been treated in the house on the other side of the gate. NR. Open M-Sa 9-5, Su 1-5. 50¢ adults, 35¢ children under 13. (601) 673-9864. ✔

Vicksburg

Eighteenth-century French missionaries were the first white settlers to come upon this spot on high bluffs overlooking the

Mississippi River. The town was not laid out, however, until 1819 when Reverend Newit Vick platted the area. He died of yellow fever in the same year, but Vicksburg flourished and soon became an important port. The Civil War touched Vicksburg as much as any city in the South, and much evidence of the conflict remains. In 1876 another disaster struck the town: the Mississippi River changed her course. The city might have gone into permanent decline, but the Army Corps of Engineers diverted the Yazoo River into the Mississippi's old bed in 1902. Today, Vicksburg is a thriving city which boasts numerous splendid examples of ante-bellum architecture. Many of the old mansions are opened to the public during the annual **Spring Pilgrimage** which is held at the end of March and the beginning of April. Write the Tourist Information Center, P.O. Box 110, 39180, or call (601) 636-9421 for further information.

CEDAR GROVE, 2200 Oak St., c. 1840. One of Vicksburg's finest ante-bellum mansions, Cedar Grove was built by John Alexander Klein, a wealthy jeweler and lumber merchant, for his bride Elizabeth. The 2½-story Greek Revival house, now a museum, has a full Doric tetrastyle portico and a two-story rear gallery. Many of the original furnishings still grace the house, and pre-Civil War magazines and texts are available for perusal. A Civil War cannonball is still lodged in the parlor wall. NR. Open M-Sa 9:30-5, Su 1:30-5. $4 adults, $1 children. (601) 636-1605.

McRAVEN, 1503 Harrison St., c. 1820, 1836, 1850. This Greek Revival house was built in three different stages by three different owners. First a cottage on the Vick plantation, and then a Federal town house, the residence was made a Greek Revival mansion when the elegant front section was added in the 1850s by John Bobb. The interior of the latter portion is beautifully finished with Greek Revival woodwork and intricate plasterwork. Bobb was the first civilian in Vicksburg to be killed by Union troops: story has it that he demanded that some soldiers leave his garden. In recent years, the house has been beautifully restored and furnished with fine period pieces. NR. Open Sept-May, M-Sa 9-5, Su 1-5; June-Aug, M-Sa 9-6, Su 1-6. $3 adults, $1.50 students 12-18, children under 6 free. (601) 636-1663.

OLD COURT HOUSE MUSEUM, 1008 Cherry St., Court Sq., c. 1861. Designed by architect William Weldon, this imposing structure was erected by skilled slaves. The 2½-story building is made of stuccoed brick and surmounted by an octagonal clocktower with a dome. Four entrance porticos are supported by thirty-foot Ionic columns. During the Civil War, this building was the symbol of Confederate resistance, and during the forty-seven-day siege of Vicksburg in 1863, Union soldiers were held prisoner in the courtroom. When the city fell to Federal forces, the Stars and Stripes were flown from the courthouse cupola. This building served as the Warren County Courthouse until 1939; today it is a museum of local and Southern memorabilia. Of note is the Jefferson and Varina Davis Room, housing artifacts which "honor the lives of Vicksburg's two most outstanding citizens." A research library in the building is open on weekdays. NR, NHL. The museum is open M-Sa 8:30-4:30, Su 1:30-4:30. $1 adults, 50¢ students, 25¢ children 6-12. (601) 636-0741.

Near the courthouse is the **Holy Trinity Episcopal Church** (1870), 900 South St. With its Belgian slate roof and lofty steeple, this is one of the finest Romanesque Revival buildings in the state. Worthy of special note are the six Tiffany windows and the window installed in memory of the soldiers who gave their lives in the Civil War. NR. Open for regular services. (601) 636-0542.

SPRAGUE, Vicksburg Harbor, 1902. *Showboat* was filmed on this, the largest and most powerful of Mississippi steam barges. The *Sprague* towed products ranging from oil and bauxite to Model T's until 1948 when she was bought from the Standard Oil Co. by the citizens of Vicksburg for the sum of ten dollars. The old towboat was converted for use as a theater, meeting place, and river museum. In 1974, most of her superstructure burned; today she is still in the process of being restored. Meanwhile, the show goes on at the **Showboat Theater,** 3101 Confederate Ave. (601) 636-0471. If you're just interested in seeing the old towboat, walk down to the banks of the Yazoo Diversion Canal and see how work is progressing. NR.

VICKSBURG NATIONAL MILITARY PARK, on the East and North edges of the city, 1863. This park commemorates the forty-seven-day siege of Vicksburg, which ended on July 4, 1863. The fall of this city was crucial to Union control of the Mississippi River. When Ulysses S. Grant succeeded in defeating the Confederate troops here and at Port Hudson, Louisiana, Federal forces moved into the leading position. Rifle pits, gun emplacements, breastworks, and the remains of nine Confederate forts may be seen at the site. Start your tour at the **Visitor Center,** where you will be supplied with literature detailing the important points on the sixteen-mile driving tour. Located near US 80 and I-20, the center offers a variety of exhibits concerning the siege. At the other end of the park, off US 61 N, the **USS Cairo** (1861) is being restored; adjacent is a **museum** containing artifacts from the ironclad gunboat. Even with armor 2½-inches thick, this 175-foot-long boat, designed by James Eads, could not survive the two Confederate mines it hit while on mission on the Yazoo River. The boat sank and remained underwater for over a century. NR. Park and Visitor Center open Sept-May, daily 8-5; June-Aug, daily 7-7. Free. (601) 636-0583. ★ ✔

Woodville and vicinity

It has been said that Woodville is the town which "best typifies the ante-bellum South"; visitors may want to take the time to pick up a walking-tour map and explore this almost untouched 19th-century town. Maps are available at the Town Hall, Main St., and at Rosemont (which see). The Civic Club also sponsors Woodville's **Fall and Spring Pilgrimages,** which occur one weekend in March and in October. Call (601) 888-6809 for further information.

OFFICE AND BANKING HOUSE OF THE WEST FELICIANA RAILROAD COMPANY, Depot St., 1834. When Mississippi was still a frontier with half its land occupied by Indian nations, a number of planters in the Mississippi Valley decided to build this rail line to facilitate transport of cotton to the river. All that remains is the office and banking house.

Built in the Greek Revival temple style, the building has six-columned porticos at either end. The rather stark interior retains all of its original hardware, including the vault; the elliptical staircase is the structure's most graceful component. Today the office and banking house is being restored for use as a museum of Southern decorative arts by the Woodville Civic Club. You may want to stop by and see how things are progressing. NR.

ROSEMONT PLANTATION, MS 24, 1 mile E. of Woodville, c. 1810. Jefferson Davis hailed from Woodville, and today his 1½-story frame and clapboard family home has been restored and is open to the public. The woodwork on the interior is finely carved, and much of the hardware is original. The house contains mementos of Davis and his family, and every two years a Davis family reunion is held at the site. NR. Open Mar-Dec 15, M-F 9-5. $4 adults, $1 students. (601) 888-6809.

Northern Mississippi

The towns of northern Mississippi are especially evocative of rural 19th-century life; those who take the time to travel on local roads will discover a fascinating variety of sites — from Jacinto in the west to Greenville on the Mississippi. The University of Mississippi is located in the center of this region, in the beautiful residential town of Oxford. William Faulkner chose Oxford as his home, and Yoknapatawpha County, a fictitious locale which appears in many of his novels, bears many similarities to this region. In the cottages, museums, battlefields, and plantations of Northern Mississippi, the traveler will discover a different and unique Magnolia State.

Amory

AMORY REGIONAL MUSEUM, 1215 Crowden Dr. Housed in this museum are a variety of collections of local interest, including the equipment of Dr. B.C. Tubb,

one of Monroe County's most venerable physicians, as well as mementos of the most decorated soldier ever to have served in the U.S. Army, Lawrence (Rabbitt) Kennedy. Open M-F 9-5, Sa-Su 1-5. Free. (601) 256-2761.

Baldwyn vicinity

BRICES CROSS ROADS NATIONAL BATTLEFIELD SITE, 6 miles W. of town on MS 370, 1864. Here on June 10, 1864, Confederate General Nathan Forrest, through brilliant tactics and hard fighting, won a battle against Union forces which numbered twice as many as his own troops. Interpretive markers at the one-acre site describe Forrest's tactics to the visitor. NR. The **Brices Crossroads Museum** is nearby on US 45 N. A collection of Americana and Indian artifacts are housed in a reconstructed pioneer home. Open M-F 10-6, Sa 9-6, Su 1-6. Free. (601) 365-9371. ★

Clarksdale

DELTA BLUES MUSEUM, 1109 State St., has a superb 90,000-volume library of books and periodicals on blues artists and music, as well as slide and sound programs on the blues. So if you've got the blues, or want to hear them, stop by June-Sept M-F 1-6, or the rest of the year by appointment. Free. (601) 624-4461.

Also in town is an **Archaeology Museum**, located in the Carnegie Public Library, 114 Delta Ave. A variety of Indian artifacts are on exhibit. Open M-Tu 9-8, W-Th 9-6, F-Sa 9-5. Free. (601) 624-4461. ✔

Columbus

In 1817 a small band of pioneers arrived at a bluff 125 feet above the Tombigbee River. Satisfied with the rich fertile earth of the Black Prairie and the proximity of three rivers (the Buttahatchee and Luxapalilia run through Columbus, too), they founded a settlement which came to be known as "Possum Town"—the innkeeper, Spirus Roach, is said to have borne some resemblance to that animal. Before long, fields were cleared and planted, and as the farmers grew wealthy, they began to build houses in Columbus. Today many of the residences are still privately owned, but fifteen to twenty historic homes are open to the public every year during the **Spring Pilgrimage** in early April. The Columbus-Lowndes Chamber of Commerce, 318 7th St. N., offers driving tour maps of the city and information about Pilgrimage. Write Box 1016, 39701 or call (601) 328-4491.

THE COLUMBUS AND LOWNDES COUNTY HISTORICAL SOCIETY MUSEUM, 316 7th St. N., 1847. The two-story Greek Revival brick Lee House, with its lovely ornamental cast-iron porch, was built by Major Thomas Blewett, passed on to his daughter, and then to his granddaughter, the wife of General Stephen D. Lee. Now a museum, the residence contains collections of clothing, portraits, silver, furniture, china, glass, and guns. NR. Open Tu, Th 1-4; other times by appointment. Free. (601) 328-5437.

RIVERVIEW (McLaran House), 514 2nd St., 1847-51. This handsome Greek Revival house was built for Col. Charles McLaran, founder of the First National Bank of Columbus. One of the highlights of the city, Riverview has columns standing thirty feet tall. The exterior walls are sixty feet long, and the tip of the belvedere is sixty feet above the ground. The interior is beautifully finished with black marble mantels, original chandeliers, and ornate plasterwork. An exceptional feature is the wall between the study and the music room which can be raised and lowered to accommodate parties of various sizes. NR. Visible from the street, but open to the public during the Spring Pilgrimage.

Corinth

CURLEE HOUSE, Jackson and Childs Sts., c. 1857. During the Civil War, this two-story frame and stucco Greek Revival house was occupied at different times by both a Confederate and a Federal General. Today the dwelling is a museum containing Indian artifacts and Civil War relics. NR. Open F-W 1-4, and by appointment. $1 admission. (601) 287-8267.

Greenville and vicinity

OLD DELTA DEMOCRAT TIMES BUILDING, 201-203 Main St., c. 1881. Floods have destroyed most of Greenville's early buildings, and, though this one has been extensively altered, it is one of the few that have survived. The structure retains such interesting architectural features as the ornate cast-iron columns on the molded arched windows on the second story. The building's real significance, however, lies in the fact that the *Delta Democrat Times,* a Greenville paper, operated here from 1943 to 1968. William Hodding Carter, Jr., the *Times's* distinguished former editor, was an ardent proponent of racial equality when that mode of thought was not yet current; he won the Pulitzer Prize for his eloquent editorials in 1946. Today the building is occupied by Mississippi Industries for the Blind. NR.

WETHERBEE HOUSE, 509 Washington Ave., c. 1875. This modest house was built by a Union soldier who never went back to his home state of Illinois. Hiram Wetherbee settled in the frame and clapboard structure after the war; the simple architecture is typical of dwellings built at that time. Sold to the Council of Greenville Garden Clubs in 1973, it now houses art exhibits. NR. Open by appointment. $1 adults, 50¢ children. (601) 332-2246 or 8148.

WINTERVILLE MOUNDS HISTORIC SITE AND MUSEUM, 3 miles N. of town on MS 1, c. 1500. These mounds are thought to be what remains of a ceremonial center used by Indians of the Mississippian era. One central mound fifty-five-feet high is surrounded by a dozen smaller ones. Excavated in 1967 by the Peabody Institute, the mounds yielded relics which are exhibited in the adjacent museum. NR. Open Tu-F 8-5, Sa-Su 1-5. 50¢ adults, 35¢ students. (601) 334-4684.

Greenwood and vicinity

COTTONLANDIA MUSEUM, US 49-82 Bypass. This museum contains an interesting collection of regional memorabilia and Indian artifacts and is surrounded by a wildflower garden. Open Tu-F 9-5, Sa-Su 2-5; other times by appointment. Nominal charge. (601) 455-1416.

FLOREWOOD RIVER PLANTATION, 2 miles W. of town on US 82. A reconstructed plantation, this living history museum includes in its collection blacksmith and carpentry tools, steam engines, sorghum and grist mills, antebellum furnishings. Open Mar-Dec, Tu-Sa 9-5, Su 1-5. $2 adults, $1.50 students. Guided tours available. (601) 455-3281.

Holly Springs

Holly Springs was once called the "Athens of the South" because there were numerous monumental Greek Revival structures in town—until Union troops descended on the community. Most of those that remain are private, but **Montrose** (1858), 212 Salem St., is open to the public by appointment. This Greek Revival mansion was

built by Alfred Brooks as a wedding present for his daughter. (601) 252-2943. Also of interest is the Italianate **Marshall County Courthouse** (1870-72), Courthouse Sq., constructed after the original 1837 frame edifice was burned by Federal forces. NR. Open during regular business hours. (601) 252-4431.

Many of the area's historic homes are opened to the public during the annual **Spring Pilgrimage.** Contact the Chamber of Commerce, P.O. Box 12, 38635, for details. (601) 252-2943.

MARSHALL COUNTY HISTORICAL MUSEUM, College Ave. and Randolph Sts. Chickasaw Indian artifacts and mementos of 19th-century Mississippi life can be found in this interesting museum. Open M-F 9-11 and 2-4. Donations accepted. (601) 252-4437.

Jacinto

JACINTO COURTHOUSE, off MS 356, 1854. This dignified late-Federal brick building, with twelve-over-twelve windows and crowned by an octagonal cupola, has been restored to its original appearance and is now used as a nature/conservation center. NR. Open Tu-Sa 10-5, Su 1-5. Free. (601) 287-4296.

Oxford

Settled in 1836 and named for the famed English university, Oxford did not succeed in attracting Mississippi's state university until 1848. Though many of the city's buildings were destroyed during the Civil War, a few have survived the years, and they contribute to the sedate aura so typical of rural Mississippi towns.

Many of Oxford's historic houses are opened to the public during the **Spring Pilgrimage** each April. For further information contact the Oxford-Lafayette County Chamber of Commerce, 440 N. Lamar, P.O. Box 147, 38655. (601) 234-4651.

AMMADELLE, 637 N. Lamar St., 1860-65. An outstanding example of Italianate residential architecture, Ammadelle was designed by architect Calvert Vaux, the man who conceived the plazas and buildings which add so much grace to New York's Central Park. The two-story brick dwelling is a beautifully proportioned assemblage of balconies and porches, arched doorways and round-arched windows. NR, NHL. Private, but visible from the street.

ROWAN OAK, Old Taylor Rd, c. 1840. William Faulkner, the Nobel Prize-winning author, lived here for thirty-four years, from 1929 until his death in 1963. His house now belongs to the University of Mississippi, and its administrators have left his belongings much as they found them. NR. The two-story frame Greeek Revival home is open to the public M-F 10-12 and 2-4, Sa 10-12. Free. (601) 234-3284.

UNIVERSITY OF MISSISSIPPI, on University Blvd., 19th and 20th centuries. Opened in 1848 with eighty students and a faculty of four, Ole Miss now has a student body of 10,000 and occupies a campus of over 1,000 wooded acres. Only three antebellum buildings have survived. The white-columned **Lyceum** was completed in 1848, and the **Old Chapel** in 1853. Most interesting is the imposing two-story three-

domed brick edifice known as the **Barnard Observatory**. This handsome Greek-Revival building is based on the design of the Pulkova Observatory in Russia. The Mississippi version was built under the direction of Chancellor Frederick A.P. Barnard between 1857 and 1859. Barnard, who wanted Ole Miss to become the "Harvard of the South" commissioned a Massachusetts firm to build the longest telescope in the world. The telescope was to have a nineteen-inch lens, four inches longer than those at Harvard and Pulkova. Though the telescope was completed, it was never delivered; the Civil War put an end to Barnard's plans for Ole Miss. **The Center for the Study of Southern Culture** is now housed in the Observatory; it specializes in research material and artifacts concerning Southern music, folk-life, and literature. NR. The center is open M-F 8:15-4:45. Free. (601) 232-5993. For university information call 232-7318.

West Point vicinity

WAVERLEY PLANTATON, 10 miles E. of town on MS 50, c. 1852. This two-story Greek Revival house is best known for its fine interior detailing and wonderful twin staircases with three tiers of octagonal balconies. Built for George Hampton Young, a prominent citizen, the house was restored in the 1960s. NR. Open daily. $2.50 adults, under 6 free. (601) 494-1399.

Historic Accommodations

An asterisk (*) indicates that meals are served.

Fayette

SPRINGFIELD PLANTATION, MS 553, 39069. (601) 780-3802. An historic site that accepts overnight guests. (See historical listing.) Advance reservations are required. NR.

Lorman

ROSSWOOD, off US 61, 39069. (601) 489-4215. An historic site that accepts overnight guests. (See historical listing.) NR.

Natchez

Historic accommodations abound in Natchez. Natchez Pilgrimage Tours will help the traveler arrange to stay in any of a number of ante-bellum buildings, ranging from restored 18th-century inns and town houses to guest houses on the grounds of mansions or the mansions themselves. For information and reservations write P.O. Box 347, 39120, or call (601) 446-6631 or (800) 647-6742.

THE BURN, 307 Oak St., PO Box 347, 39120. (601) 446-6631 or (800) 647-6742. Open all year. The first recorded Greek Revival house to have been built in Natchez, The Burn dates from c. 1832. Today it provides pleasant accommodations and relaxing, shady gardens for the visitor. Named for the brook that once traversed the property, The Burn is one of Natchez's outstanding ante-bellum houses and a delightful place to stay. Breakfast is served. NR. Reservations are made through Natchez Pilgrimage Tours.

EOLA HOTEL, 110 N. Pearl St., 39120. (601) 445-2233. Open all year. One of the grand hotels of the South built during the booming '20s, the Eola was reopened in 1982 following a multi-million dollar restoration. The handsome lobby is decorated with antiques, and the rooms have been pleasantly refurbished. *

SILVER STREET INN, 1 Silver St., Box 1224, 39120. (601) 442-4221. Open all year. Built in the 1840s, this pleasant inn was once a "bawdy house" in the dockside area of town known as "Natchez-Under-the-Hill." In more recent years the building has been restored and rooms furnished with country antiques.

STANTON HALL, 401 High St., P.O. Box 347, 39120. (601) 446-6631 or (800) 647-6742. An historic site that accepts overnight guests. (See historical listing.) A swimming pool and lovely grounds are among the amenities offered to guests at this historic mansion. NR, NHL. Reservations are made through Natchez Pilgrimage Tours.

Port Gibson

OAK SQUARE, 1207 Church St., 39150. (601) 437-4350 or 5771 or 5300. Open all year. The guest house on the grounds of Port Gibson's largest ante-bellum mansion provides comfortable accommodations for guests. A Southern breakfast and a tour of the house are included. NR.

Vicksburg

ANCHUCA, Cherry and First East Sts., 39180. (601) 636-4931. Open all year. J.W. Mauldin built this Greek Revival mansion in 1830. He named it Anchuca, an Indian word which translates as "happy home." Jefferson Davis's brother, Joseph Emory, lived here for a time; it is said that the president of the Confederacy addressed the people of Vicksburg from the little balcony above the front door. Today, handsomely-furnished rooms, a Southern breakfast, and a tour of the house and grounds are among the amenities to be enjoyed.

CEDAR GROVE, 2200 Oak St., 39180. (601) 636-1605. An historic site that accepts overnight guests. (See historical listing.) Comfortable rooms in this historic mansion are furnished in ante-bellum style. NR.

9. TENNESSEE

HERNANDO de Soto is believed to have been the first European to explore the area that is now Tennessee: in 1541 he and his soldiers raised the Spanish flag over the east bank of the Mississippi River near present-day Memphis.

The first permanent settlement, however, wasn't established until 1779, and it was located at Jonesboro, in the eastern part of the state. East Tennessee is bounded by the Great Smoky Mountains, highest range of the eastern United States. Much of the beautiful country here has been preserved in the Great Smoky Mountains National Park and Cherokee National Forest, which together stretch from Virginia on the north to Georgia on the south. The Appalachian Trail winds through much of the preserve, affording beautiful vistas of forested mountains and lakes.

Another trail, the Old Natchez Trace, roughly bisects Middle Tennessee. For part of its length (from Gordonsburg south to the Alabama line), the Natchez Trace Parkway traverses the main route taken by pioneers who first explored the southern frontier in the 16th to 19th centuries. Middle Tennessee is gentler country — a land of rolling hills, meadows, lakes, and streams, where many of the prosperous farms begun in the early 19th century are still producing goods for market, and where prominent Tennesseans like Andrew Jackson and James K. Polk left their mark. Middle Tennessee is also home to the state capital and largest city, Nashville.

West Tennessee is defined by the meandering course of the Mississippi and by the rich plantation lands along its banks, whose principal crops — cotton and tobacco — brought fortunes to many in the 19th century.

Tennessee, called the Volunteer State, received the appellation because so many of its residents volunteered to fight in the War of 1812. During the Civil War, many decisive battles were fought on Tennessee soil, including the famous engagements at Shiloh and Chattanooga.

The Tennessee Valley Authority (TVA) was created by act of Congress in 1933 to harness the power of the Tennessee River and its tributaries, producing electricity, jobs, and new farmlands during the height of the Depression. The TVA's impact can be seen throughout Tennessee and in neighboring states: the lakes and parklands created by TVA dams have been set aside for fishing, swimming, and other forms of recreation (see also Land Between the Lakes, Kentucky).

Land of Davy Crockett and Andrew Jackson, of sour mash whiskey and country music, Tennessee offers a wide variety of historic attractions for visitors of all ages and interests.

Fairvue, Gallatin

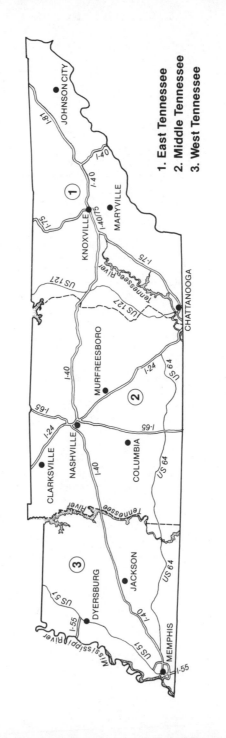

1. East Tennessee
2. Middle Tennessee
3. West Tennessee

East Tennessee

The roots of Tennessee are deeply embedded in the mountainous terrain known to locals as "First Tennessee." Davy Crockett's grandparents were among the pioneers of the area, and it was here that the first capital of the Territory of the United States South of the River Ohio was established in the late-18th century. Pioneer forts and log houses are among the eastern section's many historic attractions; more sophisticated dwellings, dating from the latter part of the 19th century, can be found in the cosmopolitan centers of Chattanooga and Knoxville.

Byrdstown vicinity

CORDELL HULL BIRTHPLACE, 1.2 miles S. on TN 42, 19th century. Member of the Tennessee legislature, U.S. congressman, and secretary of state for eleven years (1933-44), Cordell Hull is best remembered for his support of the United Nations, for which he was awarded the Nobel Peace Prize. The rude log cabin where Hull was born has been reconstructed; a nearby museum houses a collection of memorabilia relating to the statesman. NR. Open late May-Labor Day, daily 10-6. Free. (615) 864-3247.

Chattanooga

Sprawled in the Tennessee River's Mocassin Bend, and surrounded by mountains on three sides, Chattanooga is one of Tennessee's liveliest industrial centers. Remains of the city's first heavy industry, the **East Tennessee Iron Manufacturing Company Blast Furnace** (c. 1854), can still be seen downtown in Bluff City Park (NR).

Nearby **Lookout Mountain** (which see) was the site of a bloody three-day battle, one of the major engagements of the Civil War. On the lighter side, Chattanooga is justly proud of its famous "choo-choo," and throughout the city are exhibits which no railroad buff will want to miss.

CHATTANOOGA CHOO-CHOO, Terminal Station, 1400 Market St. An enor-

mous Beaux Arts structure, Terminal Station was completed in 1908 at a then-staggering cost of $1.5 million. In recent years imaginative renovation has turned the domed building into a hotel, restaurants, shops, and exhibits featuring the great age of rail travel. You can even ride a trolley! NR. Open daily. (615) 266-5000. ✔

HOUSTON ANTIQUE MUSEUM, 201 High St., 1898. An elaborately-decorated Victorian-era building houses Tiffany glass, 19th-century decorative arts and furniture, pewter, porcelains, dolls, and pottery. Open Tu-Sa 10-4:30, Su 2-4:30. $1.50 adults, 75¢ children. (615) 267-7176.

HUNTER MUSEUM OF ART, Bluff View, 1904. A superb Georgian Revival mansion perched high above the Tennessee River is the repository for the Chattanooga Art Association's extensive collection of American painting, drawing and sculpture. The collection, which ranges over three centuries, is housed both in the mansion, once owned by Coca-Cola magnate George Thomas Hunter, and in an adjoining modern annex. NR. Open Tu-Sa 10-4:30, Su 1-4:30. Donations accepted. (615) 267-0968.

LOOKOUT MOUNTAIN, Ochs Hwy. and Scenic Hwy. Certainly the most breathtaking way to reach the top of Lookout Mountain, which towers over the city, is via the **Lookout Mountain Incline,**

3917 St. Elmo Ave., constructed as a tourist attraction in 1895. Cable cars rise more than 2,000 feet on double track. NR. Open June-Labor Day daily 9 am-9:30 pm; otherwise 9-6. Round trip $3 adults, $2.25 children 6-12. (615) 821-4224. ✓

Chickamauga and Chattanooga National Military Park, which spreads across the mountain into Georgia, is accessible from the incline railway or by car; some of the Civil War battle sites within the park, such as **Missionary Ridge,** where Sherman's attack was repeatedly stymied by Confederate forces, are somewhat far afield. The assault on Lookout Mountain was a key engagement in the **Battle of Chattanooga;** the **Ochs Museum** within the park should be your first stop for information about the course of the battle and its effect on the war. The fiercest fighting on the mountain took place at the **Cravens House,** an antebellum home which has been restored, and where further information about the conflict is available. Cravens House is open Mar-Nov, M-Sa 9-5, Su 1-5. 50¢ adults, free to children under 16. The park is open May-Sept, daily 9-8, otherwise daily 9-6. Free. (615) 821-7786. ★

TENNESSEE VALLEY RAILROAD MUSEUM, 2202 N. Chamberlain Ave. Several miles of track, four railroad bridges, and historic Cumberland Tunnel which cuts through Missionary Ridge, are part of this vast railroad museum. A replica of a turn-of-the-century depot, old pullman cars, mail cars, dining cars, cabooses—most dating from the early 1900s—are still in operation. You can hop aboard for a ride through the tunnel (45 minutes), have lunch in a dining car built in 1926, and tour luxurious Pullman cars from the heyday of railroading. All aboard! NR. Open late May-early Oct, Sa 10-5, Su 1-5 and by appointment. $2 adults, $1 children. (615) 622-5908. ✓

Cumberland Gap National Historic Park (see Kentucky)

Dayton

RHEA COUNTY COURTHOUSE, Market St. at 2nd Ave., 1890-91. William Jennings Bryan and Clarence Darrow met at this brick courthouse in 1925 to do legal battle over John Scopes, a Dayton high school teacher accused of teaching the Darwinian theory of evolution in violation of a Tennessee statute which forbade the teaching of "any theory other than of the divine creation of man as taught in the Bible." The resulting "Monkey" trial became one of the most famous in American history. NR. Open M-Tu, Th-F 8-4:30, W, Sa 8-12. Free. (615) 775-0185.

Elizabethton

SYCAMORE SHOALS STATE HISTORIC AREA, US 321, 18th-20th centuries. A reconstructed fort, including a stockade and five log buildings, stands on the site of one of the earliest settlements in the Appalachian foothills. Members of the 1770s settlement called themselves the Watauga Association, and were ruled by an early written constitution. Open daily 8-5. Free. (615) 543-5808.

Gatlinburg vicinity

GREAT SMOKY MOUNTAINS NATIONAL PARK, US 441. The **Sugar-**

lands **Visitor Center,** located south of Gatlinburg at the intersection of the Newfound Gap and Little River Rds., should be your first stop for maps, brochures, and information about the trails, campgrounds, historical attractions, and recreational facilities available in this 800-square-mile preserve, which is located in both Tennessee and North Carolina (which see). Open May-Oct, daily 8-7:30; Nov-Apr, daily 8-4:30. Free. (615) 436-5615.

Cades Cove, located about twenty miles southwest of the visitor center, is an extensive museum complex whose buildings— gristmill, log homesteads, blacksmith shop —date from a settlement established in the early 19th century. The showpiece is the **John P. Cable Mill** (1868), whose waterpowered wheel is still operating. Samples of stone-ground cornmeal can be purchased daily during the summer. Buildings are furnished with rustic Appalachian pieces, and spinning and weaving demonstrations are presented. NR. Open Apr-Oct, daily 9-5. Free. (615) 436-5615. ✔

Greeneville

ANDREW JOHNSON NATIONAL HISTORIC SITE, Depot and College Sts., 19th century. Before succeeding to the presidency upon the assassination of Abraham Lincoln in 1865, Andrew Johnson had had a varied career. He began as a tailor, then became an alderman, mayor of Greeneville, state legislator, U.S. senator, and finally vice president. The small frame tailor shop and two-story brick house he owned have been restored, and contain

personal mementoes and 19th-century furnishings. NR. Open daily 9-5. Free. (615) 638-3551.

In the late 1700s, Greeneville was capital of the sovereign state of Franklin, the smallest and certainly most short-lived state in American history. Its founders, the Reverend Samuel Doak and John Sevier, led the area's secession from North Carolina in 1785, but the state lasted only three years and subsequently became a part of Tennessee. Much of the downtown area has been designated an **historic district;** a log cabin replica of the **Franklin state capitol** is located here, as are numerous buildings dating from the late 18th-early 20th centuries. NR. (615) 638-4111.

Harrogate

ABRAHAM LINCOLN MUSEUM, Lincoln Memorial University campus, US 25E. Union General O.O. Howard founded this university in the late 1800s because of a direct request from President Lincoln during the Civil War. The museum was established at the same time; its collection has grown to number more than 250,000 items pertaining to the life of Lincoln and to the Civil War. Open June-Aug, M-Sa 10-6; Sept-Nov and Feb-May, Tu-Sa 9-4, Su 1-4. $1.50 adults, $1 senior citizens, 75¢ children 6-12. (615) 869-3611.

Jefferson City

GLENMORE, off US 11E, 1868-69. John Roper Branner, who in 1861 was instrumental in getting the East Tennessee, Virginia, and Georgia Railroad built, commissioned this lavishly-trimmed Second Empire mansion. More than twenty rooms of the house are furnished with elaborate Victorian pieces. Operated by the APTA. NR. Open May-Oct, Sa-Su 1-5 and by appointment. (615) 475-3819.

Johnson City and vicinity

ROCKY MOUNT, 4 miles NE on US 11E, 1770-72. William Cobb, an emigré from eastern North Carolina, built this large two-story log house in the "Far West." He was one of the first settlers in what is now Tennessee, and his house became the temporary capitol, under Governor William Blount, of "The Territory of the United States South of the River Ohio" in 1790. The Cobb home has been restored to its original appearance; the nearby **Overmountain Museum** portrays the early history of the region. Open M-Sa 10-5, Su 2-6. $2 adults, $1 children 6-16, group rates. (615) 538-7396.

TIPTON-HAYNES LIVING HISTORICAL FARM, US 23, 18th-19th centuries. John Tipton, a native of Maryland, came to what is now Tennessee in 1783-84 and built a two-story log house which became the nucleus of a large farm complex that was expanded throughout the 19th century. The farmhouse, barn, smokehouse, and springhouse have been restored; ducks, pigs, and other livestock are tended; and chores are performed without benefit of 20th-century technology. NR. Open Apr-Oct, M-Sa 10-5, Su 2-6. $1 adults, 50¢ children 6-12. (615) 926-3631. ✔

Jonesboro

JONESBORO HISTORIC DISTRICT, 18th-19th centuries. Most of this small town has been designated an historic district, since it is the oldest community in Tennessee, founded in 1779. The constitutional convention and early legislative sessions for the state of Franklin (now east Tennessee) were held here; a number of buildings dating from the earliest days of the settlement now house shops and restaurants. A **visitor center** at 103 Main St.

offers brochures and information about the area's most historic buildings. NR. (615) 753-5961.

Kingsport

NETHERLAND INN, King's Old Boatyard, off US 11 W, 1802-18. The stone and wood Netherland Inn, along with a nearby complex of outbuildings and wharves, was first operated as a warehouse for shipping salt; later it became an inn and stage station. Today the inn has been restored and refurbished; the stable, kitchen, smokehouse, and other outbuildings have been reconstructed as part of a large museum complex, whose exhibits include 19th-century furnishings and costumes. NR. Open all year, W-Su 2-4:30 and by appointment. $1 adults, 50¢ children. (615) 247-3211. ✔

Knoxville

In 1786, North Carolinian James White moved his family to the area which is now Knoxville and constructed a crude log cabin and stockade not far from the Tennessee River. Just five years later, White sold part of his land holdings to territorial governor William Blount, who had selected the area as the site of the capital for the territory. The infant capital city was named for Major General Henry Knox, then secretary of war, and remained the seat of state government until the mid-19th century, when Nashville got the nod.

BLOUNT MANSION, 200 W. Hill Ave., 1792. William Blount's roomy two-story frame house served as the first capitol of the territory. The house and dependencies, including the old **governor's office** just behind the mansion, have been restored to their late-18th-century appearance and furnished with period antiques. The **Craighead-Jackson House** (1818), just across the street, serves as the visitor center. NR, NHL. Open Mar-Oct, Tu-Sa 9:30-5; Nov-Feb, Tu-Sa 9:30-4:30; also Su 2-5, May-Oct. $2 adults, 50¢ children under 12. (615) 525-2375.

KINGSTON PIKE AREA, 19th-20th centuries. Within a few short blocks of each other on the lovely residential thoroughfare of Kingston Pike are three historic homes which have been restored as museum houses. **Crescent Bend** (The Armstrong-Lockett House), at #2728, was built in 1834; its collections include American and English furniture, paintings, mirrors, and silver. Open Tu-Su 10-12 and 1-4. $2 admission. (615) 637-3163. **Confederate Memorial Hall,** #3148, is the former Bleak House, a spacious brick ante-bellum mansion constructed in 1858. Operated by the United Daughters of the Confederacy, Bleak House is the repository for a collection of 19th-century furniture, Confederate history, and Civil War relics. Open Apr-Sept, Tu-Su 2-5; Oct-Mar, Tu-Su 1-4, and by appointment. $1 adults, 50¢ children. (615) 522-3371. The **Dulin Gallery of Art,** is housed in the former Dulin House (1915), #3100, a frame and stuccoed Neo-classical Revival mansion designed by John Russell Pope for Knoxville businessman Hanson Lee Dulin. The gallery's collection includes painting, sculpture, graphics, and several rooms of miniatures. NR. Open Tu-F 12-4, Sa-Su 1-5. Free. (615) 525-6101.

GENERAL JAMES WHITE HOME AND FORT, 205 Hill Ave., 18th and 20th centuries. James White, founder of Knoxville, constructed a number of crude log buildings on his original homesite. Only one—the family home—remains today; it has been moved several times, and has been much restored. Other buildings from the complex, along with the log stockade, have been reconstructed by the City Association of Women's Clubs. Open Tu-Sa 9:30-5, Su 1-5. $1.50 adults, 25¢ children 6-12. (615) 525-6514.

Knoxville vicinity

MARBLE SPRINGS, 6 miles S. via US 441, TN 33, and Tipton Station Rd. on Neubert Springs Rd., 18th century. Marble Springs was the rural home from 1790 until 1815 of John Sevier, the state's first governor. Of the original buildings on the farm, only the two-story main house remains. It has been restored, and a springhouse, smokehouse, and separate kitchen have been reconstructd on the site. Sevier's home is furnished with rustic pioneer furniture; early artifacts and costumes are displayed. NR. Open Tu-Sa 10-12 and 2-5, Su 2-5. $1 adults, 10¢ children. (615) 573-5508.

RAMSEY HOUSE, 6 miles SE on Thorngrove Pike., 1797. Francis Alexander Ramsey was active in county and state government and served on the board of trustees for the University of Tennessee. His roomy two-story home was built of locally-quarried pink marble, an elegant material for the time. Rooms throughout the house are trimmed with finely-molded chair rails and other sophisticated details; furnishings date from the late-18th and early-19th centuries. NR. Open Apr-Oct, Tu-Sa 10-5, Su 1-5. $1.50 adults, 25¢ children 6-12. (615) 546-0745.

Maryville vicinity

SAM HOUSTON SCHOOLHOUSE, 6 miles N. via TN 33, 1794. Sam Houston, who was to gain great fame as governor of both Tennessee and Texas, president of the Republic of Texas, and U.S. senator from the same state, taught at this one-room log structure during the school term of 1812. The building was used as schoolhouse for more than a century and later adapted as a crude residence. Restored in the 1950s, it is the oldest school in Tennessee. Operated by the state. NR. Open M-Sa 9-6, Su 1-6. Free. (615) 983-1550.

Morristown

CROCKETT TAVERN MUSEUM, 2106 E. Main St. In the 1790s John Crockett moved his family from the banks of the Nolichucky River (present town of Limestone) to a site on the Abingdon-Knoxville Rd., where he constructed a small tavern. It was at this tavern that Davy Crockett, John's son, spent his youth. Although the original building no longer exists, a careful reconstruction was built in the 1950s only a few yards from the original site. Its six rooms are furnished with pioneer antiques, and a basement museum displays many artifacts relating to Davy, who was a humorist, bear hunter, state legislator, U.S. congressman, and martyr in the cause of Texas independence. Operated by the APTA. Open May-Oct, M-F 12-5. $2 adults, $1 children, group rates. (615) 586-6382.

Norris

MUSEUM OF APPALACHIA, TN 61, 19th century. More than two dozen log cabins and other buildings dating from the first half of the 19th century have been assembled on a 70-acre site, surrounded by farmlands, kitchen herb gardens, and barnyard fowl. Each building has been meticulously restored and refurbished with pieces original to its era. NR. Open daily 8-dusk. $2.75 adults, $1.50 children, group rates. (615) 494-7680.

Oak Ridge

AMERICAN MUSEUM OF SCIENCE AND ENERGY, 300 Tulane Ave. A closely-guarded community during World War II, Oak Ridge was the home of the Manhattan Project, whose thousands of scientists and support personnel lived here under oaths of secrecy with one major goal: to construct the nation's first uranium purifying plant. Uranium processed in the plant was to be used to produce fissionable material for the first atomic bomb. Exhibits within the museum tell the story of those years and of the peaceful uses of atomic energy. Open M-Sa 9-5, Su 12:30-5. Free. (615) 576-3200.

The nuclear reactor constructed in 1943 is located 10 miles SW on Bethel Valley Rd. It served for many years as the principal atomic research facility in the United States. NR, NHL. Open M-Sa 9-4. Free. (615) 574-4166.

Pall Mall

SERGEANT YORK HISTORIC AREA, 19th-20th centuries. The small village of Pall Mall was the birthplace and residence of Alvin C. York, whose actions in the Battle of the Argonne Forest during World War I earned him numerous citations, including the Congressional Medal of Honor. The gristmill which he operated from 1943 until the 1960s is now a museum, as is the farm where he grew up. NR. Open daily 8-6. Free. (615) 879-5821.

Pigeon Forge

PIGEON FORGE MILL, off US 441, 1830. This old gristmill has had a varied past, having been used as an iron forge, lumbermill, loomhouse and power generator through the years. These days, however, it's back to grinding cornmeal, whole wheat, rye, and buckwheat for flour; visitors can purchase the results. Guided tours are offered. NR. Open Apr-Nov, M-Sa 9-6. $1.25 adults, 75¢ children 8-12. (615) 453-4628.

Rugby

HISTORIC RUGBY, INC., TN 52, 19th century. In October, 1880, English author Thomas Hughes (*Tom Brown's Schooldays*) founded a colony in the northern Cumberland mountains, and named it after his public school, Rugby. His aim was to establish "a new center of human life, human interests, human activities . . . in this strangely beautiful solitude: a center in which a healthy, hopeful, reverent life shall grow." At its height Rugby consisted of 65 buildings housing 450 residents. Fire, flood, and disease were to cripple the colony before the turn of the century, however, and today fewer than 100 people, some descendants of the original colonists, live in the community. 17 original buildings remain, including the Thomas Hughes Public Library (1882), a small frame building containing one of the finest representative collections of Victorian literature in America; Christ Church Episcopal (1887), an outstanding example of Carpenter's Gothic architecture; and several homes originally built for members of Hughes's colony, including his own cottage, Kingstone Lisle (1884). These buildings are open to the public and furnished with many of the pieces which originally graced them. NR. Open Mar-Nov, Tu-Sa 10-5, Su 2-5. $2 adults, $1 children, group rates. (615) 628-2441.

Vonore vicinity

FORT LOUDON, N. via US 411. Built in 1757, Fort Loudoun was the first major British outpost west of the Allegheny Mountains. A thriving settlement grew up within the protective stockade, but in 1760 warring Cherokees captured the fort and massacred most of the residents. A careful reconstruction, based on archaeological excavations and historical records, has been undertaken by the state. A visitor center displays many artifacts from the site. Open daily 8-4. Free. (615) 884-6217. ★

Middle Tennessee

Rolling hills, green meadows, and picturesque streams characterize the central area of Tennessee. Some of those streams empty into the Cumberland River, which meanders along a winding course through Nashville, the state capital. Pioneer life in this area west of the mountains wasn't as harsh as in the rugged country of East Tennessee; simple cabins quickly gave way to large plantations as settlers reaped profits from the soil.

Castalian Springs

CRAGFONT, TN 25, early 19th century. General James Winchester, a hero of the Revolution, speaker of the Tennessee Senate, and one of the founders of Memphis, brought stonemasons and ships' carpenters 700 miles through the wilderness from his native state of Maryland to build this stone Georgian house. Located on a rocky hill about five miles from present-day Gallatin, Cragfont is furnished with early 19th-century antiques, some of which are original Winchester family furnishings. Operated by the APTA. NR. Open mid Apr-Oct, Tu-Sa 10-5, Su 1-6, and by appointment. $2 adults, 25¢ children, group rates. (615) 452-7070.

WYNNEWOOD, TN 25, c. 1828. Used as a stagecoach inn and a private residence, this large log structure was built to take advantage of the nearby mineral springs prized for their medicinal qualities. Among the frequent visitors to the inn was Andrew Jackson, attracted by the nearby racecourse the enterprising innkeeper set up, rather than by the soothing waters. NR, NHL. Open M-Sa 10-4, Su 1-6. $2 adults, $1 students, 50¢ children under 12. (615) 452-5463.

Columbia

JAMES K. POLK ANCESTRAL HOME, 301 W. 7th St., 1816. Samuel Polk constructed a roomy two-story brick house to accommodate his growing family. His son James, who was to become president in 1844, lived here for several years as both schoolboy and young lawyer. Some of the furniture is original to the house; other pieces were used in the Polks' Nashville home and at the White House. Next door is the Sisters' House, built for Jane Maria Polk Walker and Ophelia Polk Hays, which is also open as part of this historic museum complex. NR, NHL. Open Apr-Oct, M-F 9-5, Su 1-5; Nov-Mar, M-F 10-4, Su 1-5. $2 adults, 75¢ students, 50¢ children under 12, group rates. (615) 388-2354.

Dickson

GOVERNOR FRANK G. CLEMENT BIRTHPLACE, Frank Clement Pl., late 19th century. Frank G. Clement, Tennessee's forty-first governor, served three terms in the capitol. His grandmother was innkeeper of this depot hotel; her living quarters, on the ground floor, are adorned with the furnishings in use when Clement was born there, in 1920. Memorabilia relating to Governor Clement's terms in office are on display. Open Tu-Su 12-5. Free. (615) 446-6522.

Dover and vicinity

FORT DONELSON NATIONAL MILI-

TARY PARK, 1 mile W. on US 79, 1862. Earthworks, batteries, and reconstructed log huts mark the site of this Confederate fort, which was captured by Union troops under Ulysses S. Grant in February, 1862. The decisive battle for Fort Donelson was Grant's first major Civil War victory, greatly enhancing his prestige as a military leader and opening an avenue into the heart of the South by way of the Tennessee and Cumberland rivers. Nearby in town, the **Dover Hotel** (1853), where Grant's famous demand for "unconditional and immediate surrender" was met, has been restored and is open for tours. Civil War memorabilia are on display within. NR. Open daily 8-5. Free. (615) 232-5348. ★

Franklin

FRANKLIN BATTLEFIELD, US 31, 19th century. On November 30, 1864, Confederate General John B. Hood shattered the Confederate Army of Tennesseee with his uncoordinated, badly-planned attack on a strong Union force. The area south of town, where Hood's troops assembled, is still largely unchanged. The **Carter House** (1830), 1140 Columbia Ave., still bears the marks of bullets and shells; Union troops were stationed around it during the battle, and the small brick residence served as their command post. Restored by the APTA, the Carter House is furnished with artifacts of the ante-bellum era, Civil War relics, and 19th-century antiques. NR. Open M-Sa 9-4, Su 2-4. $1.50 adults, 50¢ children under 16. (615) 794-1733. ★

Gallatin (see Castalian Springs)

Lynchburg

JACK DANIEL DISTILLERY, TN 55, 1866. Jasper Newton Daniel bought a small distillery in a picturesque hollow in the mountains of south central Tennessee in the 1860s; the brew that he produced with pure spring water (which still flows from a cave in the hollow) won international recognition as Tennessee Sippin' Whiskey. In 1866, when the U.S. Government began licensing distilleries, Jack Daniel's was the first registered. The 19th-

century one-story **office** building where "Mister Jack" worked is now a museum. Among the other early structures remaining are sheds, the **rickyard** (where charcoal is still made from hard sugar maple), and the brick **stillhouse**, rebuilt after the end of Prohibition by Daniel's nephew. Tours are given of the facility, but samples aren't available: the county is "dry"—as it has been since 1909. NR. Open daily 8-4. Free. (615) 759-4211.

Murfreesboro and vicinity

OAKLANDS, N. Maney Ave., 19th century. This imposing mansion is actually three houses in one, each representing a different period in Tennessee history. The original structure was a simple two-story, two-room dwelling built around 1815. Enlarged five years later, Oaklands became typical of modest American brick homes of the period. But in 1850 a major addition was made, including four rooms, a spacious hallway and semi-circular stairway, making Oaklands one of the most elegant homes in the area. During the Civil War the house was alternately occupied by both the South and the North. In December, 1862, Jefferson Davis and his aide, Colonel George W.C. Lee (son of Robert E.) stayed here while visiting troops in the area. The mansion's ten acres of grounds include a 19th-century garden, a wooded bird sanctuary, and a small medical museum of wartime artifacts. NR. Open Tu-Sa

10-4:30, Su 1-4:30. $1.50 adults, 75¢ children under 16, group rates. (615) 893-0022. ★

Not far from Oaklands is **Cannonsburgh Pioneer Village,** a good place to take the kids when they get restless. Located on S. Front St., the village is a reconstruction of 19th-century life, complete with working gristmill, general store, one-room school, blacksmith shop, and craft demonstrations. Open May-Oct, Tu-Sa 10-5, Su 1-5. Free. (615) 893-6565. ✔

STONES RIVER NATIONAL BATTLE-FIELD, 3 miles NW of Murfreesboro on US 41, 1862-63. The three-day battle waged at Stones River was the first major confrontation in the two-year western campaign that cut the Confederacy in two and reached its climax in Sherman's march to the sea. Both the North and the South suffered heavy losses; both claimed victory. A national cemetery at the site contains the graves of more than 6,000 Union soldiers; the centrally-located **visitor center** is the place to find brochures and maps outlining the course of the battle. NR. Open daily 8-5. Free. (615) 893-9501. ★

Nashville

Founded in 1779 by a small group of pioneers who built a fort on the banks of the Cumberland River, Nashville grew quickly throughout the first decades of the 19th century and was made the permanent state capital in 1843. Many industries have contributed to the city's growth: the most famous, of course, is the music business, for Nashville is home to the world-renowned "Grand Ole Opry," where many of this century's most successful country and western singers got their start.

COUNTRY MUSIC HALL OF FAME AND MUSEUM, 4 Music Sq. E. Minnie Pearl's first hat, Roy Rogers' boots, Gene Autry's guitar, and Elvis Presley's "solid gold" Cadillac are among the plethora of exhibits here. The museum also conducts tours of nearby **Studio B,** RCA's first Nashville recording studio, where the process involved in transforming live music to disc form is explained. Studio B is open daily 9-5. The museum is open June-Aug, daily 8-8; Sept-May, daily 9-5. $3.50 adults, $1.25 children 6-11. (615) 244-2522.

CUMBERLAND MUSEUM AND SCIENCE CENTER, Ridley Ave. Archaeology, anthropology, natural history, and transporation exhibits are among the offerings of this huge modern facility. Children will want to see the model train exhibits, American Indian toys, and antique doll collection. Open Tu-Sa 10-5, Su 1-5. $1.50 adults, $1 children. (615) 242-1858. ✔

FORT NASHBOROUGH, 170 First Ave. N. Five accurate reproductions of the original Fort Nashborough cabins, including two block houses, have been erected by the Metropolitan Board of Parks and Recreation not far from the site of the first stockade on the Cumberland River. Common household tasks—cooking, candle-making, soap-making—are demonstrated by costumed staff members. Open M-Sa 9-4; also Su 1-4 in summer. Free. (615) 255-8192. ✔

THE PARTHENON, Centennial Park, 1896-7. Built for Tennessee's Centennial celebration, this is the only existing replica of the original Greek Parthenon. Nashville's late 19th-century copy was not intended to be a permanent addition to the city's architecture; it was almost totally rebuilt in 1931. Four enormous bronze en-

trance doors are said to be the largest such portals in the world. The basement rooms are used as galleries for art exhibits, which change monthly. NR. Open Tu-Sa 9-4:30, Su 1-4:30. Suggested donation $1 adults, 50¢ children. (615) 259-6358.

RYMAN AUDITORIUM (Grand Ole Opry House) 116 Opry Place, 1889-91. Construction of this Victorian-Gothic auditorium was the result of an ardent campaign by Nashville residents to build an assembly hall for Sam Jones, a Georgia revivalist popular in the area. In the early 1900s a stage replaced the pulpit, and the building became a hall for lecturers and entertainers. In 1941, the Grand Ole Opry

moved in and remained here until Opryland U.S.A. was completed more than thirty years later. NR. Guided tours are conducted daily 8:30-4:30. $1 admission. (615) 749-1445.

TENNESSEE STATE CAPITOL, Capitol Hill, 1845-59. In 1843, the Tennessee General Assembly selected Nashville as the permanent capital of the state and shortly thereafter commissioned William Strickland to design the new capitol building. The result, sited on a commanding hill overlooking the city, is a massive limestone structure patterned after the temples of Greece, with Ionic porticoes at each end and a 42-foot cupola crowning the whole. Strickland died several years before the building was completed and was entombed within the walls in accordance with his wishes. The spacious grounds contain monuments to a number of noted Tennesseans, among them Andrew Jackson and President James K. Polk, who is interred with his wife in a **tomb** designed by Strickland in 1850. NR, NHL. Open M-F 8-4:30, Sa-Su 9-4. Free. (615) 741-3211.

TENNESSEE STATE MUSEUM, Polk Cultural Complex, 5th and Deaderick Sts. Paintings, decorative arts, and historic artifacts commemorating Tennessee's years of settlement, political development, and industrial growth are housed in a new state facility opened in 1982. At the nearby **War Memorial Building,** 7th and Union Sts., exhibits are devoted to the state's involvement in 20th century wars. Both facilities are open Tu-Sa 9-5, Su-M 1-5. Free. (615) 741-2692.

Nashville vicinity

A number of the attractions which follow are within Nashville's city limits; they are listed here because of their distance from the downtown area.

BELLE MEADE, 7 miles SW at 110 Leake Ave., 19th century. Belle Meade, sometimes called the "Queen of Tennessee Plantations," was established by John Harding in 1807. Harding's son, William, built the present Greek Revival mansion in 1853 as the focal point of a 5,300-acre plantation on which he raised thoroughbred horses, cattle, sheep, and goats. During the latter half of the 19th century, Belle Meade was one of the most famous thoroughbred farms in the nation, producing many successful racers, including Iroquois, the first American-bred winner of the English Derby (1881). The beautiful mansion has been restored and refurbished; it is in sharp contrast to the oldest building on the grounds, the c. 1800 **log cabin** in which William Harding was born. Other structures open to the public are a large **carriage house and stable,** where the riding horses were kept (now the repository for a fine collection of antique carriages); a **smokehouse, gardenhouse,** and **dairy.** Operated by the APTA. NR. Open M-Sa 9-5. $2.50 adults, $2 students, $1 children 6-12. (615) 352-8247.

CHEEKWOOD (Tennessee Botanical Gardens and Fine Arts Center), 7 miles W. off TN 100 on Forest Park Dr., 1929. Joel Cheek originated the Maxwell House coffee blend and sold the recipe to General Foods for $45 million. With the proceeds, his heirs constructed a 60-room Georgian Revival mansion, which they filled with 18th-century antiques, priceless art, and structural oddities such as a staircase from Queen Charlotte's Palace at Kew. The mansion was donated to the Tennessee Botanical Gardens in the 1950s; the grounds are beautifully planted with flowers, trees, and shrubs, and a separate building displays exotic plants. Open Tu-Sa 10-5, Su 1-5. $2 adults, $1 children 7-17. (615) 352-5310.

THE HERMITAGE, 12 miles E. on US 70N, 1818-19. For over 40 years Andrew Jackson lived at The Hermitage, during which time he rose from a frontier militia commander to the Presidency. He bought the property in 1804 and lived with his family in a small log cabin while the present porticoed brick mansion was being constructed. The house is beautifully furnished, largely with the Jacksons' possessions; most of the outbuildings remain, including the early 19th-century **log cabin** where Jackson and his wife, Rachel, first lived, a **smokehouse,** and a **carriage house.** Jackson's **tomb** is located in a picturesque corner of the garden, still shaded by hickory trees planted in 1830. Operated by the Ladies Hermitage Association. NR, NHL. Open daily 9-5. $3 adults, $1 children 6-13, group rates. (615) 889-2941.

Tulip Grove (1836), also operated by the Ladies Hermitage Association, stands across from The Hermitage, overlooking a green valley and **"Rachel's Church,"** a small house of worship which the Jacksons helped build. Tulip Grove, a large Greek Revival mansion, was built for Andrew Jackson Donelson, Mrs. Jackson's nephew and secretary to the President. Furnishings include original pieces belonging to Donelson. NR. (Admission to The Hermitage includes Tulip Grove.)

TENNESSEE AGRICULTURAL MUSEUM, 6 miles S. off I-65, Hogan Rd. Exhibits on Tennessee farming, operated by the state department of agriculture, include hand tools, horse-drawn equipment, household implements, and early farm articles. Open M-F 9-4. Free. (615) 741-1533.

TRAVELLERS' REST, 6 miles S. off US 31, Farrell Pkwy., 18th-19th centuries. John Overton, an early Tennessee judge who helped plan Andrew Jackson's presidential campaign, built his simple frame home in several stages over the decades he owned it. His son, John Overton II, added another section in the late 1880s. Travellers' Rest served as a temporary headquarters for Confederate General John B. Hood during the Civil War. Operated by the National Society of the Colonial Dames of America, the house is furnished with Federal and early Empire antiques, Sheffield silver, 19th-century toys, decorative arts, and books. NR. Open M-Sa 9-4, Su 1-4. $2 adults, 75¢ children under 12, group rates. (615) 832-2962. ★

Smyrna vicinity

SAM DAVIS HOME, 2 miles N. off I-24, 19th century. Young Sam Davis was captured by Union troops in November, 1863. Papers containing information about the North's troops and fortifications were found on his person, and, because he refused to reveal the source of his information to spare his life, he was hanged as a spy, earning the sobriquet "boy hero of the Confederacy." The two-story frame house where Davis grew up, typical of ante-bellum middle-class farms, is furnished with simple, utilitarian pieces. The **slave quarters** and **overseer's cabin** have been rebuilt, along with stables and other outbuildings common to small plantations of the era. A **museum** adjacent to the house contains Civil War artifacts and letters from Davis to his family. NR. Open Mar-

Oct, M-Sa 9-5, Su 1-5; Nov-Feb, M-Sa 10-4, Su 1-5. $2 adults, $1 children 6-11. (615) 459-2341. ★

Winchester and vicinity

FALLS MILLS, 10 miles W. on US 64, 1873. This picturesque brick mill, with its operating water wheel, was originally used to manufacture woolen material and coarse cloth; in the early 1900s it was operated as a cotton gin. Now meal and flour, available for sale, are produced here in a bucolic setting along Factory Creek. NR. Open M-F 8-4, Sa 9-4, Su 12:30-4. 50¢ adults, 25¢ children. (615) 469-7161.

HUNDRED OAKS CASTLE, off US 64, 1889. Arthur Handly Marks, son of Tennessee's 21st governor, built this enormous brick castle, patterned after those he had seen and admired in England and Scotland. The huge two-story library is an exact replica of the one in Sir Walter Scott's castle in Abbotsford; it and Hundred Oaks's 36 other rooms are filled with antiques. NR. Open Tu-Su 10-10. $1 adults, 50¢ children. (615) 967-0100.

West Tennessee

The natural boundary of Tennessee's western reaches is marked by cypress, cottonwoods, and plains that line the mighty Mississippi River. The gentle topography was found to be ideal for growing cotton; the river's breadth and depth enabled easy shipment of the bales to distant markets and spurred the growth of the state's largest city, Memphis. Control of the Mississippi was vital to both sides during the Civil War; along its banks are remnants of many battlefields where the struggle was waged.

Fort Pillow

FORT PILLOW STATE PARK, TN 87, 1861-64. Fort Pillow was one of many Mississippi River defenses built by the Confederates in their attempt to stop Union incursions. Most of the trenches and walls are still intact. A **visitor center** in the park has exhibits explaining the two

major battles fought here: in 1862, heavy Confederate losses forced evacuation, but in 1864 the fort was regained by troops under Nathan Bedford Forrest. NR. Open daily 8-5. Free. (901) 738-5466. ★

Jackson

CASEY JONES HOME AND RAILROAD MUSEUM, 211 W. Chester St., c. 1900. Jonathan Luther (Casey) Jones was an engineer for the Illinois Central Railroad. One night he agreed to substitute for a sick cohort who couldn't make the Memphis to New Orleans run and was killed in a futile attempt to stop his speeding train from colliding with a stalled freight on the tracks ahead. The small frame home where he lived has been restored as a museum of railroadiana. NR. Open summer M-Sa 8-5, winter M-Sa 9-4, Su 1-5. $2 adults, $1 children 6-12. (901) 668-1222. ✔

Hernando de Soto is credited with having discovered the Mississippi River in 1541; it is thought that he stood on a high bluff overlooking the broad waterway only five miles from the present city of Memphis. Aside from temporary fortifications built by the French and Spanish in the 17th and 18th centuries, it was to be nearly 300 years before a settlement was firmly established here. In 1819, John Overton, Andrew Jackson, and James Winchester laid out a river-bluff town which they named Memphis for the ancient Egyptian city meaning "place of good abode." The settlement grew quickly, spurred by the success of the cotton plantations and lumber mills which sprang up around it. Still a vital river port more than 150 years later, Memphis's chief industries remain closely wedded to cotton and lumber manufacturing.

The city's most famous modern attraction is Graceland (1939), the has-to-be-seen-to-be-believed home of Elvis Presley, "King of Rock and Roll." The musical heritage of Memphis, however, is more venerable: its Beale St. (which see) is known as the "Home of the Blues."

The listings which follow are divided into two geographic sections: the downtown area, clustered along the eastern bank of the Mississippi; and the outlying district, whose attractions are more widely spread to the east and south. The Convention and Visitors Bureau, 12 S. Main St., offers many brochures describing historic sites and information about riverboat excursions on the Memphis Queen Line. (901) 526-1919.

Downtown Memphis

BEALE STREET HISTORIC DISTRICT, bounded by Main and 4th Sts., late 19th-20th centuries. The Beale St. area provided the environment that gave birth to the blues, a unique contribution of black culture to American music. When W.C. Handy (who claimed not to have invented, but only to have adapted, the music) frequented the area at the turn of the century, it was lined with saloons, sporting houses,

gambling halls, and theaters. Many of the buildings have been restored.

A. Schwab, founded in 1876, has been operated by the same family ever since. The department store contains a museum of Beale St. memorabilia, including early sheet music for "St. Louis Blues" and other Handy tunes. NR. Open during business hours. Free. (901) 523-9782.

The **Orpheum Theatre** (1927), at the corner of Main and Beale Sts., is a lavishly appointed Italian Renaissance "movie palace" which has been restored and now offers Broadway productions on a seasonal basis. NR. (901) 525-7800.

VICTORIAN VILLAGE, 600 block of Adams Ave., 19th-20th centuries. Many elaborate mansions were erected here, designed in the ornate Italianate, Second Empire, and Neo-classical styles. Many of the finest homes have been restored; several are open to the public. The most impressive is the **Fontaine House** (1870), 680 Adams St., a brick and terra-cotta Second Empire mansion built for Amos Woodruff, a successful banker and merchant. Restored by the APTA, it is furnished with 19th-century antiques. Open Jan-Mar, daily 1-4; Apr-Dec, daily 10-4. $2 adults, $1 students and children. (901) 526-1469.

The **Mallory-Neely House,** 652 Adams, is an imposing Italianate mansion built c. 1855 and remodeled in the 1880s. Its 25 rooms are decorated with antiques ap-

propriate to the period. NR. Open daily 1-4. $2 adults, $1 students and children. (901) 523-1484.

A few blocks west, at 198 Adams, is the **Magevney House** (c. 1836), said to be the oldest residence in Memphis. The small clapboard cottage belonged to Eugene Magevney, a schoolteacher, and is furnished with some of his original possessions. NR. Open Tu-Sa 10-4. Free. (901) 526-4464.

The Outlying Area

CHUCALISSA INDIAN VILLAGE AND MUSEUM, 1987 Indian Village Dr., 10th-17th centuries. Archaeologists believe that Chucalissa is one of the deserted villages de Soto discovered in 1541 just a few miles east of the Mississippi River. Chucalissa means "abandoned houses" in the Choctaw Indian language; a staff of Choctaw Indians and archaeologists operates a reconstructed village on the site, with thatch-roofed houses arranged around a town square. Some of the excavations made here have been preserved under glass to show examples of the techniques used; artifacts are displayed; and special festivals are held during the summer months. NR. Open Tu-Sa 9-5, Su 1-5. 50¢ adults, 10¢ children. (901) 785-3160. ✔

OVERTON PARK HISTORIC DISTRICT, bounded by N. Parkway, E. Parkway, Poplar Ave., and Kenilworth St. More than 300 acres of meadow and forest, relatively unchanged since they were set aside in 1900, offer an oasis in the midst of city life. Best of all, this is the location of the **Memphis Zoo and Aquarium,** which boasts more than 2,000 different species of birds, animals, and fish. NR. Open Apr-Oct, daily 9-6; Nov-Mar, daily 9-5. $1.50 adults, 50¢ children 2-11. (901) 726-4781. ✔

PINK PALACE MUSEUM, 3050 Central Ave., 1930. Clarence Saunders was the founder of the Piggly-Wiggly chain of supermarkets and, as such, the inventor of a new concept in grocery shopping. He's best remembered by Tennesseans, however, for the construction of an outrage-

ously-extravagant mansion which locals dubbed "The Pink Palace." Unfortunately, Saunders went bankrupt during the Depression and the monster was never completed. The city acquired it shortly thereafter and transformed it into a museum of history and natural science. The extensive exhibits — from a miniature circus with moving parts to an insect display — are now housed in a new, modern wing. The Pink Palace itself is used for office and laboratory space. NR. Open Tu-Sa 9-5, Su 1-5. $1 adults, 50¢ children. (901) 454-5601.

Rutherford

DAVID CROCKETT CABIN, US 45W. In 1823 Davy Crockett moved to the rugged country of West Tennessee and settled on the Rutherford Fork of the Obion River. A reproduction of his cabin has been built on the site and furnished with tools, household utensils, and simple furniture of the period. Open May-Oct, Tu-Su 9-5, and by appointment. 50¢ adults, 25¢ children. (901) 665-7166.

Shiloh

SHILOH NATIONAL MILITARY PARK, off TN 22, 1862. The decisive, bloody Union victory at Shiloh in April,

1862, led to the early capture of Corinth, Mississippi, and of Memphis, and helped the North to gain control of the Mississippi River from Cairo, Illinois, to the Gulf of Mexico. A tour of the battlefield should begin at the visitor center, where exhibits and maps plot the course of the action. A national cemetery within the park contains the graves of more than 3,000 soldiers killed during the fray. NR. Open June-Labor Day, daily 8-6; Labor Day-May, daily 8-5. Free. (901) 689-5275. ★

Historic Accommodations

An asterisk (*) indicates that meals are served.

Chattanooga

CHATTANOOGA CHOO-CHOO HILTON INN, 1400 Market St., 37402. (615) 266-5000. Open all year. An 85-foot-high skylit dome is the centerpiece of Chattanooga's Terminal Station (1908), now converted into a fine hotel. (See historical listing.) NR.*

Gatlinburg

BUCKHORN INN, Tudor Mountain Rd., 37738. (615) 436-4668. Open all year. Near the entrance to Great Smoky Mountains National Park, and with its own tranquil lake, the Buckhorn Inn (1938) and cottages, all furnished with antiques offer a peaceful respite.

Knoxville

THREE CHIMNEYS OF KNOXVILLE, 1302 White Ave., 37916. (615) 521-4970. A lovely old Queen Anne residence (1896), Three Chimneys is decorated with Victorian furniture and artifacts.

Memphis

THE PEABODY, 149 Union Ave., 38103. (901) 529-4100. Open all year. The opulent Italian Renaissance Revival Peabody was completed in 1925, and quickly gained a reputation as the most elegant hotel in the South. Recently restored and refurbished after years of neglect, it is noted for its permanent residents—a family of ducks—which waddle across to the central fountain in the lobby each morning. NR.*

Nashville

THE HERMITAGE, 231 6th Ave., N, 37219. (615) 244-3131. Open all year. Preservationists recently saved this 10-story Beaux-Arts landmark (1910) from the bulldozers. It has been painstakingly refurbished, and is once again a first-class hotel. NR.*

10. KENTUCKY

SYNONYMOUS in many minds with the Kentucky Derby and mint juleps, Kentucky is in fact far more. Explored and settled by Daniel Boone, birthplace of Abraham Lincoln, the Bluegrass State offers many attractions for the history-minded traveler. From the formidable Cumberland Mountains on the east to the awesome Mississippi on the west, there are communities of all sizes where museums, old forts, and primitive log cabins exist, sometimes cheek by jowl with modern office buildings and industrial centers.

La Salle, carrying the banner of France, sailed down the Ohio in 1669 and landed at what is now Louisville. But it was to be nearly a century before Virginian Thomas Walker, with a small party of intrepid followers, discovered the famous Cumberland Gap through the rugged eastern mountains. The first English settlement was established at Harrodsburg more than two decades later, in 1774, and Kentucky remained a county of Virginia until 1792, when it became the first state west of the mountains to join the new union.

Kentucky's participation in the Revolutionary and Civil Wars was not nearly as extensive as that of neighboring Virginia, partly because of the mountainous terrain which intervened. During the Civil War Kentuckians were divided in their loyalties, but the state remained in the Union. Kentucky's two most famous native sons—Abraham Lincoln and Jefferson Davis—were, ironically, the chief protagonists of the war.

Modern-day Kentucky prizes its historic sites. Louisville and Lexington are urban centers where historic preservation is a respected alternative to demolition. Scenic parkways crisscross the state; the traveler with a sense of adventure may want to leave the main routes for a look at some of the small towns—Bardstown, Danville, Elizabethtown, Paris—whose quiet streets are lined with early 19th-century houses.

The listings which follow have been divided into four geographic sections to facilitate short tours: the mountainous region of Eastern Kentucky includes Cumberland Gap National Historical Park; Northern Kentucky features the cities of Newport and Covington, just opposite Cincinatti, Ohio. Central Kentucky is bluegrass country, and includes the state capital, Frankfort, along with the major metropolitan centers of Louisville and Lexington. Western Kentucky, bounded by the winding Mississippi and Ohio Rivers, is a mixed agricultural and industrial center.

Henry Clay Monument, Lexington

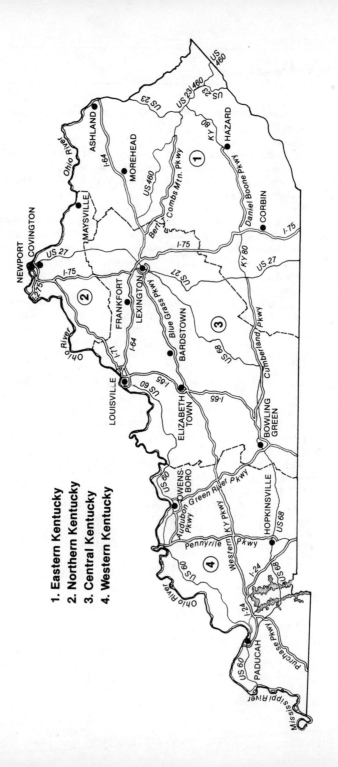

1. Eastern Kentucky
2. Northern Kentucky
3. Central Kentucky
4. Western Kentucky

Eastern Kentucky

Until the mid-18th century, when the now-famous Cumberland Gap was discovered, the rugged Cumberland Mountains between Kentucky and Virginia stymied early settlers who wished to move westward. Even today, this is one of the state's least populous regions, much of it devoted to the sprawling Daniel Boone National Forest, a nature-lover's dream. The area's historic attractions are similarly oriented, most concerned with the difficult, hardship-plagued lives of the early settlers.

Barbourville

DR. THOMAS WALKER CABIN, KY 459. Thomas Walker, physician and surveyor, was employed by the Loyal Land Company of Virginia to explore its grant of 800,000 acres in "Kentucke." With a small group of men, he traversed the Cumberland Gap in 1750 and established a base camp near a broad river, which he named the Cumberland. The camp was a crude log shelter—the first house built in Kentucky. A replica has been built on the exact site of the original, and a monument to Walker stands nearby. Operated by the state. Open Mar-Oct, daily 9-5. Free. (606) 546-4400.

Bernstadt

FIRST EVANGELICAL REFORMED CHURCH, KY 80, 1884. Built by Swiss immigrants during the late 19th century, this small frame church served the ecclesiastical needs of the community until the 1950s. It is one of the few unaltered structures remaining in the area of the original Swiss settlement. NR. Open by appointment. (606) 864-4574.

Fleming County

COVERED BRIDGES: **Goddard Bridge,** Maddox Rd., Goddard, 19th century; **Hillsboro Covered Bridge,** S. of Hillsboro on KY 111, c. 1865; **Ringos Mill Covered Bridge,** 14 miles S. of Flemingsburg on KY 158, 1867; **Sherburne Covered Suspension Bridge,** KY 11 at Licking River, 1867. Of these four 19th-century covered bridges, Goddard and Sherburne are still in use more than 100 years after their construction. The Sherburne Bridge, supported by massive stone abutments and a center pier, was strengthened by the addition of the suspension structure and cables in the early 1950s, and is heavily trafficked today. All

Ringos Mill Covered Bridge   **219**

of the bridges are of frame construction with stone supports. All are NR.

Irvine vicinity

DANIEL BOONE NATIONAL FOREST, KY 52. This enormous national preserve (more than 600,000 acres) stretches from the Tennessee border northeastward to within 20 miles of the Ohio state line. Included within its boundaries are lakes, rivers, the Red River Gorge, known for its spectacular rock formations, and several man-made historic sites as well. Near Irvine is the **Cottage Iron Furnace** (1854), a remnant of the once-profitable Kentucky iron industry. Within its rough hewn sandstone walls, cast iron was made for local markets, and pig iron shipped to other forges for transformation into bars, nails, and similar products. The furnace operated until 1879, when the industry declined both because of the obsolescence of the process and the growing competition from the northern Great Lakes area. NR. For information about the National Forest, contact Forest Supervisor, 100 Vaught Rd., Winchester, KY 40391. (606) 744-5656.

London

MOUNTAIN LIFE MUSEUM, Levi Jackson Wilderness Road State Park, US 25. A reconstructed pioneer village includes log cabins, a smokehouse, blacksmith shop, and barn, all surrounded by rough-hewn split-rail fences. Within the buildings are displays of costumes, decorative arts, glass, Indian artifacts, and other miscellany from the early days of Kentucky's settlement. Open May-mid Sept, daily 9-5. 50¢ adults, 25¢ children. (606) 878-8000.

North of London via I-75 and KY 909 is **Fort Sequoyah,** an early settlement which grew up along Skagg's Trace, a wilderness thoroughfare developed in the 19th century. An old general store, post office,

school, and Indian trading post have been restored on the site. Open M-Sa 9-6, Su 1-6. Free. (606) 843-7131.

Middlesboro

CUMBERLAND GAP NATIONAL HISTORICAL PARK, US 25E. Twenty years after Dr. Thomas Walker discovered the Cumberland Gap in 1750, Daniel Boone used the opening to lead parties of adventurers through the mountains to the beautiful bluegrass country beyond. The 20,000-acre national park is shared about equally by Kentucky and Virginia, with a small portion located to the south in Tennessee. It is in Kentucky, however, that the Gap's history is best interpreted. A **visitor center** near Middlesboro offers exhibits on botany, archaeology, and human settlement; north near the town of Cubage is the **Hensley Settlement** (1903-42), a widely-scattered group of hewn log farmsteads with shake roofs and split-rail fences surrounding them. At its peak, the community had a population of about 100. Restored by the National Park Service, the settlement is open as a museum of pioneer life and culture. NR. Open daily 8 am - dusk. Free. (606) 248-2817.

Pikeville and vicinity

HATFIELD-McCOY FEUD HISTORIC DISTRICT, 19th-20th centuries. The family feud which raged in this rugged eastern Kentucky area for more than 30 years is the stuff of legend: Hatfields against McCoys, and McCoys against Hatfields, taking potshots at each other whenever the mood struck. And all, they say, over the ownership of a single hog! Check at the Pike County Courthouse for information about the nearby **Jeremiah Hatfield house,** where three McCoy brothers bit the dust, and other sites involved with the conflict. NR. (606) 432-6000.

Northern Kentucky

Separated from Ohio and Indiana by the beautiful, winding Ohio River, Kentucky's northern reaches were primarily colonized with forts and trading outposts built along the waterway. Such outposts grew and flourished as more and more adventurers made their way westward; industry prospered, and the success of manufacturing concerns led to the construction, especially in Covington and nearby Newport, of elaborate mansions and large, ornately-detailed commercial buildings, most dating from the latter decades of the 19th century.

Carrollton vicinity

GENERAL BUTLER STATE RESORT PARK, 2 miles S. via KY 227. Within the grounds of this north-central recreation area is the beautifully-restored **Butler Mansion,** a 19th-century dwelling which was once the home of General William Orlando Butler, hero of the Battle of New Orleans during the War of 1812. NR. Lavishly furnished in the ornate Victorian style, the mansion, like the park, is open daily 9-5. Nominal admission. (502) 732-4384.

Covington and vicinity

CATHEDRAL BASILICA OF THE ASSUMPTION, 9 E. 12th St., 1895-1910. Patterned after Paris's monumental Notre Dame, (and at one-third its size no less impressive), this stone Gothic Revival cathedral is awash with flying buttresses, stained glass, marble, carved wood, and sculpture. The sculpture was the work of Clement J. Barnhorn; the three large murals which adorn the Blessed Sacrament chapel were painted by Covington's Frank Duveneck. NR. Open daily 7:30-6. Free. (606) 431-2060.

COVINGTON AND CINCINNATI SUSPENSION BRIDGE, foot of Court St., 1866. Spanning the Oho River between Covington and Cincinnati, Ohio, this is one of the great suspension bridges in the history of early American engineering, and was the prototype for the most famous—New York City's Brooklyn Bridge, designed by the same engineer. Talk about the need for such a span was begun in 1839, and John A. Roebling was selected to design it. But between political machinations and civil unrest (the War Between the States delayed construction for five years), the bridge, with its massive cables and great stone piers, took twenty-seven years to complete. NR, NHL.

RIVERSIDE DRIVE HISTORIC DISTRICT, bounded by Riverside Dr., 4th St., Licking River, Greenup and Garrard Sts., 19th century. Riverside Drive has always been the site of Covington's most elegant houses. The buildings within this district, many of which date from the early 1800s, include outstanding examples of many styles of 19th-century architecture. While the lavish mansions of this exclusive district are all privately owned, you can get a river's-eye view of them from another historic structure, the *Mike Fink,* a 19th-century paddlewheeler moored at the foot of Greenup St., which has been transformed into a restaurant. Open M-Sa 11-11, Su 2-10. (606) 261-4212. ✔

VENT HAVEN MUSEUM, 33 W. Maple Ave., Fort Mitchell. This unusual museum is dedicated to the art of "throwing the voice,"—ventriloquism. Its displays include more than 500 ventriloquists' dummies and an extensive library of books on the history and lore of the art. Some of the dummies on display are more than a century old. Open May-Sept, M-F by appointment only. Free. (606) 341-0461. ✔

Maysville and vicinity

MASON COUNTY MUSEUM, 215 Sutton St. The Ohio River town of Maysville was founded in the 1760s, and within thirty years had become a thriving port, where Kentucky settlers often stopped first on their way to their new homesteads. Most of the downtown area around the **Mason County Courthouse** (1844) on W. 3rd St. is encompassed in the **Courthouse Square** or **Maysville Downtown Historic District,** whose exuberantly-decorated cast-iron-front buildings show the influence of the city's river trade with New Orleans, far to the south. The museum displays are housed in a restored 1876 building, and feature slides, old documents, photographs, river dioramas, and other exhibits relating to the history of Maysville and northern Kentucky. NR. Open Tu-Sa 10-4, Su 2-4. $1 adults, 50¢ children. (606) 564-5865.

Maysville is now the seat of Mason County; the original county seat was **Washington,** 3½ miles south (via US 68), founded in 1784. Most of Washington has been designated an historic district, and many of its houses and public buildings date from the latter years of the 18th century and the first decades of the 19th. NR. Guided tours of the most historic buildings are available on weekends from May-Dec. $2 adults, 50¢ children. (606) 759-7814 or 759-7843.

Mount Olivet

BLUE LICKS BATTLEFIELD PARK, US 68, 18th century. In 1782, a full year after Cornwallis's surrender to Washington's armies at Yorktown, Virginia, one of the few Kentucky battles of the Revolutionary War was fought here. A museum within the park tells the story of that fierce battle and also displays pioneer artifacts, mastodon bones, colonial costumes and decorative arts, and other items of Kentucky frontier history. Operated by the state. Open Apr-Oct, daily 9-5. 75¢ adults, 50¢ children, group rates. (606) 289-5547. ★

Newport

MANSION HILL HISTORIC DISTRICT, roughly bounded by I-471, Washington Ave., 2nd and 6th Sts., 19th century. Separated from Covington by the narrow, winding Licking River, which has its outlet in the mighty Ohio across from Cincinnati, Newport was founded in the late 18th century and soon became a lively industrial and trade center. Its extensive iron and steel production supported most of the town's residents, many of whom chose to build their homes on the hills overlooking the Ohio River. The Mansion Hill neighborhood, therefore, is an eclectic mix of opulent estates and the humbler dwellings of the working class, most built during the last decades of the 19th century, and representing a wide range of Victorian architectural styles. An earlier, but certainly no less impressive house, is the **General James Taylor Mansion (Bellevue)**, at 335 E. 3rd St. Completed in 1840 from a design attributed to Benjamin Latrobe, the spacious Greek Revival dwelling sits high on a hillside with a commanding view of the surrounding area. Built for one of Newport's founders, the mansion, whose elegant interior includes a graceful spiral staircase, may be viewed by appointment with the present owners. NR. (606) 261-5795.

Union

BIG BONE LICK STATE PARK, KY 338. During the Pleistocene period enormous herbivores existed in the vicinity of the salt water spring now inside the boundaries of this 500-acre park. Mammoths, mastodons, and ancestors of the sloth, bison, and horse came to eat the vegetation and lick the salty earth around the spring; many became mired in the bogs and died. In the first organized paleontological expedition in the United States, Captain William Clark was sent by President Jefferson to recover remains from the site in 1807. The first modern excavations were begun in the 1960s, and ancient bones have been dispersed from the diggings to museums around the world. Plaques arranged throughout the park explain the history of the area; there are lifesize models of prehistoric beasts, and a model "dig" with bone samples and replicas. A small museum displays the complete skeleton of a young bison, as well as bones, claws, and a mammoth tusk. NR. Open Apr-Oct, daily 8-4:30. Free. (606) 384-3522.

Central Kentucky

Home of the state's most important cities, Lexington, Louisville, and Frankfort (the capital), Kentucky's central region is famed for its bluegrass country, home of thoroughbred racing. While the grass isn't really blue (except for a few weeks in the spring, as it first begins to grow), it seems an appropriately romantic appellation for this area of rolling farmland, white fences, and rich, beautiful horse farms.

Bardstown and vicinity

The small north-central community of Bardstown was founded in the late 18th century by David Bard, son of a wealthy Virginia landowner. One of the buildings still remaining from the first years of settlement is **Talbott Tavern** (1779), a stone and brick structure which was built as a coach stop at the end of the stage routes from Philadelphia and Virginia. Located at Court Square, the tavern was visited by such notables as Andrew Jackson, Henry Clay, William Henry Harrison, and Stephen Foster. It is still in operation as a restaurant, and is open daily for lunch and dinner. NR. (502) 348-3494.

BARTON MUSEUM OF WHISKEY HISTORY, Barton Rd. Bardstown is the seat of Nelson County, one of whose primary industries has always been the production of good Kentucky sour mash whiskey. Rare manuscripts, books, bottles, and advertising posters are among the exhibits arranged to explain the history of the American whiskey industry from its 18th-century beginnings through the close of Prohibition. Sorry, no free samples. Ask here about tours of local distilleries. Open daily 8-12 and 1-4:30. Free. (502) 348-3991.

MY OLD KENTUCKY HOME (Federal Hill), US 150, 18th-19th centuries. The earliest wing of Federal Hill was built about 1795; the main house, a fine Federal manor, was completed in 1818 by Judge John Rowan, who later became a U.S. Senator. It was here, during a visit with the Rowans in 1852, that Stephen Foster is said to have written his most famous song, "My Old Kentucky Home." Now part of a 235-acre state park which offers campground facilities and a fine golf course, Federal Hill is furnished with period antiques and portraits. NR. Open Tu-Su 9-5. $1 adults, 25¢ children. (The park is open daily, 9-7:30, admission free.) (502) 348-3502.

ST. JOSEPH PROTO CATHEDRAL AND COLLEGE COMPLEX, W. Stephen Foster Ave., 1819-42. Designed by John Rogers, the two-story brick cathedral is considered to be the first Catholic cathedral erected west of the Alleghenies, and thus one of the oldest in the United States. The Greek Revival building was completed in 1819. Nearby is **Spalding Hall** (1839), built as the main campus structure for St. Joseph's University, which was begun the year the cathedral was completed. It is now a museum, where local historical artifacts are displayed, some of which relate to the nearby cathedral. NR. Open Memorial Day-Labor Day, M-F 10:30-5:30, Su 1:30-5:30, and by appointment. 50¢ adults, 25¢ children. (502) 348-6402.

WICKLAND, ½ mile E. of Bardstown via US 62, 1813-17. Built for Charles Anderson Wickliffe, Kentucky governor and U.S. congressman, the Georgian mansion was later the home of Wickliffe's son, Robert, who was to become governor of Louisiana. Situated on a 66-acre farm, Wickland exhibits much of its original woodwork and furnishings. NR. Open June-Labor Day, daily 9-7, and by appointment. $1.50 adults, $1 students, 50¢ children. (502) 348-5428.

Berea

APPALACHIAN MUSEUM, Jackson St. Located on the campus of Berea College, one of the first mountain schools (1855), the Appalachian Museum was established in the early 1970s as a repository for historical artifacts and decorative arts of the area's mountain dwellers. Farm tools, homemaking utensils, baskets, samples of plants used for dyes—all present a vivid picture of life without modern conveniences, but where ingenuity and skill have obviated the need for such things. Open M-Sa 9-6, Su 1-6. $1 adults, 50¢ children. (606) 986-9341.

Bowling Green

KENTUCKY MUSEUM, Western Kentucky University, Russellville Rd. Administered by the University, the Kentucky Museum features a wide assortment of exhibits, from "The Changing Face of Main Street" to fashions from the past, paintings, and antique furniture. Over the years, donations of old tools, furniture, clothing and textiles, works of art, toys and rare books have made this collection one of the finest in the state. Open Tu-Sa 9:30-4, Su 1-4. Free. (502) 745-2492.

RIVERVIEW (The Hobson Mansion), Hobson Grove Park, west end of Main St., 1860. Riverview is a two-story Italianate house of brick on a native stone basement. Once the home of a prosperous Bowling Green family, it is now operated as a museum, with many of the original furnishings intact. NR. Open Tu-Su 2-5, and by appointment. $1 adults, 50¢ children 8-14. (502) 842-8957.

Bybee

BYBEE POTTERY (Cornelison Pottery), KY 52 E., 19th century. Situated in the small rural community of Bybee, in the rolling bluegrass county of Madison, this pottery complex is one of the oldest continuously operating potteries west of the Alleghenies. Currently producing a durable, practical ware, the Bybee Pottery is operated by the fifth generation of the Cornelison family. The earliest building of

the complex is a rectangular log structure (c. 1845), where much of the preliminary "throwing" work is still done. NR. Open M-Sa 9-12, 1-4. Free. (606) 369-5350.

Crab Orchard vicinity

WILLIAM WHITLEY HOUSE STATE SHRINE, 2 miles W. off US 150, 1787-94. This early brick house served as home and fortress to Colonel William Whitley, Indian fighter and pioneer scout, who built it with features to make it impregnable to Indian attack—thick walls, rifle ports, and heavily-shuttered windows. Called "the Guardian of the Wilderness Road," the Whitley house was a gathering place for frontiersmen such as George Rogers Clark, Isaac Shelby, and Daniel Boone. Furnished with late 18th-century antiques, the house is maintained by the state Department of Parks. NR. Open June-Aug, daily 9-5; Sept-May, Tu-Su 9-5. 50¢ adults, 25¢ children. (606) 355-2881.

Danville

CONSTITUTION SQUARE HISTORIC DISTRICT, bounded by Main, Walnut, 1st, and 2nd Sts., late 18th-19th centuries. Kentucky's political development began here in 1785, when the then Virginia county held its first constitutional convention, proposing withdrawal from Virginia and formation of a new state. Replicas of the original log courthouse, meetinghouse, and jail which were the center of early pioneer life have been constructed here, and the surrounding residential and commercial district contains brick and frame buildings which date from the late 18th century. The oldest **post office** in the state, relocated here, is now a museum of early Kentucky history. The first Kentucky constitution was signed in the building. NR. Open daily 9-5. Free. (606) 236-5089.

Also in the district is the **McDowell House and Apothecary Shop,** 125-7 2nd St. (c. 1795). Recognized today as the father of abdominal surgery, Dr. Ephraim McDowell successfully performed a difficult abdominal operation here in 1809. His achievement helped to overcome the widespread belief that such surgery was invariably fatal. Adjoining the doctor's frame house is the small brick apothecary shop where McDowell dispensed remedies to his patients. NR, NHL. Open Nov-Mar, Tu-Sa 10-12 and 1-4, Su 2-4; Apr-Oct, daily 10-12 and 1-4, Su 2-4. $1.50 adults, 50¢ children under 12. (606) 236-2804.

Elizabethtown

BROWN-PUSEY HOUSE, 128 N. Main St., 1825. Built as a stagecoach stop, this Georgian dwelling is now operated as a museum and historical library. It is thought that George Armstrong Custer lived here in the early 1870s. Open M-Sa 10-4. Free. (502) 765-2515.

LINCOLN HERITAGE HOUSE, Freeman Lake Park, 1789 and 1806. Two separate cabins connected by a large covered doorway, the Lincoln Heritage House is so-called because Thomas Lincoln, father of Abraham, did the joining work on the second cabin's interior. Furniture and household articles from the first half of the 19th century decorate both cabins. NR. Open June-Sept, Tu-Sa 10-6, Su 1-6. 50¢ adults, 25¢ children 6-12. (502) 769-9077.

Fort Knox

PATTON MUSEUM OF CAVALRY AND ARMOR, Fort Knox Military Reservation, Fayette Ave. Colorful (and controversial) World War II General George S. Patton was known for his flamboyance: the ivory-handled pistols he wore on each hip are displayed here, along with many other objects from his career. Military buffs will want to see the early armored vehicles, military equipment, medals, and paintings. Open daily 9-4:30. Free. (502) 624-3812. ★

(Yes, Fort Knox is the repository of a vast amount of the United States' supply of gold bullion. No, it is *not* open for public inspection.)

Frankfort

Surrounded by gentle hills along the course of the Kentucky River which divides the city, Frankfort was named for an early settler, Stephen Frank, who began to develop lands here in the late 18th century. His riverside property became known as Frank's Ford. The capital was established at Frankfort in 1786, when General James Wilkinson, commander in chief of the western division of the army, donated part of a 100-acre grant for the establishment of a government building (See Old State Capitol, following).

Frankfort's oldest residential district, a large area of 18th- to early 20th-century homes, is the location of several major museum buildings (see Liberty Hall and Orlando Brown House, following) and is known as "Corner in Celebrities" because of the unusually large number of famous people—senators, congressmen, judges—who have lived within its boundaries. Once you've visited the museums, you might like to meander through the area, whose ante-bellum charm is defined by bell towers and steeples, walled gardens, and overhanging trees.

ORLANDO BROWN HOUSE, 202 Wilkinson, c. 1836. Built by capitol architect Gideon Shryock for the son of then-Senator John Brown, whose Liberty Hall stands nearby, the brick Greek Revival residence is expertly maintained by the National Society of the Colonial Dames of America. NR. Open Tu-Sa 10-5, Su 2-5. $1.50 adults, 50¢ children. (502) 875-4952.

FRANKFORT CEMETERY, 215 E. Main St., 1844. This 100-acre cemetery contains the graves of Daniel Boone, U.S. Vice President Richard Menton Johnson, fifteen Kentucky governors, numerous national and state notables, and hundreds of soldiers from all major U.S. wars since the Revolution. NR. Open daily dawn-dusk. (502) 223-8261.

KENTUCKY MILITARY HISTORY MUSEUM, E. Main St., 1850. The old **State Arsenal,** a tall brick structure with narrow, elongated windows, was actively used during the Civil War to repulse an attack on Frankfort, and later commandeered by the National Guard. It is now the repository for a vast collection of weapons, uniforms, flags, and other military equipment displayed so as to trace the state's military history from the days of Daniel Boone through the service of the Kentucky National Guard in Vietnam. NR. Open M-Sa 9-4, Su 1-5. Free. (502) 564-3265. ★

KENTUCKY STATE CAPITOL AND GOVERNOR'S MANSION, Capital Ave., early 20th century. The center of Kentucky state government is a Beaux-Arts classical building designed by Frank Mills Andrews in 1905; he copied from Paris's Hotel des Invalides (the rotunda and interior of the dome) and from Versailles's Grand Trianon Palace (the ornate State Reception Room) in executing his plans. NR. Open M-F 8-4:30, Sa-Su 9-4:30. Free. (502) 564-3449. On the grounds is the current **Governor's Mansion** (1912), designed by C.C. and E.A. Weber to harmonize with the capitol, and patterned after the Petit Trianon at Versailles. NR. Open (in fair weather only) Tu, Th 9:30-11:30 am. Free. (502) 564-6960.

LIBERTY HALL, 218 Wilkinson St., 1796-1800. This superb Federal mansion was built by John Brown, a prominent early Kentucky lawyer and politician. In the decade prior to building his residence, Brown was active in the movement to separate Kentucky from Virginia, of which it was then a part. Liberty Hall was patterned after the sophisticated architecture of Philadelphia, a city which Brown much admired. Today operated by the National Society of the Colonial Dames of America, the mansion is furnished with many outstanding 18th- and 19th-century antiques. NR, NHL. Open Tu-Sa 10-5, Su 2-5. $1.50 adults, 50¢ children. (Combination ticket available with Orlando Brown House.) (502) 227-2560.

OLD GOVERNOR'S MANSION, 420 High St., 1797. Until the early 1900s, when the present governor's mansion was completed, this 2½-story brick Georgian residence was home to thirty-three Kentucky governors, and it now serves as the home of the lieutenant governor. Beautifully furnished with a variety of antiques and decorative arts, the mansion is open for tours. NR. Open Tu,Th 10-4, and by appointment. (502) 564-5500.

OLD STATE CAPITOL, Broadway at the St. Clair Mall, 1827-30. The first major work of local architect Gideon Shryock, Kentucky's third state house (the first two burned) is a severely simple, two-story Greek Revival landmark with an Ionic portico. In the middle of the building is a beautifully designed and executed marble staircase which rises to a square dome. The state Historical Society administers the old capitol as a museum, and in it are housed extensive exhibits pertaining to Kentucky history. NR, NHL. Open M-Sa 9-4, Su 1-5. Free. (502) 564-3016.

Harrodsburg and vicinity

OLD FORT HARROD STATE PARK, US 68/127. Captain James Harrod led a group of thirty settlers across the Cumberland Gap in 1774, and they chose this site, with its nearby springs, on which to build a permanent community — the first in Kentucky. Hostile Indians in the area necessitated the building of a fort with a protective stockade. While the original buildings no longer exist, reproductions of the early cabins and school, the first in the state (1775), have been built here. Also within the grounds of the park is the **Lincoln Marriage Temple**, which shelters the 18th-century log cabin in which Abraham Lincoln's parents were married (moved here from the original site in Beech Fork). Open Apr-Oct, daily 9-5; Nov-Mar, Tu-Su 9-5. $1 adults, 50¢ children. (606) 734-3314.

SHAKERTOWN AT PLEASANT HILL, 7 miles NE via US 68, 19th century. Settled in 1805 by members of the United Society of Believers in Christ's Second Appearing, the Pleasant Hill community is believed to be the most successful and one of the longest-lasting of America's communal religious societies (it survived into the 1920s). Group dwellings were built of native timber, brick, and limestone. Other structures within the complex (all of which survive today), included a **meeting house** (1820), **post office** (1848), **wash house** (c. 1825), **bath house** (1860), and **cooper's shop** (1847). In all, there are 27 original buildings full of functional Shaker furnishings and decorative arts. Interpreters are on hand to explain the Shaker way of life and to demonstrate broommaking, cabinetry, coopering, spinning, weaving and quilting.

One of Shakertown's recent attractions, and one guaranteed to please the children,

Centre Family House

is an old paddlewheel **riverboat** moored at the Shaker Landing on the Kentucky River, which offers hour-long cruises in mid-morning and mid-afternoon from late May to late Oct. ($4 adults, $2 students 12-18, $1 children 6-11). Shakertown includes a fine dining room in the old **Trustees' Office** (1839), where original Shaker recipes and simple country fare are offered (open daily, 8:30 am - 9 pm; reservations suggested). If you so choose, you can even stay the night in one or another of the original buildings (see Historic Accommodations). NR, NHL. Open mid Mar-late Nov, daily 9-5; otherwise daily 9-4:30. $3.50 adults, $1.50 students 12-18, 75¢ children. (606) 734-5411. ✔

Hodgenville vicinity

ABRAHAM LINCOLN BIRTHPLACE NATIONAL HISTORIC SITE, 3 miles S. via US 31E and KY 61, early 19th century. In 1808 Thomas and Nancy Lincoln bought a small farm known as Sinking Spring and moved into a one-room log cabin near a large limestone spring with their first child, Sarah; their son, Abraham, was born only three months later on February 12, 1809. The Lincolns were to stay on the 300-acre farm for only two years before moving on. The crude log house they briefly inhabited has been much restored; in 1906 John Russell Pope was engaged to design a marble and granite memorial building to house the cabin, which had been disassembled, moved, and exhibited across the country before being returned to its original site. The Lincoln family Bible is on display in the building, along with early tools and weapons, household objects, and exhibits relating to the Lincolns and to pioneer life. NR. Open Sept-May, daily 8-4:45; June-Aug, daily 8-6:45. Free. (502) 358-3874.

Lexington

Legend has it that the city of Lexington, whose first permanent settlement was established in 1779, had been named four years earlier, when a group of hunters building a shelter in the area received news of the historic Battle of Lexington. Whether or not the legend has any basis in fact, present-day Lexington is much more apt to be associated with horses than with revolution. Situated in the heart of Kentucky's famous bluegrass country, Lexington is the hub of the thoroughbred industry, and also the world's largest burley tobacco market; millions of pounds of the weed are sold each year at auction here. Because of the wealth brought by the tobacco and horse farms which surround it, the city is noted for its beautiful 19th-century homes and churches, a number of which are open to the public and are described below.

One particularly lovely residential area, where the houses are still privately-owned, is **Elsmere Park,** off N. Broadway between W. 6th and W. 7th Sts., whose elegant, generously-proportioned homes were built between 1891 and 1913, most in the then-popular Queen Anne and Neo-classical Revival styles. NR.

There are several fine examples of ecclesiastical architecture in Lexington as well: **Christ Church Episcopal,** Church and Market Sts., is an early Gothic Revival edifice designed in 1845 for the oldest Episcopal congregation west of the Alleghenies. NR. Open daily, 9-5. Free. (606) 254-4497. **Central Christian Church** is a huge Romanesque pile at 207 E. Short St., considered a direct descendant of the Cane Ridge Christian Church founded by Robert W. Finley in 1790 (which later became known as Disciples of Christ). NR. Open all year, daily 9-5. Free. (606) 233-1551.

Lexington's wealthy residents enjoyed their off hours as well as their lucrative professions: in 1886 Oscar Cobb, a leading theater architect, was hired to design an **Opera House** for the city. The result was an elaborately-designed Victorian brick building at 141 N. Broadway, which has been restored recently, and where performances (dramas, musicals, special events) are again held regularly from Sept to June. NR. (606) 233-4567.

ASHLAND, Richmond Rd., 1806, 1857. Henry Clay, who served as speaker of the House of Representatives, peace commissioner at Ghent following the War of 1812, secretary of state, U.S. senator, and three-time nominee for president, bought Ashland Farm in 1811. Clay's son, James, bought the estate at public auction in 1853, and his first act was to tear down the original house and build anew on its foundations. James Clay's choice was the current mansion, an Italianate residence which follows the plan of the original, but whose ornate detailing is vastly different. Twenty acres of woodland surround the 20-room mansion, which is furnished primarily with Clay family possessions. NR, NHL. Open daily 9:30-4:30. $2 adults, 50¢ children. (606) 266-8581.

Henry Clay is interred within an Egyptian Revival mausoleum on the grounds of **Lexington Cemetery,** 833 W. Main St. Established in 1849, this rural cemetery has beautifully-landscaped grounds that contain the graves of many prominent citizens and of more than a thousand Confederate and Union soldiers. NR. Open all year, daily 8-5. Free. (606) 255-5522.

The tiny **law office** Clay built at 176 N.

Mill St. in 1803 has been restored and is operated by the state. NR. (606) 254-9331.

GRATZ PARK HISTORIC DISTRICT, bounded by 2nd and 3rd Sts., the Byway, and Bark Alley, 18th-19th centuries. Located in the heart of the oldest part of Lexington, Gratz Park is a wonderful oasis of greenery surrounded by great Federal houses. Most are privately-owned, but the **Hunt-Morgan House** (1814) at 201 N.

Mill St., one of the finest, was saved from demolition in 1955 by the Blue Grass Trust for Historic Preservation, which operates it as a museum. John Wesley Hunt, Kentucky's first millionaire, made his fortune in banking and in the import-export business. One of his descendants, John Hunt Morgan, led the Confederate Morgan Raiders during the Civil War; another, Thomas Hunt Morgan, won a Nobel Prize in genetics. The Hunt-Morgan House is furnished with fine 19th century antiques, many the work of Kentucky artisans. NR. Open Tu-Sa 10-4, Su 2-5. $1.50 adults, 50¢ children. (606) 253-0362.

MARY TODD LINCOLN HOUSE, 578 W. Main St., early 19th century. In 1832 Robert S. Todd and his family moved to this two-story Georgian brick house; Mary Todd resided here until 1839, when she went to Springfield, Illinois. Three years later she married Abraham Lincoln. The Lincolns returned to visit in Lexington several times, and the house remained in the Todd family until the 1850s. Recently restored by the Kentucky Mansions Preservation Foundation, the house is furnished with 19th-century pieces, family portraits, and personal articles of the Lincoln and Todd families. NR. Nearby is **Parker Place**, 511 W. Short St. (c. 1860), an Italianate mansion which incorporates part of an earlier structure where Mary Todd Lincoln's grandmother once lived. Operated with the Lincoln House, Parker Place is also furnished with antiques and fine 19th-century decorative arts. NR. Open all year, Tu-Sa 10-4. $3 adults, $1 children. (606) 233-9999.

TRANSYLVANIA UNIVERSITY, N. Broadway and 3rd St., 1780. One of the oldest colleges west of the Appalachians, Transylvania was a serious rival of both Yale and Harvard in the early 19th century. Henry Clay served on the faculty as professor of law and was a trustee of the school until his death. The oldest original structure on campus is **Old Morrison** (1831), a Greek Revival building designed by Gideon Shryock, which housed the school's administration offices for many years. The **Transylvania Museum** located

inside displays 19th-century medical implements and scientific apparatus. NR, NHL. The museum administers **Patterson Cabin** (1780), one of the original settlers' homes of the area, which was relocated to the campus in the 20th century. Old Morrison and Patterson Cabin are open M-F 8:30-4:30. Free. (606) 233-8120.

UNIVERSITY OF KENTUCKY, S. Limestone St. and Euclid Ave., 1865. Two fine museums are on the University campus: **Photographic Archives** houses a collection of more than 100,000 historic photos; and **Museum of Anthropology** contains archaeological materials and human skeletal remains from sites excavated in the state. Both are open M-F 8-4:30. Free. (606) 258-4219.

KENTUCKY HORSE PARK, 6 miles N. off I-75 on Iron Works Rd. This unique park celebrates both the thoroughbred and the many varieties of work and pleasure horses which have been vital to Kentucky history. A statue of the famed racer Man O' War dominates the grounds; there is an antique carriage display, a large oval where special events such as steeplechasing and rodeos are held, and a fine museum, the **International Museum of the Horse,** which includes an extensive library and displays relating to equine history worldwide. Open Memorial Day-Labor Day, daily 9-7; otherwise daily 9-5. Combination ticket: $5 adults, $4 children 7-14. (606) 233-4303. ✔

WAVELAND STATE SHRINE, 6 miles S. off US 27 on Higbee Mill Pike, c. 1845. Built for prosperous Lexington resident Joseph Bryan on a tract of land originally claimed by frontiersman Daniel Boone, Waveland is a two-story Greek Revival mansion with a tall columned portico. Outbuildings on the tree-shaded property include servants' quarters, a country store, and a blacksmith shop. Operated by the state as a museum of country life, the mansion contains exhibits of silver, china, toys, clothing, farm and craftsmen's tools, kitchen utensils, and military relics dating from pioneer days to the recent past. NR. Open Tu-Sa 9-4, Su 1:30-4:30. $1 adults, 50¢ students, 25¢ children, group rates. (606) 272-3611.

Loretto vicinity

BURKS' DISTILLERY, E. of Loretto off KY 49 and KY 52, 19th-20th centuries. A whiskey distillery was begun here in 1805, shortly after a water-powered gristmill was erected on the site. The mill no longer exists, and for more than fifty years the distillery business was dormant, but it was revived in 1890 and continues to this day. Most of the buildings, now owned by Maker's Mark, date from the early 20th century; they have been restored, and the company welcomes visitors to tour its operations. NR. Open M-F 10:30-3:30. Free. (502) 865-2881.

Louisville

George Rogers Clark, who gained fame for his exploration of the Northwest Territory, led thirteen families to the site of Louisville in 1779. The city's present name was bestowed in 1828 to honor Louis XVI of France for his aid during the American Revolution.

Today Kentucky's largest city is best known as host to the jewel of American horseracing, the Kentucky Derby, which is held each year on the first Saturday in May. While the raising, training, and selling of Kentucky thoroughbreds is a vital part of Louisville industry, the city's leading businesses are concerned with the manufacture of whiskey and tobacco, as they have been since the 19th century. In the period following the Civil War, Louisville grew quickly; many of its most notable commercial and residential areas were developed after 1870, as businessmen prospered and poured fortunes into their companies and their homes.

Stop first at the **Louisville Convention and Visitors Bureau,** 5th and Muhammad Ali Blvd., for information about the listings which follow and other attractions. Open M-F 8:30-5, Sa 8:30-3 (also Su May-Oct 11-3). (502) 582-3732.

AMERICAN SADDLE HORSE MUSEUM, 730 W. Main St. The history of the American saddle horse, a breed developed in the 1830s in Kentucky, is explained here in one of the old cast-iron-front buildings along W. Main near the river. Trophies, ribbons, saddles, bridles and bits, riding costumes, and a gallery of world champions are among the exhibits. NR. Open M-Sa 10-4, Su 1-5. $1 adults, 75¢ students and senior citizens, 50¢ children. (502) 585-1342. ✔

THE ART CENTER ASSOCIATION AT THE WATER TOWER, 3005 Upper River Rd. One of Louisville's most famous old buildings is the water company pumping station, comprised of the engine and boiler room and a 169-foot-high standpipe tower, which was designed in 1858 by Theodore R. Scowden. These utilitarian structures feature exuberant Classical Revival details: the tower sports a domed cupola at its apex, while the base is surrounded by columns topped by life-size classical statues of mythological figures. The Art Center Association, which maintains the buildings, schedules monthly exhibits of regional art. NR, NHL. Open M-F 9-5, Su 10-4. Free. (502) 896-2146.

BELLE OF LOUISVILLE, Riverfront Plaza, at 4th St, 1914. The Belle is an authentic, operating Mississippi sternwheeler. Her gingerbread trim and the pilot house above the top deck have been restored; and during the summer she's available for 2½-hour cruises along the Ohio. Don't miss this! NR. Open Memorial Day-Labor Day, Tu-Su 1-4:30, Sa also 8:30 pm for dance cruises with orchestra. Nominal admission. (502) 582-2547. ✔

CAVE HILL CEMETERY, 701 Baxter Ave., 1848. 300 acres of rolling hills, valleys, and lakes, beautifully landscaped with many rare shrubs and trees, form the grounds of this rural cemetery, where George Rogers Clark and other notables from the Louisville area are buried. The cave for which the cemetery is named, originally part of a large, prosperous farm, is close by. NR. Open daily 8-4:45. Free. (502) 584-2121.

CHURCHILL DOWNS, 700 Central Ave., 19th century. Established in 1874, Churchill Downs was the brainchild of Colonel Meriwether Lewis Clark, a prominent Louisville thoroughbred breeder and grandson of William Clark, famed explorer. Colonel Clark modeled the track after England's Epsom Downs; it was his hope (which turned out to be well justified) that construction of the Downs would stimulate the faltering thoroughbred industry. In 1875 the first Kentucky Derby was held. Clark's original grandstand and clubhouse were replaced in 1895 by the present buildings, spanking white structures whose most notable feature are the twin Gothic spires which crown them.

One of Churchill Downs's most famous trademarks is the series of gardens and floral displays located throughout the 147 acres. The **Kentucky Derby Museum,** located at the track, sponsors summer tours of the grounds and gardens, and exhibits murals, racing memorabilia, saddles, bridles, and the elaborate Derby trophy. NR. Open late Apr-June and mid Oct-late Nov, daily 9-11; otherwise daily 9:30-4:30. Free. (502) 634-3261.

THE FILSON CLUB, 118 W. Breckinridge St., 19th century. A Louisville town house is the repository for a fine collection of Kentucky historical artifacts, including silver, portraits, prints, photos, textiles, costumes, guns, and household items. Open Oct-June, M-F 9-5, Sa 9-12, otherwise M-F 9-5. Free. (502) 582-3727.

The club also administers **Brennan House,** 631 S. Fifth St., an Italianate mansion built in 1868 for Francis Ronald, a wholesale tobacco merchant, and later the residence of Thomas Brennan, industrialist and inventor. NR. Open W 10-2. $2 admission. (502) 582-3727.

JEFFERSON COUNTY COURTHOUSE, 527 W. Jefferson St., 1842-58. Although not completed as envisioned by the architect, Gideon Shryock, this courthouse is considered his major architectural achievement in Louisville. It is an imposing Greek Revival edifice with a projecting Doric portico on the main façade and pilasters framing each window. The rotunda with dome that Shryock planned as the centerpiece of the courthouse was never built. The courthouse and its neighbor, the Beaux-Arts **Louisville City Hall** (1870), are two of Louisville's most favored build-

ings. NR. Open M-F 8:30-4:30. Free. 581-5701.

KENTUCKY RAILWAY MUSEUM, Ormsby Station Site. Trains and engines of all shapes and sizes, from tiny models to giant old locomotives such as the **L & N No. 152,** which remained in service from its completion in 1905 well into the 1950s (NR), are displayed at this transportation museum. Don't forget to bring the kids. Open May-Sept, Sa-Su 12-5; Oct, Su 12-5. $1.50 adults, $1 children. (502) 245-6035. ✔

MUSEUM OF NATURAL HISTORY AND SCIENCE, 727 W. Main St. Five contiguous buildings in Louisville's historic riverfront cast-iron district have been transformed into a large museum which will be sure to interest just about everybody. From archaeology to the Apollo 13 space capsule; from mineralogy to artifacts exhibited in the style of a turn-of-the-century museum; from fashion to stuffed polar bears, alligators, and dinosaurs, it's all here. NR. Open M-Sa 9-5, Su 1-5. $1 adults, 75¢ students, 50¢ children. (502) 587-3138. ✔

UNIVERSITY OF LOUISVILLE, 3rd St. and Eastern Pkwy., 1798. This large school was the first co-educational college in Kentucky and remains one of the state's largest and best-known schools. Two museums on the campus are worth a visit: the **Photographic Archives** boasts 750,000 pictures relating to Kentucky history and to photographic technique. Open M-F 8:30-12 and 1-5. Free. (502) 588-6752. The **J. B. Speed Art Museum** houses Kentucky's foremost collection of English, European, and American paintings. Open Tu-Sa 10-4, Su 2-6. Free. (502) 636-2893.

Louisville vicinity

FARMINGTON, 6 miles SE via US 31 E., 3033 Bardstown Rd., 1810. The design for this outstanding Federal house has been attributed to Thomas Jefferson, although historians have been unable to confirm it beyond doubt. The well-proportioned brick house was built for Judge John Speed, a prominent local jurist. Operated by Historic Homes Foundation, Farmington is furnished with early 19th-century antiques; on the grounds are a fine old stone barn and blacksmith shop. NR. Open M-Sa 10-4:30, Su 1:30-4:30. $2 adults, $1 students. (502) 458-5486.

LOCUST GROVE, 6 miles NE via River Rd. at 561 Blankenbaker Ln., c. 1790. From 1809 to 1815 General George Rogers Clark, western military leader of the Revolutionary War, lived in the handsome two-story Georgian home built by

his brother-in-law, Major William Croghan. The beautifully-restored brick residence retains much of its original interior paneling and many furnishings; the surrounding 65 acres contain nine outbuildings which have also been restored. Operated by the Historic Homes Foundation. NR. Open M-Sa 10-4:30, Su 1:30-4:30. $2 adults, $1 students. (502) 897-9845.

Mammoth Cave

MAMMOTH CAVE NATIONAL PARK, KY 70. Mammoth Cave is a system of underground passages totaling more than 200 miles in length. In the late 19th century, visitors were transported to the park via *Hercules and Coach* (1888). Now on display, the steam locomotive with baggage car was designed to look like a streetcar so that horses, used to such contraptions but not to steam engines, wouldn't panic and bolt. NR. A **visitor center** within the park offers a series of tours, varying in length from half an hour to all day. Open June-Aug, 7:30-7; Mar-May, Sept-Nov 8-5:30; Dec-Feb, 8-5. Admission varies depending on tour selected. (502) 758-2328. ✔

Paris

DUNCAN TAVERN HISTORIC SHRINE, 323 High St., 1786-88. Because of its proximity to the county courthouse, this two-story stone tavern was the scene of many depositions in early land suits and also functioned as the Paris community social center. Adjacent to the tavern is the **Anne Duncan House** (1800), built by the widow of the tavern owner. Both the old hostelry and the frame and log residence have been restored and are furnished to their original periods. NR. Open Tu-Sa 10-12, 1-5, Su 2-5. $1.25 adults, 75¢ children. (606) 987-1738.

Perryville

PERRYVILLE BATTLEFIELD STATE SHRINE, US 150, 1862. This was the site of Kentucky's major Civil War battle, in which Union troops under General D. C. Buell forced General Braxton Bragg to retreat into Tennessee, ending the Confederate invasion of the state. **Crawford House**, where Bragg made his headquarters, and **Bottom House**, around which the battle was waged, still stand in the park. (Both are NR.) A museum on the site displays artifacts from the battle and offers interpretive exhibits to explain the course of the fighting. Open Apr-Oct, daily 9-5. 50¢ adults, 25¢ children. (606) 332-8631. ★

Richmond vicinity

FORT BOONESBOROUGH STATE PARK, 12 miles N. via I-75 and KY 627. In 1769, land speculator Judge Richard Henderson engaged Daniel Boone to explore the wilderness west of the Cumberland Mountains, purchase lands from the Cherokees, and escort new settlers along the Wilderness Road to their new homes. Fort Boonesborough, where the explorer and colonists built thick stockades to defend themselves against Indian attack, is long gone, but the state has reconstructed the early buildings. Craft shops, a museum of Boone memorabilia and other historic items; cabins and blockhouses are located here close by the Kentucky River; the paddleboat **Dixie Belle** is available for hour-long trips along the waterway (additional charge). Fort Boonesborough is open Apr-Labor Day, daily 10-6:30; Labor Day-Oct, W, Th, Su 10-6:30. $2 adults, $1 children. Combination ticket available with White Hall State Shrine, following. (606) 527-3328. ↙

WHITE HALL STATE SHRINE, 7 miles N. via US 25 and US 421, 1798, 1864-68. Cassius Marcellus Clay, abolitionist, newspaper publisher, and minister to Russia, made White Hall one of the grand estate houses of post-Civil War Kentucky. He was born (1810) in the older section of the house, built by his father in the Federal style, and he died in the same bed 93 years later, having enlarged the mansion considerably, embellishing it with Italianate detailing. Restored by the state and furnished with 19th-century antiques, many original, White Hall is surrounded by lovely grounds and gardens. NR. Open Apr-Labor Day, daily 9-5. $1 adults, 25¢ children 6-12. (606) 723-9178.

Springfield vicinity

LINCOLN HOMESTEAD STATE PARK, 5 miles N. via US 150, on KY 528. 18th-19th century. The original two-story log structure on this site was the home of Mordecai Lincoln, Abraham Lincoln's uncle, from 1797 to 1815. Shortly after the Lincolns moved out of the dwelling, the present frame Federal structure was constructed over the log section. Guided tours are offered. NR. Open May-Sept, daily 8-6. 50¢ adults, 25¢ children. (606) 336-3083.

Tompkinsville vicinity

OLD MULKEY MEETING HOUSE STATE SHRINE, 1½ miles S. on KY 1446, 1804. The walls of this meeting house, one of the earliest log churches in Kentucky, are in almost perfect condition, and the interior contains huge crossbeams, peg-leg benches, and a rough, handmade pulpit. A nearby pioneer cemetery contains the graves of Hannah Boone, the explorer's sister, and of fifteen Revolutionary War soldiers. NR. Open daily 9-5. Free. (502) 487-9481.

Western Kentucky

Bounded by the Ohio and Mississippi Rivers on the north and west, and by an arbitrary, unnaturally-straight border with Tennessee on the south, Kentucky's western part is largely an industrial area today, in which several sites of historic interest have survived to be explored.

Columbus

COLUMBUS-BELMONT BATTLEFIELD STATE PARK, KY 58 and KY 123, 1860-72. During the Civil War, Confederate General Leonidas Polk envisioned these high bluffs overlooking the Mississippi River as a strategic area of defense. In 1861 a garrison of more than 12,000 men created the fortification which became known as the "Gibraltar of the West"; a mile-long chain was anchored on the bluffs and stretched across the river on rafts to prevent Union steamers from using the Mississippi. Parts of the chain, which broke under its own weight, remain on display in the park, which contains a museum of Civil War relics. NR. Open June-Aug, daily 9-5; May, Sept Sa-Su 9-5. Free admission to the park; museum: 50¢ adults, 25¢ children. (502) 677-2327. ★

Fairview

JEFFERSON DAVIS MONUMENT, KY 115, 1917-24. Erected in honor of Confederate President Jefferson Davis, this 351-foot-high obelisk is one of the tallest in the country. An observation deck at the top offers a superb view of the surrounding countryside. NR. Open Mar-Nov daily 9-5; Dec-Feb, Sa-Su 9-5. 50¢ adults, 25¢ children. (502) 886-1765.

Golden Pond

LAND BETWEEN THE LAKES, off US 68, 19th century. Operated by the Tennessee Valley Authority, this is one of the country's newest and most expansive (170,000 acres) recreational areas. Located between Kentucky Lake and Lake Barkley, it overlaps the border between Kentucky and Tennessee. Within its grounds, some 250 acres have been developed as a living history farm, where crops are raised, livestock tended, and special programs, from tall-tale telling to hog slaughtering, are offered throughout the year. Sixteen original log structures have been reconstructed here; a visitor center explains 19th-century farming techniques. NR. Open daily 9-5. Free. (502) 924-5602.

Mayfield

WOOLDRIDGE MONUMENTS, Maplewood Cemetery, US 45, 1892-99. A group of sixteen wonderfully eccentric

limestone statues commemorate the life, interests, and closest relatives of Henry G. Wooldridge, a wealthy, obviously self-involved horse breeder, who commissioned the folk art to grace his tomb. NR. Open daily 7-6. Free. (502) 247-6101.

Owensboro

OWENSBORO MUSEUM OF FINE ART, 901 Frederica St. Housed in the 1905 Carnegie Library building, this collection of American art includes painting, sculpture, textiles, graphics, and decorative arts, most of 19th-century origin. Open M-F 10-4, Sa-Su 1-4. Free. (502) 685-3191.

Paducah

WILLIAM CLARK MARKET HOUSE MUSEUM, 2nd and Broadway, 1905. General William Clark laid out the town of Paducah in 1827 and set aside this block for a market house. The current structure, third on the site, is a red brick building which now houses mementoes of early town life — the first motorized fire truck, antique tools and furnishings, and the complete, reconstructed interior of the 19th-century Dubois Drug Store. NR. Open Tu-Sa 12-4, Su 1-5. Admission 50¢. (502) 443-7759.

The Market House also contains exhibits relating to Paducah's most famous native, Alben Barkley. More information about Barkley, a state legislator, U.S. senator, and vice president, can be obtained at the Alben Barkley Museum, Madison at Sixth St. Located in a mid-19th-century Greek Revival residence, the museum features memorabilia of the Barkley family and of famous men from the Paducah area, along with period furnishings and decorative arts. NR. Open Sa-Su 1-4, and by appointment. 50¢ adults, 25¢ children. (502) 554-9690.

South Union

SHAKERTOWN AT SOUTH UNION, US 68 at KY 73, 19th century. The South

Union community founded in 1807 by the United Society of Believers in Christ's Second Appearing retains only 8 of 200 original buildings. **Centre House** (1835) is the largest structure, a four-story brick dwelling once home to nearly 100 members. Today it contains a fine museum, with more than 2,000 items of Shaker furniture, tools, and textiles. Other buildings include a **general store and post office** (1859), a **wash house** (1854), the **ministry shop** (1846), and a **tavern** (1869) which is now privately owned. NR. Open late May-Labor Day, M-Sa 9-5, Su 1-5; Sept-Oct, Sa 9-5, Su 1-5. $2 adults, $1 children 6-13. (502) 542-4167.

Wickliffe

ANCIENT BURIED CITY, US 51/62 and US 60, c. 900 A.D. The Temple Mound People flourished in the western Kentucky area more than 1,000 years ago. Excavations have uncovered remnants of their civilization, including pottery, tombs, and crude toys. Open M-W, F-Sa 8-6, Su 12-6. $2 adults, $1 children, group rates. (502) 335-3681.

Historic Accommodations

An asterisk (*) indicates that meals are served.

Bardstown

TALBOTT TAVERN, 107 W. Stephen Foster Ave., 40004. (502) 348-3494. Open all year. (See historic listing for description.) The hostelry is renowned for its fine dining. NR.*

Berea

BOONE TAVERN HOTEL, Main St., 40403. (606) 986-9358. Open all year. Students at Berea College helped to construct the brick Georgian Revival Boone Tavern in 1909; today they still participate in its operation, from helping to serve and prepare meals, to building some of the furniture which decorates the rooms.*

Brandenburg

DOE RUN INN, US 2, 40108. (502) 444-2982. Open all year. Constructed as a woolen mill in 1792, and enlarged in the first quarter of the 19th century, Doe Run Inn has been owned by the same family for the last five generations.*

Harrodsburg and vicinity

BEAUMONT INN, 638 Beaumont Dr., 40330. (606) 734-3381. Open Mar-Nov. The late Greek Revival structure (c. 1851) which has functioned for the past 60 years as Beaumont Inn achieved its greatest distinction in the late 19th century as Daughters' College, one of the leading women's schools in the South. NR.*

SHAKERTOWN AT PLEASANT HILL, KY 4, 40330. (606) 734-5411. Open all year. Fourteen 19th-century buildings located throughout the Shaker Village (see historic listing) include pleasantly-furnished guest rooms. NR, NHL.*

Louisville

SEELBACH HOTEL, 500 Fourth Ave., 40202. (502) 585-3200. Open all year. The opulently-decorated Beaux-Arts Seelbach was opened in 1905, the product of efforts by German immigrants Louis and Otto Seelbach. Restored in the late 1970s, it is conveniently located at the center of downtown Louisville. NR.*

Index